TURKISH COAST

Hints for using the Guide

Following the tradition established by Karl Baedeker in 1844, buildings and works of art, places of natural beauty and sights of particular interest, are distinguished by one ★ or two ★★.

To make it easier to locate the various places listed in the "A to Z" section of the Guide, their co-ordinates are shown in red at the head of each entry: e.g., İstanbul **D/E 2/3**.

Coloured lines down the right-hand side of the page are an aid to finding the main heading in the Guide: blue stands for the Introduction (Nature, Culture, History, etc.), red for the "A to Z" section, and yellow indicates Practical Information.

Only a selection of hotels and restaurants can be given; no reflection is implied therefore on establishments not included.

In a time of rapid change it is difficult to ensure that all the information given is entirely accurate and up-to-date, and the possibility of error can never be entirely eliminated.

Although the publishers can accept no responsibility for inaccuracies and omissions, they are constantly endeavouring to improve the quality of their Guides and are therefore always grateful for criticisms, corrections and suggestions for improvement.

Preface

This guide to the Turkish Coasts is one of the new generation of Baedeker guides.

Illustrated throughout in colour, they are designed to meet the needs of the modern traveller. They are quick and easy to consult, with the principal sights described in alphabetical order, and practical details and useful tips shown in the margin. The information is presented in a format that is both attractive and easy to follow.

The subject of this guide is the whole of Turkey's extensive coastline, particularly the areas and places of interest on the Aegean Sea and the Turkish south coast on the eastern Mediterranean, but also covering the Black Sea Coast, the great city of İstanbul, the Bosphorus, the Sea of Marmara and the Dardenelles.

The guide is in three parts. The first part gives a general account of the area, its climate, flora and fauna, population, state and society, history, notable personalities and culture and art. A brief selection of quotations and some suggested routes lead into the second part, in which the principal places of tourist interest are described in detail. The third part contains a variety of practical information designed to help visitors to find their way about and make the most of their stay. Both the sights and the practical information are listed in alphabetical order.

Ruined buildings, such as the Celcus library in Ephesus, and peaceful sailing on the bay of Antalya make the Turkish coast an ideal holiday area

The new Baedeker guides are noted for their concentration on essentials and their convenience of use. They contain numerous specially drawn plans and colour illustrations; and at the end of the book is a large map making it easy to locate the various places described in the "A to Z" section of the guide with the help of the co-ordinates given at the head of each entry.

Contents

Nature, Culture, History
Pages 10–81

Sights from A to Z
Pages 84–281

Practical Information from A to Z
Pages 284–326

Baedeker Specials

Welcome

İzmir

Clocktower in Konak Square

The Greek poet Musaeus tells how the youthful Leander swam across the Hellespont every night to visit his beloved Hero, a priestess at Sestos on the western shore. To make the eastward crossing today, by ferry over the Dardanelles or by one of two modern bridges suspended high above the Bosphorus at İstanbul, is to leave one continent, Europe, behind and set foot on another, Asia, and in particular Asia Minor. This travel guide focuses on the coastal regions of Asia Minor.

Those who travel overland through the Balkans to that friendliest of destinations Turkey, are greeted on the final lap of their journey by some delightful scenery, driving for part of the way between Edirne and İstanbul past sandy beaches on the northern shore of the Sea of Marmara. No visit to İstanbul, most uniquely situated of all the world's great cities, should end without a boat trip to the enchanting Princes' Islands in the eastern Sea of Marmara or through the Bosphorus to the Black Sea. Who could ever forget the passage of this famous waterway, its shores clad in Mediterranean vegetation and lined with delightful villages and mighty fortresses.

Linking the Sea of Marmara to the Aegean Sea is the long, narrow strait of the Dardanelles, ever-busy with shipping. While a trip on the water is particularly to be recommended, fine views of the fascinating Dardanelles scenery can be had from many places on land.

Kuşadası

A dream island with the remains of a Byzantine Castle

Pergamon

The Trajan Temple enthroned on the highest point of the Acropolis

Antalya

Panorama of the old town, a delightful seaside resort on the south coast

among Friends!

The west coast of Turkey bordering the Aegean is fissured by large bays and numerous peninsulas. South of the gulfs of Edremit and Çandarlı lies the deep indentation of the Bay of İzmir, at its head the city of that name, capital of the Ege region. Enclosed to the west by the Çeşme peninsula with its abundance of lovely bathing spots, the bay has been developed with an eye to tourism. To the south is the well-known holiday resort of Kuşadası (with a marina and beaches), and further south still another lively holiday centre, Bodrum. Picturesquely situated in a pleasant bay, on the site of ancient Halicarnassus, Bodrum too boasts a fine marina and good diving as well as a Crusader castle. Along the southern side of the Gulf of Bodrum runs a narrow hilly peninsula with, at its tip, the ruins of ancient Knidos.

The almost land-locked Gulf of Marmaris, another popular holiday area, marks the start of the mountainous Lycian section of the coast (Fethiye, Ölüdeniz, Kaş, Kekova, Finike) extending round into the Gulf of Antalya, on the western side of which the narrow, mountain-backed coastal strip between Kemer and the port of Antalya offers some excellent beaches.

The scenery of the eastern Mediterranean coast beyond Antalya has earned it the title of Turkish Riviera. While the best beaches are around Side, Alanya, Gazipaşa and Anamur, and between Silifke (Cape İncekum) and Mersin, the Gulf of İskenderun also offers good bathing and watersports.

Aphrodisias

The reconstructed Propylon which originally led to the Temple of Aphrodite

İstanbul

The power of the Sultan of the Bosphorus, once the fear of Europe, lies behind the magnificent decoration of the Sultan's throne

Nature, Culture History

Facts and Figures

General

Turkey

Territory

At its peak in the 16th and 17th c. the Ottoman Empire extended over a vast area of more than 5,000,000sq.km/1,900,000sq. miles; by the beginning of the 20th c. this had fallen to just under 3,000,000sq.km/ 1,200,000sq. miles; further territory was lost in the Tripolitanian and Balkan wars; and after the First World War there were even more drastic reductions. Not only were the great expanses of the Syro-Arabian tableland permanently lost but large areas of present-day Turkish territory had also to be given up: the whole of the north-east to Armenia, the south-east to the Mosul region and a strip 50–100km/ 30–60 miles wide west of this to Syria, then under French Mandate, while Smyrna (İzmir), with a hinterland of some 100 by 150km/60 by 90 miles on the west coast of Asia Minor, and almost the whole of Thrace in European Turkey, as far as the Çatalca Line only 40km/25 miles from İstanbul, were assigned to Greece, which now extended along a broad front to the Black Sea.

This last slashing reduction in the national territory, imposed under the Treaty of Sèvres (August 20th 1923), was bitterly resisted by the Turkish people under the leadership of Mustafa Kemal Paşa (Atatürk), who succeeded in recovering all these areas under the Treaty of Lausanne (July 24th 1923), which gave Turkey a unified natural *Lebensraum*. This territory was subsequently enlarged by the addition of the Hakkârı area in the extreme south-east (1926) and the important Sanjak of Alexandretta, the Hatay region (1939). Altogether 67 provinces.

The territory of Turkey as thus constituted form a long rectangle extending from east to west with good frontiers. As against the unwieldy expanse of the Ottoman Empire with its far-flung peripheral territories the compact territory of present-day Turkey makes a more unified nation and has transformed an empire dominating a wide range of peoples and territories, from the Balkans to the Syro-Arabian tableland, into a national State, with Ankara as the capital since 1923.

◀ *Ölü Deniz near Fethiye*

Frontiers

More than two-thirds of Turkey's frontiers are on easily defensible coasts – fully 6000km/3730 miles of coastal frontiers (not counting the Sea of Marmara, which is wholly enclosed by Turkish territory) against only 2753km/1710 miles of land frontiers. So heavily indented is the coastline and so contorted the land frontiers that the perimeter of Turkey is twice as long as that of a circle of equivalent area.

Division of territory

With a total area of 779,453sq.km/300,868sq. miles, Turkey is divided into a European part and an Asiatic part 32 times greater, Anatolia (from Greek *anatole*, "rising (of the sun)"), separated by the Dardanelles, the Sea of Marmara and the Bosphorus. There is no real separation, however, since the territories and the peoples on both sides of the divide are similar.

Turkey as a bridge between Europe and Asia

As a peninsula projecting from the western end of the Asiatic land mass and with some of its territory extending into Europe, Turkey, lying between longitude 25° 45′ and 44° 48′ E and between latitude 42° 06′ and 35° 51′ N (between the farthest points in each direction), occupies an important position as a link and mediator between regions with different economies and cultures. The seaway through the straits has been of particular importance since ancient times as a bridge between Europe and Asia. The straits also provide a means of communication between the eastern Mediterranean (Aegean) and the Black Sea, and thus contributed, from the time of the early Greek colonies in the Black Sea, to the diffusion of influences towards the north-east, the most important being the establishment of Byzantium, from which Christianity was later to spread to eastern Europe.

In geographical terms the greater part of Turkey belongs to the highlands of western Asia; but, brought from time immemorial into close contact with the West by its bridge position, present-day Turkey is strongly influenced by European culture. Politically this is given expression by its association with the European Community and its membership of NATO.

With its considerable area, Turkey has a large population of some 60,000,000 with a high degree of national unity. It is thus by far the most powerful of the Near Eastern and south-eastern European States. With its very varied geographical pattern, with great natural differences between the warm, wet coastal regions and the arid interior, between the narrow but fertile strips of land along the coasts, the vast upland plateaux and the great mountain ranges, and with its mineral wealth, Turkey has a range of resources which harmoniously supplement one another and hold the prospect of further development in years to come.

Coastal Regions

Marmara region

Thrace and the Marmara region – the Thracian steppe-land and the area south of the Sea of Marmara with its alternating pattern of hills and low-lying basins – are two territories of very different character which through proximity and close connections of many kinds can be seen as forming a larger unity.

The Thracian tableland is continued beyond the Bosphorus (once a river valley running from the Golden Horn to the Black Sea) by the Bithynian Peninsula (in Turkish Kocaeli), a region of very similar topography. The Dardanelles were once also a valley traversed by a river, and here, too, the rolling uplands of the southern Marmara region continue on the Gallipoli (Gelibolu) Peninsula on the north side of the straights.

The northern part of the Sea of Marmara (length 280km/174 miles, width 80km/50 miles, area 11,500sq.km/4439sq. miles) is a rift valley extending from west to east and going down to considerable depths (much of it below 1000m/330ft, with maximum depths reaching 1350m/4430ft), the most westerly element in a sequence of troughs and basins known as the Paphlagonian Seam some 1000km/600 miles long which plays an important part in the conformation of northern Anatolia. Out of the shallow (under 50m/165ft) area along its northern coast emerge the Princes' Islands, built up of hard quartzites which have resisted erosion. In the shallow waters of the southern part of the sea are the island of Marmara and a number of smaller islands. The Sea of Marmara, a typical inter-continental sea, is wholly surrounded by Turkish territory.

Thrace consists mainly of an area of flat steppe-land between 100m/330ft and 200m/660ft in height traversed by broad valleys: an erosion plain thrust upwards in geologically recent times overlaying Late Tertiary marine sediments, mainly Miocene limestones, marls and clays, with sands and gravels brought down from the Istranca Hills by rivers. The Istranca range, rising in the forest zone to a height of 1031m/3383ft to the north-east of the Thracian tableland, consists basically of Palaeozoic rocks and represents a continuation of the dome formation of the Balkan mountains. To the south-west of the tableland, between Tekirdağ and the Gulf of Saros, is the Genos range, an upland region of flysch and limestone with recent folding which rises to some 945m/3100ft; this is continued by lower hills along the Gallipoli Peninsula, which has a broad strip of Late Tertiary sediments along the Dardanelles. Raised beaches at different heights (ranging between 6 and 7m/20 and 23ft and 110m/360ft above sea-level) bear witness to changes in the level of the sea. A last post-glacial rise in sea-level associated with world oceanic changes converted the estuaries of rivers flowing into the Sea of Marmara into coastal lagoons extending far inland, as at Büyük Çekmece and Küçük Çekmece to the west of İstanbul. To the west of the Bosphorus and on the Kocaeli Peninsula on the Asiatic side of Traco-Bithynian erosion plain, thrust upward at a late geological period, cuts Early Palaeozoic (Silurian, Devonian) folded rocks. In the eastern part of the Kocaeli Peninsula the tableland is thrust up higher, much dissected and extensively forested.

With a continental temperature pattern and annual precipitation between 40 and 60cm/16 and 24in., falling mainly in winter, the Thracian tableland is a great expanse of arable and pasture land, stripped of its forests by 6000 years of human activity (with only the Ergeni area perhaps originally unforested), where the traditional agriculture has been improved by the growing of sugar-beet and sunflowers.

Except for the Istranca Hills, the Black Sea coast and the interior of the Kocaeli Peninsula, which are thinly settled, Thrace is well populated, with numbers of small and medium-sized towns distributed fairly regularly over its area. Two places merit special mention – the great city of İstanbul, with its many layers of history, its busy present-day development and its influence reaching out over the Bosphorus into Anatolia, and Edirne (ancient Adrianople), the first Ottoman stronghold in Europe, with its outstanding works of art and architecture.

As a result of geologically recent upward and downward movements the region south of the Sea of Marmara shows a mixed pattern of hills and depressions, mostly running from west to east. The Gulf of İzmit, a recent depression, is continued eastward by Lake Sapanca and, beyond this, the Adapazarı basin on the Lower Sakarya. A first ridge of hills to the south is followed by a second depression, consisting of the Gulf of Gemlik and its continuation, Lake İznik. A second ridge, extending farther west along the Sea of Marmara as a range of coastal hills of moderate height, is succeeded by a third depression consisting of the

Bursa Basin and Lakes Apolyont and Manyas. In the mountains to the south of this depression the highest peak is Ulu Dağ (2543m/8344ft), the Mysian of Bithynian Olympus, in the summit region of which are corries formed by two small glaciers during the Ice Age. Farther west, in the Troad, the pattern of relief is more irregular.

The Marmara region already enyoys the climatic privileges of the Mediterranean. While the hills are covered with pine and oak forests and scrub-oak, the fertile basins between them have flourishing olive-groves, fig and fruit orchards, vineyards, tobacco plantations and corn-fields, but also great expanses of grazing for cattle and sheep. In these basins, accordingly, the density of population is above the average.

Most notable among the region's towns is Bursa, superbly situated on the slopes of Ulu Dağ, with its mosques and sultans' tombs. The Troad can claim a prestigious monument of the past in the site of ancient Troy, with its successive occupation levels extending from prehistoric to Classical times.

Aegean coast

The Aegean region extends from the coast of the Aegean to the ranges of hills that make up the mountain barrier of western Anatolia, the watershed between the coastal region and the arid interior. Here, too, the land is broken up by depressions running from west to east, between which are mountain ranges, mostly of ancient rocks and often steeply scarped, rising to considerable heights (1000–2000m/3300–6600ft); Boz Dağ (2157m/7077ft). To the west the hills are continued by long peninsulas with much-indented coasts and by the Greek islands. The fertile rift valleys are watered by large rivers – the Gediz, the Küçük Menderes and the Büyük Menderes (the classical Maeander) – and covered with huge fig plantations, olive groves, vineyards (used for the production of raisins as well as wine) and fields of cotton, grain and tobacco.

Favoured by its mild Mediterranean climate, this area has been settled and developed by man since the earliest times and has a great range of magnificent remains of the past – Pergamon, Ephesus, Priene, Miletus, Didyma, Hierapolis and many more. It takes in the territories of ancient Mysia, Lydia and Caria. In the various parts of the region the main centres are industrial towns of medium size. Of particular importance is the great port and industrial city of İzmir, Turkey's third largest city, with some 2,500,000 people in the conurbation. A natural phenomenon of extraordinary beauty and interest is offered by Pamukkale ("cotton castle"), on the site of ancient Hierapolis (opposite Denizli in

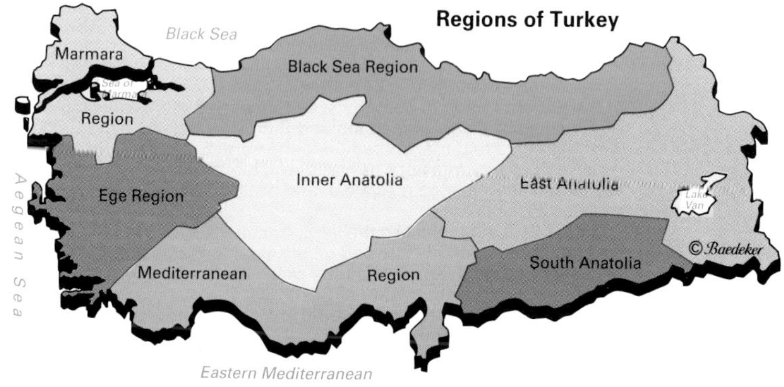

the valley of the Büyük Menderes), with its fantastic terraces of limestone concretions.

Mediterranean coast

After its much-indented western section, towards which extend the ranges of the Western Taurus, here running almost due north–south, the south coast of Anatolia has only two large, widely arched bays between here and the Gulf of İskenderun – the Gulfs of Anatalya and Mersin. The limestone mountains of the Western Taurus rear up steeply, directly from the coast, to heights of 2000m/6500ft or more, with some peaks towering to over 3000m/9800ft. Farther north they rise out of the large coastal plain of Antalya and continue into the upland region of the interior with its numerous lakes. Here the Western Taurus gives place to the great arc of the Central Taurus, also built up of limestones, which runs south-east, east, north-east and finally north-north-east, and after a zone of lesser peaks reaches its highest points between Karaman and Silifke, attaining 3583m/11,756ft in Bolkar Dağ (Medetsiz) and to over 3800m/12,500ft in the Cilician Ala Dağ.

East of Alanya, between the limestone mountains of the Central Taurus and the coast, is a lower range of wooded hills, formed of Palaeozoic crystalline schists and much dissected by valleys, which falls steeply down to the sea, leaving room only round the estuaries of rivers for small areas of cultivated land – rice-fields, banana plantations, groundnuts, vegetable culture in hothouses. There is a striking contrast between the seaward slopes of these hills, with their plentiful supply of rain, and the arid inland side. On the southern slopes a lower vegetation zone reaching up to 700m/2300ft and in places up to 1000m/3300ft, with plants sensitive to cold, olives and Aleppo pines (in the subspecies *Pinus brutia*), gives way to a belt of coniferous forest (Austrian pine) interspersed with deciduous trees (oaks, planes, nut trees), followed by a zone of pines, cedars and juniper trees extending up to the tree-line at 2200–2400m/7200–7900ft). The highest parts (Ala Dağ) reach up into the region of permanent snow, with glaciers and glacier-like patches of snow. On the northern side the pattern is very different: a region of steppe-land extends to the foot of the mountains, and only above 1200–1400m/3900–4600ft, where there is sufficient moisture for trees, is there a zone of natural forest – of which, however, only fragments are left.

The western part of the large coastal depression round the Gulf of Antalya consists of extensive travertine plateaux, in two stages (200–250m/660–820ft and 40–120m/130–390ft). To the east of this are large river plains which, favoured by the climate, are intensively cultivated with citrus fruits (particularly in the western part, near the coast), cotton, groundnuts and cereals. In winter this is used as grazing land by nomads who move into the hills in summer. On the travertine plateaux in the western half of the depression large modern industrial installations (textiles, rubber, chromium) have been established.

The Antalya Plain, settled by man at an early stage, was the heartland of the ancient region of Pamphylia and preserves impressive remains of the cities of Perge, Aspendos and Side. The upland region to the west belonged to Caria, the region to the north to Isauria. The town of Antalya (formerly Adalia), was founded in the 2nd c. B.C. by Attalos II of Pergamon, who named it Attaleia, and it still preserves some notable remains of the past.

On the Gulf of Mersin lies the large Adana Plain, a recent infill plain which together with the low and gently sloping plateaux of Late Tertiary limestones and the hilly country of the hinterland forms the fertile and densely populated region of Çukurova. The rivers Seyhan (with a large dam and hydro-electric station) and Ceyhan flow down from the Central and Eastern Taurus, with their abundance of rain. The Çakit Çay cuts through the Taurus in a narrow gorge which is also used by the Baghdad Railway, on a boldly engineered stretch of line. This passage

The beautiful Bafa lake situated in the hinterland of the Aegean coast

through the mountains is within the Cilician Pass region, but the original pass – known in antiquity as the Cilician Gates – is a narrow gorge in a little valley which runs up from the Adana Plain to the Tekir Pass (1200m/3900ft) and continues from there to meet the Çakit Çay at Pozantı. Here, too, the road and railway meet. The main road and the railway then continue together, running west and then north-west on the line of an old caravan route and drove road, going north over a low pass into a large basin on the west side of Ala Dağ and from there continuing farther into the interior. Pozantı is thus the focal point of the Cilician Pass region.

In the Çukurova region plantations of citrus fruits and olives, vineyards, market gardens and the production for export of water-melons, aubergines, tomatoes, etc., which ripen very early here, bear witness to the gentle climate. In winter cereals (wheat, barley, oats) are grown, and the nomads come down to their winter grazing grounds. Çukurova is most notable, however, as Turkey's largest cotton-growing area. Most of the cotton is grown by large producers in the plain, but there are also small peasant holdings on the lower plateaux and upland regions, up to a height of about 500m/1640ft. The cotton harvest brings in large numbers of seasonal workers, and the crop provides the basis for a considerable cotton industry in the region, with numerous factories. The villages in the plain have square houses built of mud brick with flat roofs, given their distinctive mark by the wooden structures on the roofs which provide sleeping accommodation on hot summer nights. The principal towns are Mersin with its large modern port, ancient Tarsus and Adana on the River Seyhan. In antiquity the region was part of Cilicia, bounded on the west by Pisidia.

Black Sea coast

From the mouth of the Sakarya in the west to the Soviet frontier in the east Turkey's Black Sea coast is flanked by an 1100km/685 mile long barrier of hills and mountains, ranging in width between 150km/

Mountain passes lead inland to the Taurus Mountains

95 miles and 200km/125 miles and consisting of a series of chains, mostly running parallel to the coast, with large longitudinal valleys and basins forming part of a long rift valley (the Paphlagonian Seam). The coastal region is well supplied with rain, which is particularly heavy in autumn and winter, but rainfall declines towards the interior. At the west end the annual rainfall is 1000mm/40in., at higher levels in the coastal chain 1500mm/60in., round Samsun, where the coast runs south-east, it falls below 800mm/30in., and at the east end, in the Pontic region, it is over 2000mm/80in. The favoured climate of the coastal areas is reflected in the vegetation, with the olive, a tree susceptible to frost, growing at the lower levels. Mixed deciduous forest, with a dense undergrowth largely consisting of rhododendrons, extends up to 1000m/3300ft, to be succeeded by hardy firs and pines. Inland the forest consist of fir and scrub-oak; and, finally, forest cover is found only on the northern slopes of the hills with their better supply of rain.

In the western section of the mountains between the rivers Sakarya and Kızılırmak, in the hinterland around Zonguldak where the smooth coastline curves gently northwards, there are extensive coal deposits. Here, too, with the opening out of the Sakarya Valley into a basin at Adapazarı, begins a succession of large basins enclosed by hills -- Düzce (100m/330ft), Bolu (700m/2300ft), Reşadiye (900m/2950ft) and Gerede (1300m/4256ft), with a marked variation in the agricultural pattern according to height, from the maize, tobacco and other crops intensively cultivated in the lower basins to the barley and wheat fields and the pasture land of the highest (Gerede). The Kastamonu Basin (700m/2300ft) lies slightly farther north. While the coastal hills are still under 2000m/6560ft, the Ilgaz Massif south of Kastamonu rises to 2565m/8416ft, and Köroğlu Tepe south-east of Bolu to 2378m/7802ft.

Round the mouths of the Kızılırmak and the Yeşilırmak is an area of fertile low-lying land in which tobacco is grown. In this area lies

Samsun, the principal town on the Black Sea coast, with an important export trade.

The Zigana region, to the east, rises in its higher ranges to over 3000m/9850ft, reaching 3937m/12,917ft in the Kaçkar range. Here the mountains take on an Alpine character, with rugged forms carved out by glacial action – begun during the Ice Ages but still continuing today. In the densely populated coastal region valuable high-quality crops are grown. Of particular importance is tea, which not only meets domestic requirements but provides a surplus for export. Here, too, and indeed all along the Black Sea coast, are considerable plantations of hazelnuts.

Climate

The coasts of Turkey fall into two different climatic zones: on the one hand the Black Sea coast, with a temperate climate and regular high rainfall, and on the other Mediterranean coast, with a typically Mediterranean climate marked by dry and very hot summers and mild rainy winters.

Mediterranean coast

On the Turkish south and west coasts spring often begins as early as the end of February. Summer lasts from April to September, with little rain, high temperatures and, usually, a brilliantly blue sky. The weather in autumn is also usually fine. The good weather normally ends in November, when heavy falls of rain announce the coming of winter; but temperatures remain mild, and snow hardly ever falls on the Turkish Mediterranean coast.

The total annual rainfall is about 700mm/28in. in İzmir (1050mm/41in. in Antalya), with almost 500mm/20in. – 800mm/31in. in Antalya – falling between November and February. Rain is a rarity in July and August; during these months the rainfall is often less than 10mm/½in. The humidity of the air ranges between 60 and 75 per cent in winter and 52 and 60 per cent in summer.

The mean annual temperature at İzmir is 17.5 °C/63.5 °F. The hottest months, with means averaging 26.8 °C/80.2 °F, are July and August. The coldest month is January, when the thermometer averages only 8.7 °C/47.7 °F. Temperatures are higher on the south coast, with a mean annual temperature in Antalya of 18.5 °C/65.3 °F. Here summer maximum temperatures as high as 44 °C/111 °F are sometimes recorded. The summer heat in the western and southern coastal regions is made tolerable by fresh sea-breezes.

Black Sea coast

Spring comes later to the Black Sea coast than to the Mediterranean, with the full flush of vegetation appearing only in April. Temperatures during the summer are pleasant; only at the east end of the coast is it sometimes unpleasantly close, when warm moist sea-winds are brought up against the barrier of the Pontic Mountains. The landscape along the Black Sea coast remains green into autumn, thanks to its abundant rainfall. The winter can sometimes be severe, and snow is not uncommon.

With its temperate climate, the Black Sea coastal region has sufficient rainfall throughout the year, with a maximum in autumn. There are, however, considerable variations within the region: while at the west end (from Ereğli to Sinop) the mean annual rainfall is about 1200mm/47in., it is only 735mm/29in. at Samsun and 820mm/32in. at Trabzon, while at Rize, near the east end, it is as much as 2400mm/94in. The humidity of the air is uniformly high throughout the year, at 72 per cent.

The highest temperatures are in August, averaging 22–24 °C/71.6–76.1 °F – İstanbul 24.3 °C/75.7 °F, Trabzon 23.4 °C/74.1 °F. In winter the temperatures are about 6–7 °C/43–44.5 °F. The coldest month is February, when temperatures can fall below –10 °C/+14 °F.

Climate

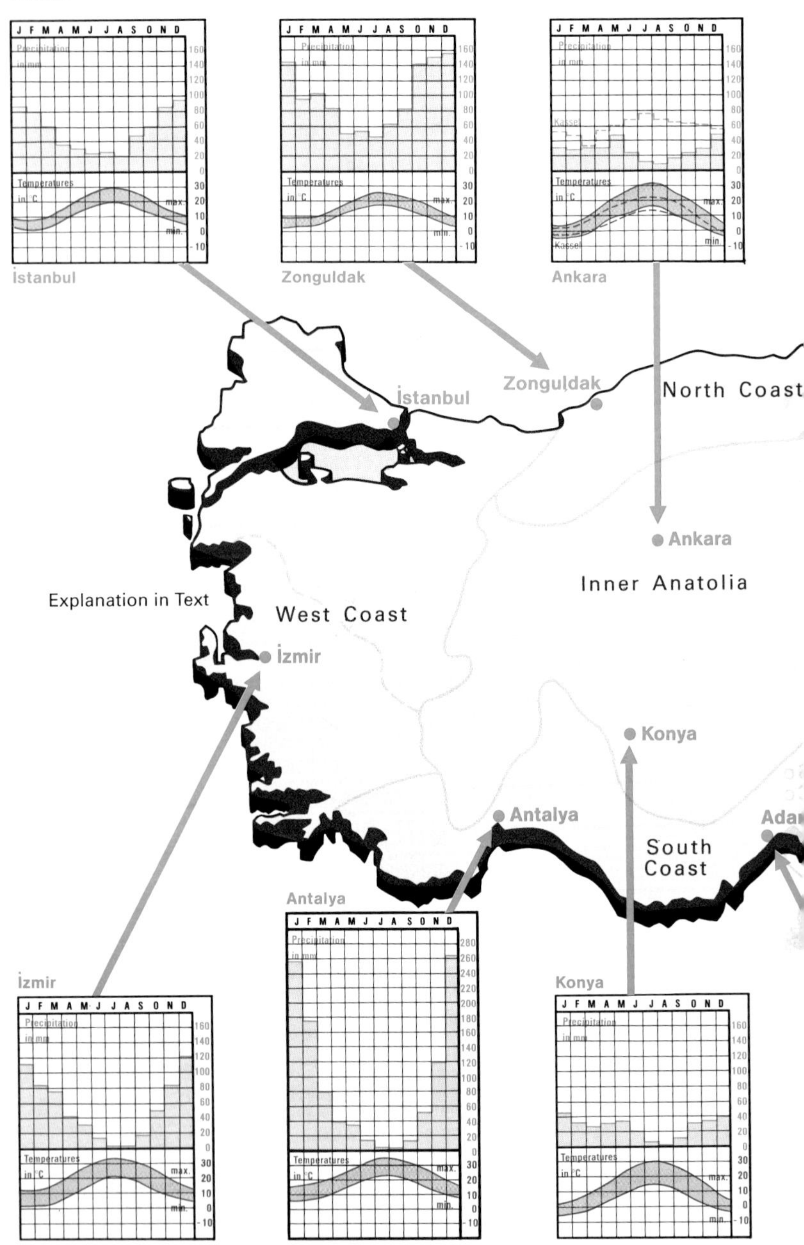

İstanbul
Zonguldak
Ankara
Kassel
Precipitation in mm
Temperatures in °C
max.
min.
J F M A M J J A S O N D
North Coast
Inner Anatolia
Explanation in Text
West Coast
İzmir
Konya
Antalya
South Coast

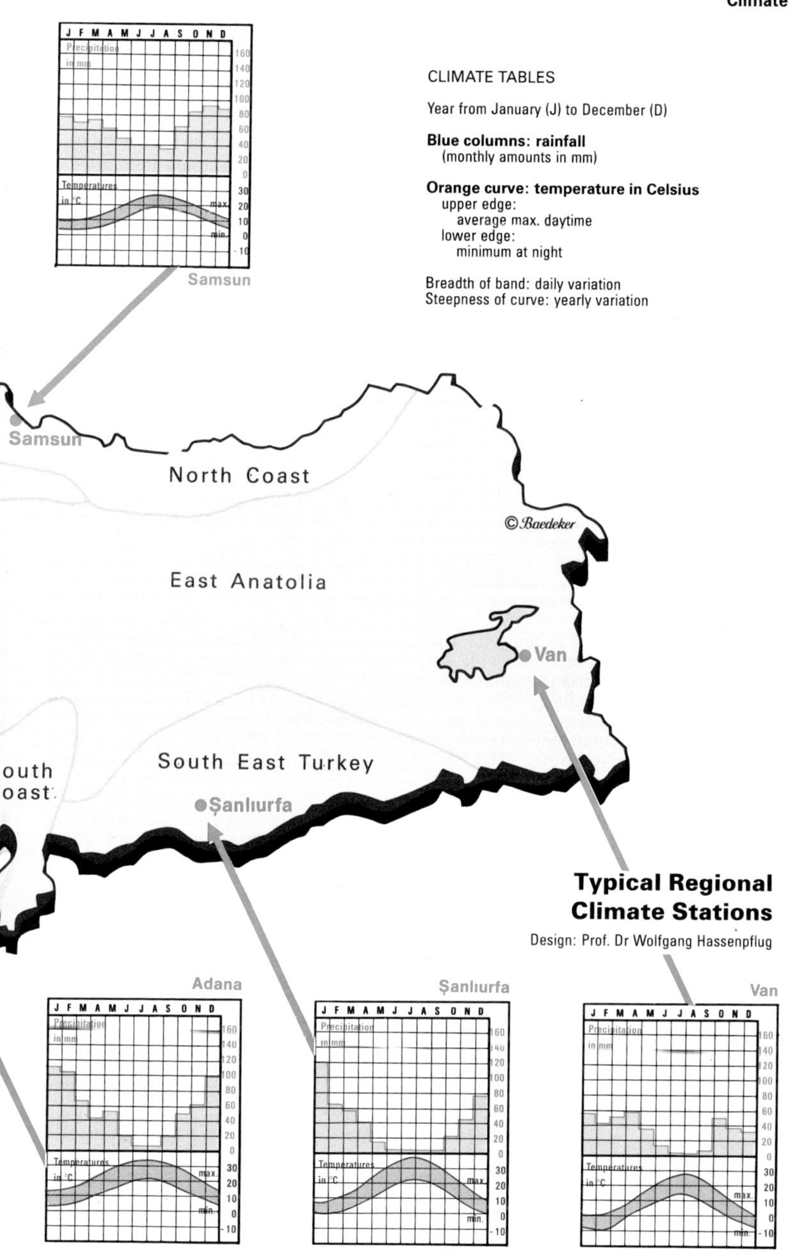

CLIMATE TABLES
Year from January (J) to December (D)
Blue columns: rainfall
(monthly amounts in mm)
Orange curve: temperature in Celsius
upper edge:
average max. daytime
lower edge:
minimum at night
Breadth of band: daily variation
Steepness of curve: yearly variation
Samsun
North Coast
© Baedeker
East Anatolia
Van
South East Turkey
Şanlıurfa
South Coast
Typical Regional Climate Stations
Design: Prof. Dr Wolfgang Hassenpflug
Adana
Şanlıurfa
Van
J F M A M J J A S O N D
Precipitation in mm
Temperatures in °C
max.
min.

Flora and Fauna

Flora

The climatic differences between the coastal regions on the Black Sea and on the Mediterranean are naturally reflected in their different patterns of vegetation.

The Black Sea coast has a vegetation pattern of almost Central European type. In those wooded areas that have survived in spite of the intensive cultivation of the coastal region fir, spruce, beech, oak, plane, elm, lime, ash and maple still flourish. Rhododendrons are found everywhere. Among evergreen shrubs the laurel and the arbutus (strawberry tree) are prominent.

As a result of population pressure in the Black Sea region the once-luxuriant natural vegetation is now steadily being displaced by the advance of cultivation. The crops to which the largest areas of cultivated land are devoted are hazelnuts and maize. The fig, which is not particularly sensitive to cold, is widely grown all along the Turkish north coast. Mandarins grow in the more sheltered coastal areas. Tea is cultivated round Rize. The olive also flourishes in certain parts of the region, but rarely above 100–200m/330–660ft.

The south and west coasts of Turkey show a typically Mediterranean vegetation pattern. The landscape in these regions is dominated by the macchia, a dense scrub-forest of evergreens, most of them leathery leaved. The whole spectrum of Mediterranean flora is found here, in particular the holm-oak with its small, shining, prickly leaves, the arbutus, the carob, the tree heath and the myrtle. The macchia is interrupted here and there by patches of woodland and areas of cultivation. Although centuries of slash-and-burn cultivation have much reduced the original forest cover the Turkish coast has preserved larger areas of forest than other Mediterranean countries. The predominant forest tree is *Pinus brutia*, a variant of the Aleppo pine. Also common is the stone pine, with large round cones which yield edible seeds reminiscent of hazelnuts. Among cultivated plants a place of predominant importance is occupied by the olive, which flourishes on the west coast up to about 400m/1300ft, on the south coast up to 700m/2300ft and in sheltered spots as high as 1000m/3300ft. In the fertile plains of this region other crops – grown with or without artificial irrigation – include citrus fruits, vines, figs, Mediterranean vegetables and increasingly also cotton and bananas.

Fauna

The fauna of the Turkish coastal regions include a wide variety of species, but their numbers have been greatly reduced in recent decades. As a result of forest fires and the uncontrolled shooting of any kind of game at any time of year red deer and roe deer, wild goats and wild sheep are now rarely encountered; only in the forests on the Black Sea coast are deer and smaller mammals to be seen in any numbers. Bears, red deer and wild boar still live in the mountains, and in the Taurus the occasional leopard as well as other wild cats. Donkeys and mules, traditionally valued as beasts of burden, are much in evidence throughout the country.

Tortoises are found in remarkable numbers along Turkey's southern and western coasts, while loggerhead turtles breed in the Dalyan Delta.

Kites are a familiar sight around İstanbul; white storks breed in a great many wetland areas of Turkey.

Although fishing is not uncommonly done with explosives and drag-nets, some coastal areas have preserved a surprising variety and surprising numbers of fishes and other marine animals. Among those found in the eastern Mediterranean are dolphins, mackerel, bass, moray, species of sea-bream, crustaceans and – rather more unusually – the dark red parrot-fish, the only representative of a tropical family of fishes to have established itself in the Mediterranean.

Aleppo pine

Reed beds and forest

Hisbiscus

Oranges ripening

Population

Development

Formed in the course of a development which has covered many millennia and can be traced back in the historical tradition for 4000 years – a development which has seen massive movements of peoples, ethnic overlays and assimilations involving Hittites, Phrygians, Persians, Macedonians, Greeks, Galatians (a Celtic people), Romans, Arabs, Seljuk and Ottoman Turks – Turkey has evolved a remarkably uniform human type showing a certain predominance of western Asiatic characteristics, usually of medium size and sturdy build, with a short skull and dark eyes and hair.

After the reduction of Turkish territory to its present frontiers the national unity was enhanced by the emigration and controlled resettlement of the Greek population of about 1,500,000, who were allowed to live only in certain specified areas (İstanbul, the islands of İmroz and Bozcaada), the expulsion of Armenians and the restriction of the Kurdish settlement areas on the one hand and by the return of over 1,000,000 Muslims (the muhacirs) from Bulgaria, Yugoslavia, Greece and Romania on the other.

The Kurds

The Kurdish peoples have no state of their own. They are Muslim, with an Iranian language, and live in the mountainous frontier regions of south-east Turkey, Syria, Iraq and Iran, an area known as Kurdistan. Almost half the Kurds are domiciled in Turkey, concentrated around their stronghold of Diyarbakır; the number of Syrian Kurds is, by comparison, small.

The Turkish State does not recognise the Kurds as a national minority, considering them "mountain Turks" with no claim to special rights. The Turkish Language Law of 1983 forbids the use of Kurdish in public. Rigorous suppression of Kurdish aspirations for independence has resulted in the radicalisation of their struggle for autonomy. The militant Kurdish Workers' Party (PKK) is banned in Turkey and its members and sympathisers ruthlessly hunted down by the national security forces.

Turkish nationalities

Over 90% of the population are Turks, at least 7% Kurds (officially "mountain Turks") and an estimated 1.6% Arabs; other ethnic minorities living in Turkey include Circassians (Cherkess), Georgians, Laz, Armenians, Abkhazians, Chechens, Yezidians, Greeks, Bulgarians, Albanians and Jews

Numbers, growth and distribution

Mainly as a result of the substantial excess of births over deaths, Turkey's population more than trebled in the fifty or so years between 1927 (when it stood at just over 13.6 million) and 1980 (just over 44.7 million); by 1993 it had risen to more than 59 million, with an annual rate of growth between 1980 and 1990 of 2.4%. Something over 10% of the population live in European Turkey (Avrupa Türkiyesi).

More than 1.3 million Turks live and work abroad, many of them in Germany.

Density

Density of population over the country as a whole is 76 per sq.km/197 per sq. mile. This bald statistic masks the huge divergence between areas of low population density in the interior, particularly the mountainous east and arid south-west, and those of high density around the country's perimeter. Chief among the latter are the eastern Black Sea coast, the coastal area between Ereğli and Zonguldak, the lowlands of

Typical scene of Turkish men meeting together

the Marmara and Ege regions, the plains in the hinterlands of Antalya, Adana and İskenderun, and the Hatay (Antakya), all of which also exhibit particularly high rates of population increase.

Some statistics

Average life expectancy in Turkey is 67 years, infant mortality 5.4%, the literacy rate 19%, and the official unemployment figure 8.6% and inflation is 70%.

Urban population

The proportion of the population living in towns has risen from 18.8% in 1927 to 64% in 1992.

Workforce

Turkey has a working population of over 20 million, of whom 45% make their living from the land, 32% in the service sector and 23% in industry.

Religion

Over 97% of Turks are Muslims, predominantly Sunni with about 22% Alevi (Shiite); there are small Jewish and Christian (Orthodox, Roman Catholic and Protestant) minorities.

Language

The official language is Turkish; the minorities use their own language among themselves.

Education

Under Atatürk's secular reforms, school attendance is officially compulsory between the ages of six and fourteen but in practice this only applies to the primary school years. Schooling is free and co-educational.

Although vocational training is not wholly in place, there are adequate secondary schools.

Overall the country has close on 30 universities and colleges. Particular emphasis is placed on teacher training, and adult education also plays an important role.

State and Society

Constitution and Government

According to its constitution the Republic of Turkey, officially "Türkiye Cumhuriyeti", is a "national, democratic, secular and socialist republic".

The legislature is the Greater National Assembly, consisting of the Parliament, with 450 members elected every four years by proportional representation, and the Senate, with 150 directly elected members, 15 members appointed by the head of state, and a number of life senators.

The head of state is the President, elected by the Greater National Assembly. The presidential period in office is restricted to one 7-year term.

Appointments to the Cabinet (prime minister and ministers) require a vote of confidence from the Assembly as a whole.

Political parties

Turkey's main political parties, in descending order of size according to the number of seats won in the 1991 parliamentary election, are the True Path Party (DYP), the Motherland Party (ANAP), the Social Democratic People's Party (SHP), the People's Workers' Party (HEP), the Party of the Democratic Left (DSP), the Nationalist Labour Party (MÇP) and the pro-Islamic Welfare Party (RP).

Legal system

Under the reformist constitution of 1923 the Turkish legal system was restructured and secularised; new criminal and civil codes were introduced modelled chiefly on Italian and Swiss law respectively.

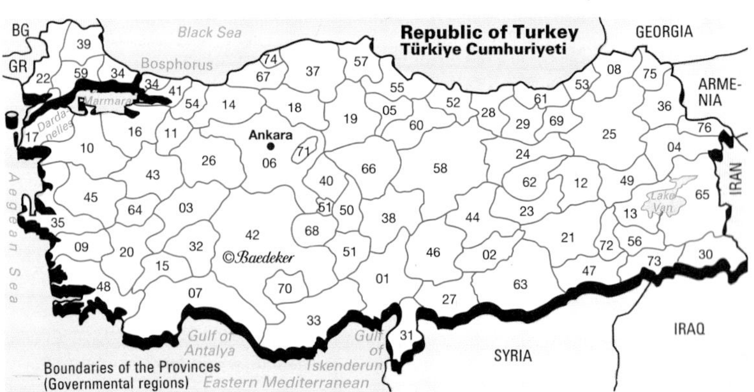

Boundaries of the Provinces (Governmental regions)

Administrative Districts

01 Adana
02 Adiyaman
03 Afyonkarahisar
04 Ağri
05 Amasya
06 Ankara
07 Antalya
08 Artvin
09 Aydın
10 Balıkesir
11 Bilecik
12 Bingöl
13 Bitlis
14 Bolu
15 Burdur
16 Bursa
17 Çanakkale
18 Çankırı
19 Çorum
20 Denizli
21 Diyarbakır
22 Edirne
23 Elâziğ
24 Erzincan
25 Erzurum
26 Eskişehir
27 Gaziantep
28 Giresun
29 Gümüşhane
30 Hakkâri
31 Hatay (Antakya)
32 Isparta
33 İçel (Mersin)
34 İstanbul
35 İzmir
36 Kars
37 Kastamonu
38 Kayseri
39 Kırklareli
40 Kirşehir
41 Kocaeli (Izmit)
42 Konya
43 Kütahya
44 Malatya
45 Manisa
46 Kahramanmaraş (Maraş)
47 Mardin
48 Muğla
49 Muş
50 Nevşehir
51 Niğde
52 Ordu
53 Rize
54 Sakarya (Adapazarı)
55 Samsun
56 Siirt
57 Sinop
58 Sivas
59 Tekirdağ
60 Tokat
61 Trabzon
62 Tunceli
63 Şanlıurfa (Urfa)
64 Uşak
65 Van
66 Yozgat
67 Zonguldak
68 Aksaray
69 Bayburt
70 Karaman
71 Kırıkkale
72 Batman
73 Şırnak
74 Bartın
75 Ardahan
76 Iğdır

Administrative divisions

Turkey's primary administrative unit is the province or, in Turkish, "il" (formerly "vilayet", "elayet" or "sancak"). Until a few years ago there were 73 such provinces, numbered alphabetically from Adana (01) to Zonguldak (73). Since then another three have been created: Bartin, Ardahan and Iğdır. The 76 provinces are subdivided into a total of 600 smaller units known as "ilçe" (formerly "kaza"), which in turn are further subdivided into some 900 rural districts or "bucak" (formerly "nahiye"). Special development projects are planned in respect of the provincial capitals which between them are responsible for the administration of more than 35,000 towns and villages.

Membership of international organisations

Turkey is a member of or signatory to, inter alia, the United Nations (UN) and various UN affiliated bodies, the World Health Organisation (WHO), the General Agreement on Tariffs and Trade (GATT), the International Monetary Fund (IMF), the Organisation for Economic Co-operation and Development (OECD), the North Atlantic Treaty Organisation (NATO; since 1952) and, since 1990, the European Conference on Security and Co-operation.

Turkey is linked to the European Union (EU) by a Treaty of Association negotiated with the European Common Market (as it was then) in 1963. Long sought-after membership of the EU Customs Union was finally achieved in 1996, a boost to pro-Western elements in the Turkish administration. Turkey played a leading role in the setting up in 1991 of an "economic community" of Black Sea states, which has its headquarters in İstanbul.

Diplomatic relations

Turkey maintains diplomatic relations with most of the world's countries.

History

Prehistory — Asia Minor is already settled by man in the Stone Age. The first evidence of unified settlements dates from the Neolithic (4th/3rd millennium B.C.); small, well-fortified settlements with the residence of the chieftain or prince. This culture, which is still without the art of writing, is influenced by the Sumerians.

2000 B.C. onwards — The Hittites – an Indo-European people – push into Anatolia in a series of waves and thereafter establish their authority over the natives.

c. 1650–*c.* 1460 — Labarna (whose name becomes the title of later Hittite kings) founds the Hittite Old Kingdom, or Kingdom of Hatti. Under his successors the original territory round the capital, Hattusa (some 200km/125 miles east of Ankara), is considerably extended.

c. 1460–*c.* 1200 — After a period of weakness the Hittite kingdom takes on a fresh lease of life under a new dynasty: establishment of the New Empire, whose greatest ruler Suppiluliuma I (1380–46) reorganises the Hittite State and greatly extends its frontiers.

In the late 13th c. Hittite power begins to decline. The end comes with an attack by the "Sea Peoples", coming from Thrace. An attack from the same quarter brings about the fall of Troy VIIA (identified with Homer's Troy).

c. 1200–*c.* 1000 — During the great Aegean Migration the west coast of Asia Minor is settled by Greek peoples (Ionians, Aeolians, Dorians). The further development of the Greek cities in Asia Minor runs broadly parallel to that of mainland Greece, and they take a major part in the Greek colonising movement (700 B.C. onwards). Miletus alone – the political and cultural leader among the cities on the west coast of Asia Minor – is credited with the establishment of more than 90 colonies on the shores of the Black Sea.

c. 800–*c.* 680 — The Phyrgians, an Indo-European people, amalgamate the smaller political units in Central Anatolia into a large kingdom with its capital at Gordion. During the reign of King Midas, famed for his legendary wealth, the kingdom eventually falls to the advancing Cimmerians.

c. 680–546 — After the expulsion of the Cimmerians the Kingdom of Lydia succeeds Phrygia as a leading power in Asia Minor. The Greek cities on the west coast, with the exception of Miletus, come under Lydian control.

The Lydians were probably the first people to replace the pieces of metal used in payment for goods by stamped coins (7th c.).

546 — A pre-emptive attack on the Persians by King Kroisos (Croesus) of Lydia is defeated. The Lydian kingdom and soon afterwards the whole of Asia Minor, including the Greek cities on the west coast, are incorporated in the Persian Empire.

500–494 — A rising by the Ionian cities on the west coast of Asia Minor under the leadership of Miletus marks the beginning of the Persian Wars, which continue until 478. After years of fighting the rising is put down by the Persians and Miletus is destroyed.

334–323 — The structure of the Persian Empire has become gradually looser, and the satraps (provincial governors) and the subject peoples have become increasingly independent. As a result Alexander the Great is able to gain control of Asia Minor in one rapid victorious campaign.

After Alexander's death Asia Minor becomes a bone of contention between the Diadochoi (Successors). 323–281

After a period during which none of the Diadochoi is able to establish his authority on a durable basis the Seleucids gain control of almost the whole of Asia Minor. The cities on the south-west and south coasts at first fall to the Seleucids, but then come under Egyptian influence. 281–263

Thanks to the loose administrative control exercised by the Persians, a number of independent principalities (Pontos, Bithynia on the north coast of Asia Minor, etc.) are established.

The Kingdom of Pergamon becomes the dominant power in western Asia Minor. In their struggle against the Seleucids the rulers of Pergamon ally themselves with Rome. The last King bequeaths his kingdom to Rome. 263–133

The Romans declare the western part of Asia Minor a Roman province under the name of Asia. 129

The Roman general Pompey (Pompeius) reorganises the administration of Asia Minor. A series of "client States" are established bordering the Roman provinces which ring almost the whole coastline of Asia Minor. 63 B.C.

Under Roman rule western Asia Minor enjoys a period of economic prosperity and cultural flowering.

Paul's missionary journeys to Asia Minor. from A.D. 250

In subsequent decades the political centre of gravity moves increasingly to the north-west. After the administrative division of the Empire into an eastern and a western half Diocletian (284–305) makes Nikomedeia (now İzmit) his preferred place of residence. c. A.D. 250

Constantine the Great (324–37) makes Byzantium, renamed Constantinople, capital of the Empire. 330

After the division of the Empire by Theodosius the Great Asia Minor becomes the heartland of the East Roman (Byzantine) Empire. The bases of the State are Roman law and administration, Greek language and culture and the Christian faith. 394–95

At the death of the Emperor Basil II (976–1025) the Byzantine Empire is at the apex of its power. Thereafter conflicts between the administrative and the military aristocracy lead to a decline in fiscal and military power. 1025

On August 19th Emperor Romanus IV Diogenes and his Byzantine army are decisively defeated by the Seljuk Turks of Rum under Sultan Alp Arslan at the Battle of Mantzikert (Manzikert; present-day Malazgirt, in the Ararat highlands north-west of Lake Van). The Seljuks proceed to conquer large areas of Central Anatolia, even advancing as far as the Mediterranean. 1071

The Fourth Crusade becomes a catastrophe for the Byzantine Empire. The Crusaders capture Constantinople and establish a Latin Empire, with territory in north-western Asia Minor. The Byzantine Emperor regains control of these territories only in 1261. 1203–04

The Ottomans, whose expansion has been a growing threat since the end of the 13th c., take Constantinople (May 29th) and put an end to the Byzantine Empire. The city, renamed İstanbul, becomes capital of the Ottoman Empire. 1453

History

1520–66 During the reign of Suleiman the Magnificent the Ottoman Empire reaches its highest peak. As well as the whole of Asia Minor it controls Mesopotamia, Syria, Egypt and North Africa as far west as Morocco (1580); its outposts in the north are Hungary and Transylvania (a vassal State); it exerts influence, directly or indirectly, over extensive territories on the north coast of the Black Sea; and in the east its authority extends as far as the Caspian Sea.

1683 After the failure of the Second Siege of Vienna (following a first unsuccessful siege in 1529) the decline of Ottoman power begins. Over the next two centuries the Empire is compelled to give up large areas of territory. In parallel with this external decline goes an internal decay: the sultans increasingly withdraw from the direction of Government business and from active participation in military campaigns, while in the provinces the local governors become increasingly powerful.

from 1800 The Ottoman Empire becomes more and more dependent on the western European Powers, which increasingly offer it protection against Russia (Russo–Turkish Wars). This political rapprochement also influences the domestic situation: reform of the army with the help of Prussian officers, administrative and legal reforms, increasing influence of European culture.

1841 The Dardanelles Treaty between the Ottoman Empire, Britain, France, Austria and Prussia bans the passage of all non-Turkish warships through the Dardanelles.

1856 The Treaty of Paris, which ends the Crimean War (1853–56), guarantees the independence of the Ottoman Empire. The Empire's financial dependence on the Western Powers, however, increases.

1876 A new constitution (abrogated only a year later) provides for the equality of all religions and peoples within the Ottoman Empire.

1878 The Ottoman Empire is compelled to cede the sovereignty of Cyprus to Britain.

1908 The Young Turk movement, an opposition group directed against abritrary rule by the Sultan and control by foreign Powers, secures the restoration of the 1876 Constitution.

1914–18 The Ottoman Empire enters the First World War as an ally of the Central Powers and gains some successes during the earlier phase of the war: in 1915–16 an Allied attempt to occupy the Dardanelles is defeated. But the final year of the war brings defeat and surrender.

The armistice signed at Moudros on October 30th 1918 in effect marks the end of the Ottoman Empire.

1919 Mustafa Kemal Paşa (b. 1881 in Salonica, d. 1938 in İstanbul) organises national resistance to Allied control over extensive areas of Turkish territory.

1920 A large National Assembly, meeting in Ankara, refuses to recognise the Sultan's authority and establishes a new government led by Mustafa Kemal.

1920–22 During the Greek–Turkish War the Greeks rapidly occupy large parts of western Anatolia but are then compelled by Turkish forces to withdraw. The evacuation of Smyrna (İzmir) in September 1922 ends 3000 years of Greek settlement on the west coast of Anatolia.

1922 Mustafa Kemal proclaims the abolition of the Sultanate (November 1st).

Under the Treaty of Lausanne (July 24th) the Allies recognise Turkish sovereignty, but Turkey is compelled to give up the non-Turkish parts of the former Ottoman Empire. On October 29th the Republic of Turkey is proclaimed. Mustafa Kemal (on whom, eleven years later, in 1934, the title "Atatürk" – father of the Turks – is bestowed) becomes its first President, and in subsequent years carries out comprehensive reforms: displacement of Islamic law, abolition of polygamy, political equality of women, introduction of the Latin alphabet, modern labour and social legislation, etc. Ankara become capital of the Turkish Republic. 1923

İsmet Inönü succeeds Atatürk as President. During his period of office greater democracy is introduced. 1938

During the Second World War Turkey at first remains neutral, but later draws closer to the Allies. On February 23rd 1945 it declares war on Germany. 1939–45

An aid agreement (arms credits) with the United States fosters the association of Turkey with the Western system of alliances. 1947

Celal Bayar, leader of the Democratic Party, which wins a general election, becomes President, with Adnan Menderes as Prime Minister. 1950

Turkey joins NATO. 1952

Violent student riots against anti-democratic measures introduced by Menderes (Press censorship, etc.) are followed by a military rising under General Cemal Gürsel, who takes over the government. Bayar, Menderes and other politicians are arrested, and some are executed. 1960

Cyprus is granted independence by Britain (August 16th). Since the Turkish Cypriot minority is given rights of self-government only in religious and cultural matters, there is subsequently much fighting between Turkish and Greek Cypriots.

Adoption of a new constitution which guarantees the basic rights of the individual and provides for far-reaching educational and social reforms. 1961

After the victory of the Justice Party in an election Süleyman Demirel becomes Prime Minister. 1966

Cevdet Sunay succeeds the gravely ill Cemal Gürsel as President. Increasing radicalisation of political life. 1966

Admiral Fahri Korutürk is elected President. On October 30th, almost 50 years to the day from the inauguration of the Republic (September 29th 1923), the first bridge over the Bosphorus (İstanbul Boğazı Köprüsü) opens to traffic. 1973

In an election in October the Republican People's Party gains a simple majority and its leader, Bülent Ecevit, forms a coalition government with the Islamic and conservative National Salvation Party. 1974

In Cyprus the National Guard, with the support of the military régime in Greece, rebels against President Makarios. When Ecevit, the Prime Minister, sends Turkish troops to the island the revolt collapses; but the Turks nevertheless occupy the northern part of the island.

The conflict over Cyprus compels Ecevit to resign (September).

The six-month-old Government crisis is ended by the formation of a coalition of the right led by Demirel, the Prime Minister (March 31st). 1975

1977 Further Government crisis: neither Ecevit nor Demirel is able to form a stable government.

1978 Ecevit becomes Prime Minister again (January 5th). Terrorist attacks by extremist groups of both right and left increase in number. The Government puts many provinces under martial law.

1979 Demirel succeeds Ecevit as Prime Minister.

Pope John Paul II makes an official visit to Turkey (November 28th) – the first Pope to do so. He has conversations with the Orthodox Patriarch of Constantinople on the possibility of a rapprochement between their two Churches, in schism since 1054.

1980 The army seizes power in a bloodless *coup d'état* (September 12th). Parliament is dissolved and the National Security Council established as the supreme organ of government, headed by General Kenan Evren. A new government is formed, with Bülent Ülüsü as Prime Minister. It proclaims martial law in all the country's provinces, prohibits the operation of parties and trade unions, restricts Press freedom and arrests many politicians.

Amnesty International accuses the military junta of torturing prisoners detained in the fight against left- and right-wing terrorists.

1981 President Kenan Evren inaugurates "Atatürk Year". Dissolution of all political parties (October 16th).

1982 In a Referendum on November 7th an overwhelming majority of the population approves a new draft Constitution. In voting for the Constitution they are also voting for the election of General Evren as President for a seven-year term. Although the Constitution guarantees the basic human rights it leaves the military with great influence on policy.

1983 Subject to certain conditions, the establishment of political parties is permitted from May 16th (new parties and electoral laws).

A general election on November 6th is won by ANAP, the Motherland Party; a technocrat, Turgut Özal, becomes Prime Minister.

On November 15th the Parliament of the Turkish-held part of Cyprus proclaims the "Independent Turkish Republic of Northern Cyprus" with Rauf Raşit Denktaş as "President"; Turkey is the only country to grant recognition. The UN Security Council does not accept the legal validity of this action.

1984 In protest against inhuman conditions in Turkish prisons hundreds of political prisoners go on hunger strike; some die. Martial law is suspended in certain provinces.

1985/86 A "freedom of movement" provision in the 1963 Treaty of Association linking Turkey with the European Union (as it now is), grants Turkish nationals the right to seek employment in any EU country. As the effective date (December 1st 1986) approaches, these rights of entry become an issue between Turkey and the Federal Republic of Germany.

1987 In the controversy with Greece over the exploration of the Aegean Sea Turkey withdraws temporarily from the planned search for oil in the international waters of the continental shelf in the area of the Greek Islands.

On April 14th the Republic of Turkey officially applies to join the European Community (EC; now, since 1993, the European Union – EU).

A controversial change in electoral law enables the ANAP to retain power in the parliamentary elections. Özal continues as Prime Minister.

Following an international conference on economic reform, held at the end of January at Davos in Switzerland, the Turkish Prime Minister Özal and the Greek Prime Minister Papandreou declare that in future Greece and Turkey will strive for peaceful relations between the two countries. 1988

On July 3rd the second Bosphorus bridge (Fâtih Sultan Mehmet Köprüsü) opens.

Local elections result in victory for the Social Democratic People's Party (SHP) led by Erdal Inönü. 1989

Over 200,000 Turks are expelled from Bulgaria (July).

In October Turgut Özal is elected President and Yıldırım Akbulut Prime Minister.

The EC Commission turns down talks on Turkey's membership of the European Community (December).

The Turkish Parliament agrees to the deployment of Turkish troops in the Gulf. At the special Paris Summit on European Security and Co-operation in November, Turkey is a signatory to the "Paris Charter for a New Europe" pledging to uphold democracy and the rule of law, to observe human rights, and to promote friendly relations with other signatories. 1990

Turkey strengthens its relations with the states of the former Soviet Union and also Iran. 1991

By the end of April more than 200,000 Kurds have crossed into Turkey to escape from persecution in Iraq during and after the Gulf War.

In the parliamentary elections held on October 20th the conservative DYP, the Party of the Right Way, emerges victorious with 27% of the votes cast, as against 24% for the Motherland Party (ANAP) which has been in power for eight years. The DYP's Süleyman Demirel heads the new coalition government.

An agreement on economic co-operation among countries bordering the Black Sea, an initiative launched by President Özal, is initialled in İstanbul on February 2nd and signed by eleven states on July 25th. 1992

Following continual raids by Kurdish guerillas on Turkish garrisons and police stations, the air force steps up attacks on Kurdish villages near the Turkish–Iraqi border.

Agreement is reached with Syria on joint exploitation of the waters of the Euphrates following the official opening on July 24th of the Atatürk Dam.

After the sudden death of President Turgut Özal (on April 17th, in Ankara), Süleyman Demirel is chosen (May 16th) to succeed him for a seven-year term. 1993

Elected on June 13th to the chair of the True Path Party (DYP), economist Tansu Çiller (b. 1946) becomes Turkey's first woman Prime Minister.

Following local elections, municipal leaders in İstanbul and Ankara come from the pro-Islamic Welfare Party (SP). 1994

Repeated attacks by the Kurdish Workers' Party (PKK) on south coast tourist resorts lead to a dramatic fall in the number of visitors. Policing is stepped up as an additional safety measure.

Turkish troops cross the border into northern Iraq to search out and destroy PKK bases, withdrawing after a few weeks. Following a lull in terrorist attacks the number of tourists shows signs of tentative recovery. 1995

In the parliamentary elections at the end of December the pro-Islamic Welfare Party (SP) make the greatest gains, winning 158 of the 550 parliamentary seats and a coalition government is formed.

1996 In January Turkey is admitted to the customs union of the EU (European Union).

In June, Prime Minister Muset Yilmaz (Motherland Party leader), resigns as head of minority coalition government formed with the True Path Party.

Historic Kingdoms and Provinces of the Anatolian Coast (Map p. 38)

Bithynia

Characteristics

The ancient province of Bithynia centred on the fertile plain of north-west Anatolia, bordered in the west by the Bosphorus and Sea of Marmara and in the north by the Black Sea and inland extending eastwards as far as the mountain passes beyond Bolu and southwards to the Ulu Dağ mountains south of the Gulf of İzmit and the Köroğlu Dağları hills. Geologically speaking parts of its north-western edge still belong to Thrace, while to the east and south, chalk and palaeozoic slate and limestone come together to form hills and mountains reaching their greatest altitude in the Ulu Dağ (2500m/8205ft). Verdant forests of beech, pine, fir, oak and rhododendron grow on Bithynia's well-watered Black Sea slopes, while farming prospers in the sunshine higher up. In some parts agriculture of a more intensive kind is practised by relatively recent settlers such as the muhacir who made their homes in the region after being driven from the Balkans, Caucasus, Crimea and elsewhere when the Ottoman Empire was stripped of its provinces there in the late 19th c. One of Turkey's most densely populated areas, the Bithynian plain today carries the principal routes from İstanbul to Ankara as well as forming part of the industrial zone of the country's north-west, much of it concentrated around İzmit, Adapazarı and Bursa.

History

Lying at the crossroads of Europe and Asia Minor, the territory of ancient Bithynia was constantly being fought over. Originally settled by the Thracians, it was taken by the Lydians in around 550 B.C. and later by the Persians. Since the wooded mountains of the north lay outside the hegemony of Alexander the Great and his successors, Bithynia was left to develop more or less independently under the Seleucids and by the 2nd c. B.C. had become a kingdom in its own right, flourishing around its ancient capitals of Nikomedeia (İzmit) and Nicaea (İznik). In 74 B.C. it was made a Roman province. Under the Romans, the Greek city colony of Chalcedon, founded on the Bosphorus around 675 B.C. and situated where the İstanbul suburb of Kadıköy stands today, became the provincial capital. During the Byzantine era Chalcedon was the seat of an important archbishopric and was the venue in 451 of the Fourth Ecumenical Council. In the 11th c. Bithynia was ruled by the Seljuks. Since the 14th c. it has been Ottoman and, in Bursa, furnished the Ottomans with their first capital.

Caria

Characteristics and History

The ancient coastal province of Caria in the south-western corner of Asia Minor lay more of less between the Maeander (Büyuk Menderes) and the Dalaman/Koca Çayı rivers. Somewhat of a backwater today, Caria enjoyed considerable importance in ancient times on account of the many harbours along its deeply indented coastline, its relatively dense population, and the well-trodden trade route through the Maeander valley, with Miletus at its mouth. No clear picture has yet emerged of the Carians who originally lived there and whose inscriptions are still to be deciphered. Their national shrine was the temple of Zeus Labrayndos (with the double axe) at Mylasa (Milas).

Ancient authors speak of the Carians as early pre-Greek seafarers, pushed south from their island homes and the coasts of the Troad by the Greeks and living in loose federations of tribes with their own culture in only a few cities (Mylasa/Milas, Alinda/Çina, Alabanda). In the late 7th c. B.C. Caria's cities were ruled by the Lydians and in the 6th c. by the Persians, achieving independence only in 387 B.C. when they joined other regions of Asia Minor in the Delian League. The subsequent Persian satrap dynasty and later struggle for power among the Diadochoi (which brought a measure of Hellenisation in terms of speech and writing to Caria in the period after Alexander), were finally ended by Rome in 129 B.C. From 27 B.C. onwards Caria was to enjoy over two centuries of prosperity under Roman rule while managing to preserve its own culture, writing and pre-Indo-European language.

Cilicia

Characteristics

The ancient kingdom of Cilicia in Asia Minor was the area the west of which was known to the Assyrians as Khilakku and the east as Kue. The western half, Cilicia Tracheia or "rough" Cilicia, comprises the rugged and still largely undeveloped and inaccessible range of the Taurus Mountains which drop steeply down to the sea, while to the east lies the fertile Cilician plain with its fields of grain and cotton and its banana and citrus groves. Administratively, a somewhat similar division still persists today, this flourishing modern agricultural region with its well-developed industrial base being split between the two Turkish provinces of İçel and Adana, the former having Mersin as its capital and the latter the industrial city of Adana at the very heart of the Cilician plain.

Cilicia was never a kingdom in its own right for very long, being too much of a buffer state and continually prey to the rivalries of neighbouring powers. There is no doubt, on the other hand, that from very earliest times this was one of those regions which served as a cradle of ancient civilisations. On the Çukurova plain alone, between Mersin and Toprakkale, there are 150 historic sites, some dating back as far as the neolithic, chalcolithic and bronze ages, others representing important legacies from the Hittite period right up to Classical Greece and Rome.

Fashioned by the Seyhan and Ceyhan – the "rivers of Paradise" as the Arab geographers called them – the fertile alluvial plains of the Taurus foreland have been inhabited for many thousands of years.

History

Cilicia was probably in part and for a time incorporated into the independent kingdoms of Arzawa and Kizzuwadna (later, from about 1650 B.C.), buffer states between the Hittites and the Mitanni. For some 400 years, from 1196 B.C., it belonged to the late Hittite Kueli kingdom. After the established order in Anatolia was destroyed in the late 7th c. B.C. by invading Scythian and Cimmerian "barbarians" from southern Russia, one of the new political entities to emerge as the regions sought to establish their own identity was a kingdom of Cilicia south of the Taurus. The Cilician kings, ruling in Tarsus as vassals of the Persians, contrived to retain a degree of independence and succeeded in expanding their territory as far as Cappadocia and Pamphylia.

Around 103 B.C. Cilicia came under the sway of the Romans. It was not until 66 B.C. however, after Pompey had rooted out and vanquished the fearsome pirates from their lairs in the west, that Tarsus became the capital of the Roman province of Cilicia. This ushered in a long period of prosperity which ended only in the 7th c. A.D. when the Arabs swept up from the south. The Armenian kingdom of Cilicia (Little Armenia, until 1375) took root in the late 11th c., from 1199 enjoying Crusader support. Thereafter Armenians continued to live in the Taurus mountains north-east of Adana and in Kahramanmaraş (Maraş) around Hacin right up until their deportation earlier this century.

Between 1352 and 1378 the Ramazanoğlu nomads succeeded in establishing their own independent principality in the face of the Turcoman tribes who, ever since 1185, had been gradually moving into the area from the north-east. Despite being absorbed into the Ottoman

Empire in 1517, this was to survive for about 250 years. In time, and against a background of increasing political instability (uprising at Celäli and Saruca/Sebkan), the demands of these wandering herdsmen led to the flatter parts of Cilicia near the coast being turned over to winter grazing, with fewer and fewer settlements. It was only when the nomadic way of life was abruptly terminated in the late 19th c. that cultivation resumed on the coastal plain.

Ionia

Characteristics and History

The offshore islands and fertile plain along Turkey's south-western Aegean coast formed the ancient region of Ionia. The people who colonised the area in the 1st millennium B.C. were probably the first Greeks to move into Asia Minor. Immensely rich in culture, especially in Archaic times, Ionia originally embraced the cities of Ephesus, Erythrae, Clazomenae, Colophon, Lebedos, Miletus, Myus, Priene and Teos, these being later joined by Chios, Phocaea and Samos to form the Ionian League. The Ionians' religious centre was the shrine of Poseidon in the Panionion on Mount Mykale. The cities were quickly blessed with immense prosperity thanks to their position on the trade routes from the east. This contact with the old civilisations of the Orient led to a great flowering of cultural life in Ionia, which became the home of poets (Homer probably lived in Smyrna around 800 B.C.), philosophers (Thales, Heraclitus of Ephesus, Pythagoras of Samos), historians (Herodotus) and physicians (Hippocrates). Ionian artists were equally gifted, producing paintings and sculptures of a breathtaking lightness and grace. It is to the supple spirit of the Ionians that Greek architecture owes its originality, elegance and charm. On the darker side, internal feuding undermined their great democracies and opened the way to rule by tyrants. Ionia was to play its last major role on the stage of world history with the Ionian uprising of 500–494 B.C., which saw the destruction of Miletus by the Persians. Following Alexander's conquest of Asia, the Ionian cities enjoyed a second flowering, producing such marvels as the Temple of Diana (Artemis) at Ephesus, one of the seven wonders of the ancient world.

Isauria

Characteristics and History

The Taurus mountain country north of Pamphylia and Cilicia, around the modern-day small towns of Mut, Ermenek, Hadım, Bozkır, Seydişehir and Beyşehir, was known to the ancients as Isauria. With its landscape of mountains and basins surrounding Lakes Beyşehir (Kireli Gölü) and Suğla (Karaviran Gölü), Isauria forms, together with Pisidia adjoining it to the west, part of Anatolia's upland lake district. Merging gradually into the high plateau of Lycaonia further to the north and east, Isauria's relative remoteness only ended with the building of the Anatolian railway and the Eğridir line along the Maeander valley.

Comparatively little is known of the original Isaurians except that they were a rough people, a law unto themselves, feared far and wide as notorious pirates. Around the middle of the 1st c. B.C. Marcus Aurelius Polemo, one of the high priests of the temple city of Olba on the Taşili plateau, succeeded in uniting the savage tribes of the Taurus into one independent kingdom. Later the Byzantine emperor Leo I used these warlike tribesmen to break the power of the Ostrogoths. Following his death in 474, Leo was succeeded by a former Isaurian leader, Tarsikodissa, who had changed his name to Zenon. The early years of the Byzantine era had at long last seen the Isaurians become more civilised, but under Zenon they contrived to be as much of a nuisance as the Ostrogoths before them; indeed, in Byzantine eyes, their level of culture remained well below that of the Goths. Despite Zenon having

Ruins of a Byzantine church near Alanya

built the Byzantine basilica over the catacombs of St Thekla at Silifke, his successor Athanasius, after prolonged hostilities, was forced to despatch the unruly Isaurians to Thrace and settle them there.

Lazistan

Characteristics and History

Lazistan, the land of the Laz and most easterly of the Pontine provinces, occupies the narrow scenic Black Sea coastal strip to the east of Trabzon, extending to beyond Artvin. Until the early Middle Ages it was the ancient kingdom of Colchis, the same green and rainsoaked land to which, in the days of King Aietes, Jason and the Argonauts came in search of the Golden Fleece, and where lived Medea, legendary princess-progenitor of the Medeans. The principal town on the coast is Rize. Further inland lies the lovely little mountain town of Artvin (see entry) on the Çoruh Nehri.

The Laz still form a sizeable ethnic minority in the area to the south and south-west of Batum (Georgia), mostly in Turkish territory. The "Lazoi" were Orthodox Christians from the early 6th c. and until the 10th c. had their own kingdom. Conquered by Mehmet II in 1461, the kingdom fragmented into as many valley principalities as there were valleys. The people also converted to Islam and today are as zealous Sunnites as they were once Christians. The Turks called the country Çengelistan, "land of the barbed hook", on account of its inaccessibility and the contrariness of its inhabitants. Until the 19th c. Lazistan was an Ottoman province in its own right, enjoying considerable independence from Istanbul; even at that time the Laz were in the habit of moving abroad in search of work, travelling to neighbouring Georgia.

The Acropolis of Pergamon ▶

Historic Kingdoms and Provinces of the Anatolian Coast

Lydia

Characteristics

Many scholars, when referring to ancient Lydia, include the Ionian fringe around İzmir (Smyrna) on the Aegean coast. And not without reason. Similar in landscape and closely interwoven historically with the Lydian heartland, its influence lent a finer gloss to the innately less refined architecture and sculpture of the Lydians. Here are found Anatolia's largest and most densely populated lowland plains, matched only by the Çukurova plain in Cilicia, plains which, within Lydia as the seat of early civilisation, attained political and economic significance earlier than the hinterland. This coastal region, the most heavily indented section of the Turkish coast and thus blessed with the most harbours, divides naturally into a number of distinctive, self-contained units which, in ancient times, set themselves apart from Lydia proper as the twelve Ionian city states. The ancient Lydian capital of Sardis, its wealth founded on gold from the river Pactolos (Sart Çayı), foreign trade, and the skill of its artists and craftsmen (paintings, bronze and gold jewellery) was situated in central western Lydia. The Ionian heartland, by contrast, with the ancient centre of Ephesus, lay between the Gediz (Hermos) river in the north and Küçük Menderes (Caestros) in the south. The less densely populated hill country of eastern Lydia, with its upland pastures and fields of grain interrupted by the Katakekaumene, the "burnt land" of the ancients, the badlands of basalt clinker and lavafields around Kula, heralds the transition to the steppe-like landscape of neighbouring Phrygia.

History

Originating in the 14th/13th c. B.C., Lydia's early history is shrouded in legend. It first makes its appearance as a historical entity in the early 7th c. B.C. when, following the destruction of the Phrygian kingdom by the Cimmerians, the Mermnades dynasty headed a large and powerful realm with its capital at Sardis. It is said to have been ruled by the famous Atyad dynasty, identified with the Assuwa referred to in Hittite inscriptions. Their successors, following the Thracian invasion in around 1200 B.C., were the mythical Heraklides dynasty, descendants of Hercules. Lydia later became a Persian satrapy and thereafter shared the fate of the rest of Asia Minor.

The Lydians' language, known only from 65 inscriptions dating from the 6th/4th c. B.C., reveals clear Hittite influence. As a people they were famous as much for their craftsmen as for their legendary King Croesus, defeated by the Persians in 546 B.C. Culturally as well as geographically they occupied an intermediate position between Greece and the Near East.

Lycaonia

Characteristics and History

Few travellers will be familiar with the name of Lycaonia, the ancient province once situated high on the great plateau of Central Anatolia, bordered by the Central Taurus to the south and having at its heart the classical Iconeum (Konya). Ringed by mountains, Lycaonia's arid plains are by far the driest on the plateau (annual precipitation less than 300mm/12in.) and in summer its limitless vistas of treeless steppe recall nothing so much as the deserts of Arabia. In spring however, largely through artificial irrigation, this dry-farming country is transformed into a sea of green, as befits one of the great breadbaskets of Turkey. A mountain town, a garden-like oasis, guards each of the main passes leading out of Lycaonia – Konya, on the route to Pisidia and Phrygia, Niğde and Aksaray on the roads to Cappadocia, Ereğli keeping watch before the Cilician Gates, and Karaman on the way taken by Frederick Barbarossa to Kalykadnos.

Although Lycaonia may well have been the cradle of Anatolian pre-history (Çatalhüyük), it was never of great importance in classical times. Only under the Seljuks and their successors, the Karaman dynasty, did powerful and enduring independent kingdoms emerge.

Lycia

Characteristics

The broad peninsula in the extreme south of what was the Turcoman Tekke principality in south-western Anatolia, and which now takes in parts of the provinces of Antalya, Muğla, Burdur and Denizli, was known to the ancients as Lycia. Exceptionally rich in culture and history and with a coastline only recently opened up to tourism, it has one of Turkey's most contrasting and varied landscapes. Western Lycia, where three limestone massifs underpin a plateau-like countryside, is still largely devoid of traffic, while on its sea-facing flanks, clumps of many different kinds of trees, colourful fruit groves and fields of grain are interspersed with marshy humid swamps which stubbornly persist in defiance of modern drainage.

Inland Lycia's high pastures, 900–1200m/2954–3938ft above sea level, are markedly drier by contrast and its roads wind hither and thither, up, down and around the bare hill country, largely treeless but by no means monotonous. Eastern Lycia is taken up with the vast mountain wall of the Bey Dağları, towering up to 2375m/7795ft above the Gulf of Antalya. The town of Termessos, high among the wooded slopes, was for a long time the refuge of the ancient Solymians after they had been driven out by the Lycians.

The real cultural centre of the region is undoubtedly southern Lycia, an area full of contrasts, not unlike Lazistan. Nowhere does such a rapid topographical transition take place within so narrow a coastal belt as here; bare mountain heights at 3000m/9846ft swiftly give way to pasture- and pine, oak and juniper-covered hills and these to chalk cliffs clad in pine, myrtle and laurel maquis with, beneath them, valleys and coastal lowlands glowing in the heat of summer.

History

The Lycians, who emerged as the dominant force among the heavily fragmented population groupings living here in the 6th/5th c. B.C., came originally from Crete, and according to classical tradition called themselves "Tramils". The Pisidians and Solymians, long resident on the peninsula, were driven further inland into the mountains. From 540 B.C. Lycia was ruled by the Persians and then by the Seleucids. In the 5th c. the Lycian cities gained a degree of independence, banding together to form the Attic League; fine seafarers, the Lycians were notorious for piracy until the Second Pirate Wars finally put an end to that particular scourge.

Separated by the mountains into diverse small units, Lycia and its peoples were never easily welded into a unified realm. Hence, from the most distant past, Lycian history has been marked by feudalism, vested interest and fragmentation, although it did develop its own writing and language. As late as the 10th c. A.D. the Lycian language, which had much in common with the Indo-European Hittite dialect of Luwian, was still being used in some isolated valleys. The region also evolved a distinctive Lycian style of art, heavily influenced by Ionian and Anatolian forms, seen at its best in the reliefs and architecture of the monumental Lycian rock tombs dating from the 6th c. B.C. onwards.

Mysia

Characteristics

The hill country of what used to be ancient Mysia makes few concessions to farming. Manufacturing industry is scarce and restricted to one or two centres such as Bursa, Balıkesir and Bandırma. Intensive use is made of the coastal lowlands (Biga, Bergama, Edremit, the Skamander plain) and some of the large intramontane basins (Bursa, Apolyont, Manyas, Balıkesir), which are more densely populated as a result.

Mysia effectively falls into a western and an eastern half either side of the Simav Çayı (Makestos), which through the ages has provided a route between İzmir and the Marmara region; the extension inland of the Gulf of Edremit creates a second divide, this time running west to east. Whereas the two northerly sections benefit from the rainfall generated by the Sea of Marmara, the south-east of the region is much drier. The coastal foothills are thickly planted with olive trees and oak groves (*quercus aegilops*), while the well-watered hills of the hinterland are clad in part with lovely forests of summer oak, shady beech and rhododendron. Southern Mysia, once the province of Pergamum, lends itself more readily to farming, settlement and lines of communication; here pines and sweet chestnuts add further variety to the tree cover on the hills.

The mountainous south-east and north-west still have few roads and are sparsely populated (increasingly so as people leave the mountain villages to work in the big cities or the tourist resorts on the coast). Towering massifs like those of Kaz Dağı (Mount Ida; 1769m/5806ft) in the west, Alaçam Dağı (2089m/6856ft) in the south, the twin peaks of Eğrigöz Dağı (2072m/6800ft) towards the plains of Phrygia in the east, and Ulu Dağ, the Mysian Olympus where Hadrian once trapped bears (2543m/8346ft) in the north, provide the setting for a rugged landscape of wooded mountains and hills.

History

Mysia lay at the heart of the great kingdom of Pergamum which also embraced the Troad (Biga peninsula). It experienced its heydey in the 3rd c. B.C. at the time of Alexander's successors, the Diodochoi, when it was ruled by the powerful Attalid kings. Other important cities of that time included Kyzikos (near Bandırma), Lampsakos (Lapseki, on the Dardanelles), and Adramyttion (Edremit).

Relatively little is known of the Mysian language and culture, though it would appear from a short inscription dating from the 4th/3rd c. B.C. that Mysian was a dialect somewhere between Lydian and Phrygian

Pamphylia

Characteristics

The sunbaked plain of Pamphylia curves around the head of the Gulf of Antalya between Antalya (Adalia, Attaleia) in the west and Gazipasa (classical Selinus) and Alanya (classical Coracesium, the "crow's nest", famous for its pirates) in the east. With the Bey Dağları (over 2000m/6564ft) an impressive backdrop to the west and the Central Taurus to the north, it nestles almost like a piece of North Africa between its mountains and the Mediterranean. In the north the white chalkfaces of the low foothills of the mountain country of Pisidia are covered with pines and maquis, their lower slopes dotted with ruins of ancient castles and classical cities; numerous villages crowd the well-watered valley floors. The Pamphylian plain itself is rich alluvial farmland given over to intensive cultivation of vegetables, cotton, citrus fruits and bananas. Further west towards Lycia however the subsoil is of limestone tufa; here the cultivated travertine terraces start right at the foot of the mountains, falling steeply to the sea and the ancient harbour of Antalya.

History

In classical times the most important of Pamphylia's 40 settlements were Adalia, Alanya, Perge, Aspendos and Side. The main period of settlement is thought to have occurred late in the 2nd millennium B.C. when Greek refugees, fleeing here following the fall of Troy, mingled with the local peoples (the name Pamphylia in ancient Greek means "land of all the tribes", an indication perhaps of the ethnic variety existing at that time). Ruled in turn by the Lydians, Persians, Alexander the Great, Antigonos I (one of Alexander's successors), the Seleucids and the Ptolemies (rulers of Egypt), it enjoyed a brief period of independence until the west of the region was ceded to the king of Pergamum in 188 B.C. The Romans made it the heart of the military province of Cilicia, then merged it with Lycia in the 1st c. A.D. to form a single province reaching the height of its prosperity in the 2nd c. A.D. Earlier, this part of the coast had also been notorious for its pirates, a constant thorn in the flesh of the Romans until their reign of terror was ended by Pompey. He also took the local cult of Mithraism back with him to Rome, and for a long time Mithras was the official protector of the Roman empire and the great rival of the Christian religion. The local attachment to Mithraism proved a considerable initial stumbling block to the spread of Christianity, as a consequence of which the Crusaders later set up numerous small Christian enclaves, each with its castle, along the coasts of Pamphylia and Cilicia. During the Turkish War of Liberation earlier this century this fact was seized upon by the Italians who, as "heirs to the Roman Empire" and representatives of the Church of Rome, laid claim to these coasts.

Paphlagonia

Characteristics

The westernmost of the ancient countries of the Pontus, with mountains up to 2000m/6564ft high, Paphlagonia lies between the Filyos (Yenice İrmağı) in the west, with the coalfields of Ereğli–Zonguldak, and the Halys (Kızılırmak) in the east. Its high wide plains are framed by the Küre Dağları 2019m/6626ft in the the north, the Ilgaz Dağları 2546m/8356ft in the south and the Köroğlu Dağları 2013m/6607ft in the east. Harbours are few along its steep coast, while the hinterland becomes less forbidding only with the start of the ancient Pontus proper east of the Kızılırmak. Immediately beyond the narrow woodland zone of coastal hills the dry interior begins. Three farmland belts with hamlets and small weaving towns run parallel to the evergreen coastline; here on the undulating chalk uplands irrigation is used to enrich pastureland and cultivate grain, maize, cotton, rice, fruit and tobacco. The valleys of the Araç Çayı and Gökırmak on the drier southern side of the mountains are Paphlagonia's economic backbone. At the heart of the plateau lie the high plains of İflani/Devrekanı on which are located the province's ancient capital, Kastomonu, and Safranbolu, gateway to western Paphlagonia and once Anatolia's centre for saffron-growing. A line of little market towns extends along the valleys of the Ulu Çay (Gerede Çayı), Devrez Irmak and section of the lower Kızılırmak in the south. There the rainfall can be as little as 400mm/15in. a year in parts, and dry steppe gradually comes to predominate with the transition to Central Anatolia. The people of this sparsely settled region have long been considered wild and strange, the ancient Greeks who colonised the area calling them "Paphlasians", i.e. speakers of a barbaric tongue.

History

Paphlagonia came under Lydian rule in the 6th c. B.C. and then Persian and, following Alexander's campaigns, Macedonian. It became a kingdom in its own right only during the Hellenistic period when the local Ariarathes dynasty held power. Conquered by the Romans under Augustus it was incorporated into the province of Galatia.

Phrygia

Characteristics

Occupying the west of the Anatolian plateau around the sources of the Sakarya Nehri within the triangle of the modern-day cities of Afyon, Eskişehir and Ankara, ancient Phrygia was named after the western Indo-Europeans who came here from Europe around 1200 B.C. and left their mark as skilled craftsmen with a culture of their own. Straddling the routes to the east from Lydia and Caria, it was evidently a country of many towns and cities. Today it has just three major centres: Afyon, the opium city, Eskişehir, a hub of industry and important rail junction, and Kütahya, a centre for ceramics and the mining of brown coal. Across much of Phrygia, westerly and southerly winds still carry rain deep into the mountains, bringing with it denser settlement and a greater degree of cultivation. Even in early classical times this agricultural potential enabled Phrygia to develop into a powerful independent kingdom, with many centres of population. Its marches, where East met West, were a battleground for Persians and Lydians, Romans and Galatians, Arabs and Romaioi, Crusaders and Seljuks, Ottomans and Mongols, Byzantines and Turks. Though signs of settlement nowadays are few and far between, ruins and age-old monuments abound on the rolling plateau around the upper reaches of the Sakarya, with here and there towering rock outcrops and a scattering of scraggy trees.

Language

The Phrygian language, which died out in the 6th c. A.D., was closely related to Greek, as is clearly shown by 80 ancient Phrygian inscriptions (7th–4th c. B.C.) written in a script reminiscent of Greek, and over 110 neo-Phrygian writings in Greek from Roman times.

History

As Thracian invaders, the Phrygians played a decisive role in the destruction of the Hittite kingdom and the fall of Troy. Their independent Phrygian kingdom of the 8th and 7th c. B.C. maintained close contacts with the Aryans in the east and the Greeks in the west. Its early history is chronicled only briefly (Herodotus), telling of the suicide of its last king, Midas, in Gordium when it fell to the Cimmerians (676 B.C.). With the establishment of the Galatians in eastern Phrygia in the 3rd c. B.C., the orgiastic fertility cult of the mother goddess Cybele and her consort Attis became widespread amongst town dwellers, while countryfolk tended to worship Men the moon god, ruler of Paradise and the Underworld. In 188 B.C. Phrygia came under Pergamum and afterwards Rome, being made a province in 133 B.C.

Montanism
Novatianism

While the early spread of Christianity in the region was largely due to St Paul, the 2nd c. A.D. witnessed the emergence of two extreme sects: Montanism, founded by the Asia Minor-born prophet Montanus who preached that the end of the world was nigh; and Novatianism, named after the Roman theologian and later bishop Novatian whose adherents called themselves "the pure" (Greek: "katharoi" – hence the Cathar heresy of the Middle Ages) and refused to allow lapsed Christians back into the Church.

Pisidia

Characteristics

The ancient Central Taurus mountain country of Pisidia lies between the coastal Pamphylian plain and the Phrygian plateau on the one hand, and the massifs of Lycia and "rough" Cilicia on the other, beginning in the south where the mountains and valleys become impassable and ending in the high mountain ranges of the interior (Sultan Dağları, Karakuş Dağları, Söğüt Dağı, Dedegöl Dağları). Divided today between the provinces of Burdur, Isparta, Denizli and Antalya and stretching from Lake Beyşehir in Isauria to Kastel Dağı on the Phrygian border, it is a high plains country, dotted with lakes and shallow depressions, with patchy soils and pastureland. In the middle and on the eastern side of the central plateau is a region of chalk escarpments rising above poljes and karst chasms where entire lakes drain away underground. The south sees little traffic and its sparse population live in a few islands of cultivation. Despite having remained largely free of foreign cultures until the coming of the Romans, Pisidia is rich in antiquities, many of them the ruins of fortified strongholds. Rushing rivers bite deep into rugged mountains cleft by narrow canyons, caves, and underground streams, and where beech, cedar, pine, spruce and oak are interspersed with "yayla" (summer pastures).

History

The mountain fastnesses of the Pisidians, a long-established and proverbially warlike people, remained for centuries untouched by outside influences. Its inaccessibility and the fierce resistance of its people meant that Pisidia avoided outright conquest by the Persians and Alexander the Great; Greek and Roman culture only succeeded in gaining a foothold when the Pisidians became allies of the Romans. While the interpretation of Pisidian is still in dispute, only short fragments having so far been found, it seems to have some similarity to languages of the Indo-European group.

Pontus

Characteristics

The heartland of the ancient kingdom of Pontus lies between the mouth of the Halys (Kızılırmak) and the Çoruh Nehri. So as to distinguish it from western Pontine Paphlagonia, this particular strip of Black Sea coast between Trabzon and Samsun (the only two Pontic ports of note) has from time to time been known as "East Pontus". Narrow and mountainous, it was for centuries exposed to the influence of Greek colonists and the seafaring peoples of the Black Sea.

Despite its deep-cut mountain valleys, the western part, the Canık ("land of life") with its flat, andesitic and trachytic lava tablelands, presents an inviting landscape of fields, pastures and parkland. Here the alluvial plains of the Iris (delta of the Yeşilırmak and setting for the Amazon legend) provide the only fertile coastal lands of any size in the northern Pontus; here too lies the town of Bafra, until 1806 capital of an independent Canık with its tiny mountain strongholds, feudal castles and ruins. The eastern part of the Pontus is more a region of spectacular natural beauty, rich in forests and minerals, where three mountain ranges, towering up to 3000m/9846ft, stand between the dry hinterland and the sea.

Maize and hazelnuts grow on the rain-soaked slopes of the northern and eastern Pontus, in places thickly clad right down to the sea with dense forests and undergrowth of beech, pine, rhododendron and azalea. This is the land of the classical Chalybe, the ironsmiths, its woods dotted with the remains of ancient mine workings and furnaces (Gümüşhane). Also typical of the Pontus are the scattered hamlets and farmsteads clinging to the steep valley sides and mountain slopes. More extensive farmland, and hence greater density of population, is found only in the southern basins: Hart Ovası (Bayburt), Suşehri Ovası,

Suluova (Merzifon), Taş Ovası (Erbaa), Niksar Ovası, Kaz Ovası (Tokat), Turhal and Zile, Amasya Ovası.

History

The Greeks had founded city colonies including Sinope (Sinop), Amisos (Samsun), Kerasos (Giresun) and Trapezius (Trabzon) on the Black Sea coast in the 6th c. B.C. Following the Persian defeat by Alexander the Great, a larger kingdom with its capital at Amaseia (Amasya) was created in 281 B.C. by Mithridates II, the first to call himself King of Pontus. Later, Mithridates VI Eupator, the Great (120–63 B.C.), who chose Amisos (Samsun) for his capital, extended his realm into neighbouring territory and began to threaten the Roman Empire in Greece. Julius Caesar put an end to the expansionist ambitions of the Pontine rulers and their allies (Tigranes, Pharnaces II) at the battle of Zela (Zile: "Veni, vidi, vici") in 47 B.C. The western Black Sea coast (Bithynia and Paphlagonia) became the Roman province of Bithynia et Pontus, while the section east of the Halys (Kızılırmak) was handed over to the Galatian ruler Deiotarus and a local ruler Polemo, before these lands too become Roman (province of Galatia) in 32 and 63 B.C.

After Constantinople fell to the Crusaders in 1204, two fleeing princes of the Imperial Comnenos dynasty, David and Alexius I, established a flourishing Pontic empire of their own with its capital at Trebizond (Trabzon). It survived for over 250 years until absorbed into the Ottoman empire in 1462.

Thrace

Characteristics

To the very earliest Greeks Thrace was the whole of the Balkan Peninsula east of Illyria, including Macedonia; then later just its eastern half south of the Danube. The Roman province of Thrace only covered the region between the Balkan mountains and the Sea of Marmara (Propontis), and from the time of the Ottoman conquest it has simply been the area south of the Rhodope Mountains, Greek in the west and Turkish in the east.

Turkish Thrace (today consisting of the provinces of Edirne, Kırklareli, Tekirdağ and İstanbul) is a dry region, the high mountains to the north and west keeping the rainfall at bay. The İstranca hills (Yıldız Dağı) in the north-east and the Kuru Dağı/İşıklar Dağı in the south-west are the only upland areas of note; even here there is little in the way of tree cover. The "Thracian triangle" between Edirne, İstanbul and Gelibolu (Gallipoli) is made up of a kind of broken tableland, drained by the Maritza, Ergene Nehri and their tributaries; it is a countryside of heath and steppe – and intensive grain production on the approaches to İstanbul. Lying as it does at the crossroads of the land routes between Europe and Asia and the sea routes between the Black Sea and Mediterranean through the Bosphorus and the Dardanelles, Thrace has always been of greater strategic importance than economic.

History

King Teres founded the first great kingdom of Thrace around 450 B.C. Under his successors it reached to the Danube, the Sea of Marmara, the Aegean and the Black Sea but ceased to be an independent country after 342 B.C. Despite becoming part of the Roman and then the Byzantine Empire, its strategic position meant it was often the prey of other nations – Huns, Goths, Slavs, Bulgarians – until finally falling to the Ottomans in 1358. Although Bulgaria captured large parts of Thrace in the first of the Balkan Wars, in the second it lost the western section around Kavala to Greece, followed by the whole of the coastal strip during the First World War.

Famous People

Listed below in alphabetical order are famous personalities who, associated with the coastal regions of Turkey by birth, sojourn, career or death, attained international importance.

Alexander the Great
(356–323 B.C.)

Alexander the Great, one of the world's greatest military commanders, was born in Pella in northern Greece, the son of King Philip II of Macedon and Olympiás, daughter of King Neoptolemos. Between 342 and 340 B.C. his tutor was the philosopher Aristotle. Alexander had already distinguished himself in battle at Chaironaia in 338 B.C. when he secured the throne as Alexander III by eliminating his rivals following the death of his father in 336 B.C. at the hands of Pausanias, a Macedonian, possibly a hired assassin.

Appointed Commander of the Corinthian League he moved first against the Thracians and the Illyrians and put down a rising by the Thebans (335 B.C.). As supreme commander of the Greeks Alexander embarked in 334 B.C. on a campaign of "Hellenistic revenge" against the Persians. He crossed the Hellespont (Dardanelles) with an army of 35,000 men, winning the battle on the Granikos in the spring, occupying Gordium (the story of him cutting the legendary Gordian knot is without historical foundation), then marching over the Taurus mountains to Cilicia and defeating the Persian king, Darius III, in a cavalry battle in November of 333 B.C. at Issus, north of present-day İskenderun. This left the way open to Egypt where he founded the city of Alexandria and had his divine origins and claim to power confirmed by the oracle of Zeus Ammon at the Siwa oasis.

From Egypt Alexander and his army marched to Babylonia, where he again defeated Darius, this time decisively, at Gaugamela on the Mossul plain, now in Iraq. He carried on into Persia (Iran) and finally began his Indian campaign (327–325 B.C.), penetrating as far as the River Hyphasis (the River Beas in the Punjab) where his exhausted men forced him to turn back. At the end of the long march down the Indus, some of the army returned by sea through the Persian Gulf while Alexander and the rest of his men made the gruelling crossing of the desert, eventually reaching Babylon where he died of a fever while preparing for an Arabian campaign.

Alexander's declared policy, in part already embarked upon, of conciliation and of consolidating the great new empire he had created from so many disparate pieces, was doomed to failure. His empire fragmented almost immediately as rival claims were lodged by his successors.

Anaxagoras
(*c.* 500–428 B.C.)

The Greek natural philosopher Anaxagoras was born about 500 B.C. in the Ionian city of Klazomenai near Smyrna (İzmir). He went to Athens as a young man and gained a considerable reputation. Later, however, he was accused of impiety and fled to Lampsakos (on the south side of the Dardanelles/Hellespont), where he died in 428 B.C.

Anaxagoras believed that all life was derived from tiny particles of qualitatively distinct substances which he called *spermata* ("seeds"). These were set in motion by an all-commanding cosmic mind (*nous*) and, by the separation of unlike particles and the combination of like particles, formed into things. His writings have come down to us only in very fragmentary form.

Anaximander
(*c.* 610–*c.* 546 B.C.)

The Greek natural philosopher Anaximander (Anaximandros) of Miletus, disciple and successor of Thales, is regarded as the founder of scientific geography. Taking up Hesiod's concept of "chaos" he held that all things originated from a primal immortal substance which he called the *apeiron* ("Infinite"), developing out of this in stages through a series of contrasts or oppositions (warm–cold, moist–dry, etc.). His prose work "On Nature" ("Peri Physeos") was lost at an early period, but one passage has come down to us. "To that from which all things come, all things will one day return." Anaximander thought of the earth as cylindrical in form, originating in some cosmic whirling movement, and of man's soul as made of air. He devised the first map of the inhabited world, a celestial globe and a sundial with which he determined the solstices.

Anaximenes
(*c.* 588–*c.* 524 B.C.)

The Ionian natural philosopher Anaximenes of Miletus is believed to have been a pupil of the great Anaximander. Like him, he believed that all things originated from some primal substance, which in his view was air – infinite, eternally in motion and condensing or rarefying to create all things on earth. He is believed to have been the first to assert that the moon drew its light from the sun. His writings have survived only in one small fragment.

Kemal Atatürk
(1880/81–1938)

The Turkish statesman Mustafa Kemal Paşa was born in 1880 or 1881 in Salonica (Macedonia), attended the Military Academy in Constantinople, took part along with Enver Paşa in the Young Turk Rising of 1908–09, fought against Italy in Cyrenaica in 1912 and commanded a Turkish force in Gallipoli in the First World War. When western Turkey was occupied by the Greeks in 1918 he withdrew to Anatolia, where he organised resistance to Allied and Greek forces in May 1919 and broke off relations with the Sultan's government. In 1920 he became President of the National Assembly, and in 1921–22 drove the Greeks out of Asia Minor. In 1921 he was granted the honorific title of Gazi. In November 1922 he abolished the Sultanate, and in the following year he proclaimed the Republic of Turkey, of which he was elected first President on October 29th 1923.

Kemal Paşa's aim was the creation of a Turkish National State on a secular basis; and the national renewal was to be achieved by a fundamental Europeanisation of Turkish society. He made Ankara the new capital of Turkey and carried through comprehensive political and cultural reforms – legal codes, social position of women, educational policy, introduction of the Latin alphabet, reform of the calendar, etc.

In 1934 he changed his name to Kemal Atatürk ("Father of the Turks"). He remained President of the Republic until his death on November 10th 1938 (in İstanbul). His remains, originally buried in the Ethnographic Museum in Ankara, were transferred in 1953 to the Atatürk Mausoleum.

Atatürk's ideas, given the name of Kemalism, are – subject to certain restrictions – still valid in Turkey today.

Beyazıd I
(*c.* 1354–1403)

The Ottoman Sultan Beyazıd I Yıldırım, the Thunderbolt, who ruled from 1389, was the eldest son and heir of Sultan Murad I. Conqueror of Bulgaria and Serbia, he made Wallachia a vassal state and penetrated down into Greece, although he failed to capture Constantinople. In the autumn of 1396 he defeated the crusader army led by Sigismund, King of Hungary, at Nicopolis on the Danube, but was defeated in turn by Tamerlane and his Mongol hordes at Ankara in the summer of 1402. He died Tamerlane's prisoner at Akşehir on March 8th 1403.

N.B.

There are numerous alternative spellings of the name Beyazıd, e.g. *Beyazıt* · *Bayezıt* · *Bayazıt* · *Bayazıd* · *Bayasid* et al.

Beyazıd II
(*c.* 1448–1512)

The Ottoman Sultan Beyazıd II Veli, the Holy One, was born in Demotika (now Didimotichon, in the Greek district of Evros), and succeeded his father Mehmet II Fâtih (see entry) in 1481. He waged frontier wars in the Balkans (1482 conquest of Hercegovina) but was unsuccessful against the Egyptian Mamelukes in Cilicia, brought Moldova (now part of Romania) under his sway and moved against Venice, capturing its Greek outposts. It was during his Sultanate that the Ottomans first attacked Transylvania and Austria. In 1512 his son Selim I (see entry) rose against him and, with the help of the janizaries, forced him to abdicate.

Beyazıd II died on May 26th 1512 close to his birthplace.

Constantine the Great
(*c.* A.D. 288–337)

The Emperor Constantine I, the Great, was born in what is now Niš in Serbia about A.D. 288. In 330 he moved the capital of the Empire from Rome to Byzantium, which then became known as Nova Roma or Constantinopolis (now İstanbul). The Edict of Milan which he promulgated in 313, granting Christians freedom of worship, was the first step towards the adoption of Christianity as the State religion of the Empire.

During Constantine's reign the foundation-stone of Hagia Sophia (Ayasofya) was laid, the Forum of Constantinople was completed and the Serpent Column from Delphi set up in the Hippodrome. Constantine is a saint of the Armenian and the Greek and Russian Orthodox Churches.

Diogenes
(413–323 B.C.)

The Greek philosopher and itinerant teacher Diogenes was a native of Sinope on the Black Sea. A pupil of Antisthenes, he belonged to the school of Cynics, who sought the assimilation of man into nature by the rejection of all cultural values and social norms. Diogenes is said to have put these ideas into practice by living a life of extreme asceticism. His fame does no rest on learned works but on numerous anecdotes (e.g. Diogenes' tub) illustrating his unconventional character and on the ready wit ascribed to him. He dies in Corinth.

Epictetus
(*c.* A.D. 50–140)

The Stoic philosopher Epictetus (Epiktetos), born about A.D. 50 in the Phyrgian city of Hierapolis (now Pamukkale), was originally a slave but was given his freedom at the request of Nero. After Domitian expelled the philosophers from Rome in A.D. 94 he taught a large circle of disciples at Nikopolis (Epirus), where he died about A.D. 140.

In his exposition of Stoicism Epictetus confined himself to questions of ethics. His call for humility, brotherly love, modesty and independence of mind ("Endure and abstain!") anticipates some of the ideas of Christianity. Epictetus himself wrote nothing, and his teachings were recorded by his pupil Arrian in the fragmentarily presrved "Diatribai" ("Conversations") and short moral catechism "Encheiridion".

Mehmet Afık Ersoy (1873–1936)

Born in İstanbul, the writer Mehmet Akıf Ersoy received a first class traditional Islamic education, attended the Veterinary Academy in 1894, worked in the border provinces of what was then the Ottoman Empire, and spent some time in Germany during the First World War. Though initially a supporter of Pan-Islamism he later joined the freedom movement and was a member of the newly created Turkish Republic's first parliament. He spent the last ten years of his life in Egypt as a lecturer in literature in Cairo.

In his early years Ersoy wrote lyric poetry of a religious nature. Throughout his collected poetical works (seven volumes of poems between 1911 and 1933) he employs the classical Turkish metre while presenting his material in a naturalistic way. His freedom song "İstiklâl Marşı" was adopted as the Turkish national anthem in 1921.

Mehmet Akıf Ersoy died in his home city of İstanbul on December 27th 1937.

Eudoxos (*c.* 408–*c.* 355 B.C.)

The Greek mathematician, astronomer, scientist and philosopher Eudoxos came from Knidos in Asia Minor. After stays in Egypt and at Kyzikos (near present-day Erdek on the south coast of the Sea of Marmara) he went to Plato's Academy in Athens, where he founded his own school.

The outstanding astronomer of his day, Eudoxos compiled a widely used calendar with climatic information, recognised the curvature of the earth's surface and put forward the theory of concentric spheres to explain the varying movements of the planets. As a mathematician he created the general theory of proportion, concerned himself with the problem of the Golden Section and devised a means of determining the volume of a pyramid or a cone. In a geographical work he described the three continents of Europe, Asia and Africa.

Eyüp Ensarı (7th C. A.D.)

Eyüp Ensarı was a trusted companion of the Prophet Mohammed and standard-bearer of the first Holy Army of Islam. He is said to have been killed while in command of the Arab forces during the first seige of Constantinople (674–678) and to have been buried on the site of the present mosque (Eyüp Sultan Camii) in the İstanbul suburb of Eyüp on the west bank of the Golden Horn. This remains İstanbul's most sacred mosque, especially revered as one of the holy sites of Islam.

Colmar Freiherr von der Goltz (1843–1918)

Colmar Freiherr (Baron) von der Goltz, born in East Prussia in 1843, served in the wars of 1860 and 1870–71 (the Franco–Prussian War) and thereafter in the Military History Section of the General Staff. From 1883 to 1895 he played a major part in the rebuilding of the Turkish Army and as a much-respected military adviser was granted the title of Pasha (Goltz Pasha). In 1911 he was appointed Field-Marshal, and in 1914 became Governor-General of Belgium. In 1915–16, commanding the Turkish First Army, he successfully bottled up a British force in Kut el-Amara in Mesopotamia.

His ideas were frequently in conflict with the prevailing views of his day, and at one time he was posted away from the General Staff. He died in Baghdad in 1916, and is buried in the grounds of the West German Ambassador's summer residence at Tarabya on the Bosphorus.

Heraclitus (*c.* 540–480 B.C.)

The Greek philosopher Heraclitus (Heracleitos), a recluse with a thorough-going contempt for mankind, was born and lived in Ephesus. Among the most important of the early Greek thinkers, he held the world to exist in a state of continuous change, all things coming to be and passing away through strife ("polemos", war) which Heraclitus considered the divine guiding principle (logos) of the universe. He believed fire to be the primordial substance and saw in the phenomenon of flowing water a manifestation of the elements' perpetual flux, in which the human soul is also caught up. Though the famous dictum "panta rhei" (all things flow) was probably a later attribution, Heraclitus' belief in the fruitfulness of opposites and opposition receives expression in the statement "War (more accurately, strife, dispute, struggle) is the father of all things".

Through his pupil Cratylus, Heraclitus' ideas influenced Plato and the Stoic school of natural philosophy, and in the modern period Renaissance thought. Hegel and Nietzsche both took up elements of his doctrine. Heraclitus' own writings have come down to us only in the form of fragments.

Herodotus (*c.* 490–*c.* 425/420 B.C.)

Herodotus, called by Cicero the "Father of History", was born in the Dorian city of Halikarnassos (Bodrum), but was compelled to leave the town after taking part in a rising against the tyrant Lygdamis. He travelled a great deal – to Egypt and Africa, Mesopotamia, the Black Sea coast and Italy – and thereafter lived for a time in Athens, greatly respected and honoured. In 444 B.C. he moved to the newly founded Athenian colony of Thourioi (Thurii) in southern Italy. His "History" – divided after his time into nine books named after the Muses – is a critical consideration and assessment of the countries in which he had travelled as well as a record of political events. Its high point is the account of the Persian Wars. Later study has confirmed in many respects the accuracy of his work, which is a valuable source of information on the Greek settlements in Asia Minor as well as on the lands and people of Africa and the Near East.

Nazım Hikmet (1902–1963)

Born January 20th 1902 in Saloniki (Greek Thessaloniki) the son of a doctor from an aristocratic family, Nazım Hikmet (Nâzım Hikmet Ran) attended the Naval College in İstanbul before spending the years between 1921 and 1928 in the Soviet Union, studying at the Communist University for "Eastern Workers" in Moscow. Having joined the banned Turkish Communist Party in 1924, on his return to Turkey he was arrested many times for subversive activities, eventually being sentenced in 1937 to 28 years imprisonment. Freed under an amnesty in 1950, he lived in Sofia, Warsaw and Moscow, where he died on June 3rd 1963.

Hikmet's poetry has earned him recognition as the founder of the new Turkish verse. Having begun by writing patriotic poems, he became acquainted with Expressionism and Dadaism in the experimental literary circles of Moscow in the Twenties. He was the first Turkish poet to abandon the classical metre, turning increasingly to free verse liberally sprinkled with slang and a more colloquial style of language.

The influence of the Russian poet Mayakovsky clearly had a hand in Hikmet's emergence as the leading writer of poetry among the Turkish moderns around 1930, though during his years in exile it was inevitably his political activism which captured the headlines. His extensive corpus has been translated into many languages; from 1950 to 1964 his work was banned in Turkey and is still viewed with unease there even today.

Hippodamos (5th c. B.C.)

The great architect and town-planner Hippodamos of Miletus gave general validity and authority, in both theory and practice, to the gridiron plan which had already been adopted in the layout of early Greek colonies. The Hippodamian system proceeded in a strictly rational way: it divided the area of the city into a rectangular grid of building plots of equal size, taking no account of variations – even quite considerable variations – in ground-level and topography. Sites were reserved within the grid for public buildings and squares, while the residential quarters were allowed to develop outward from the centre. Hippodamos himself planned the cities of Piraeus (the port of Athens), Thourioi (Thurii) in southern Italy and Rhodes, as well as his home town of Miletus.

Homer
(*c.* 8th c. B.C.)

The city of Smyrna (İzmir) in Asia Minor claimed – probably with justice, though there were other contenders for the honour – to be the birthplace of Homer (Homeros), the legendary author of the "Iliad" and the "Odyssey", the earliest epic poet of the West. Tradition has it that he was a blind rhapsode (reciter of epic poems) who travelled round the princely Courts of the Ionian cities. The guilds of rhapsodes which developed about 700 B.C. in Ionian territory, particularly on the island of Chios, honoured Homer as their founder and teacher and called themselves Homerids. Nevertheless there was always controversy about the existence of Homer as a historical figure; in particular it was doubted whether any one man was capable of composing two such mighty works. In 1795 the German scholar Friedrich August Wolf raised what became known as the "Homeric question", suggesting that the "Iliad" and the "Odyssey" were collections of separate songs by different poets. On this theory the name of Homer became a collective designation for early Greek epic poetry. The prevailing view now is that there was a historical Homer, who lived and composed his poems on the west coast of Asia Minor and that he had many links with the island of Chios. In writing his great works he probably based himself on earlier and shorter epic poems. The "Iliad" is thought to have preceded the "Odyssey". Both works underwent much alteration and expansion after Homer's time. Homer is also credited with the authorship of a number of hymns and epigrams and two comic epics, "Margites" and "Batrachomyomachia" ("War of the Frogs and Mice").

İsmet İnönü
(1884–1973)

Born Mustafa İsmet Paşa on September 25th 1884 in the then Greek Aegean port of Smyrna (now İzmir in Turkey), this Turkish soldier and statesman took part in the Young Turks' revolution of 1908. In 1920 he joined the freedom movement led by Mustafa Kemal Paşa (Atatürk, see entry), becoming Chief of General Staff to the Kemalist forces in the wars with Greece (1920–22/23). In 1921 he won several battles around İnönü in the province of Bilecik, subsequently taking the name of the village for his surname.

As Turkish Foreign Minister (1922–24) he signed the 1923 Treaty of Lausanne, and as Prime Minister (1923/24 and 1925–37) had a large say in the internal reforms carried out by Atatürk in Turkey. After Atatürk's death in 1938 İnönü became President of the Republic and chairman of the CHP, the Republican People's Party. With great single-mindedness he continued the programme of reform (greater press freedom, introduction of the multi-party system, etc.) and contrived to keep Turkey largely out of the Second World War, coming in on the side of the Allies only in 1945.

After defeat by the Democratic Party in the 1950 elections he became leader of the Opposition. Following the military putsch in 1960 he returned as Prime Minister from 1961 to 1965. An opponent of Bülent Ecevit's increasingly social democratic party line, he eventually stood down from chairing the CHP and left the party. He had been serving (from 1972) as a senator in the Grand National Assembly when he died on December 25th 1973 in Ankara.

Mausolos (4th c. B.C.)

Mausolos of Maussolos, Satrap (Provincial Governor) of Caria under Persian rule, achieved independence in the Satrap's Rising of 362 B.C. and founded a kingdom of his own with its capital at Halikarnassos (now Bodrum). His magnificent tomb, the Mausoleion (Mausoleum), was begun during his lifetime and completed after his death (353 B.C.) by his sister and wife Artemisia. It was one of the Seven Wonders of the World. The name mausoleum came subsequently to be applied to other large tombs.

Mehmet II the Conqueror (1432–81)

Sultan Mehmet II Fâtih (Mehmet the Conqueror), born in Adrianople (Edirne) in 1430 and, from 1451, seventh Sultan of the Ottoman Empire, captured Constantinople after a two-month siege in 1453, renaming it İstanbul (or Stamboul as it afterwards became known in the West). He took possession of the famous church of Hagia Sophia for Islam but allowed the Genoese in Galatia to continued to trade freely subject only to the surrender of all weapons and the payment of official taxes and tolls. He also granted recognition to the Greek Orthodox Church, transferring jurisdiction over Greek Christians to the Orthodox Patriarch Gennadios, an opponent of Rome. Greeks who had fled İstanbul before the Ottoman advance were invited back to help repopulate the city, so bringing into being the Phanariotentum (named after Phanar, the Greek quarter).

Mehmet II made İstanbul the capital of the Ottoman Empire (building, in the course of his reign, the first Ottoman palace to be erected on the European side of the Bosphorus), and the spiritual centre of Islam. He died in the city on May 3rd 1481; his türbe (tomb), reconstructed in the 18th c., stands within the great Mehmet Fâtih mosque.

Mehmet Namık Kemal (1840–88)

Born December 21st 1840 in Rodostó (now Tekirdağ), scion of an aristocratic line of officials, Mehmet (Mehmed) Namık Kemal is considered one of Turkey's greatest popular poets. After receiving a private education, he worked as a civil servant in İstanbul where he was also employed on "Tasvir-i Efkâr", the journal published by İbrahim Şinasi but which Namık Kemal himself took over in 1865.

Already in his youth a fierce opponent of the despotic Sultans, the critical nature of Namık Kemal's journalism led to his being forced to flee to Paris in 1867 and thereafter to London where, together with Ziya Pasha, he published "Hürriyet" (Freedom), the Turkish exiles' anti-government journal. An amnesty in 1870 brought his return to Turkey where the performance of his freedom play "Vatan yahud Silistre" (Homeland or Silistria) at İstanbul's Gedikpaşa Theatre early in April 1873 resulted in civil unrest, the banning of the play, and his banishment to Cyprus where he spent the years until 1876 in prison in Famagusta (now Turkish Gazimağusa). Released following the deposing of Sultan Abdul Aziz, he left Cyprus and helped to found the Young Turks in Paris in 1876. After serving briefly on the constitution commission, in 1877 he was banished to the Aegean island of Midilli (Greek

Mytilíni/Lesbos), becoming governor there in 1879. In 1884 he was transferred to Rhodes, and in 1887 to Chios, where he died from tuberculosis on December 2nd 1888.

With its pretentious romanticism and often blatant sentimentality, Namık Kemal's poetry and prose, including "İntıbah", the first "modern" Turkish novel, served as a clarion call to the stirrings of Ottoman patriotism and helped to give impetus to the Young Turk movement, thus paving the way for Atatürk's revolutionary reforms.

St Nicholas (3rd/4th c.)

According to tradition St Nicholas (Feast Day December 6th) was born at Patara in Lycia and at the beginning of the 4th c. was Bishop of Myra (now Demre), also in Lycia, where he became known for his compassion and to help those in distress. The legend, however, probably developed round a historical figure, Abbot Nicholas of Sion (near Myra), of whose death on December 10th 564 there is documentary evidence. His tomb in Antalya was plundered in the early medieval period, and in 1087 his relics were carried off to Bari in southern Italy. The veneration of St Nicholas as protector of seamen, merchants. prisoners and particularly children originated in the Greek Church in the 6th c. and was adopted also by the Russian Church. In the 9th c. it reached Italy, and from there spread to other European countries. St Nicholas has become better known to English-speaking children as Santa Claus.

Osman I (1258–1326)

Osman I, who gave the Ottoman dynasty its name ("Osman" being pronounced "Othman" in Arabic), was the son of Ertoğrul, a famous tribal chief and warlord of a small Bithynian fiefdom in western Anatolia (around present-day Söğüt). By seizing Byzantine strongholds Osman extended his father's domain and by 1290 had established his own independent emirate from which the great Ottoman Empire was destined to grow.

Bearer of the title "Ghazi" (warrior of Islam), Osman I died in 1326 in Söğüt.

Aristoteles Onassis (1906/07–75)

The Greek businessman Aristoteles Sokrates Homeros Onassis was born on January 15th 1906 or 1907 in Smyrna (İzmir). In 1923 he emigrated by way of Greece to Argentina, where he reorganised his family's tobacco business. Later he became Greek Consul in Buenos Aires. In 1932–33 Onassis began to build up the shipping line which was later to own the world's largest commercial shipping fleet. During the Second World War he put his ships at the disposal of the Allies, and after the war concentrated on increasing the tanker capacity of his fleet. In addition in 1957 he established Olympic Airways (State-owned since 1975), engaged in international banking business, ran casinos and dealt largely in property.

His first wife (1946–60) was Athina Livanos, daughter of another shipping magnate. He later married Jacqueline Kennedy, widow of the murdered President. Onassis died in Paris on March 15th 1975. He is buried on his private island of Skorpios which lies off the Ionian island of Lefkos. Here, too, are buried his son Alexander, who was killed in 1973 in an aircraft crash, and his daughter Christina who died in 1988.

Heinrich Schliemann (1822–90)

The archaeologist Heinrich Schliemann was born in Mecklenburg, in eastern Germany, in 1822. Family circumstances compelled him to leave school and seek a career in business. A great asset in his subsequent career was his gift for languages, of which he finally mastered 15. After achieving great success in an Amsterdam commercial house he founded his own business in St Petersburg (Leningrad) in 1847. This enabled him to build up a considerable fortune, which allowed him to devote himself entirely to archaeology from 1858 onwards. After travelling widely and studying languages and archaeology in Paris he settled in Athens in 1868. Convinced that Homer's works were based on historical facts, he anticipated modern archaeological practice in studying the literary sources, examining the topography of the site and where necessary carrying out test digs before undertaking actual excavation.

Schliemann, assisted by Wilhelm Dörpfeld from 1882 onwards, carried out excavations at Troy (1870–82 and 1890), Mycenae (1876), Orchomenos (1880–86) and Tiryns (1884–85). He presented his principal finds, the gold "Treasure of Priam" from Troy (now in Moscow) and the gold jewellery from the royal tombs at Mycenae, to the Museum of Prehistory in Berlin and the National Archaeological Museum in Athens. He died in Naples on his way back from Germany to Athens, and is buried on Athens.

Selim I (1467 or 1470 –1520)

Ottoman Sultan from 1512, Selim I Yavuz, the Grim, who came from Pontic Amasya, established the supremacy of Sunni orthodoxy by his ruthless suppression of Shiite uprisings in Anatolia. This brought him into conflict with the Shiite Safavid dynasty, rulers of Persia, whom he forced to relinquish territory in Azerbaidjan before proceeding to conquer Mesopotamia, Syria, Palestine and Egypt (taking the capital Cairo in May 1517 and executing the last of the Mamelukes the following month). The holiest sites of Islam thus fell under his sway and he assumed the title of Caliph.

Selim I, who was also the author of Persian verses, died near Çorlu en route from İstanbul to Edirne in 1520, probably from the plague.

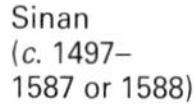

Sinan (*c.* 1497–1587 or 1588)

Hoca Mimar Sinan, the Ottoman Empire's greatest architect, is thought to have been born in an Anatolian village near Kayseri. The son of Christian (Greek or Armenian) parents, he was taken from his family and sent to İstanbul to receive a Muslim education and train as a janizary. From 1521 he served Suleiman the Magnificent (see entry) as an engineer on various military campaigns before, in 1538, he was appointed chief architect of the Ottoman Empire, a position he held under three Sultans, Suleiman I, Selim II and Murad III.

Between 1528 and 1588 he was responsible for the construction of no less than 477 buildings including some of the largest and most perfect Ottoman mosques and a host of other important public edifices. Of this total, more than 150 mosques, some large (*camii*), some small (*mescit*), over 70 medreses, 38 palaces, over 30 caravanserai, 25 mausoleums, and innumerable schools, public baths (*hamam*), almshouses, hospitals and dervish cloisters are still standing today, not to mention bridges and aqueducts (one of which, 265m/870ft long, brought water from Mağlova into İstanbul). More than half Sinan's buildings are situated in or around İstanbul, at that time the glittering capital of the Ottoman Empire. It was not until he was nearly 50 that this "Ottoman Michelangelo" felt adequately equipped to undertake the construction of mosques. While drawing much of his inspiration from the multi-domed design of the Hagia Sophia, the well-travelled Sinan was also familiar with the work of the Seljuks, the tombs of Anatolia, the early Christian cave churches of Cappadocia, and traditional Armenian architecture.

Among his most outstanding buildings are the Prince's Mosque (Şehzade Mehmet Camii) and Mosque of Suleiman the Magnificent (Süleymaniye Camii), both in İstanbul, and the Mosque of Selim II (Selimiye Camii) in Edirne. By then much venerated, Hoca Mimar Sinan died in İstanbul in 1587 or 1588.

Suleiman the Magnificent (1494–1566)

The only son of Selim I (see entry), Suleiman I was probably born on November 6th 1494 at Trebizond (Trabzon) on the Black Sea. He became Sultan in 1520 and is known in his homeland as "Kanuni", the Lawgiver; to Europeans, on the other hand, this most expansionist and accomplished of the Ottoman rulers has always been "Suleiman the Magnificent". In the course of substantially enlarging the Ottoman Empire he captured Belgrade in 1521 and Rhodes in 1522 (forcing the Knights of the Order of St John to leave the island for Malta), defeated and killed King Lewis of Hungary at Mohács in 1526, took Buda in 1529 and, between September 27th and October 15th the same year, unsuccessfully laid siege to Vienna; in 1534 he captured Baghdad and in 1562 took possession of Transylvania. His domain extended eastward as far as Persia (Iran), while his fleet gave him mastery of the Red Sea (including Yemen and Aden) and virtually the whole of the Mediterranean, ravaging the coasts of North Africa, Italy, Greece and Dalmatia under the command of Suleiman's fearsome corsair admiral, Kair ad-Din (Barbarossa), a Greek from Mytilene (Lesbos).

During his sultanship Suleiman was responsible for transforming the imperial army and judicial system. Under his rule the capital İstanbul flourished as never before, becoming a great centre of intellectual life (Suleiman himself wrote poetry under the pseudonym "Muhibbi"). The city itself was enriched by a spate of building supervised by Suleiman's chief architect, Sinan (see entry). Suleiman died on September 6th 1566 during the war with Austria while beseiging Sziget (Hungarian at that time, now Sighetul Marmaţiei in Romania) which the Ottomans took two days later. His *türbe*, the largest of Sinan's many mausoleums, is situated in the cemetery of İstanbul's great mosque complex, the Süleymaniye Külliyesi.

Thales (*c.* 625–*c.* 545 B.C.)

The Greek philosopher, astronomer, mathematician and natural scientist Thales of Miletus is said to have been of Phoenician origin. He founded the Ionian school of natural philosophy, which held that all living things originated from water. He believed that there was life even in inorganic matter, and attributed all motion to an all-directing soul. As an astronomer he is said to have predicted an eclipse of the sun in 585 B.C. The proposition attributed to him – that all triangles inscribed in a semicircle are right-angled – was already known to the Babylonians.

Thales triangles

Thales was one of the Seven Sages of antiquity

Xenophanes (*c.* 565–*c.* 470 B.C.)

The Greek poet and philosopher Xenophanes of Kolophon (now Değirmendere, near İzmir) left Ionia at the age of 25 and led a wandering life as a rhapsode (reciter of epic poems) in Greece and Sicily. He finally settled at Elea in southern Italy, where he died. His poems and songs are concerned with philosophical and ideological themes. Xenophanes rejected Greek mythology and polytheism and believed in a single perfect divinity which had nothing in common with mortal beings – in this anticipating the Eleatic school of philosophy. Xenophanes was also interested in natural science, and his observation of fossils led him to conclude that animals and plants developed over long periods of time.

Xenophon (*c.* 430/425–*c.* 355 B.C.)

The Greek historian Xenophon, an Athenian by birth and in his youth an adherent of Socrates, took part in 401 B.C. in the campaign of the Persian Cyrus the Younger against his brother King Artaxerxes II Mnemon. After Cyrus had been killed at Kunaxa, Xenophon led the Greek rearguard on a long and heroic return march through Armenia in the depths of winter, eventually reaching the Black Sea coast at Trapezús (Trebizond; modern-day Trabzon). He joined with the Spartan king Agesilaus in campaigning against the Persians in the west of Asia Minor, and also fought on the Spartan side in the battle of Koroneia (394 B.C.) which led to his banishment from Athens. Thereafter he lived and wrote on the estates given to him by the Spartans at Scillus, south of Olympia, until forced to flee to Corinth following the collapse of Spartan rule. It is not clear whether he was ever allowed to return to Athens before his death, which probably occurred in Corinth.

All of Xenophon's writings have survived. Chief among them are "Anábasis" (eight volumes on the Persian expedition under Cyrus and the long homeward march of "the 10,000") and "Hellenicá", a history of Greece from 411/410 B.C. following on from Thucydides' "History of the Peloponnesian War". He also wrote various pedagogical works including treatises on horsemanship and statecraft ("Kyrupädie", "The Spartan State" and "Póroi", the latter on the subject of the state revenues of Athens) and, no less importantly, several works relating to Socrates, "Memorabilia", "Apology", "Oikonomikós" and "Sympósion" (a Socratic disputation).

Culture and Art

Rich cultural heritage

Numerous finds have shown that the coastal fringe of Anatolia has been settled by man since the earliest times. From the Stone Age to the present day an extraordinary variety of peoples and cultures have left their traces on the peninsula of Asia Minor. Nowhere else, surely, will the traveller find the changing pattern of human culture down the ages so impressively demonstrated: in many places remains of Greek, Roman, Byzantine, Seljuk and Ottoman building can be seen side by side, and churches and houses will often be found built on the foundations of earlier buildings.

Periods and Cultures

Prehistoric period

The oldest Stone Age settlement so far known in Anatolia was found near Antalya, with implements, weapons and unpainted pottery which give some impression of the life lived by the people of this early culture.

During the Copper and Bronze Ages numerous regional cultural centres developed in Asia Minor. Among them were those of Troy I (from 3000 B.C.) and Troy II (from 2500 B.C.). In Troy II Schliemann found what he called the "Treasure of Priam", with forged tools and jewellery of precious metals.

Hittites

The historical period in Anatolia begins with the Hittites, who moved into Asia Minor towards the end of the 3rd millennium B.C. They were the first people in Anatolia to use a written script – the cuneiform script which they introduced from Mesopotamia in the 18th/17th century B.C. They also used a hieroglyphic script which shows some analogies with the Cretan hieroglyphs.

Hittite art developed out of the interaction of the cultures of the incoming Indo-Europeans and the native Hattians. By the 18th c. B.C. it shows all its essential characteristic; its great flowering, however, is between about 1450 and 1200 B.C. During this period large temples and palaces were built, and imposing works of fortification. The most distinctive feature of Hittite architecture is the total asymmetry of the layout. The Hittites were ignorant of the column, using square pillars for support. Characteristic of Hittite architecture, too, are large windows with low balustrades.

Large sculptured reliefs are frequently found at the gates of palaces or on rock faces. Their detailing shows that Hittite artists worked to established formulae and prescriptions. Not only the hair-style and the dress but the limbs of the persons represented are always depicted in accordance with an accepted pattern.

Lydians, Lycians, Carians

After the fall of the Hittite Empire about 1190 B.C. there was a Dark Age, varying in length in different parts of Asia Minor. In the 8th c. B.C. the Lydians, Lycians and Carians came to the fore in south-western Anatolia. Of the art and architecture of these peoples little is left but funerary structures (magnificent funerary monuments, rock tombs with richly decorated façades, burial caves, etc.). By mid 7th c. these cultures had come under Greek influence, but until the time of Alexander the Great they still preserved their own characteristic styles. Only then did the Greek style become dominant in Anatolia.

Greek art

The early Greek settlements on the west coast of Asia Minor (1050–750 B.C.) were the first primitive, and in the field of art they were still under the influence of their homeland. In subsequent centuries, however, the Eastern Greek world achieved a great political development and, in parallel with this, a flowering culture in which the Ionians played the leading part. Their culture, which evolved from the cohabitation of the Greek and native populations and was subject to a variety of Oriental influences, reached its peak between 650 and 494 B.C. The Ionian art of this period is markedly different from that of mainland Greece. Specific characteristics of the sculpture, for example, are the radiant expression on the faces of figures and the elaborately patterned folds of the drapery. Much more important, however, is the Ionian contribution to Greek architecture. With its slender proportions Ionian architecture mitigates the rather squat and heavy character which Greek architecture acquired from the Doric order. But it is difficult now to get any real impression of Ionian architecture itself, which survives only in fragments to be seen in the museums of İstanbul, İzmir and Selçuk (Ephesus) and elsewhere.

Although after the destruction of Miletus (494 B.C.) Eastern Greek art produced little work in its own distinctive style, the cities of western Asia Minor were still among the leading artistic and cultural centres of Hellenistic times (the last three centuries B.C.). The Ionic style continued to exist alongside Doric. A distinctive feature of the Hellenistic period as compared with earlier centuries is that the individual building was not considered in isolation but as one element in a total architectural conception: this can be seen, for example, in the layout of Priene. In this period, too, the functional aspect of the various structural elements was of less concern than their ornamental effect, producing architecture designed for ostentatious display: the classic example of this is Pergamon, with buildings which were overcharged with decoration.

Roman art

The Greek tradition of Asia Minor continued almost without interruption into Roman times, and the Roman art of Asia Minor shows no distinctive character of its own. From this period survive the finest and best preserved theatres of antiquity (Aspendos, Miletus, Ephesus).

Byzantine art

Byzantine art developed during the 5th c. out of the Roman culture of late antiquity, the Hellenistic foundations of which had been further enriched by Christianity, and achieved its first great flowering in the reign of Justinian (526–65). There followed a period of stagnation and,

The Seven Wonders of the Ancient World

Mausoleum of Halicarnassus

Temple of Diana at Ephesus

Statue of Zeus at Olympia

Colossus of Rhodes

Pyramids at Giza

Pharos at Alexandria

Hanging Gardens of Babylon

Of the "Seven Wonders" of classical antiquity, designated thus in the 3rd c. B.C., two were on Greek territory in Asia Minor, now part of Turkey – the Mausoleum, tomb of the Carian King Mausolos at Halicarnassus (Bodrum), and the great Temple of Artemis/Diana at Ephesus (Selçuk).

A further two were also Greek – Phidias' statue of Zeus at Olympia on the Pelopponese peninsula, and the Colossus of Rhodes, a gigantic bronze figure of the sun god Helios standing astride the entrance to the harbour on the Aegean island of Rhodes.

Two of the remaining three were in Egypt – the Pyramids at Giza (near Cairo) and the Pharos (lighthouse) just outside Alexandria; the seventh wonder – the Hanging Gardens of Semiramis – were in the palace of King Nebuchadnezzar II at Babylon (in what is today Iraq).

Apart from the Egyptian pyramids next to nothing of these famous structures has survived.

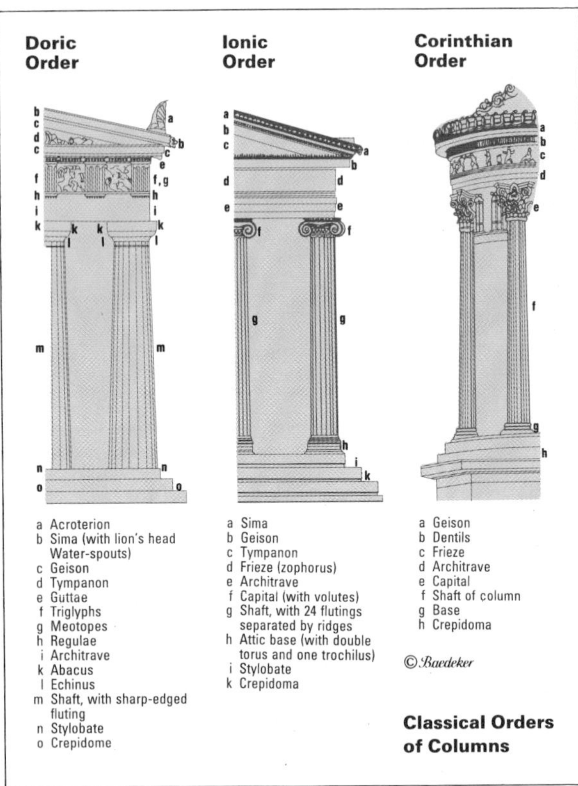

Classical Orders of Columns

during the Iconoclastic Controversy (726–843), of decline. Then, in the late 9th c., there was a fresh flowering of Byzantine art under the Macedonian dynasty.

Although art was still primarily in the service of the Church, the Iconoclastic struggle produced one positive effect in the emergence of a school of secular art alongside religious art. This new heyday of Byzantine culture continued into the 12th century, and thereafter there was a further period of brilliance under the Palaeologue emperors (1261–1453). The end came with the capture of Constantinople by the Turks.

The various phases of Byzantine art are reflected particularly in architecture, mainly of course Church architecture.

Before the time of Justinian the commonest type of church was the basilica, a rectangular building with a flat roof borne on columns or pillars, usually dividing it into three aisle, which had developed out of the market hall and court-room of Hellenistic times. The church proper was entered by way of a square forecourt surrounded by colonnades (the atrium) and a vestibule or narthex. The church was divided into two parts, the first part, for the lay congregation, being separated by a high screen from the part reserved for the clergy. This latter part ended in the apse, which contained the altar, the bishop's throne and benches for the officiating priests. The central aisle had a gently arched barrel roof, the side aisles pent roofs. There may be variations from the standard type; for example the atrium may be missing, or there may be four side aisles.

After architectural techniques for the construction of domes of considerable size had been devised, a second type of church, the domed basilica, came into favour in the time of Justinian. This was a hybrid between a rectangular and a circular structure. The dome was conceived as an interruption of the central aisle or nave, and the desire to enhance its effect led to the incorporation in the structure of barrel-roofed transepts, lateral semi-domes, relieving arches and other features. Although the original basilican form was thus considerably modified the basic structure of the basilica can still be recognised in the narthex, lateral aisles and apses. These new architectural features reached their full development in the world-famed Hagia Sophia (532–37).

The third type of Byzantine church, the domed cruciform church, developed from the 6th c. onwards but did not reach its fully matured form until the Macedonian dynasty; thereafter it predominated over all earlier forms. The basic structure of this type of church is a Greek cross (i.e. one with arms of equal length). At the intersection of the nave and transepts is the main dome, and there are other domes at the ends of the arms of the cross, and frequently also at the corners of the square of rectangle within which the church is inscribed. In subsequent centuries, as the domes became increasingly inconspicuous, attempts were made to give them more prominence by raising them on drums; but this destroyed their organic connection with the structure as a whole.

Byzantine art also excels in the fields of applied art and paintings. Painting is represented by icons, miniatures and wall-painting; another form of wall decoration is mosaics. In these fields of art the Iconoclastic Controversy – a conflict started by the Iconoclasts, who opposed what they saw as the excessive veneration accorded to images – marks a decisive break. It is only after the defeat of the Iconoclasts, in the latter part of the 9th c., that representational art recovers its momentum. The object of this art is not mere decoration: it is to direct the thoughts of the faithful, by these pictorial representations, to the message of salvation. Particularly effective in achieving this is the mosaic, with the durable qualities of its materials and its striking effects of light and colour.

Although the selection of subjects and their disposition in the church had previously been left to the artists, after the Iconoclastic Controversy certain rules became established. For example the highest point in the church – the dome, which was seen as a symbol of the vault of heaven – must always have a representation of Christ enthroned, surrounded by the Archangels and attended, on a lower level, by the Evangelists and by Apostles or Prophets.

The earliest portraits of saints may have been in the encaustic technique (burnt in wax paint) brought in from Egypt. Later they were painted in tempera on wood, and finally also in oil. The earliest surviving icons of this kind date from the 11th c.; more numerous are those of the 14th–16th c.

The art of the Byzantine miniature-painters is found in illuminated manuscripts – though those we have today are copies of earlier models. These book illustrations are less narrowly confined to prescribed forms than the mosaics, and are constantly in quest of new ornamental forms.

In the field of applied art, apart from goldsmith's and silversmith's work and textiles, ivory-carving is of particular importance.

Seljuk art

In the time of the Seljuks Byzantine Asia Minor entered the Islamic World. The occupation of Anatolia began in 1071 with the celebrated

Battle of Manzikert in eastern Asia Minor, after which the victorious Seljuks advanced rapidly along the peninsula to the Mediterranean coast. Seljuk art could thus find expression all over this area; its main base, however, was in inner Anatolia, and particularly in the capital, Konya.

The heyday of Seljuk art was in the first half of the 13th c. Within this brief 50-year period the Seljuks were active builders, erecting numerous mosques and medreses (theological colleges) with their tile-faced minarets, fortress-like caravanserais (inns), castles and türbes (tombs).

The mosques show a surprising variety of architecture. In addition to types, such as the courtyard mosque, which had already been developed in other Islamic countries, Asia Minor produced a distinctive type of its own, the basilican mosque. Instead of the usual wide prayer-hall this was a longitudinal structure with three or more aisles. Characteristic features of this type are the system of domes and the elaborate doorway which is normal only in Asia Minor. Doorways of this kind, which are found also in medreses, caravanserais and türbes, are distinctive features of Seljuk architecture, and with their arabesques, calligraphic inscriptions and geometric decoration they display the whole repertoire of Seljuk ornament. A surprising feature in the use of figural motifs, which are not found in other Islamic religious art.

In secular architecture the predominant type of building is the saray (palace), which is not a single large building but a juxtaposition of a series of smaller "kiosks" or pavilions. Also characteristic of Islamic secular architecture are the caravanserais or hans which were constructed at regular intervals on the main trade routes. Built in the style of fortresses and defended by massive towers, these replaced the primitive earlier rest-houses. Like the mosques, they have imposing and elaborately decorated doorways which show, even more strikingly than in the sacred buildings, the Seljuk delight in figural ornament. Carvings of lions are particularly popular. The Seljuks were also masters in the art of fortification. A particularly striking example of a walled Seljuk town is Alanya. In the field of applied art mention must be made in particular of the fine Seljuk carpets. Asia Minor must have become at an early stage the leading area for the manufacture of knotted carpets. The oldest examples, made wholly in wool using the so-called "Turkish knot", are notable for the contrast between the borders and the closely patterned central panels. Very commonly the colour schemes are based on different shades of the same basic colour – for example different tones of blue, red or green.

Ottoman art

After the conquest of Constantinople in 1453 the rise of the Ottoman Empire into a World Power began, a development which was accompanied by a great cultural and artistic flowering. In the history of Ottoman art a number of phases can be distinguished; the early period (14th and 15th c.), showing a variety of trends, is followed in the 16th and 17th c. by the classical period of Ottoman art, which shows a high degree of uniformity; this in turn is succeeded by a final phase, under strong European influence.

The variety of Early Ottoman art is shown particularly in the architecture of the mosques, in which a completely new phase begins. In place of the basilican type characteristic of the Seljuks the wide prayer-hall returns to favour, combined with the courtyard and with the vestibule first introduced in Asia Minor. The dome gains increasing importance, and rows of domes cover the colonnades in the courtyards of mosques and medreses. The façade is given a new note: it is enlivened not only with the elaborate Seljuk doorway but also with bands of windows and facings of coloured marbles.

The classical period of Ottoman art (16th and 17th c.) is characterised by a strikingly uniform imperial style, which extends into the remotest regions of the vast Ottoman Empire but displays its finest achievements in İstanbul, the centre of power and culture.

The most strikin g features of the Ottoman mosques are their imposing central domes and the exaggeratedly slender minarets. The trend towards the monumental is evident everywhere, with gigantic structures which are clearly inspired by Hagia Sophia. The finest of the Ottoman mosques were designed by the great architect Sinan (see Famous People), the "Ottoman Michelangelo", who is credited with

The Serefeddin Camii in Konya

the construction of no fewer than 477 buildings. His domed buildings show great variety of plan.

Secular as well as religious buildings were now given their distinctive character by domes. Domes dominate the spaciously planned hamams (bath-houses), which like Roman baths are tripartite in design with a changing and rest room, a warm room and a hot room but have no cold room, as do the palaces. In the loosely planned layout of their palaces the Ottomans followed the Seljuk model, though the palaces now occupied a considerably larger area.

Tiles now played a major part in the decoration of buildings, being used to cover large areas of both the exterior and the interior. They show a new ornamental style, influenced by Europe and markedly more realist. The decoration reflects the country's extravagant profusion of flowers. The new decorative forms are not only applied to architecture but are found in other types of applied art – for example, in the decoration of fine porcelain. Ceramic production in general developed on an extraordinary scale in the famous workshops of İznik from the first half of the 16th c. onwards, and the reputation of Turkish products spread as far afield as Europe.

Our knowledge of the earliest products of Turkish carpet-making workshops comes from 15th c. European paintings, which depict, among other types, the so-called "Holbein carpets", with purely geo-

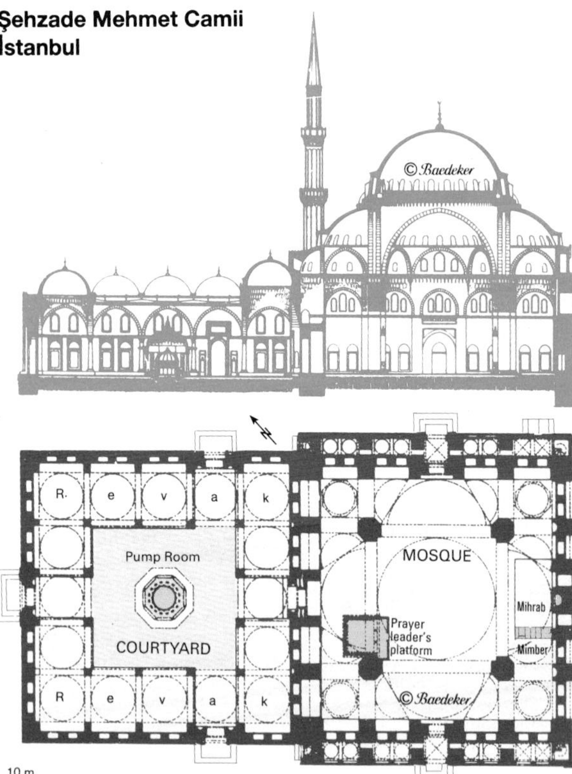

İstanbul's Princes' Mosque, Şehzade Camii, by the great Sinan (see Famous People)

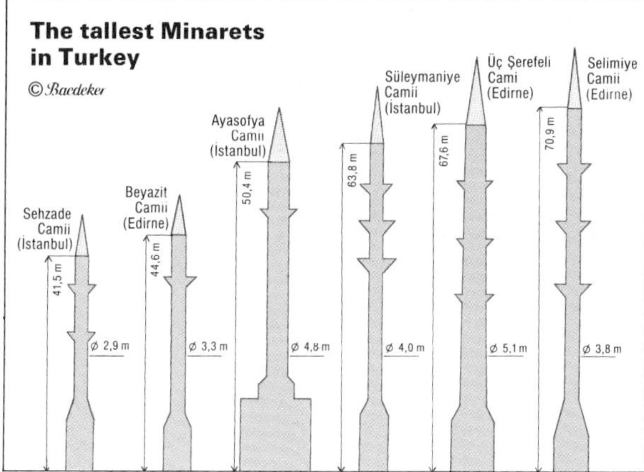

metric designs. An important type is the prayer rug with a representation of the mihrab (prayer niche in a mosque), on which the faithful say their prayers, turned in the direction of Mecca.

Other valuable textile products are precious fabrics including Ottoman silk brocades, velvets and velvet brocades. These, too, show the characteristic Ottoman floral patterns.

Tulip period

In a final flowering of art in the early 18th c. – the "Tulip period" – Western influence is evident. Features of European Baroque are readily recognisable – most obviously in the curving roofs and dome structures.

Turkish Rococo

Rococo came to the Ottoman Empire from France in the mid 18th c. and was enthusiastically received both by the Court and by Turkish artists, who developed the style into a distinctively Turkish form.

Modern period

In the 19th and 20th c. the influence of European architecture became steadily more marked. Oriental influences can be detected only in the decoration of buildings.

Settlements and Urban Development

Ancient sites

With a history of human settlement going back 700 years, Asia Minor is richly stocked with remains of the past, many of them outstanding in interest and beauty. Many parts of the country are dotted with hüyüks, the prehistoric settlement mounds, frequently more than 30m/65ft high, which have yielded and are still yielding a rich harvest of finds. Among major sites of archaeological interest are Troy, Pergamon, Sardis, Ephesus, Priene, Miletus, Hierapolis, Perge, Aspendos and Side, but there are countless others of lesser fame, and many existing towns preserve buildings of the Byzantine, Seljuk and Ottoman periods.

Traditional housing

Traditional types of houses still prevail – timber and half-timbered houses with many large windows and hipped or other types of pitched roofs in the western and northern regions, mud-brick or stone houses with small windows in the interior and the south-east. In these areas the village houses are all flat-roofed, hipped or pitched roofs being found only in the towns. Stone building is characteristic particularly of the volcanic regions and of the arid areas in the east.

The villages and the old parts of towns show the planless layout characteristic of the Oriental town. The older areas are closely built up, the residential districts with their winding lanes, almost windowless house-fronts, walled gardens and courtyards, being separated from the business quarters with their lively bazaars and craftsmen's workshops, while the more recent extensions have a more regular layout and a more spacious atmosphere. Characteristic features of the townscape are the mosques with their minarets. In villages and smaller towns and in the suburbs of the larger towns the houses are interspersed with gardens.

Explosion of building

In recent years there has been a great wave of building activity, particularly in the towns but also in the country. All over Turkey visitors will see work in progress on the improvement of the infrastructure (roads, drainage, etc.), new housing and industrial developments and the construction of holiday villages and hotels in regions of particular attraction to meet the demands of the holiday and tourist trade.

Typical Islamic Buildings

Mosques

The principal Islamic sacred building is the mosque – Turkish "mesçit", from the Arabic "masjid" meaning "place of prostration" (in prayer). The main mosque in any town or city, where the faithful gather for Friday prayers, is the "cami" (from the Arabic "jemaa" = "place of congregational worship").

Courtyard

The outermost aisles of the mosque extend beyond the length of the prayer hall to form covered galleries each side of the courtyard.

Entry to the courtyard is through an often elaborately decorated doorway set in a substantial outside wall. A grand fountain, frequently of marble, in the centre of the courtyard, is used for the obligatory ablutions which precede prayer.

Minaret

At a corner of the outer wall or side galleries stands the minaret – Turkish mosques often have two or more – from which the muezzin calls the faithful to prayer.

Prayer hall
kiblah
mihrab

The prayer hall, the main part of the mosque, is square or rectangular. In the centre of the kiblah wall (Turkish "kıbla") which faces towards Mecca, is an often lavishly appointed prayer niche (mihrab; Turkish "mihrap"). Next to the mihrab, usually set at right angles to the kıbla wall, stands the pulpit (mimbar or minbar; Turkish "mimber").

Medreses

A second important category of religious building is the medrese (from the Arabic "darasa" meaning "to study"). These colleges of higher education teach science and medicine as well as Koranic studies and Islamic law. They incorporate both accommodation for students and a mosque-like prayer hall.

The two or even three storey-high medrese buildings are normally grouped around a rectangular courtyard with a fountain in the centre and a prayer hall at one end. Lecture rooms, library and administrative offices occupy the ground floor and the students' rooms, often no more than small cells, the floor(s) above.

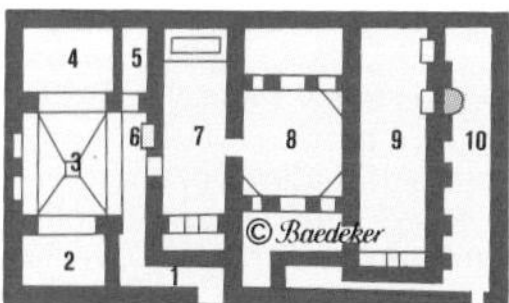

Turkish Bath – Hamam

Typical plan of a bath-house

1 Entrance
2 Supervisor's lodge
3 Inner courtyard
4 Rest room
5 Toilet
6 Well
7 Cold room
8 Warm room
9 Hot room
10 Heating area with stove and tank

Hamams

Turkish baths

As in the rest of the Islamic world, there are public and private bath-houses throughout Turkey. These "hamams" as they are called in both Arabic and Turkish, are really intended for Muslim purification.

The baths, many of them domed, are modelled on those of the Romans, and divided into a cold room, a hot room, a steam bath, and a rest room, together with a fountain, often of marble, and toilets.

The way into the hamam is always circuitous to prevent passers-by from seeing in from outside. An attendant is on hand in the usually tiled interior to see that the proprieties are observed. The sexes are always segregated.

Quotations

Kemal Atatürk (1880–1938)

Antalya is, without any doubt, the most beautiful place on earth. (March 6th 1930)

Baedeker's "Constantinople and Asia Minor" (1914)

. . . Special equipment for the journey is not necessary. For Constantinople a good, fairly light, suit is recommended in normal circumstances, supplemented on windy boat or carriage trips and in the cooler period after sunset by a greatcoat. A soft felt hat is the most convenient form of headgear. The fez denotes a subject of the Sultan, and is therefore, not appropriate for foreigners. During the rainy season rubber shoes are indispensable in Turkish towns which lack drainage. A black coat should be worn only for visits to high Turkish officials. Laundry competently washed, the charge being frequently based on the number of articles of whatever kind – approximately four francs the dozen. For travel in Aisa Minor a suit must be of durable material, and sturdy footwear is necessary. Each traveller will come provided with binoculars, water-bottle, compass, flannel shirts and a heavy felt cloak. For long rides and overnight stops in peasants' houses, etc., a travelling-rug, cutlery, aluminium plates and cups, gaiters, a neck scarf, a tin of insect powder and a stout, easily lockable travelling-bag of soft leather which can be tied to the saddle are required. The local fare can be supplemented by tea, chocolate and biscuits brought from home. The offer of a cigarette (*sigâra*) is a good way of expressing thanks for small courtesies, a cup of coffee, etc. To carry weapons with you merely creates difficulties.

Ernle Bradford, "Ulysses Found" (1963)

The island of Tenedos lies a bare two miles off the coastline of Asia Minor. Between the island and the shore the fast-running current still sluices down from the Dardanelles, just as it did when the Greeks set sail from Troy. Now known as Bozcaada, it is one of the only two Turkish islands in the Aegean and is of little importance today. Indeed, its whole history has been a happy one – happy in that it has hardly featured in the bloody chronicles of the Aegean, except on the one famous occasion when the Greeks pretended to abandon the siege of Troy. When, on the instructions of Ulysses, the Greeks had burned their camp and retreated to their boats as if in defeat, it was towards Tenedos that they set sail. It was nightfall when they left, and on the following morning the Trojans coming out of their city found the Greek camp burned and deserted, and only the mysterious wooden horse left behind on the shore in front of Troy. The Trojans looked seaward, but there was no sign of the enemy fleet, so they assumed that the Greek ships were already hull-down, bound for their homeland. Little did they know, as they dragged the horse across the sun-dried land and into the walls of Troy, that the greek fleet was lying concealed behind the low bulk of Tenedos.

It is not a mountainous island, and its most prominent feature Mount Sana is less than 400 feet high. In those days, though, like the rest of the Aegean islands, it was doubtless green and spiky with trees. Little more than three miles long, it could still afford anchorage to quite a large fleet on its south-western coast. On this side of the island there are innumerable small bays and coves where the ships would be safe from northerly winds, and from the southward-flowing current of the Dardanelles. If the stratagem of the wooden horse was largely the product of Ulysses' fertile mind, it was undoubtedly he who pointed out to Agamemnon where the ships could lie in safety out of sight of the Trojans. Not for nothing had Ulysses spent his youth in the Ionian islands – the home of pirates right up to the 19th century. There can have been few Greeks who knew more than Ulysses about winds and weather, suitable places for ambush, and anchorages where sea-raiders could bide their time.

On the night when Ulysses and the other Greeks emerged from the belly of the wooden horse to open the gates of Troy, Agamemnon and the fleet rowed silently back from their shelter behind Tenedos. They beached their ships, and made their final victorious assault on the sleeping city of their enemies. It is likely that the Greeks anchored their fleet in the small bay just south of Yukyeri Point. It is still a good anchorage for small vessels, with bottom of sand and weed, and a beach protected from the north by a small headland on which now stands the ruins of an old fort. Even though the coastline may have changed a little during the past three thousand years, it was probably here that the Greek fleet was drawn up during the siege of Troy. The low peninsula still provides shelter from the prevailing winds, and the current runs more slowly at this point. Out in the centre, between Tenedos and the mainland, it can run as fast as two and a half knots, a considerable hazard for ships which under sail or oar are unlikely to have made more than four or five.

It was from this beach that Ulysses embarked with his comrades after the sack of Priam's capital. Behind them the city on the plain still smoked, and the ruined walls collapsed with a sighing fall. A south-easterly wind was blowing, hot off the mainland, as they hauled in the sleeping-stones which served them for anchors and cast off the stern anchors that they had made fast to rocks on the beach.

George Gordon, Lord Byron (1788–1824)

. . . I have been in all the principal mosques by virtue of a firman, this is a favour rarely permitted to infidels, but the ambassador's departure obtained it for us. I have been up the Bosphorus into the Black Sea, round the walls of the city, and indeed I know more of it by sight than I do of London. . . .

. . . I have seen the ruins of Athens, of Ephesus and Delphi, I have traversed great part of Turkey and many other parts of Europe and some of Asia, but I never beheld a work of nature or art which yielded an impression like the prospect on each side, from the Seven Towers to the end of the Golden Horn.
(Letter of June 28th 1810)

Colmar Freiherr von der Goltz (Prussian and Turkish General) "Anatolian Excursions" (1896)

The place where I begin these notes is one of those that have long been forgotten. Nowadays who knows much about the Baths of Yalova, or Coury-les-Bains, as the Frenchified society of Stamboul now likes to call it, or Pythia, to give it its Greek name, or Ilidja ("Hot Bath"), as it is called in Turkish? It is only within the last few years that it has been heard of again in the capital, where it is held to be a duty and an obligation to know the most insignificent European spa, and of course to visit them during their season. And yet in antiquity these were the most celebrated baths in the East. How much more have less favoured places, in themselves more important, fallen into oblivion!

Near the entrance to the Gulf of Ismid, opposite Cape Tuzla to the south, the site of an ancient city is occupied by the modest little coastal town of Yalova, a place of mixed but mainly Turkish population, which can be reached from Constantinople in a four-hour steamer trip. A well-preserved highway which begins here is the only thing that suggests anything out of the ordinary. It leads to the hot springs of Kuru, which lie in the valley of the Hamandere ("Valley of Baths"), a tributary of the Samanlydere, 12 kilometres south-west of Yalova in the foothills of Samanlydagh, the ancient Argonthonion Oros.

. . . Below, the Hamandere surges through the rocky gorge, and the steam rising from its water is the first sign that we have reached our goal. A horseshoe-shaped spa building with a shady square in front of it, a hotel facing it, a few Swiss-style villas, surrounded by parks and gardens: that is all there is. . . .

. . . between the wooded slopes of Gökdagh and the lake of Sabandja. . . .

Here already you feel their effect. The primeval subtropical forest, with creepers forming an impenetrable net to the tops of the highest trees, begins to disappear. Fires have created large clearings, leaving the blackened stumps of trees, and the local Cherkesses have begun to cultivate this new land. A scene of devastation, some will say; others will see it as the advance of culture. Those who know the Far West will see a resemblance to it here; others will be reminded of India. All areas where new land is being opened up are likely to be similar. The disappearance of low-lying forest is a natural thing, however much lovers of natural beauty may deplore it. The flat country round the lake is destined by its situation for agriculture and horticulture; the dense marshy forest was the haunt of fever, and now the cleared land will gradually be covered by other plantations, for Sabandja and the surrounding area live by fruit-growing. The land will be made healthier and more profitable. One could wish only that in the higher mountain regions a halt might be called to this devastation of the forests.

Herodotus
(5th c. B.C.)

Now the Ionians of Asia, who meet at the Panionium, have built their cities in a region where the air and climate are the most beautiful in the whole world: for no other region is equally blessed with Ionia, neither above it nor below it, nor east nor west of it. For in other countries either the climate is over cold and damp, or else the heat and drought are sorely oppressive. The Ionians do not all speak the same language, but use in different places four different dialects. Towards the south their first city is Miletus, next to which lie Myus and Priene; all these three are in Caria and have the same dialect. Their cities in Lydia are the following: Ephesus, Colophon, Lebedus, Teos, Clazomenae and Phocaea. The inhabitants of these towns have none of the peculiarities of speech which belong to the three first-named cities, but use a dialect of their own. . . .
("History", I, 142; translated by George Rawlinson.)

Homer
(*c.* 8th c. B.C.)
"Iliad" I, 1–32

Of the wrath of the son of Peleus – of Achilles – Goddess, sing
– That ruinous wrath, that brought sorrows past numbering
Upon the host of Achaea, and to Hades cast away
The valiant souls of heroes, and flung their flesh for prey
To hounds, and all the fowls of air – yet the will of Zeus was done.
Sing it from that first moment when fierce disunion
Sundered the noble Achilles and Atrides, king of men.
What God was it first caused them to clash in conflict then?
The Son of Zeus and Leto. For wroth with the high king's pride,
With an evil plague he smote the host, that fast the people died,
Because the son of Atreus had put his priest to shame.
To the swift Achaean galleys that old man, Chryses, came,
Bringing a priceless ransom for his daughter's liberty,
While high on a golden sceptre he bore for all to see
The wreath of the Archer Apollo, and prayed the Achaean lords
– All, but most the Atridae, the marshallers of swords:
"O Atreus' sons, O Achaeans glittering-greaved, I pray
That the Gods who hold Olympus' halls grant ye one day
The sack of King Priam's city, and a happy homecoming.
Yet ransom me my dear daughter, receive these gifts I bring,
Revering the Son of Zeus, Apollo, the Archer-king."
Then the other lords of Achjaea in the old man's cause spoke fair –
'Twere well to honour his priesthood and take the gifts he bare.
But the heart of Agamemnon, son of Atreus, brooked it ill
And he spurned old Chryses from him, with words of evil will:

"Never again let me find thee loitering in the way
Here by our hollow ships, old man – now nor another day –
Lest the God's own wreath and sceptre protect thee not at all!
I will *not* set free thy daughter – nay, in my palace-hall
In Argos, far from her homeland, old age shall bow her head,
Plying her loom and serving to cheer her master's bed.
Begone! – and beware my anger, if home thou wouldst come whole!"
(Translated by F. L. Lucas)

Alexander von Humboldt
German scientist and geographer
"Kosmos"
(1845–62)

What distinguished the Greek colonies from all others, particularly the rigid Phoenician colonies, and influenced the whole organism of their community came from the individuality and the ancient variation of the peoples which made up the nation. There was in the colonies, as in the whole of the Greek world, a mixture of binding and separating forces. These contrasts generated variety of ideas and feelings, differences in poetry and the melic art [poetry meant to be sung]; they generated everywhere the rich abundance of life in which apparently hostile elements were reduced to harmony and concord.

Miletus, Ephesus and Colophon were Ionian; Cos, Rhodes and Halicarnassus were Dorian, Croton and Sybaris Achaean; but within this variety of culture, and indeed even where colonies founded by different peoples lay close together in southern Italy, the power of the Homeric songs, the power of the inspired and deeply felt Word, exerted its all-conciliating magic. In spite of all its deeply engrained differences in manners and political structure, and of all changes in these structures, the Greek world remained undivided. A great realm of ideas and artistic types won by the various peoples was regarded as the property of the whole nation. . . .

Pierre Loti
"Aziyadé"
(1879)

. . . On the following evening we arrived at Ismid (Nicomedia) as night was falling. We had no passports and were arrested. Then some pasha or other was good enough to issue two false passports, and after a long palaver we managed to avoid sleeping in the cells. Our horses, however, were confiscated and spent the night in the police stables.

Ismid is a large and reasonably civilised Turkish town situated on the shores of a beautiful bay. The bazaars are busy and picturesque. The inhabitants are prohibited from going out, even with a lantern, after 8 o'clock in the evening. I preserve a very pleasant recollection of the morning we spent here – one of the first mornings of spring, with a sun which was already warm shining in a blue sky. Fortified by a tasty peasant midday meal, fresh and cheerful, our papers in order, we set out to climb to the Orhan Cami. We made our way up on narrow lanes, overgrown with weeds and steep as goat tracks. The butterflies frolicked round us, and there was a buzzing of insects. The birds were celebrating the coming of spring, and the breeze was mild. The decrepit old wooden houses were painted with flowers and arabesques, and the storks nested with such entire freedom on the roofs that they prevented some of the inhabitants from opening their windows.

From the highest point of the Orhan Cami the eye ranges over the blue water of the Gulf of Ismid and over the fertile plains of Asia to Mount Olympus above Brusa, whose mighty snow-covered peak can be seen rising in the far distance.

Rose Macaulay
"The Towers of Trebizond"
(1956)

When we saw Trebizond lying there in its splendid bay, the sea in front and the hills behind, the cliffs and ravines which held the ancient citadel, and the white Turkish town lying along the front and climbing up the hill, it was like seeing an old dream change its shape, as dreams do, becoming something else, for this did not seem the capital of the last Byzantine empire, but a picturesque Turkish port and town with a black beach littered with building materials, and small mosques and houses climbing the hill, and ugly buildings along the quay.

Quotations

Lady Mary Wortley Montagu (1689–1762)

'Tis also very pleasant to observe how tenderly he and all his brethren voyage-writers lament the miserable confinement of the Turkish ladies, who are perhaps freer than any ladies in the universe, and are the only women in the world that lead a life of uninterrupted pleasure exempt from cares; their whole time being spent in visiting, bathing, or the agreeable amusement of spending money, and inventing new fashions. A husband would be thought mad that exacted any degree of economy from his wife, whose expenses are in no way limited but by her fancy. 'Tis his business to get money and this noble prerogative extends itself to the very meanest of the sex. Here is a fellow that carries embroidered handkerchiefs upon his back to sell, as miserable a figure as you may suppose such a mean dealer, yet I'll assure you his wife scorns to wear anything less than cloth of gold; has her ermine furs, and a very handsome set of jewels for her head. They go abroad when and where they please. 'Tis true they have no public places but the bagnios, and there can only be seen by their own sex; however, that is a diversion they take great pleasure in. . . .

. . . The second day after we set sail [from Constantinople] we passed Gallipolis, a fair city, situated in the bay of Chersonesus, and much respected by the Turks, being the first town they took in Europe. At five the next morning we anchored in the Hellespont, between the castles of Sestos and Abydos, now called the Dardanelli. These are now two little ancient castles, but of no strength, being commanded by a rising ground behind them, which I confess I should never have taken notice of, if I had not heard it observed by our captain and officers, my imagination being wholly employed by the tragic story that you are well acquainted with:

The swimming lover, and the nightly bride.
How Hero Loved, and how Leander died.

Verse again! – I am certainly infected by the poetical air I have passed through. That of Abydos is undoubtedly very amorous, since that soft passion betrayed the castle into the hands of the Turks, in the reign of Orchanes, who besieged it. The governor's daughter, imagining to have seen her future husband in a dream (though I don't find she had either slept upon bride-cake, or kept St Agnes's fast), fancied she afterwards saw the dear figure in the form of one of her besiegers; and, being willing to obey her destiny, tossed a note to him over the wall, with the offer of her person, and the delivery of the castle. He shewed it to his general, who consented to try the sincerity of her intentions, and withdrew his army, ordering the young man to return with a select body of men at midnight. She admitted him at the appointed hour; he destroyed the garrison, took her father prisoner, and made her his wife. This town is in Asia, first founded by the Milesians. Sestos is in Europe, and was once the principal city of Chersonesus. Since I have seen this strait, I find nothing improbable in the adventure of Leander, or very wonderful in the bridge of boats of Xerxes. 'Tis so narrow, 'tis not surprising a young lover should attempt to swim it, or an ambitious king try to pass his army over it. But then 'tis so subject to storms 'tis no wonder the lover perished, and the bridge was broken.
("Letter from the East", 1716–18)

St Paul

. . . For I hear him [Epaphras] record, that he hath a great zeal for you, and them that are in Laodicea, and them in Hierapolis.
(Colossians 4,13)

Heinrich Schliemann (1871–73)

. . . His trenches cut ever deeper into the mound of rubble; it became ever more difficult to remove the rubble, after it had been sifted through, from a depth of 10 metres or more; work in the bottom of the trench, between high walls of loose earth, became ever more dangerous. It was only by a miracle that six workmen who had been buried under a falling wall of earth were saved. The trench had passed through a thick layer of ash and other traces of a fire, but had brought to light no significant remains of walls. Quantities of loosely packed stones were removed, and that these were the walls of the Pergamos was realised only later, when similar structures of rough undressed stone were found at other points on the site.

When the large trench which was driven across the shorter axis of the mound, starting from the north side, failed to reveal the sought-after foundations of the Temple of Ilian Athena Schliemann began to cut trenches into the mound from other points. He had been given permission by Mr Calvert to dig on his property, and work had scarcely begun on the north-west of the site than a beautiful relief slab was found near the surface. It depicted the sun god Helios, clad in a flowing robe and with a crown of beams round his head, mounting into the firmament on his four-horse chariot. Even more important than this fine piece of sculpture, no doubt a relic of the Hellenistic Temple of Athena, were the discoveries made to the south and south-west. On the south, 60 metres into the side of the mound, the workmen came upon a thick and massive wall, based directly on the native rock and still rising, with a slight batter, to a height of 6 metres; the rubble round it showed that it must originally have been still more formidable. The structure of the wall, built of undressed stones laid loosely over one another, with only earth filling out the joints, suggested the highest antiquity, as did its siting and the objects found round it. The wall could be traced continuing to right and left. It was built on virgin soil; and so this wall, if any wall on the site, must be the ring-wall of the Pergamos, said to have been built for the Trojan King by Poseidon and Apollo. The masses of rubble, 15 metres high, were removed to allow the line of the wall to be followed, and 30 metres farther on, on the south-west side of the mound, a broad and handsome ramp leading up to the walls was discovered. In order to protect its large paving slabs from the acquisitiveness of the natives, who if left to themselves remove the remains of any ancient structure, which they regard as excellent building material, Schliemann spread the story that Christ had made his way up this ramp to the palace of King Priam. It was at any rate true that the ramp – majestic for all the primitive crudeness of its construction – must have led up to the gateway of the citadel and beyond this to the palace of the ruler. The hundred workmen whom Schliemann now assembled at this point dug through masses of burned clay – only later identified as sun-dried bricks from the superstructure of the walls and gate – and thus it was established that this fortress has been destroyed in a great conflagration. And so this was the destroyed city of Troy! Here, at this gate, the fairest of women, for whose possession men had fought for ten years, showed to the elders of Troy the heroic figures of their god-descended enemies; this was the Scaean Gate! All the long endurance, all the effort had been worth while, and enthusiasm for the old legend, which he now seemed to have made reality, triumphed in the discoverer's breast. "May this sublime and sacred memorial to the heroic fame of Greece," he wrote at this time, "now and forever attract the attention of all who sail through the Hellespont; may it become a place of pilgrimage for the young of all succeeding generations and arouse their enthusiasm for knowledge, more especially for the magnificent language and literature of Greece." "May it," he went on, "be followed by the rapid and complete clearance of the ring walls of Troy, which must be connected with this tower, and very probably also with the walls brought to light by me on the north side, the excavation of which will now be an easy task."

He himself was concerned in the first place to explore the interior of the citadel, in which traces of the fire were everywhere to be found. When, near the gate, he discovered the scanty remains of a house consisting of several rooms of modest size he concluded from its situation that this was the house of Priam himself. It was discovered much later that the house was built on the ruins of the second city, the one which was destroyed by fire, and that the palaces of the Pergamos had a much more imposing aspect. But first a new and unexpected find near the building appeared to confirm the original identification. This was the great and much discussed "Trojan treasure".

In May 1873 a trench driven in from the west side of the mound cut through various ring walls and encountered the continuation of the mighty walls of the Pergamos. In Schliemann's own words: "While we were advancing along this enclosure wall and steadily uncovering more of it, I stumbled on a large copper object of highly unusual form close to the old house, a little way north-west of the gate. It at once attracted my whole attention, more particularly because I seemed to see the glimmer of gold inside it. Above the object was a rock-hard 5 foot thick layer of reddish and brown calcined rubble, and above this again was the wall, 5 feet thick and 20 feet high, which must have been built shortly after the destruction of Troy. It was urgently necessary, if this object was to be preserved for the benefit of archaeological science, to bring it into a place of safety where it would be secure from the greed of my workmen. Accordingly, although it was not yet time for the breakfast break, I immediately called for work to be suspended, and while my people were engaged in eating and resting I cut the treasure out of its rock-hard setting with a large knife – an enterprise which involved not only much effort but also a grave danger to life, since the great fortification wall under which I had to dig threatened to collapse on top of me at any moment. But the view of so many objects, each of which must be of incalcullable value to archaeology, made me greatly daring and prevented me from thinking of the danger. Even so I should not have been able to recover the treasure had not my wife helped me, standing beside me while I worked, ever ready to wrap the objects I discovered in her scarf and carry them away." Heavy gold cups, large silver jugs and golden diadems, necklaces and bracelets painstakingly composed of thousands of tiny pieces of gold – this splendid treasure could have belonged only to some mighty ruler of this land.

Rarely have the dreams of imaginative youth been so brilliantly fulfilled. After years of searching the discoverer now believed that he held in his hands the treasures of which Homer had sung. He had spent many days in Priam's proud fortress, and could now call the unfortunate King's treasures his own. After such successes he felt sated, and on June 17th 1873 he stopped work on the site – as he thought, for ever – and returned to Athens with his finds. At once he set about publishing his results, and by New Year 1874 had completed his "Trojan Antiquities" – essentially a collection of the reports he had sent to "The Times" from Hisarlik. Attached to the book was an album of more than 200 photographs of the excavations and the objects recovered.
(From the "Autobiography", published by Schliemann's wife Sophia in 1891)

Emil Wendt
"Illustrations of Geography and Ethnography"
(1846)

Asiatic Turkey:
Of the countries, once splendid but now fallen totally into ruin, which are governed by the Turks we first come to Asia Minor, the finest part of the Ottoman possessions. Here we find the famous temple city of Kabira in Pontus; Magnificent Chalcedon; Nicaea, capital of Bithynia and the meeting-place of the great Council of 325; the ancient royal city of Troy, celebrated by Homer; Phocaea, mother city of Marseilles; Sardes, the brilliant capital of Lydia, where Croesus lived in proverbial luxury; Ephesus, whose temple of Diana, now vanished, was once one of the wonders of the world; Magnesia, Tralles, Priene, Miletus, Cnidos, Pergae, Seleucia, Lystra, Laodicea, Colossae and many other important cities have been reduced to the state of imposing ruins or are so covered with ruins that it is difficult to establish their exact site. Other once famous cities, like Trebizond, which under Genoese rule was still a trading town of some consequence; Amafia and Sinope;

Nicodemia (Ismid), the first capital of Bithynia; Cyzicus (Balkir) and Mitylene (Castro); Pergamum (Bergama), once capital of a kingdom; Thyatira (Akfa), where, as at Sinope, beautiful capitals, friezes and other works of sculpture are used as building material; Halicarnassus (Bodru); Rhodes, in antiquity an important commercial city and later the well-fortified stronghold of the Knights of St John; Tarsus, the splendid capital of ancient Cilicia; Iconium (Konya); Caesarea (Kayseri), long the principal market town in the interior of Asia Minor; Malatia and many more – these still survive, but reduced in size and in wealth, with only a few remains of the splendid buildings of the past.

The two cities which have preserved most of their former importance are Brusa (Bursa), the ancient seat of the kings of Bithynia, which still has a population of 60,000, and, even more notably, Smyrna, with a population of 120,000.

Suggested Routes

Preface

The routes below, several chosen specifically because they avoid the major roads, offer some ideas for touring the coastal regions of Turkey by car. Plenty of scope is left for visitors to plan a detailed itinerary of their own with the aid of the map provided with this Guide. The routes are designed to take in all the major sights, though detours are sometimes necessary to reach particular places mentioned. See map p. 38 for ancient place names.

N.B.

Places assigned separate entries in the "A to Z" section of the Guide are shown here in **bold**.

General

Out-of-town driving

Driving in Turkey today presents far fewer of the problems regarding fuel, road conditions and journey times that used to dog anyone setting out on a tour of Anatolia. New roads are being built and existing ones upgraded. Nowadays it is possible to drive to even the remotest villages, though in some cases the roads leading to them still present quite a challenge.

Unleaded petrol is still not always easy to find, though the situation in this respect is improving all the time. Generally speaking, filling up only becomes a problem when driving for long periods/distances away from the main roads, in which case it is necessary to carry sufficient fuel in reserve or use a diesel-powered vehicle (derv is available everywhere in the countryside, being used by farmers to run their tractors).

Local people can generally advise about the state of roads. Apart from the inter-city highways, traffic remains far lighter than on Europe's overcrowded highways. Offering a villager a lift may result not only in the inevitable invitation to tea but also the forging of lasting bonds of friendship. Country folk are usually relatively poor and unable to afford the price of a dolmus (shared taxi) while demand may be insufficient to sustain a proper local bus or minibus service.

In breaking a journey into manageable stages be sure to choose as stop-over points places with hotels – ports or seaside resorts on the coast, sizeable towns or tourist centres inland. Accommodation of a good standard is not necessarily to be found everywhere, tending to be concentrated in some areas and not others (see Practical Information, Motoring and Hotels).

Thrace (European Turkey)

General

Apart from Edirne or the main highways from Greece and Bulgaria to İstanbul and Gallipoli, Thrace is probably one of the least known parts of Turkey. It appears at first sight to offer few attractions, and its rolling, largely treeless landscape, in many places a sea of grain, makes little positive impact on the visitor. All the more rewarding then to embark on a journey of discovery away from the beaten track into the altogether delightful hinterland of this underrated region. In addition, many places along the main highway have more to offer than might be initially apparent.

Nor does exploration of this south-eastern tip of Europe have to begin from the Balkans. İstanbul is every bit as good as a departure point. If heading for the Dardanelles or Turkey's Aegean coast, the route through Thrace with a ferry crossing at the end of it might be an alternative to the drive through the south Marmara region.

1. From İstanbul to the Dardanelles on minor roads

From ★★**İstanbul** a largely traffic-free route, rich in history, winds north through changing scenery and at times on narrow country roads along the shores of the ★★**Bosphorus** to Kilyos. There it turns westward, through the Belgrade Forest and along the southern foothills of the still wooded Istranca Mountains, via the little towns of Saray and Vize to Kırklareli and on to ★**Edirne** or, continuing south, to the ★**Dardanelles.** Along this latter part of the route, stretches of prairie-like wheatland alternate with wooded valleys harbouring tiny villages until, at Uzunköprü, the broad expanse of the Ergene Valley with its rice paddies opens up, followed, further south, by the tree-covered mountains of the Koru Dağı (National Park) around Kesan.

On the Gallipoli Peninsula every mile is steeped in history; there is good bathing in the Aegean on one side, and equally good bathing in the ★**Sea of Marmara** and Dardanelles hardly any distance away on the other, plus superb views over the straits. Two car ferries make the crossing to Asia Minor: one, very busy, from Eceabat to **Çanakkale,** the other from Gelibolu to Lapseki.

2. From İstanbul to Bulgaria via Edirne

Favoured by migrant workers heading out of Turkey, the E80 is by far the busiest route across Thrace. Already almost motorway standard between İstanbul and Çorlu, once the improvements planned for the western section through Lüleburgaz and Edirne are completed, this is certain to become the preferred fast route to and from ★★**İstanbul** and Europe. Heavy traffic makes it a road best avoided in the peak season. Though destined to be an express trunk route and already used as such, there are plenty of interesting things to see along the way at Çorlu, Lüleburgaz, Babaeski and above all ★**Edirne.**

3. From İstanbul to Greece via Tekirdağ

Those who would rather head back to Europe on a quieter road should opt for the longer but certainly more interesting and, in the western section, substantially more traffic-free route via the Greek part of Thrace. The first leg of the journey, from İstanbul as far as Silivri, can be made on the E80 as if heading for Edirne. The alternative is to leave ★**İstanbul** on the much more pleasant road which follows the north shore of the Sea of Marmara through the city's green suburbs to Küçükçekmece, keeping off the new motorway as much as possible thereafter. This is the only way to become acquainted with the summer vacation homes of the residents of İstanbul, stretching in a more or less unbroken line of coastal resorts and holiday apartments fringing the ★**Sea of Marmara** all the way from the capital to the provincial centre of Tekirdağ, after which the hills and reservoirs around Malkara provide a welcome change. The stretch via Keşan and İpsala to the Greek frontier is less interesting, ending as it does in the broad valley and rice paddies of the Maritza (Meriç Nehri).

If heading for Gelibolu or beyond, this particular route provides an alternative to Route 1 (İstanbul to the ★**Dardanelles**), with a particularly delightful variation after Tekirdağ, following the newly built coast road through the seaside resorts of Barbaros–Kumbağ to Şarköy and thence to Gelibolu.

From the Bosphorus into South-eastern and Eastern Anatolia

General

Turkey's main highways offer plenty of opportunities for exploring the vast hinterland of Asia Minor. There are various possible starting out

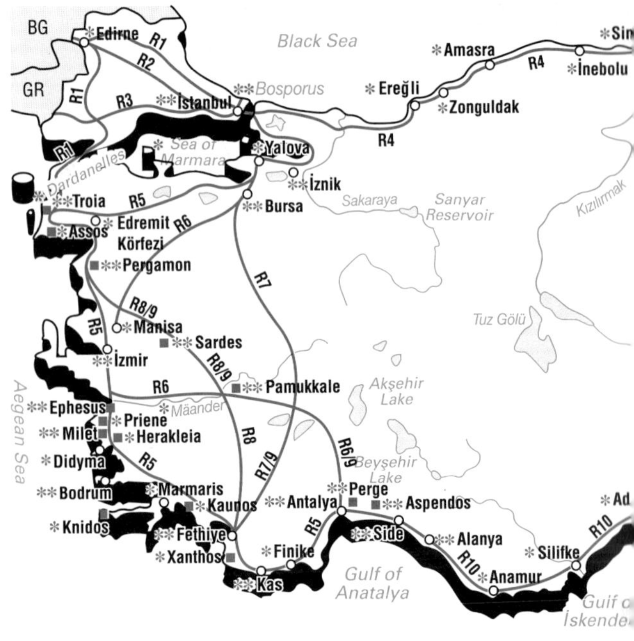

points (suitably endowed with hotels), but the two most obvious are İstanbul and İzmir on the Aegean coast.

Unless willing to trust to luck and the uncertain standards of accommodation in the more isolated parts, journeys should be planned so that any overnight stops are made in a provincial centre or one of the hotel complexes found chiefly in tourist highspots. Variations to the routes are suggested where appropriate to ensure inclusion of the finest scenery and as many of the principal sights as possible, sometimes requiring small detours or excursions.

4. From İstanbul to Artvin along the Black Sea coast

Main itinerary

The ★**Black Sea coast** has been gradually opened up to traffic in the last few decades and it is now possible to drive almost uninterrupted the length of the Pontic shores from İstanbul in the west to Artvin in the east.

Along the way, as well as Turkey's lovely northern beaches, less popular with tourists because of the climate (Karasu, Akçakoca, ★Amasra, Cide, ★İnebolu, Abana, ★Sinop, the deltas of the Kızılırmak and Yeşilırmak and the inviting bays of the eastern Black Sea coast), there is the entire north side of the northern Anatolian mountains to be explored in all their cultural and scenic variety. The subtle nuances of climate, the jungle-like forests of beech, oak, pine, rhododendron, fern, tree heather, arbutus and laurel, and the abrupt transition to cultivated crops (maize, hazelnuts, tea, tobacco), make this journey of discovery from İstanbul through İzmit and Adapazarı and then along

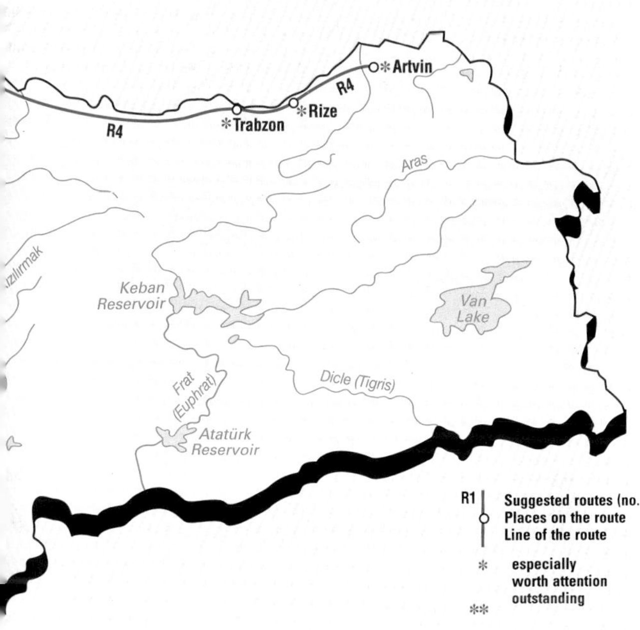

the delightful Black Sea coast via ★Ereğli, ★**Zonguldak**, Amasra, Cide, İnebolu, Sinop, Samsun, Ünye, ★Ordu, ★Giresun, Tirebolu, ★**Trabzon**, ★Rize and Hopa to ★**Artvin** especially fascinating.

Variations

At a couple of places along this Black Sea coast itinerary, there is a chance to turn aside onto an alternative, roughly parallel, route. Both options are well worth considering. The first comes at Ereğli where, by branching off inland, the mining city of **Zonguldak** is circumvented before the road arcs coastwards again to Bartın; here a second departure can be made from the tourist trail, driving through the Eflânı uplands and the Küre Dağları to Devrekânı and thence to the coast again at Abana. The main route, passes through historic Bithynia, Paphlagonia, Pontus, Colchis, the ancient Trapezunt empire, Lazistan and south-west Georgia, there are inviting and intriguing towns, villages and historic sites at almost every turn, rich in cultural history and impossible to ignore.

Detour

Should a change from the long coastal route be desired, a detour can always be made southwards into one of the mountain valleys.

5. From İstanbul to Antalya along the Aegean coast

Setting out from ★★**İstanbul** for the Aegean coast via the Dardanelles, one possibility is to take Route 1 or 3 through Thrace; the alternative is to cross to the Asiatic side and drive through the south of the Marmara region, which also has plenty to offer.

To speed up the early stages you can take the ferry from the ★★**Bosphorus** to Mudanya, or from Darıca to ★Yalova, and from there proceed to ★★**Bursa**. Here on the border between Bithynia and Mysia, at the foot of the Mysian Olympus (Ulu Dağ), the classic western Anatolia coastal tour begins, continuing westward at first and then south on good, though busy, roads to Antalya. Between Bursa and Gönen the route crosses the lowland plain with its two attractive lakes, Apolyont and Manyas.

Both can be passed either to the north or the south, though the smaller, more winding roads on the south side are scenically more interesting, particularly the road round Lake Apolyont which traverses the foothills of the Kızılelmadağı to Mustafa Kemalpaşa. The southern route around Lake Manyas offers a glimpse of some of the more recent muhacir settlements and a chance to visit the little-known historical site of Eski Manyas.

The next stretch, taking in rice plains, the lower reaches of the Gönen Çayı river and the Biga hills, leads down to the southern shore of the ★**Dardanelles** and on to **Çanakkale** and ★★**Troy** (*Truva*), crossing the scenic mountain landscape of the Troad.

Anyone who has already visited Troy and enjoys seeing unspoilt Turkish countryside can forgo the next section of coastal route and head south direct from Biga through the Troad hills via Çan and Bayramıç to Ezine, thereafter taking the narrow and occasionally somewhat rough minor road via Geyikli, Alexandria Troas, ★**Assos** (Behramkale) and Ayvacık to rejoin the main route at Küçükkuyu on the ★**Edremit Körfezi**.

The Gulf of Edremit marks the start of the succession of Aegean seaside resorts now so popular with foreign tourists; most lie at the end of small access or single-carriageway side roads (Ören, Ayvalık, Dikili, Çandarlı, Foça, the Çeşme peninsula with Urla, Ilıca and Çeşme, Gümüldür, Kuşadası, Didim).

Also strung out along this part of the Turkish coast are a host of classical Ionian, Lydian and Carian cities and sites, including some of the most famous: ★★**Pergamum** (Bergama), ★★**Sardis** (further inland), ★★**Ephesus**, ★★**Miletus**, ★**Priene**, ★**Didyma** and ★**Herakleia under Latmos**.

With its many bays and rocky headlands, the whole length of the coastline of south-western Anatolia around **Milas**, Muğla, ★★**Fethiye** and ★★**Kaş** is far more scenic, though less sandy, than the northern and western Aegean coast. Especially along the stretch south-east of Muğla, ancient capital of the Menteşe emirs, tourist development is still in its infancy, which has hitherto recommended it to discerning visitors. Quite the opposite is true of already overcrowded resorts such as ★★**Bodrum**, ★**Marmaris** and even Fethiye. Other places such as Kalkan, Kaş and ★**Finike**, once well off the beaten track, are also rapidly gaining in popularity.

The mountainous, occasionally wooded, often maquis-clad Mediterranean countryside of ancient Caria and Lycia, especially Lycia, is awash with historic sites including such evocative names as ★**Cnidos**, Halicarnassus, ★Caunus, Termessos, ★**Xanthos**, Patara, Myra, Kekova, Limyra, Olympos and Phaselis. Here again, many lie at the end of smallish side roads (Bodrum, Marmaris, Kekova, Olympos), but generally speaking driving is no problem.

Once round the corner into the Gulf of Antalya, extended sandy beaches again reappear, especially along the foot of the mighty Bey Dağları between western Pamphylia's tourist highspots of Antalya and Kemer.

A highly recommended alternative on this final section of the journey is to take the road inland from Kumluca up to Altınyaka, from there continuing on mountain roads through the Bey Dağları National Park, before dropping down again to ★★**Antalya**.

6. From İstanbul to Antalya through the mountain interior of Western Anatolia

This route, on good roads throughout, runs along the Gult of **İzmit** to Adapazarı (Sakarya) then follows the Sakarya river upstream to Geyve, through Pamukova and on over the Kaynarca Pass to ★★**İznik** (Nicaea) on the lake of the same name.

The next stretch, by-passing the Biga peninsula, cuts diagonally across the hills of northwestern Anatolia via Yenişehir, ★★**Bursa**, Balıkesir and Akhisar, through the hinterland of Bithynia, Mysia and Lydia to ★**Manisa** and ★★**İzmir**, the road being shared for much of the journey with long-distance coaches and tourist buses, traffic otherwise being much lighter than on the coast-hugging Route 5. Except for İznik, Bursa, Manisa, İzmir and Ephesus, places of historic interest along the way (such as Yenişehir, Balıkesir and Akhisar) are less spectacular and attract less attention. The ever changing scenery, however, is a constant source of delight, not least because of the contrasts between wooded mountain areas, inland basins, lakes and river gorges.

Beyond İzmir the route reverts to one of the traditional tourist trails, following the long, broad and fertile valley of the Menderes, the classical ★**Maeander**, on its slow but steady climb to the obligatory tourist highspot of ★★**Pamukkale** near Denizli. Thereafter it continues through the salt lake and limestone scenery of Western Pisidia and on via Dazkırı to the source of the Maeander at Dinar, almost on the border of Lycaonia.

Here the road swings south on the line of an old caravan route to **Burdur** and Bucak, through the poljes of south-western Pisidia and north-western Pamphylia, before dropping down from the cooler uplands to the hot and humid plain of ★★**Antalya**.

7. From the Black Sea to Lycia on minor roads

Avoiding main roads as far as possible apart from the initial stretch from ★★**İstanbul** to **İzmit** and Karamürsel, this route heads cross-country through the agreeably varied landscapes of western Bithynia, Phrygia and Pisidia to Lycia. Though the state of the road on one or two sections leaves something to be desired, this is more than made up for by the still generally unspoilt rural landscape of Western Anatolia, largely neglected by visitors apart from ★★**İznik** (Nicaea) and ★★**Pamukkale** (Hieropolis), but with its fair share of history nevertheless. The naturalness of the western Anatolian hinterland goes hand in hand with ever-changing scenery: the green forests of the north, the dry summer scrub of the hills, the grain-rich prairie steppes of Central Anatolia, the high mountains and maquis of the Mediterranean. Among particular highlights to be enjoyed are wonderful views of Lake İznik from the road over Samanlı Dağı from Karamürsel, the crossing of the wooded eastern foothills of Ulu Dağ from İnegöl to Domaniç, the hill country around Emet, and the mountainous limestone slopes of Yaylacı Dağı on the road via Çameli to ★★**Fethiye**.

Other stopping places of interest en route include **İzmit**, Yenişehir, İnegöl and Tavşanlı.

8. From the Dardanelles to Lycia on minor roads

Main itinerary

Anyone arriving in Turkey from Greece and already familiar with the Aegean coast might care to consider this parallel, inland route to Lycia from **Çanakkale** on the ★**Dardanelles**. Start out by following Route 5 from Çanakkale through the Troad as far as **Edremit**, then turn inland to İvrindi across the forested northern slopes of the Sabla Dağı.

Variations

From İvrindi there is a choice of routes south over the foothills of the Madras Dağı to the little towns of Soma and Kırkağaş, then down into the northern arm of the Gediz rift system and the fertile Akhisar Ovası.

Either option, the one via Balıkesir and Savaştepe, the other via Bergama (★★ **Pergamum**) and Kınık, means making use of delightfully remote and hence relatively slow and somewhat sub-standard roads through the border country of Mysia and Lydia. There follows a speedy run via Gölmarmara, down past the tombs of the kings of Sardis, to Salihli in the Gediz rift valley, and then on to ★★ **Sardis**. The next stage involves some rather more challenging driving through lovely mountain country, the road zig-zagging up to the pass above the high-level Lake Gölçük in the Boz Dağları, descending into the valley of the Kücükmenderes, the Little Maeander, at Birgi and Ödemis, only to climb once more to cross the wooded mountain barrier of the Aydın Dağları before dropping down again, this time to **Nazilli** in the intensively cultivated valley of the ★ **Great Maeander** (Büyükmenderes).

East of Nazilli a minor road makes its way along the picturesque Dandalas valley and over the wooded Kazıbeli passes to Tavas, Serinhisar and Acıpayam, skirting the ancient ruined city of ★★ **Aphrodisias** and displaying to advantage the many shallow upland depressions in the karst landscapes of western Pisidia and eastern Caria on the upper reaches of the Dalaman Çayı.

Two options present themselves for the final leg down to the coast and the main Antalya–Fethiye road. One is to take the new E87 via Çavdır to Kızılcadağ, the other the older, narrower and exceptionally scenic route via Gölhisar and the Dirmil pass. Thereafter follow the road southwestward down the valley of the Koca Çayı, mostly through the magnificent mountain landscape of the Ak Dağları spurs, as far as Kemer where the tang of the Mediterranean is already in the air. From there it is only a stone's throw across the final pass to ★★ **Fethiye** and the coast.

9. From Çanakkale to Antalya on minor roads

This particular tour follows a seldom-used cross-country route from the Dardanelles to Antalya. Although for the most part narrow and winding, the roads are generally well-surfaced, the majority with asphalt. Like Route 8, this itinerary, too, offers a wealth of variation, while terminating on the Turkish Riviera in the heart of Pamphylia instead of in Lycia.

It begins by crossing the lonely Troad hill country from **Çanakkale** via Çan, Balya and İvrindi to **Balıkesir** before, eschewing the direct route south, taking the old road through the mountains of the Ulu Dağ and the Simav Dağları, over two forested passes between Bigadiç and Sındırgı, into the Akhisar basin. Keeping well away from the main traffic routes, it then arcs eastward via Gördes through a region of the western Anatolian mountain country untouched by tourism, then south again past the Demirköprü barrage to the vineyards of the almost Tuscany-like Alaşehir depression which merges into the Gediz rift valley east of Salihli. A further stretch of scenic mountain road then crosses the Boz Dağları and Aydın Dağları where the two ranges meet, arriving, after Buldan, in the Menderes valley with its thermal springs around ★★ **Pamukkale**, Sarayköy and Denizli.

Every bit as impressive as Route 7 (which passes by here heading south-west), the final leg of the journey traverses the limestone mountain country of Pisidia, but in an easterly direction, crossing the extensive polje systems of Yeşilova, Tefenni and Korkuteli. North of the Bey Dağları, the road descends in a great curve through the forested and maquis-covered highlands, uncultivated apart from fruit orchards, around the former summer pastures of the Pamphylian coastal cities, past Termessos, high up in the mountains, to Döşemaltı and then at last

★★**Antalya**, pearl of the Turkish Riviera, with its fascinating old town and lovely harbour.

10. From Antalya through Pamphylia to Cilicia

Another classic route is the drive along the length of Turkey's south coast from ★★**Antalya** in Pamphylia through southern Pisidia and "rough" Cilicia to the Cilician Plain and ★**Adana**.

Even without the highly recommended detour into the Taurus (following the Köprülü upstream to the Köprülü Canyon and over the gravelled road to Selge), this route takes in a string of famous and not so famous ruined sites of antiquity, including ★★**Perge**, ★★**Aspendos**, ★★**Side**, Anamurion (★**Anamur**), Seleukia, Kanlıdıvane, Kız Kalesi and Pompeiopolis. There are also handsome Armenian and Crusader castles, some great reminders of the heyday of the Ottoman Empire (Antalya, caravanserais, Alanya), and natural beauty spots (waterfalls at Antalya, Manavgat and Tarsus; the Corycian Caves, "Cennet ve Cehennem"/Heaven and Hell, near Silifke), while on both sides of the road can be seen glass and plastic covered hothouses and hectare after hectare of exotic Mediterranean crops – citrus fruit, bananas, pomegranates, cotton, peppers and groundnuts. But above all there are the superlative beaches, the inviting bays, and the exceptional hospitality; be warned though that prices can be sky high and beds in desperately short supply in the peak season when the resorts are far too overcrowded anyway.

Apart from **Antalya** and ★★**Alanya**, the main tourist centres on the Turkish Riviera are the thriving seaside resorts around Manavgat, Sorgun and **Side**, together with the coastal towns of Rough Cilicia between Taşucu (near ★**Silifke**), Kızkalesi and Erdemli.

Despite the holiday apartment blocks mushrooming at an alarming rate around Mersin, and the heavily industrialised road from there to Adana, this stretch of coast is certainly the ideal choice for anyone who loves the summer heat, enjoys the excitement of Mediterranean beach life, but is also looking for spectacular scenery. Just the tour of the southern Taurus uplands between Alanya and Silifke, past ★**Anamur**, can hardly be bettered from a scenic point of view, though it is very winding.

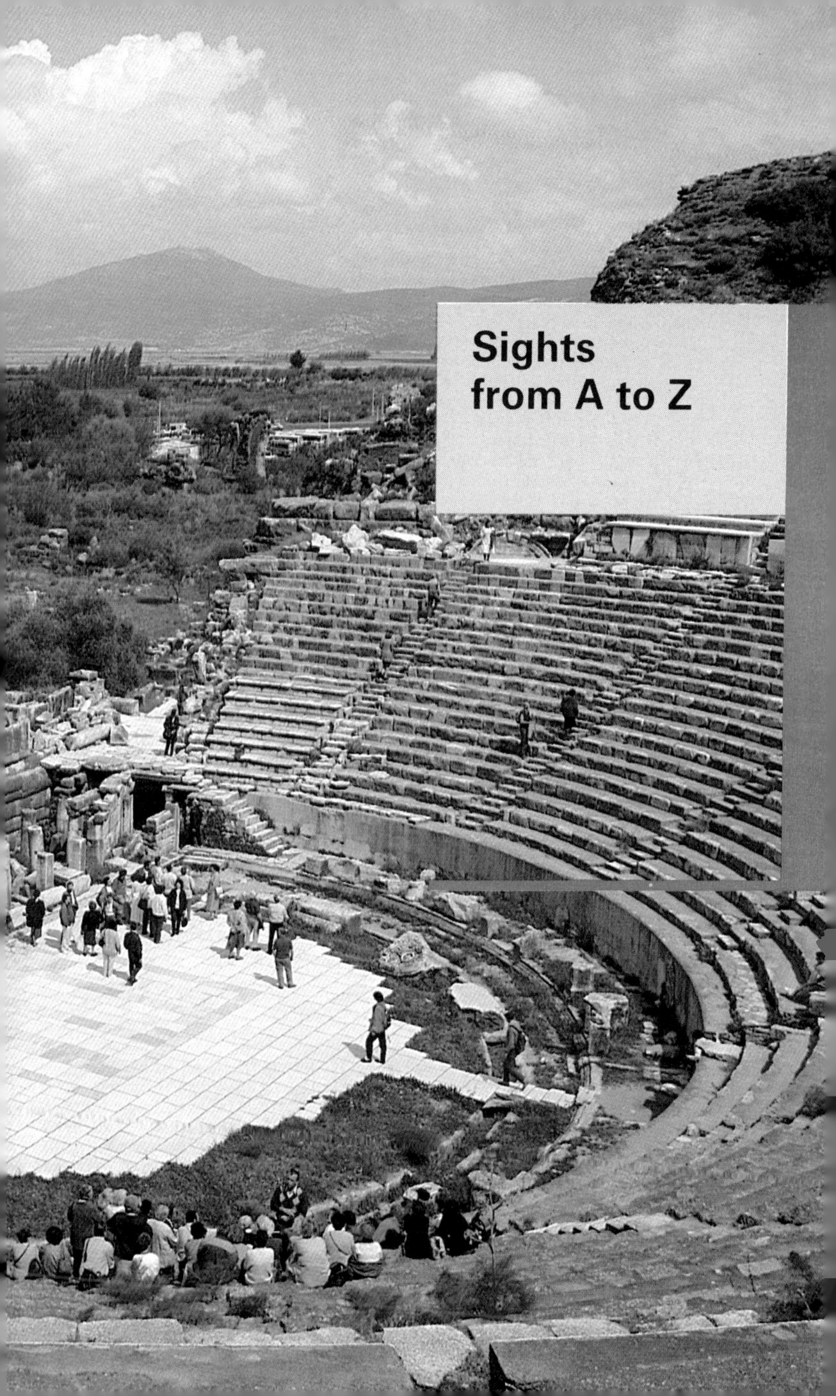

Sights from A to Z

Adana

L 6/7

South coast (eastern Mediterranean)
Province: Adana
Altitude: 25m/80ft
Population: 916,000 conurbation 1.9 million

Situation and ★ importance

The provincial capital of Adana, Turkey's fifth largest city (after İstanbul, Ankara, İzmir and Konya) and one of its wealthiest economic centres, lies in the south-east of the country in the Cilician Plain (now known as Çukurova or "Hole Plain" and in antiquity as Aleion Pedion), below the southern slopes of the Taurus. It is built on the right bank of the Seyhan (the ancient Saros), which is spanned by a number of bridges, some of them ancient, and a railway bridge.

The town draws its subsistence from the plain, with its rich citrus plantations and fertile arable land, which extends in the form of a delta towards the Mediterranean, 50km/30 miles away; and its situation near the southern exit of the "Cilician Gates", from time immemorial the principal pass through the Taurus, and on the Baghdad Railway provided the basis of its econopmic development. In recent years, therefore, Adana has enjoyed an upswing in its economy (university since 1971) and a considerable increase in population. The principal places of employment are food-canning and preserving factories, spinning- and weaving-mills, engineering plants, cement works and the railway workshops. The corn and cotton trades are also important (Cotton Exchange). The climate is very hot, but dry and unhealthy (malaria).

History

Human settlement at Adana reaches far back into pre-Christian times. The Hittite town of Ataniya may have been situated on Velican Tepe, a hill 12km/7½ miles outside the town; the present town is built on a relatively recent settlement mound. Under the Seleucids the town was known as Antiocheia on the Saros. In Roman times Adana, then called by its present name, was overshadowed by the regional capital, Tarsus, and therefore played a fairly modest role. Its real development began under Ottoman rule and, even more markedly, under the Turkish Republic.

Sights

Stone Bridge (Taç Köprü)

Practically nothing remains of ancient Adana. All that it has to show is the 310m/340yd long Stone Bridge over the Seyhan, frequently destroyed and restored in the course of its history, which preserves 14 out of its original 21 arches, including one (at the west end) which is believed to date from the time of the Emperor Hadrian (117–138).

Archaeological Museum

The Archaeological Museum contains a fine collection of prehistoric pottery from Cilicia, some Hittite items and interesting Turkish ethnographic material.

Ulu Cami

In the centre of the town stands the 16th c. Ulu Cami (Great Mosque), enclosed within a high wall, with a medrese (theological college), türbe (tomb) and dersane (Koranic school). The main entrance is on the east side. On this side, too, is a minaret (1507–08) with a polygonal shaft, blind arcading and roofed gallery reminiscent of Syrian models. Along the north side runs a triple arcade of pointed arches, off which the various rooms of the medrese open. The türbe, with Syrian-style decoration, is faced with Ottoman tiles from İznik. On the west side are the dersane and a gatehouse with a conical dome.

Other mosques

Also of interest are the Akça Mesçit (1409: a mescit is a small mosque) and the 15th c. Ramazanoğlu Camii, both in Syrian style.

◄ *Open-air theatre in Ephesus*

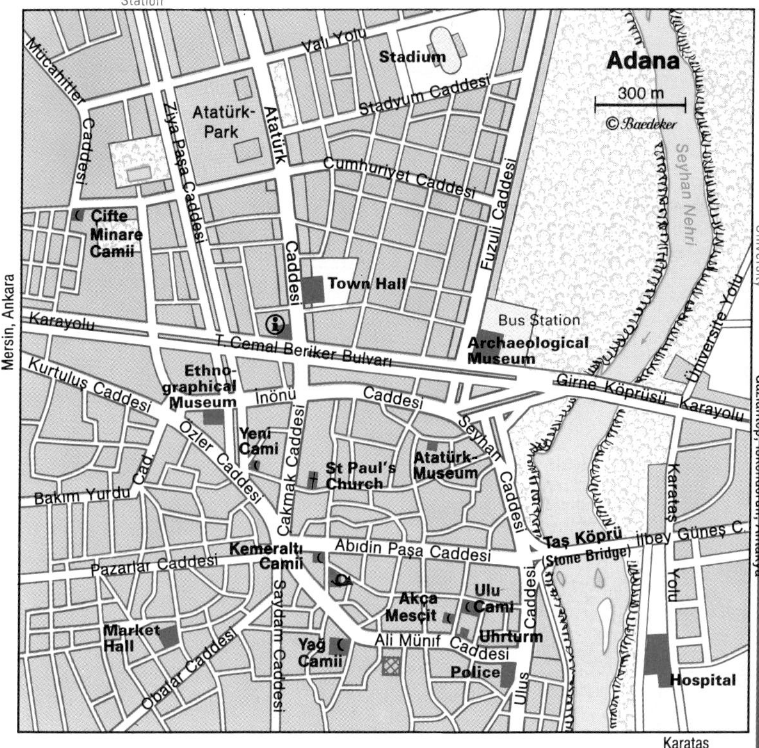

Surroundings of Adana

Seyhan Dam

8km/5 miles north of the town is the Seyhan Baraji (Seyhan Dam), which has created a double lake 25km/15 miles long on the Seyhan (water-sports).

Karataş

1km/¾ mile east of Adana a side road goes off the main İskenderun road on the right and runs south (50km/30 miles) too the little port of Karataş, near the site of ancient Magarsus. Near here is Karataş Burun, a promontory which marks the southernmost point of the alluvial plain of Çukurova. Beyond the turning for Karataş the İskenderun road continues over the Cilician Plain (Çukorova) and in 25km/15 miles comes to Misis (Yakapınar), the site of ancient Mopsuestia. The town lies on both banks of the Seyhan, here spanned by a nine-arched Roman bridge.

★Misis (Mopsuestia)

The main feature of interest in Misis is the Mosaic Museum, built over the mosaic pavement of a small church which was presumably destroyed during the Arab incursions of the 8th c. The mosaics, built up from pieces of differently coloured stone and glass, date from the time of Bishop Theodore (4th c.).

Yılanlıkale "Snake's Castle"

11km/7 miles east of Misis, on the left of the road immediately beyond a bridge over a tributary of the Seyhan, a smooth rock face with a carved figure of the Hittite king, Muwatalli (1315–1282 B.C.) rises out of the river. To the rear, on a steep-sided crag, stands the Yılanlıkale ("Snakes Castle"), an Armenian stronghold and Crusader castle of the 12th c. According to legend this was the residence of Sheikh Meran, half man and half snake, who was killed in the baths at Tarsus when seeking to carry off the King's daughter.

Ceyhan

Yumurtalık

The main road continues to the chief town of the district, Ceyhan (off road to right). Some 35km/22 miles south, on the Gulf of İskenderun, lies the little port of Yumurtalık (previously called Ayas), which in the time of Marco Polo was known as Layaze and was once the most important port in Lesser Armenia; terminal of two oil pipelines from Iraq.

★Anavarza (Anazarbus)

Beside the Sumbaş Çayi, near the village of Anavarza in Upper Çukurova, to the east of the Ceyhan–Kozan road, lie the easily recognised walled ruins of Anazarbus, at one time the minor capital of Lesser Armenia. Perched dizzily on an isolated crag some 200m/650ft directly above the town (and reached by steps from near the theatre) are extensive remains of the fortress (upper and lower fort). In addition to the ancient main street other town ruins include a Roman stadium, a theatre, an aqueduct, several churches and a fine gate to the south. The local open-air museum (situated away from the site itself, in the centre of the village) has some famous mosaics from the 3rd c.

Founded in the 1st c. B.C. Anazarbus was a Romano-Byzantine town. In the 12th c., after numerous disputes with Byzantium and with the aid of the Crusaders, it passed to Lesser Armenia, the principal capital of which was Sis (Sisium/Kozan). Although from 1199 onwards the Armenian princes styled themselves kings, they were always forced, in the final resort, to acknowledge Byzantine supremacy. While close links between the royal house and the Mongols preserved Anazarbus from destruction, in 1297 a Mongol prince had 40 Armenian noblemen, together with Hetum their king, murdered at a banquet in the town.

Hierapolis Kastabala

5km/3 miles beyond the village of Yenice on the road from Osmaniya to Karatepe stand the ruins of Hierapolis (Kastabala). Between 52 B.C. and

Anavarza, the scene of a turbulent history

17 B.C. this Cilician town became the centre of an independent principality under Tarcondimotus I. Rome (under Augustus) then restored its influence by making Tarcondimotus II, the new king, Governor of Cilicia in Anazarbus.

Kozan

Kozan (70km/43 miles north-west of Adana; pop. 50,000) occupies the site of ancient Sisium and in the 19th c. was still known as Sis. The fort, on a hill-top south-west of the town, dates from the Byzantine period. The Armenian victory over Manuel I Comnenus (1143–80) led in 1199 to the establishment of the kingdom of Lesser Armenia, of which Sis became the capital. By 1375 however, shortly after the coronation of the last king, Leon V, it fell to the Mamelukes. Despite the schism in the Church (1441), Sis remained the centre of the Armenian Church until shortly after the First World War, the Catholicos of Sis being determined to preserve the status of his seat. Eventually, in 1921, increasing Islamic repression forced the head of the Armenian Church to flee the town, the patriarchate being transferred to Beirut. In the 19th c. Sis also became the capital of the Kozanoğulları, leaders of a large nomadic tribe forcibly resettled there from Cevdet Paşa.

Toprakkale Pass, Toprakkale

About 27km/17 miles east of Ceyhan the road to İskenderun branches off to the right over the Toprakkale Pass. Describing Darius' march along this route through the foothills of Mount Amanos and the Misis Hills, the 2nd c. historian Arrian refers to the 2km/1¼ mile-long defile between sheer rock walls 40–50m/130–165ft high as the Amanian Gates (Amaniae Pylae). Just off the Osmaniye road to the north, on a steep-sided basaltic cone some 76m/250ft high, are the conspicuous remains of a medieval settlement, possibly built on the site of ancient Augusta.

★★Karatepe

Further along the Osmaniye road, a side turning branches off on the left to Karatepe (Black Hill), some 28km/17 miles north on the right bank of the Ceyhan Nehri. Excavated from 1949 onwards, the site has been extensively restored.

Karatepe was the walled stronghold of an 8th c. Hittite ruler called Azitawadda. The two main gates, on the north and south sides, are flanked by massive sphinxes while reliefs on the sills depict various gods, battle and hunting scenes, a ship with oarsmen, etc. There are two parallel inscriptions, one in Hittite hieroglyphic script, the other in Phoenician; these proved a valuable starting point for deciphering the hieroglyphic script. Little survives of the buildings within the town.

Hemite Kalesi

From Sakarcalı (on the Ceyhan, 30km/19 miles south of Kadirli) a track follows the river to Hamide and, 70m/330ft above the village, the medieval Armenian castle of Amuda. In 1212 the Lesser Armenian King Leon I handed over the fortress with its massive keep and large courtyard to the Knights of the German Order. They built the tower, continuing in occupation (at Akkon's behest) until about 1291 (no later). Down at river level below the south side of the fortress can be seen the poorly preserved remains of a Hittite rock relief. Carved in the 13th c. B.C. it shows a warrior armed with a bow and lance.

Alanya G/H 7

South coast (eastern Mediterranean)
Province: Antalya
Altitude: 0–120m/0–395ft
Population: 59,000

Situations and ★★importance

Alanya, previously called Alaja, lies on the east side of the Gulf of Antalya at the foot of a rocky marble promontory crowned by a Seljuk castle, on either side of which are sandy beaches curving back to the mainland. From the coast the land rises almost without transition to the summit of a bare karstic

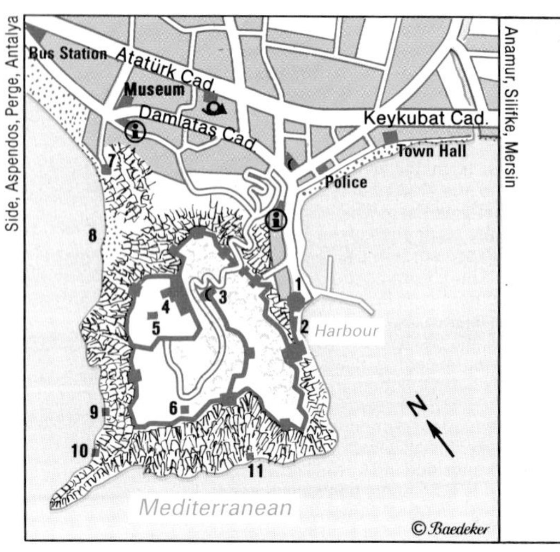

hill, Ak Daği (2647m/8685ft), which forms part of the Taurus range. Alanya lies in a region of subtropical climate and winter rain, with very mild winters and hot dry summers. In consequence the luxuriant fruit orchards end at the point where they reach the limit of the ground-water of the coastal plain and are not artificially irrigated. There they give place to a sparse macchia of oleanders, wild olive trees and euphorbias which extends over the whole of the coastal hills. For a brief period in spring the landscape is gay with the lush green of the grasses and the colourful flowers of the macchia, but in summer and autumn the arid slopes of the hills take on a dull grey hue, adding a more sombre note to the beautiful coastal scenery.

The town's picturesque situation and subtropical climate make it a popular winter resort, and its good beach attracts many visitors in summer. It is also well worth visiting, however, for the sake of its Seljuk remains.

History

Alanya, known in antiquity as Korakesion (Coracesium), was a Cilician frontier fortress on the border with Pamphylia. In the 2nd c. B.C. a pirate chief named Diodoros Tryphon built a fortress on the hill, which was destroyed by Pompey at the end of his campaign against the Mediterranean pirates. The place then passed into Roman hands, and Antony later presented it to Cleopatra. It did not become a place of any consequence, however, until it came under Seljuk rule in 1221. Alaeddin Keykubad made it one of his winter residences, under the name of Alâye, built a great stronghold on the promontory in 1226–31 and developed the town into a naval base which made an important contribution to Seljuk naval strength. The exposed seaward side and the narrowness of the coastal plain, however, prevented any economic development.

Sights

Old town

The cramped old town of Alanya, dating from Seljuk and Ottoman times, lies on the eastern slopes of the promontory between the lower wall and the middle (south) wall of the fortress, which is built on ancient founda-

Red Tower and harbour ▶

Beach and view of the fortress

tions. To the north-east is the more modern part of the town, extending along the beach and ending among the fruit orchards.

Castle hill

A road winds its way through the old town up the castle hill (120m/395ft), along the south wall and, turning north, to the upper ward, at the north end of which is the Castle Mosque (Kale Camii). At the south end stands a lighthouse erected in 1720.

★★Views

Against the west wall is the citadel proper, which is reasonably well preserved and affords superb panoramic views of the Mediteranean, the coastal plain, with the scattered houses of Alanya, the fruit orchards and the Ak Daği Massif. In the inner ward of the castle is a ruined Byzantine church on a cruciform plan.

Red Tower

Another road runs south along the coast of the promontory to the Red Tower, on the quay. This is an octagonal structure 46m/150ft high, each side 12.50m/40ft long, which was built for Alaeddin Keykubad in 1225 by the Aleppo architect Ebu Ali, who was also responsible for the castle at Sinop. Built to protect the Seljuk dockyard, it makes a massive corner bastion in the castle's defences and a prominent Alanya landmark. It was restored in 1948.

Seljuk dockyard

The Seljuk dockyard, hewn from the rock about 1227 and recently restored, has five vaulted galleries 42.5m/140ft long and 7.7m/25ft wide, linked with one another by arched openings. Here Alaeddin Keykubad built the warships with which he sought to extend his power over the eastern Mediterranean. Timber for shipbuilding came from the Taurus, then abundantly wooded. The dockyard is still in use.

Stalactitic cave

At the foot of the north-west side of the promontory, at the end of the west beach, is the Stalactitic Cave (Damlataş Mağara), discovered by quarry workers in 1948, which has stalagmites almost 15m/50ft high. The temperature of the cave remains at a constant 22°C/72°F in both summer and winter. The high carbon dioxide content (five times as high as in the open) and the radioactivity of the air make the cave a favourite haunt of local people seeking a cure for asthma or bronchitis.

At the entrance to the cave are a number of souvenir shops and a restaurant; near by is a beautiful bathing beach.

Museum

A little way north of the cave can be found a small archaeological and ethnographic museum, opened in 1967.

Surroundings of Alanya

★★Beaches

The wide bays on the stretch of coast round Alanya, below the foothills of the Taurus, are fringed by miles of beautiful beaches which rank among the finest in the whole of Turkey.

Hamaxia, Augae, Ptolemais

Leaving Alanya continue westwards along the coast road to the ancient sites of Hamaxia, Augae and Ptolemais (in the foothills of Figla Burum), past which, in 16km/10 miles, is the fortress-like caravanserai Sarapsahanı (13th c.). In a further 12km/7½ miles a by-road leads northwards to the caravanserai of Alkarahanı.

Gazipaşa

Some 50km/30 miles south-east of Alanya on the coast road along the "Turkish Riviera" is the little town of Gazipaşa, situated 3km/2 miles from the coast on an alluvial plain formed by a number of streams which flow into the sea here.

Here the promontory known to the ancients as Cape Selindi falls down to the sea in almost vertical cliffs. On the highest point of the promontory is a ruined castle; below is a good bathing beach flanked by banana plantations in the coastal plain. The town, known in antiquity as selinous, was probably founded by the Phoenicians on this strong defensive site (sela="rock"). In A.D. 117 the Emperor Trajan died here on the way back from his Parthian campaign, and thereafter the town was known for some time as Traianopolis. Many ancient remains have been discovered here. The terraced western slope of the hill was defended by a wall with numerous towers extending from the top of the hill to the mouth of the river. Farther down was the theatre, partly hewn from the rock; the seating is now missing. Another large structure may have been the Cenotaph of Trajan. An aqueduct brought water to the city from the Taurus.

Anamur H 7

South coast (eastern Mediterranean)
Province: İçel
Altitude: 0–50m/0–165ft
Population: 37,000

Situation

Anamur is beautifully situated in a plain below the foothills of the Taurus between the Sultansuys and the Tatlısu Nehri, 4km/2½ miles above the mouth of the Sultansuyu (small harbour), on the east side of Cape Anamur (ancient Anamurion), the most southerly point in Asia Minor.

★Anamur Kalesi

7km/4½ miles east of Anamur, beyond the road to Ermenek, is Anamur Castle (Anamur Kalesi, Mamure Kalesi), imposingly situated on a promontory extending out into the sea. The castle, originally dating from the early medieval period, when it was one of the most notorious and most feared corsair strongholds, was later enlarged and strengthened by the Crusaders. It is surrounded by a formidable wall with 36 round or square towers, most of them excellently preserved, with parapet walks reached by staircases inside the walls. The main entrance to the castle, which has three

courts or wards, is through a tower on the west side. At the entrance is an Arabic inscription which, as translated by Admiral Beaufort, runs: "Aladin, son of the valiant Mehmet, captured this castle through his own valour and his strong army for the noble Sherif Tunisi, the true servant of his prince, and gave the second command to the pilgrim Mustafa Esmer". According to Beaufort, who visited Anamur in 1812, the castle was then the residence of an Aga. Comte Albert Pourtalès, visiting the castle in 1843, reported that there were two mosques within the walls and that a Cypriot merchant had also set up a shop from which he supplied the inhabitants with sugar, coffee and other necessities. The castle is now abandoned, olive trees and oleanders growing in its empty courts.

Antakya (Hatay) M 7

South coast (eastern Mediterranean)
Province: Hatay
Altitude: 0–92m/0–300ft
Population: 125,000

Situation and ★★importance

Antakya, known in antiquity as Antioch (Antiocheia) and more recently as Hatay, chief town of the frontier province of that name in south-eastern Turkey, lies some 30km/20 miles from the Mediterranean in the alluvial plain of the Asi (the ancient Orontes) at the foot of Mount Habib Neccar (ancient Mons Silipius). It is surrounded by extensive olive groves which extend up to the scree slopes flanking the hill. The barren hills above Antakya, with their sparse vegetation, are an intimation of the nearness of the great Syrian Desert.

Little is left of Antioch's one-time importance as one of the commercial and cultural centres of the Hellenistic World. It now gains a relatively modest subsistence from its administrative functions, its garrison and the traffic passing through the town on the way to the countries of the Levant. It is not on the railway and no longer has a harbour.

History

In 307 B.C. Antigonos, one of Alexander the Great's generals, founded the town of Antigoneia on a site rather higher up the Orontes than present-day Antakya; the town, however, did not prosper, no doubt because it was poorly situated from the point of view of communications, and in 301 Seleukos Nikator (305–280), founder of the Macedonian dynasty in Syria, established a new settlement on the site of the present town, naming it Antiocheia in honour of his father. The new town flourished, thanks to its situation at the intersection of the road along the Mediterranean coast and the caravan route from its port of Seleukeia into Mesopotamia. In the 2nd c. B.C. it was said to have a population of some 500,000 and to be exceeded in size only by Rome itself; it had aqueducts, a street-lighting system and a colonnaded street 6.5km/4 miles long, and was criticised by contemporaries for its luxurious way of life. It was celebrated throughout the East for its games in honour of Apollo. Even after its conquest by Rome in 64 B.C. it continued to enjoy a large measure of autonomy.

Antioch played an important part in the history of early Christianity. The Apostle Paul made several missionary journeys here (Acts 11:26; 15:30, 35; 18:22), and the term "Christians" (Christianoi) was first used in Antioch (Acts 11:26). In the reign of Diocletian the Christians were ruthlessly persecuted and their churches destroyed, but his successor Constantine made Christianity the State religion and caused the churches to be rebuilt. Antioch became the seat of a Patriarch ranking after the Patriarchs of Rome, Constantinople and Alexandria, and between 252 and 380 ten Church Councils were held here.

In 525 Antioch was completely destroyed by an earthquake, and in 538 it was captured by the Persian king, Khusraw I, who deported many of the

◀ *Anamur Kalesi*

inhabitants to Mesopotamia. After its recovery from the Persians the Emperor Justinian rebuilt the town on a smaller scale, giving it the name of Theoupolis (City of God). In 638 the town fell into the hands of the Arabs, and it was not recovered by the Byzantines until 969. In 1084 it fell to the Seljuks, and in 1098 it was retaken, after a bloody battle, by a Crusading army. The Crusaders then established a princedom which was to last for 170 years.

The decline of Antioch began with its conquest and destruction by the Mamelukes in 1266. Thereafter the town's flourishing trade in the export of silk, glass, soap and copper articles fell off, with the loss of a considerable part of its revenue; the harbour of Seleukeia silted up, and Antioch gradually declined into a provincial town of no importance.

In 1516 Sultan Selim I incorporated the town in the Ottoman Empire. In 1872 it suffered heavy damage in an earthquake. In 1918 it became part of the French Protectorate of Syria; and in 1939, following a plebiscite, it was transferred to the Turkish Republic together with the Sanjak of Alexandretta (İskenderun) – a change which has not yet been recognised by Syria.

Sights

The repeated destructions it has suffered in the course of an eventful history have left Antakya with little to show of the splendid buildings of the ancient city, which occupied an area more than ten times the size of the present town. One notable feature that has survived, however, is the four-arched bridge built by Diocletian (284–305) over the Asi, which in spite of repeated restorations has substantially preserved its original form. On one of the piers is a carving of a Roman eagle.

Roman bridge

Aqueduct

Between the hospital and the Habib Neccar Camii are the ruins of an aqueduct, known as the Memikli Bridge, built in the reign of Trajan (2nd c.).

Habib Neccar Mosque

In Kurtuluş Caddesi stands the Habib Neccar Camii, a mosque converted from a Byzantine church which still contains the tombs of saints. The minaret is 17th c.

★★Archaeological Museum

Near the bridge over the Asi can be found an interesting Archaeological Museum. It is notable particularly for its collection of 50 very fine mosaics from Roman houses in the surrounding area – the largest such collection in the world – with lively representations of mythological scenes. The museum also contains a variety of finds from the Amuq Plain (particularly from Tell Açana) and a number of Roman sarcophagi.

Citadel

On a rocky plateau on the south side of the town are the ruins of the Citadel, originally built in the 11th c. and later enlarged. Only scanty remains of the

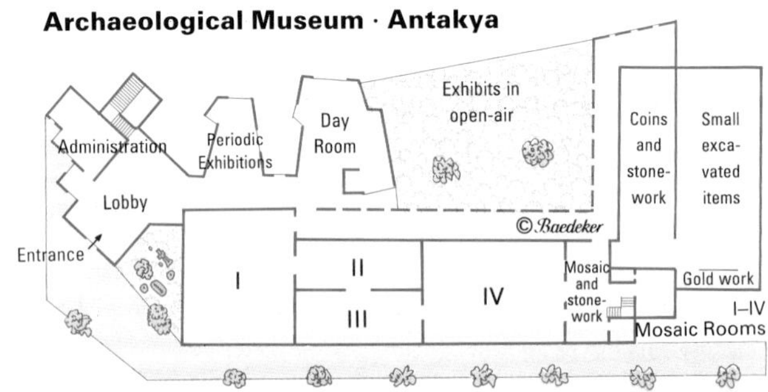

Roman mosaic in the Archaeological Museum

fortifications survive, since during the occupation of the town by the troops of Mehemet Ali, the Egyptian Viceroy who led a rising against the Sultan between 1830 and 1840, great stretches of the walls were pulled down and the stone used for building barracks. From the top there are fine views.

Town walls

The town walls, built of fine limestone from Mons Silpius, have totally disappeared from the plain. They reached from the Orontes up on to the high ground and beyond, and were said to have 360 towers up to 25m/80ft high on the hills and to be broad enough to allow four-horse chariots to be driven along the top.

Surroundings of Antakya

Grotto of St Peter

The Grotto of St Peter is reached by taking the road which runs east to Aleppo from the bridge over the Orontes. In some 3km/2 miles a narrow road (signposted) goes off on the right and leads up through suburban gardens to a hill with a car park. Near by, on a terrace commanding extensive views, is the Grotto of St Peter, a cave in which the Apostle is said to have preached and which in the 13th c was converted into a church with a Gothic façade. At the far end stands an altar, behind which, to the right, is a trickle of water which is regarded by both Christians and Muslims as having curative virtues. From the cave a narrow rocky path leads in some 200m/220yd to a likeness carved from the rock, about the origin and significance of which nothing is known. The relief was described in the 11th c. by the Byzantine historian Malalas.

Alalakh

The site of Tell Açana (Alalakh) is also reached from the Aleppo road. 21km/16 miles from Antakya, beyond the bridge over the Orontes, is the mound of Tell Açana (off to the right: no road access), site of ancient Alalakh, capital of the kingdom of Mukish (3rd–2nd millennium B.C.), which was excavated by Sir Leonard Woolley between 1936 and 1949. The earliest of the 17 levels date back to the 4th millennium B.C., the most considerable buildings (palaces, temples) to the 2nd millennium. The town was abandoned in the 12th century B.C. Material from the site is in Antakya Museum.

Demirköprüköy

Near the village of Demirköprü, 15km/9½ miles east of Antakya, the Orontes is spanned by a medieval limestone bridge, which Baldwin IV renovated in 1161. An earthquake in 1837 left the two towers of the bridge in ruins. Immediately south of the bridge lies the Tell Açana archaeological site and on the south side of the Reyhanlı road a few kilometres further east the Tell Taynat settlement mound. The latter, extending for some 500m×620m/547yd×678yd, was excavated between 1935 and 1938 by McEwan and Braidwood. First settled around 3000 B.C. it remained inhabited for about a thousand years during which time the summit plateau came to be occupied by a citadel with a large south-facing palace and a temple with a vestibule. Magnificent column bases found here can be seen in the Archaeological Museum in Ankara. At Tell Cüydeyde, another site in the vicinity, archaeologists have uncovered levels forming a continuous series from 4500 B.C. through to A.D. 600 (ceramic finds).

Reyhanlı

The town of Reyhanlı (population: 37,000) sprang up in the 19th c. following the enforced settlement of the Reyhanlı nomads. Near by, in addition to numerous rock tombs, are the ruins of the Roman town of Emma (Yenişehir; 2km/1¼ miles), scene of many a crucial conflict down the centuries. Here Aurelian defeated Queen Zenobia of Palmyra in 272 and, in 1134, Baldwin III vanquished the Arabs. The fortress, burnt down in 1139, was rebuilt only to be destroyed for a second time by an earthquake in 1171. Some few remains can still be seen.

Grove of Daphne

From the old bridge over the Orontes the Yayladağı road runs 8km/5 miles south to the residential suburb of Harbiye. 1km/¾ mile farther on is a car park, below which, on the right, is the Grove of Daphne. In this shady grove of laurels, oaks and cypresses a beautiful waterfall tumbles down over the rocks in an intricately patterned sheet of water. To this grove, according to the Greek legend, the coy nymph Daphne was pursued by Apollo, and here Zeus changed her, at her own request, into a laurel tree; in compensation for his loss Apollo was to have a temple in his honour. The grove was revered by the local people as a sacred place, and important games were held here. The town was a favoured place of residence for upper-class Greeks and Romans, and "Daphnici mores" became a synonym for relaxed moral standards.

Yoğun Oluk

About 8km/5 miles beyond Karaçay a poor road turns off towards the Musa Dağı, leading after 11km/7 miles to a 13th c. Crusader church. After the Armenian pogroms which followed the First World War the Armenian minority took refuge in the Musa Daği. The story of their suffering is told by Franz Werfel in his historical novel "The Forty Days of Musa Daği". On the 1281m/4202ft high summit is a basilica dedicated to Saint Simeon Stylite the Younger who, inspired by the example of an older namesake (Qaalat Siman/St Simeon in Syria) reputedly spent his life perched on top of a tall column erected on the spot now occupied by the church.

★Samandağ/ Seleukeia Piereia

From the fork at the western end of Samandağ (Seleukeia; 26km/16 miles), a metalled road leads north-west over an alluvial plain and past a beautiful beach to the village of Mağaracık (7km/4½ miles). Here can be seen the remains of the once-considerable town of Seleukeia Piereia, the port of Antioch, founded by Seleukos Nikator about 300 B.C. In its heyday Seleukeia had a population of 30,000. To the right are a ruined aqueduct, with tombs cut in the rock face above, and the old harbour, now silted up. A notable feature is the canal, driven through solid rock at the time of the Roman emperors Vespasian and Titus in an unsuccessful attempt to save the harbour.

Bakras Kalesi

Some 8km/5 miles west of the İskenderun road about 28km/17 miles north of Antakya stands the ruined Crusader castle "Gaston" at Bakras. It fell to Saladin in 1188, to the Lesser Armenian King Levon II in 1191 and to the Mamelukes under Baibar in 1268. The site is thought by many historians to be that of Pagrae, to which Strabo refers.

Terbezek

Reached via a poor track running west off the Maraş road a few kilometres north of Kırıkhan are the ruins of the Templar Crusader castle of Trapesak (Terbezek or Darbsek Kale-si; about a kilometre north of the village). The castle played a key role in defending the Crusader kingdom of Antiochia (Antakya) against Saladin who, after a hard fought struggle, managed to take it for a short time in 1188. In 1268 it fell to the Mamelukes. Their leader Baibar garrisoned troops there, renaming it Darsak.

Gündüslü

Near the village of Gündüslü about a kilometre west of the Maraş highway north of Kırıkhan there are three cave tombs with long inscriptions in Greek and some badly damaged reliefs.

Sultankalesi

About 20km/12½ miles due north of Kırıkhan stands a third castle, Sultankalesi, with an impressive south gate (bastions), square north tower, chapel and cistern. Situated high up (1250m/4102ft) in the Amanus Mountains near the village of Cıvlan (Sıvlan), it was probably built during the Byzantine period to guard the pass, one of the routes through the Amanus from the Maraş trench to İskenderun.

Antalya F 7

South coast (eastern Mediterranean)
Province: Antalya
Altitude: 0–40m/0–130ft
Population: 1.1 million

Situation and ★★importance

The provincial capital of Antalya is picturesquely situated at the innermost point of the Gulf of Antalya on the south coast of Turkey. To the west of the town the bare limestone massif of the Lycian Taurus plunges steeply down to the sea from a height of 3086m/10,125ft, while to the east the Lower Cilician Taurus reaches the sea only at some distance from the town. Between the two ranges, which meet at a sharp angle, is an area of coastal plain on which Antalya is situated.

The town is built on a limestone terrace which falls sharply down, in a 23m/75ft high cliff, to the bay containing the Old Harbour. Between the town and the high ridge of hills to the west the broad beach of Konyaaltı – a major attraction for holiday-makers – extends in a wide sweep. The grandiose backdrop of the Taurus, the Mediterranean vegetation of the coast plain (citrus fruits, pears, apricots, figs, olives, bananas) and the town itself on its height form a magnificent frame for the beautiful beach.

The new harbour (Setur Marina 10km west) of Antalya is the only one of any size between İzmir and Mersin. The town marina Turban Kaleıçı has won several awards, and is considered to be one of the finest in Turkey.

Climate

Thanks to its sheltered situation Antalya has a subtropical climate with very mild and wet winters (January mean temperature 9.9°C/49.8°F, July 28.1°C/82.6°F and almost rainless summers. Spring comes early, and the summits of the hills are still covered with snow at the beginning of the bathing season, which lasts from the beginning of April to the end of October.

History

In the 12th c. B.C. Achaeans from the Peloponnese moved into Pamphylia, the region in which Antalya lies, and overlaid the indigenous population. A second wave of Greek immigrants followed in the 7th c., when the Ionians

The beach at the foot of the citadel

occupied the existing settlements and established new ones. After periods of Lydian and then Persian rule Pamphylia was annexed by Alexander the Great in 334 B.C. During the struggles between Rome and Antiochos the Great the area became part of the Kingdom of Pergamon, the ruler of which, Attalos II Philadelphos (159–138), founded the city of Attaleia, now Antalya, and made it capital of Pamphylia. In 133 Attalleia, together with the rest of the kingdom of Pergamon, passed into Roman hands, and thereafter formed part of the province of Asia. The Apostle Paul landed at Attaleia with his companions Barnabas and Mark on his first missionary journey to Asia Minor in A.D. 45–49. In the time of Hadrian the town was surrounded by a strong defensive wall. The Byzantines developed it still further and surrounded it with a double ring of walls to repel attacks by the Arabs in the 8th and 9th c. During the Second Crusade (1147–49) Attaleia was the last Byzantine stronghold in southern Asia Minor to hold out against the Turks and provide a refuge for the Crusading army. From here King Louis VII of France set sail with its knights for Antioch.

In 1207 the town was taken by the Seljuks under Sultan Kai-Khusraw I, who made it a winter capital. During the Seljuk period a number of handsome mosques were built and the defences of the town were strengthened. After the fall of the Seljuk Empire Antalya became independent under a prince of the Hamid Dynasty, but was incorporated in the Ottoman Empire in the time of Sultan Murat I (1359–89). In 1472 it withstood an attack by the last Crusading fleet: the chain guarding the harbour was broken (this was deposited in the sacristy of St Peter's in Rome as a trophy of war) and the harbour itself was occupied, but the Crusaders could not gain entry to the fortress with its double walls and moats.

In Ottoman times the town – then also known as Adalia or Satalia – was divided into three parts, for Christians, Muslims and men of other faiths. The iron gates between the three sections were closed every Friday from noon to 1pm, for a prophecy had foretold an attack by the Christians at that time.

View of the Old Town, with the Yivli Minaret in the foreground

Sights

★Old Harbour

Since the recent restoration of the picturesque harbour quarter below the Citadel (Kaleiçi) the Old Harbour, nestling in a recess in the cliffs, and the surrounding area with its hotels, restaurants, boutiques and bazaar have become a busy centre of tourist activity. Other parts of the Citadel, above the boating harbour, have been renovated.

★Yivli Minare (Fluted Minaret)

A little way north-east of the Old Harbour is Antalya's most striking landmark, the Yivli Minare (Fluted Minaret), a vigorous example of Seljuk architecture with a square base surmounted by an octagonal drum bearing the fluted shaft with its corbelled gallery round the top. The minaret, which is faced with brown tiles, belongs to a mosque converted by Alaeddin Keykubad (1219–36) from a Byzantine church.

Karatay Mosque

A few paces south is the Karatay Mosque, built in 1250 by a Seljuk Vizier named Karatay.

Old Town

Other features of interest in the old town with its narrow bazaar streets are a fortified gate with a Clock-Tower in the busy main square, the nearby Tekeli Mehmet Paşa Mosque and, farther south, the Kesik Minare (Truncated Minaret), by the ruins of an abandoned mosque which was originally a Byzantine church.

★Hadrian's Gate

Considerable stretches of the Hellenistic and Roman town walls on the east side of the old town have been preserved, sometimes incorporated in later building. The most notable part is the well-preserved Hadrian's Gate, erected in honour of the Emperor Hadrian on the occasion of his visit to the town in A.D. 130. This imposing marble gateway, with two massive towers flanking three arched openings, has rich sculptural ornament.

Along the east side of Hadrian's Gate and the old town walls extends a broad avenue, Atatürk Caddesi, with two carriageways separated by a

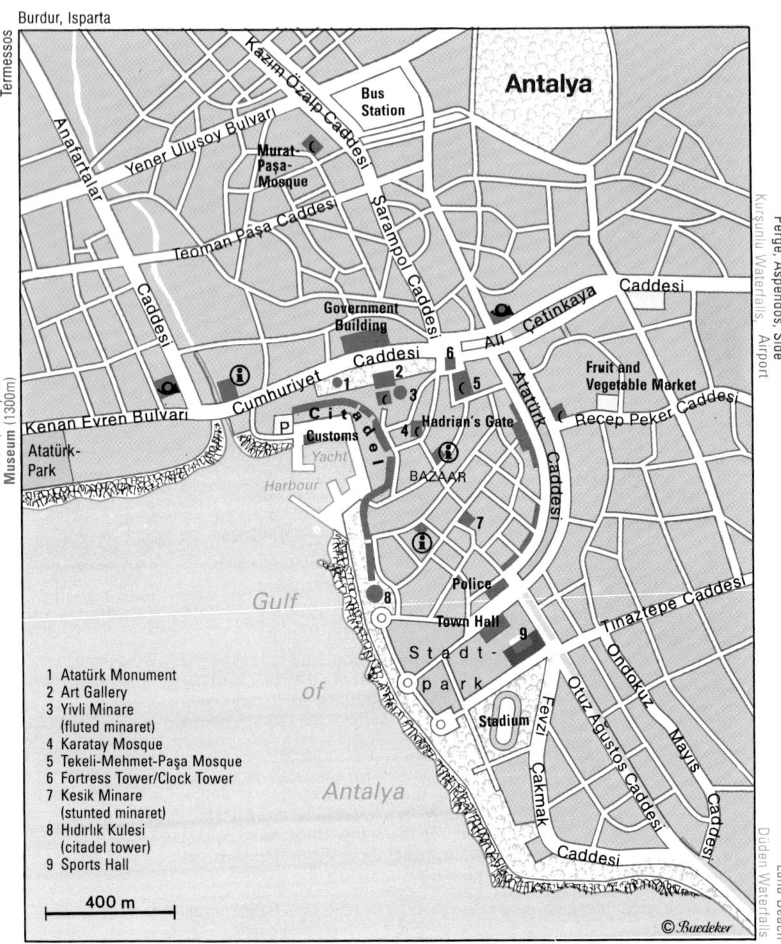

double row of stately date-palms. It runs south in a wide arc to the Town Hall, beyond which is the Municipal Park (Karaolioğlu Parki), extending to the edge of the cliff above the Gulf of Antalya. The park is worth visiting for the sake of its lush subtropical vegetation, pleasant shady walks and beautiful view over the gulf, with the Konyaaltı Beach, the new commercial harbour at the far end and, as a magnificent backdrop, the mountains of the Lycian Taurus.

Municipal Park

★View

It also has a tea garden. Round the bay are a variety of restaurants, places of entertainment, picnic areas and children's playgrounds.

At the north-west corner of the park (i.e. at the south-west corner of the citadel) can be seen the 13m/43ft high Hıdırlık Kulesi, the stump of a tower which way have been a Roman lighthouse.

Archaeological Museum

1 Children's Hall
2 Prehistory
3 Small works of art
4 Hall of Gods
5 Small works of art
6 Imperial Hall
7 Sarcophagi
8 Icons
9 Mosaics
10 Coins
11–13 Ethnological department

★Museum

Antalya's very interesting Museum of Archaeology and Ethnography is on the western outskirts of the town, 2km/1¼ miles from the centre. Founded in 1919, it was originally housed in the mosque beside the Fluted Minaret but was moved to new premises in 1972.

The large archaeological section presents an excellent survey of the great ages of the past in Pamphylia from the Neolithic by way of the Bronze Age (urn burials) to the Hellenistic and Roman periods. Particularly notable features are the gallery containing statues of divinities (mostly from Perge), items recovered by underwater archaeology, the Gallery of Roman emperors, a series of magnificent sarcophagi, mosaics from Seleukeia and the fine coin collection, with the Hoard of Probus, the Aspendos hoard (silver), a Byzantine gold hoard found at Finike in 1959 and the Side Hoard (silver). There are also a number of icons.

The rich ethnographic section of the museum displays a great variety of material of the Turkish period – weapons, clothing, stockings, jewellery andornaments, domestic equipment, books, tiles, glass, porcelain, locks, musical instruments, carpets.

Konyaaltı

The road which runs west from the museum towards Kaş and Fethiye skirts for some miles the broad Konyaaltı Beach (fine shingle; motels, camping site, restaurants), which attracts large numbers of holiday-makers in summer.

Surroundings of Antalya

★Termessos

Termessos, another important ancient site (Pisidian not Pamphylian) is situated in the mountains 30km/19 miles north-west of Antalya on the gentle slopes of Güllük Dağı (Solymos; 1650m/5415ft). This area is now a National Park. Little is known about the town's origins except that it was a Pisidian hill-fort reputedly besieged without success by Alexander the Great. The ruins seen today date from the 2nd and 3rd centuries A.D.; most notable are the theatre, the agora, a gymnasium, several pillared halls and a number of graves. A mountain road leads up to the site but the final two kilometres must be covered on foot. From the top there is a magnificent view of the Gulf of Antalya.

Saklıkent

In the last few years a small winter-sports centre has been built at an altitude of 2000–2400m/6500–7875ft near the village of Saklıkent (1850m/6071ft) in the northern Bey Dağları, about 70km/43 miles west of Antalya (via Çakırlar). Although chair-lift facilities are still modest the resort offers more than 2500 beds.

★Karst springs
Düdenbaşı Mağarası

The limestone country around Antalya is rich in karst springs, swallow-holes and waterfalls. Two large karst springs, Kırkgöz (close to a huge caravanserai dating from 1236) and Pınarbaşı, are located not far to the north-west of Antalya (follow the Burdur road for 11km/7 miles to where it forks, then take the old Korkuteli road instead of the fast new highway, continuing for a few kilometres beyond Döşemaltı). Water pours in abundance from these springs before disappearing behind the *regülatör* in the Bıyıklı Düdeni cave system. Some of the sink holes are massive, large

The ruins of Termessos

enough to engorge a river or lake (up to 30,000 litres/6600galls per sec.). The lime deposits from these and other karst springs on the edge of the Taurus north and west of Antalya have built up, over a period of 1.5 to 2 million years, into vast travertine terraces similar to those at Pamukkale. Sometimes as much as 275m/900ft high and extending into the sea in places, they are found across a wide area approximately 35=20km/22=12½ miles, or 650sq.km/250sq. miles. The spring water from Bıyıklı flows underground for 14km/8½ miles, briefly surfacing again at Varsak Obruk (huge sink-hole) before resuming its subterranean course for a further 2km/1¼ miles, re-emerging finally with tremendous power at Düdenbaşı. Here it joins forces again with the water channelled off at the Bıyıklı *regülatör* and, together with the waters of the Düden Cayı, tumbles in a series of lovely cascades down a narrow gorge in the travertine. The upper falls (Düdenbaşı Şelalesi), 14km/8 miles to the north-east of Antalya, are reached via a small road (Kızılırmak Caddesi) off the northern by-pass. The lower Düden Çayı falls (Düden Selaleşi), in the south-east part of the town itself, near a small park immediately beside the Lara Plajı coast road, plunge 20m/65ft over the edge of the travertine into the sea.

★Karain Mağarası

The Karain cave, 27km/17 miles north-west of Antalya, near Döşemaltı, in the karst country around Şam Dağ, was inhabited by prehistoric man. It has yielded finds from both Lower and Middle Palaeolithic, including bones and teeth belonging to Neanderthal man. Some of the finds are on show in a small but remarkably comprehensive museum on the site.

Kocain Mağarası

This cave lies hidden in the karst mountains 45km/28 miles north of Antalya, two hours away on foot from the village of Ahırtaş (turn north-east off the Burdur road a few kilometres beyond Döşemaltı, thence via Karataş or via Kovanlık, Camiliköy and Kilik). The cave, 600m/656yd long, 75m/82yd across and 35m/115ft high, with some colossal stalagmites, was investigated by K. Kökten, whose finds showed it to have been inhabited in prehistoric times. At the entrance is a huge cistern, also traces of a very early settlement.

Turkish Riviera

With one lovely beach giving way to another, the 220km/137 miles of coastline on the Gulf of Antalya, from Kemer eastwards to beyond Gazipaşa, is known as the "Turkish Riviera".

★West coast of the Gulf of Antalya

The west coast of the Gulf of Antalya, running almost due north–south, is fringed for some 50km/30 miles by a virtually uninterrupted line of delightful beaches, with the wooded hills of the Taurus rising immediately behind (Olimpos Bey Dağları National Park). About 50km/30 miles south of Antalya lies the up-and-coming holiday centre of Kemer, with hotels, holiday clubs, a modern yacht marina and good facilities for water sports. About 10km/6 miles further on there are more holiday facilities at Göynük and Beldibi (Stone Age site nearby).

Phaselis

Only 3km/1¾ miles south of Kemer are the ruins of the old Lydian port of Phaselis where, in 334–333 B.C., Alexander the Great set up his winter quarters. There are remains of a theatre, an aqueduct, temples, and a Hadrian's Arch erected in A.D. 114. There is also a museum.

★Chimaera and Olympos

Immediately west of the Gulf of Antalya, the 700sq.km/270sq. mile Olimpos Beydağları Milli Parkı (National Park) stretches from the coast into the nearby mountains. Ancient Olympos, near the village of Çıralı in the southern section of the Park, about 50km/30 miles south of the new resort of Kemer, is the site of one of Nature's curiosities, the eternal flame of Chimaera (the fire-breathing monster of Greek mythology), a phenomenon mentioned in A.D. 300 by Bishop Methodius and by Beaufort on his travels in 1811. To reach the spot a strenuous climb of some 150m/500ft must first be made, followed by a further 150m/500ft of ascent above the ruins of Olympos. Natural gas escaping from eighteen or so holes and

Ruins of Olympos

crevices in the rock has burned here since ancient times. Although barely discernible in daylight the flames are said to be visible far out to sea at night. The gases are still to be properly analysed but are known to include methane.

Olympos was once one of the most celebrated cities of the Lycian League before falling into the hands of pirates. They continued to plague it even after the successful campaign waged against them by the Romans in 78 B.C. In the end the city simply slipped into irreversible decline. During the imperial period Olympos was widely known as a cult site dedicated to the fire god Hephaistos (with a temple to Hephaistos at Chimaera, see above). There are also references in Plutarch to ritual feasts in honour of Mithras, Persian god of light.

The remains include those of a Roman theatre, a Byzantine basilica, a Roman temple, a bridge, defensive walls and chamber tombs. All are badly ruined and very overgrown; but standing in picturesque surroundings in a valley near the sea they are definitely worth a visit.

North coast of the Gulf of Antalya

From the eastern outskirts of Antalya a series of splendid beaches extend along the north shore of the Gulf (see above, "Turkish Riviera"). Lara Plajı is perhaps the best of them, with a number of new hotels.

★★Perge
★★Aspendos
★Side

Eastwards from Antalya are the ancient sites of Perge, Aspendos and Side (see entries)

Aphrodisias D 6

Western Anatolia (Menteşe highland)
Province: Aydın
Altitude: 548m/1800ft
Nearest place: Geyre (3km/2 miles north-west; population: 1000)

Situation

The ruins of ancient Aphrodisias lie 82km/51 miles south-west of Denizli, where the heavily wooded southern foothills of Ak Dağ border on the broad valley of the Kekre Çayı. The site itself is located high in a side valley of the upper Dandalas Çayı (Vandalas Çayı), a tributary of the Büyük Menderes Nehri (Great Maeander River).

History

Chalcolithic finds show the area to have been settled in the 4th millennium B.C.; early Bronze Age pottery also suggests there was an Assyrian trading colony here during the Hittite period. There is a tradition that the settlement took its earliest recorded name, Ninoe, from the Assyrian King Ninos (Tukulti-Ninurta I, 1245–1208 B.C.); a more likely derivation however is from Nin (Ishtar) the Old Oriental goddess of love and war, with whom Venus, the Roman goddess of love, later became identified. Nin, daughter of the moon god Sin, was sister of the sun god Shamash and wife of Anu god of heaven. Her attributes were bestowed by the Greeks upon Aphrodite, goddess not simply of beauty and love but also of the Morning and Evening Star. The town only took the name Aphrodisias in Hellenistic times, having been known previously as Lelegonpolis, Megalopolis and probably also Plarasa. Through its sanctuary it became the centre of the wide-spread cult of Aphrodite, in addition to which it had famous schools of sculpture, medicine and philosophy. The pinnacle of its fortunes was reached under the Julian emperors when Aphrodisias enjoyed the patronage of Sulla, Caesar, Antony, and Augustus; it was Antony who granted sanctuary status to the temple. This is reflected in the fact that the surviving remains are almost all Roman, an exception being the town walls which are of later date (4th c.).

In the Early Christian-Byzantine era the town was first a bishopric and then the seat of the Metropolitan Bishop of Caria; it was also rechristened Stavropolis. From 540 (in the reign of Justinian), as capital of the province

Head of Apollo

Seated Aphrodite

of that name, it became known simply as Caria (of which the name of the present village, Geyre, is a corruption). Despite having its fortifications strengthened in the latter part of the 7th c., in the 8th and 9th centuries the town succumbed to the Arabs. Its decline was accelerated by Ottoman rule until, in 1402, Tamarlane found no more than a village in the shadow of the ruined city. Excavation has proceeded in several stages, at first under the Turks in 1904/05, 1913 and 1937, then since 1961 by US archaeologists led by Kenan Erim.

Sights

★★Ruins

The sprawling ruins of Aphrodisias lie at the foot of the 2308m/7575ft Baba Dağ (formerly Salbakos) to the south of the small modern village of Geyre (Geira, Gere; the old village was situated actually among the ruins). Finds from recent excavations are housed in a little museum built with American assistance. Modern research has transformed Aphrodisias from a place which few visited into one of the most important historic sites in Turkey. A partially excavated processional way equipped with a drainage system leads to the ruins.

The Roman agora, 120m/131yd wide and 205m/224yd long, with Doric portico along the north side and Ionic portico along the south, was renovated under Tiberius (14–37). Some of the columns still have their architraves in place. Twelve columns also survive from the colonnaded Portico of Tiberius.

To the south, on the far side of a large square, stand the ruins of the domed Byzantine Martyrs' Church (6th c.).

Acropolis

The so-called "acropolis" is actually a hüyük or settlement mound. Excavation has shown it to have been inhabited in prehistoric times (from the 4th millennium B.C.).

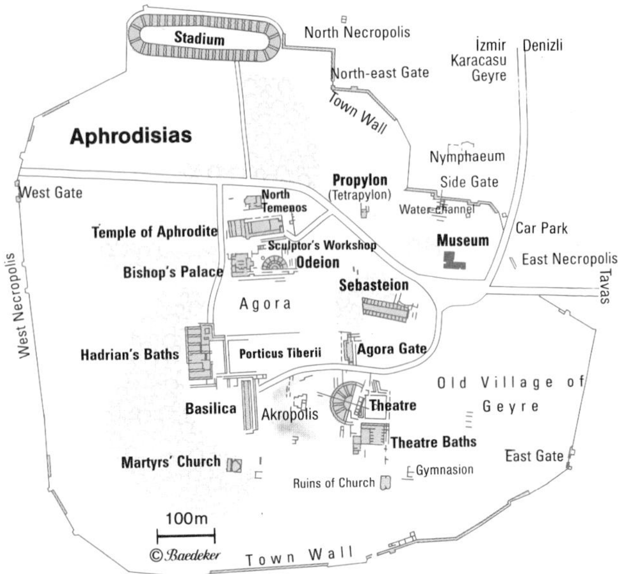

Temple of Aphrodite

The Temple of Aphrodite, an Ionic pseudo-dipteros of 8×13 columns, was built in about 100 B.C. over an earlier shrine (3rd c. B.C.) from which mosaics have survived. The temple, with pronaos and cella only, boasted a huge statue of Aphrodite, more than 3m/10ft tall, of which parts have been recovered. Of the fourteen columns still standing, two have their architrave in place. Like other temples dedicated to Aphrodite, this one can be presumed to have fulfilled a therapeutic sexual role, prostitution being a feature of the Aphrodite cult practised by priestesses and female temple slaves (hierodules). Following instructions from the Delphic Oracle, the patrons of the temple donated cult objects of various kinds: Sulla for instance gave a gold crown and double axe, Caesar a statue of Eros.

In the 5th c. the Byzantines converted the pagan temple into a three-aisle basilica. Two centuries later the town was renamed Stavropolis (City of the Cross), further severing the links with its pagan past.

Sculptors' Workshop

Between the Temple to Aphrodite and the odeion are the remains of a sculptor's workshop – the school of sculpture at Aphrodisias contributed greatly to the cultural splendour of the city. Marble for use locally and almost certainly for export was quarried from the slopes of Baba Dağ to the east of the town.

Bishop's Palace

Excavation adjacent to the sculptors' workshop has uncovered a 5th c. bishop's palace with a peristyle court with columns of blue marble, kitchen quarters with a fine dining-room, and an audience chamber with three conchas and marble intarsia floor.

Hadrian's Baths

On the west side of the agora are baths built at the time of Hadrian (117–138), with interesting basins, heating system, changing rooms and a latrine. Some fine sculptures were uncovered here during excavation.

★Museum

In addition to small archaeological finds the museum on the site mainly houses sculptures from the celebrated Aphrodisias school – heads of

The well preserved ancient stadium of Aphrodisias

muses, statues of emperors, clothed figures, etc. Particularly noteworthy are the Zoilos frieze, the portrait statue of the writer Pausanias, a reproduction of Polyclitus's famous discus thrower and a copy of the statue of Aphrodite from the temple.

Odeion

The best preserved structure on the site is the Roman odeion to the south of the Temple of Aphrodite. The little concert hall almost certainly doubled as a buleuterion (council chamber) and was decorated with reliefs and statues. Today the orchestra with its mosaic floor is usually flooded, leaving frogs to croak their own chorus from among the water plants.

★Propylon

The now reconstructed 2nd c. tetrapylon (pylon or gateway), originally with four rows of four columns, led to the Temple of Aphrodite. The columns on the east side have spiral fluting.

Sebasteion

Not far from the museum are the remains of a shrine dedicated to the worship of the Roman emperors. The complex, built in A.D. 50, consisted of a podium temple reached via steps from the east end of an elongated court. Along the north and south sides of the court ran three-storeyed porticoes, the columns in each tier being of a different Classical Greek order – Doric (lower tier), Ionic (middle tier) and Corinthian (upper tier). Between the columns of the middle and upper tiers on the south side were reliefs depicting scenes from mythology and history.

★★Stadium

The stadium at Aphrodisias ranks as perhaps the best preserved of all those surviving from antiquity. Built around an arena 270m/295yd long and 54m/59yd wide with semi-circular ends, its 22 rows of seats could accommodate more than 30,000 spectators.

The walls

The best preserved sections of the 3.5km/2 miles of defensive walls are found along the north-east of the site. Erected at the time of Constantine the

Ancient theatre in Aphrodisas

Great (306–37) they incorporate masonry from the ancient buildings. Above the northernmost of the three gateways is an inscription which originally read "May fortune favour the glorious metropolis of Aphrodisians". In the 7th c. "Aphrodisians" was changed to "Stavropolitans".

★Theatre

Large enough to seat an audience of 10,000 the Late Hellenistic theatre with double proscenium, situated on the eastern slope of the "acropolis" mound, was restored and enlarged under Marcus Aurelius (161–180). The lower part of the stage and auditorium are well preserved. In a side entrance are carved transcriptions of imperial decrees and letters addressed to the city and its chief luminary and magistrate Zoilos. They include the so-called "Diocletian Price Edict" which, in an attempt to curb runaway inflation, introduced a regime of fixed prices. The large court in front of the theatre was paved with marble slabs in the 4th c. South-east of it lie the ruins of a columned, three-aisled basilica and a gymnasium; closer at hand are the remains of the theatre baths.

Artvin R 2

Black Sea region (East Pontus)
Province: Artvin
Altitude: 500m/1641ft
Population: 20,000

Situation and ★importance

The small provincial capital of Artvin is situated in the far north-east corner of Turkey, separated from the coast by the first of the Pontic mountain ranges. It makes an excellent base for forays into the surrounding countryside in search of some of the province's many ruined Early Christian and 9th–11th c. churches. These often lie off the beaten track, accessible only on foot or along dirt roads.

Located in the very heart of Turkish Georgia, this charming old town is also known as Çoruh (from the Çoruh Nehri) or Lazin (from Lazistan i.e. land of the Laz). Ascending in a series of south-west facing terraces, it clings to a steep hillside above the mouth of the Çoruh gorge.

Despite the steepness of its mountain slopes the area around Artvin – the "rain-covered Kolchis" of the Argonaut legend – is blessed with conditions ideal for the cultivation of a wide variety of fruit, vines, olives, hazelnuts and tea.

The history of Georgia

Relatively little is known about Artvin's past. Although the Muslim Laz (Chani) who inhabit the Black Sea coastal region form a distinctive ethnic group, they nevertheless share a common history with the other Caucasian peoples of Georgia. Once fought over by Romans and Sassanids (Persians), the area was conquered by the Arabs in the 7th c.; it remained under Arab rule for nearly three hundred years.

Turkish Georgia was the homeland of the Bagratid dynasty, who came from İspir. In the 10th c. the Armenian branch siezed control of parts of Armenia and the Transcaucasus; in the 12th and 13th centuries the Georgian Bagratids left an indelible mark on the whole of Christian Georgia.

The Arab invasions signalled the start of a lengthy period of decline, following which the Persians, Turks and Russians each sought to dominate the region. In 1071 the Artvin area, which from the 9th c. onwards, under the Bagratids, had became the political and cultural heartland of Georgia, fell to the Seljuk Alp Arslan. After the Seljuks had been driven out it became, under David the Restorer (David III, 1098–1125), the flourishing Bagratid kingdom of Georgia. This period of prosperity was cut short by the Mongols who laid waste the land in 1386. In the 15th c. Tao Georgia became part of the Ottoman Empire. Following the Turko-Russian War of 1877/78 Artvin was in Russian hands until 1918.

Sights

Artvin's 16th c. Georgian fortress, perched on a cliff high above the river, is out of bounds to the public (military zone). The Salih Bey Camii, in the Çayazı area of the town, was built by Sivan in 1793(?). Salih Bey was Governor of the town.

Surroundings

Ardanuç

On a cliff top overlooking the Köprüler Deresi gorge, not far from the little town of Ardanuç (about 30km/19 miles east of Artvin), are walls and stumps of towers belonging to a once mighty 12th c. fortress. Within the fort lie the ruins of an Armenian-Georgian church, a reminder that this was once the capital of the principality of Tao Georgia. Ashot Bagrationi the Great (780–826), founder of the ruling dynasty, skilfully preserved his relative independence by maintaining good relations simultaneously with Byzantium, the Emirs of Tiflis and the Caliphate. He styled himself Kuropalat (Guardian of palaces) and built numerous churches in his small realm.

Borçka

West of the mining town of Borçka there is an Ottoman bridge spanning a tributary of the Çoruh Nehri. Above the town, which in earlier times was also known as Yeniyol (New Way), stands a completely ruined fortress. In autumn the narrow gorge of the Çoruh Nehri between Artvin and the Turkish-Armenian border is visited by vast numbers of migrating birds.

★Dört Kilise

In Dört Kilise, a village overlooking the Çoruh about 5km/3 miles south of Yusefeli (the district town), are a ruined fortress and chapel. About 8km/5 miles further on, in a side valley, stands the Ohta Eklesia, a three-aisle Georgian basilica, rectangular in plan, dating from the 10th c. The ornate exterior and part of the stone-tiled roof have survived. Fragments of paintings can be seen inside the choir and a medallion portrait of the church's patron adorns the vaulting of the east window. The ruin north of the basilica was a chapel. These two are all that remain of the four churches which once stood here (Dört Kilise meaning "four churches").

Hamamlıköy

31km/20 miles east of Artvin in the valley of the Okçular Deresi is a ruined monastery, one of the most important of all those in the İmerhevi valley (see below). The chief point of interest today is a well preserved domed church, cruciform in plan, originally endowed by Smbat (923–85). Part of the church is now used as stabling, another part as a mosque. Note the south window, with figures of the Archangels Michael and Gabriel, also the relief of the founder on the drum.

★İmerhevi valley

About 12km/8 miles south-east of Artvin, the Okçular Çayı flowing into the Çoruh Nehri from the north-east marks the entrance to a valley known locally as the İmerhevi Deresi. Because of its numerous churches and monasteries it used to be called the Sinai or Mt Athos of Georgia. A road runs the length of the valley, first to Şavşat and then past the 2640m/8664ft-high Çam Gecidi to Ardahan. Along the route, particularly around Şavşat and Ardanuç, are several architecturally extremely interesting ruined churches (though some can only be reached on foot).

★Kaçkar Dağları

Parallel to the eastern Black Sea coast runs a wall of mountains rising to heights in excess of 2000m/6500ft. This northernmost of the Pontic ranges forms the backbone of Turkish Georgia. Merging in the north into the Little Caucasus (now the Republic of Georgia), it attains its greatest altitude (3932m/12,905ft) in the Kaçkar Dağ massif, a triangle of mountains lying between Rize, Artvin and Bayburt. Bounded to the south-east by the deep Çoruh trench, from the coast the massif rises sharply to 2000m/6500ft, at which height the surface has been extensively eroded, creating a kind of tableland. The main summit (Kaçkar Dağ) lies only 35km/22 miles as the crow flies from the coast and the Çoruh valley.

Flora and flora

Caucasian spruce, Nordmann fir, forest pine, deciduous oak and Asian beech all flourish throughout the region, as do rhododendrons – the white-bloomed Caucasian rhododendron occuring extensively, the purply-violet and yellow-flowered Pontic variety forming an undergrowth beneath the beeches and pines. Both the woodland and high altitude zone are rich in wildlife, and brown bears, Caucasian chamois, bearded vultures, Caspian partridge and Caucasian black grouse are still found.

Hill walking

The Kaçkar range is magnificent mountain walking country, Parhal, a sprawling village in the Barhal Çayı valley, being a particularly good starting point. One six hour walk, filled with interest, goes from Parhal, via Kumru, Naznara and Amaneskit, first to a waterfall and then to Karagöl, a cirque lake 2600m/8533ft up. Another walk (of about ten hours) follows a track which can be used by vehicles as far as Olgunlar (Yaylalar), then continues upstream onto the Dilber Düzü (Dilber plateau; 2950m/9682ft); beyond, at 3250m/10,666ft, lies Deniz Gölü (full day's walk) and beyond that the summit of Kaçkar Dağ (3932m/12,905ft; two days needed).

★Parhal

From the Çoruh Nehri at Yusufeli a side valley runs north, penetrating deep into the mountains. About 15km/9 miles beyond Sarıgöl lies another village, Altıparmak (also called Barhal or Parchali), its square graced by a well-preserved 10th c. monastery church, still in use as a mosque. Founded by David Kuropalat and built in stone of different hues, the church resembles the basilica at Dört Kilise, even in much of its detail. Some traces of wall paintings survive. The windows are embellished with figurative motifs and reliefs. A path climbs up from the village to two more chapels. The lower of the two has only walls remaining, but the little basilica higher up boasts two small apses.

In a side valley off the Barhal Çayı, near to the village Yüksekoba, are the remains of another monastery, the Gudaschewi Manastırı.

Şavşat

Şavşat, also known as Yeniköy or Zavsat, a district centre about 63km/39 miles east of Artvin on the scenic road to Ardahan, is dominated on its east side by a massive ruined Georgian fortress. This is a relic of the days when it was the seat of the princes of Chavchetien, one of the small Georgian principalities which came into being when the country was partitioned in the 9th and 13th/14th centuries.

Yeni Rabat

About 15km/9 miles south-east of Ardanuç, the ruins of the Georgian Schatberdi Manastırı (or Yeni Rabat ie. new monastery) lie almost out of sight in a wooded hollow in the Yalnızçam Dağları, above the Köprüler Deresi. The church, endowed by Gregory Chandstili, has beautifully ornate window frames. Yeni Rabat was famous for its school of manuscript illuminators and some exquisitely illuminated Gospels produced here in the 9th and 10th centuries can be seen in the museum in Tiflis (in the Georgian Republic).

Aspendos G 7

South coast (eastern Mediterranean)
Province: Antalya
Altitude: 20–60/65–195ft
Nearest place: Belkıs

Location of the ★★ruins

The site of Aspendos, in antiquity probably the most important city in Pamphylia, and now notable particularly for its splendidly preserved theatre, lies some 50km/30 miles east of Antalya and 15km/9 miles from the coast near the village of Belkıs in the alluvial plain of the gravel-bedded River Köprüımağı, the ancient Eurymedon.

Like most of the ancient cities in Asia Minor, Aspendos had an acropolis built built on a steeply scarped hill, to which a lower town was added in the Hellenistic period. The acropolis hill, some 800m/880yd long by 500m/550yd across, rises some 40m/130ft above the fertile surrounding

Theatre at Aspendos

Orchestra of the theatre

plain. The lower town which came into being several centuries later lay under the south-east side of the hill.

History

Aspendos was founded by the Greeks – according to tradition by the legendary Mopsos about 1000 B.C. As with other towns on the coast of Asia Minor, the factors which determined the choice of site and promoted the prosperity of this Greek colony were the fertile arable land and a good harbour. On the south coast where there were few harbours the navigable lower course of the River Eurymedon, which flowed past the site, offered the inestimable advantage of a sheltered river harbour. About 465 B.C. the Athenian General Kimon won a double victory over Persian land and sea forces at the mouth of the Eurymedon, and Aspendos also played an important part during the Peloponnesian War between Athens and Sparta. Like the neighbouring cities of Perge and Side, it had its most prosperous period under the Romans, and, as with those cities, its eventual decline was due to the silting up of its harbour and the centralising policy of the Byzantine Empire.

The Site

★★Theatre

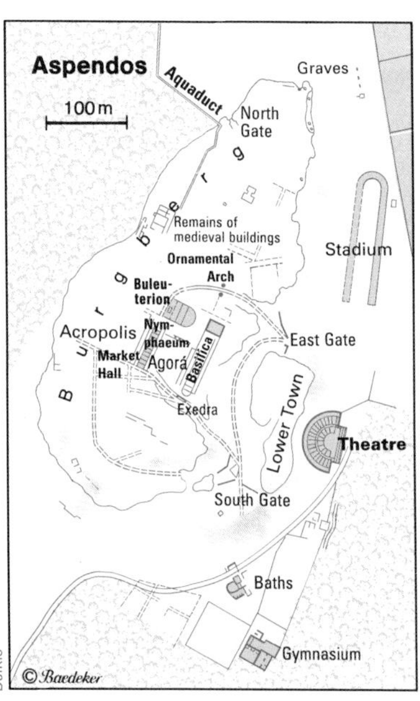

The outstanding feature of Aspendos is the theatre in the lower town, the best preserved and one of the largest Roman theatres in Asia Minor. Built in the 2nd c. A.D. by Crespinus Arruntianus and Auspicatus Titianus, the theatre has seating for an audience of betweenn 15,000 and 20,000. it has recently been restored and is now used for musical and dramatic festivals. The semicircular auditorium, divided into two sections by a broad passage half-way up, has 20 tiers of seating with 10 staircases in the lower half and 19 tiers with 21 staircases in the upper part. Round the top runs a barrel-vaulted colonnade. At either end of the auditorium are vaulted passages giving access to the stage and orchestra. The two-storey stage wall was articulated by slender double columns, with Ionic capitals on the lower order and Corinthian capitals on the upper one. The two double columns flanking the central entrance to the stage had a common broken pediment. The stage building had a wooden roof suspended on ropes. Probably the auditorium could also be covered by an awning.

Acropolis

Immediately above the lower town rises the acropolis hill. Its sides are so steep that its defences required to be strengthened by a wall only at certain points. There are only scanty remains of the buildings which once stood on the acropolis. It is entered by the south gate, the main access to the city, which is flanked by steep slopes. There were three gates of lesser importance on the other three sides. After passing the remains of a small temple and the agora we come to the nymphaeum (fountain shrine), once a monumental structure articulated by double columns but now represented only by a wall 32m/105ft long with ten niches for statues. Adjoining this on the north are the foundations of another building, probably the bouleuterion or council chamber.

Aqueduct

To the north of the acropolis hill can be seen remains of an ancient aqueduct and two water-towers to which the water was piped up under gravitational pressure.

Surroundings

National Park Köprülü Kanyon

Near the fork off the road to Beşkonak, 10km/7 miles east of Aspendos, a long Seljuk hump-back bridge with Roman foundations crosses the Köprülü Irmak. 46km/29 miles further north behind the village of Alabalık near Beşkonak, the river narrows, marking the point where the mountainous and impressive Köprülü Kanyon (Bridge Gorge) National Park begins. Behind some small fish restaurants a track leads off to Selge (within the park) across a Roman bridge which spans the gorge. Remains of an ancient cobbled road can be found on the road from here to Selge.

★Selge

High up in the Taurus Mountains about 60km/37 miles north of Aspendos lies the village of Altınkaya Köyü (Zerk; 1050m/3444ft) and the ruins of Selge. The road via Beşkonak beyond Alabalık is very poor, but quite an experience. It is said that the town was founded by Kalchas, the blind prophet of the Trojan war, and the rest of his army from Troy. Until Roman times the remote location of the settlement served to protect the town's inhabitants from foreign rule. Yet trade flourished thanks to some good relations with the towns of Pamphylia and other regions of Asia Minor and the Pisidian town of Selge enjoyed great prosperity during Imperial Roman times. The extensive ruins contain many interesting remains, but the principal sights are the Roman theatre with a Greek auditorium (10,000 seats) and the adjacent stadium. Some distance to the south-west on a mound lie the remains of a Temple of Zeus and a Temple of Artemis and just beyond a cistern-like round vessel for the town's water supply. About 500m/550yd to the east on another hillock stands the agora, at one time surrounded on three sides with rows of shops and from which a colonnaded street runs to the north. The remains of a triple-aisled basilica and a hall 120m/394ft long can be found nearby. The course of a town wall with a gate can be clearly discerned.

Assos B 4

West coast (Aegean Sea)
Province: Çanakkale
Altitude: 0–235m/0–770ft
Place: Behramkale

Location of the ★★ruins

The site of ancient Assos lies on the north side of the Gulf of Edremit, which cuts deep into the mainland of Asia Minor to the north of İzmir, and on the strait between the Troad and the Greek island of Lesbos (Turkish Midilli).

Assos can be reached on a reasonably good secondary road (about 20km/12½ miles) which branches off the E87 at Ayvacık (80km/50 miles south of Çanakkale) and runs south to end at the village of Behramkale.

History

Behramkale occupies only part of the site of the ancient city of Assos, which once covered an area of 2.5 sq.km/1sq. mile. It is situated on the summit and the terraced slopes of a steep-sided trachyte hill (235m/770ft) between the sea and the Tuzla Dere, 1km/¾ mile north of the Gulf of Edremit. In ancient times it was considered to be the most finely situated Greek city in either Europe or Asia. In the 2nd millennium B.C. Assos was the capital of the Leleges. Later it became an Aeolian colony; from 560 to 549 it belonged to Lydia, and for a hundred years it was held by the Persians. Aristotle lived in the town from 348 to 345, and in 331 the Stoic philosopher Kleanthes (d. 233 B.C.) was born here. About A.D. 58 the Apostle Paul called in at Assos on his way south (Acts 20: 13 ff.).

Restored columns in Assos

Excavations

Excavations by the American School in Athens in 1881–83 brought to light remains of structures dating from 12 centuries. Among them were the 3km/2 mile long city wall (mostly 4th c. B.C.), a particularly fine example of Hellenistc military engineering, which originally stood 19m/60ft high, the main lines of the Hellenistic layout of the town and, on the highest point of the acropolis, the foundations of an Archaic Temple of Athena, on which restoration work has been carried out in recent years. Works of art from the temple are now in İstanbul and Paris.

★View

It is well worth while climbing up to the acropolis for the sake of its far-ranging views of the island of Lesbos and the mainland to the north and east.

Behramkale

The village of Behramkale clings to the side of the hill, with steep narrow streets. At the lower end is a modest inn.

Surroundings of Assos

Baba Buran

Some 30km/20 miles west of Behramkale is Baba Burun (Cape Baba), the most westerly point in Asia Minor, with a lighthouse and the village of Babakale. Near here were the ancient cities of Polymedion and Hamaxitos. The village of Gülpınar probably occupies the site of ancient Chrysa, which had a Sanctuary of Apollo Smintheos, with a statue of the god by Skopas.

Aydın C 6

Western Anatolia
Province: Aydın
Altitude: 64m/210ft
Population: 107,000

Situation and ★importance

The provincial capital of Aydın, largely modern but with an older nucleus, is situated on the northern edge of the Büyük Menderes plain, on the alluvial fan of the Tabakhane Deresi (the ancient Eudon). The town lies just off the Denizli highway, on the İzmir–Denizli–Afyon branch of the Anatolian railway. Located west of the Tabakhane are what were the old Turkish and Jewish quarters, to the east the Armenian and Greek. Driving in from the south however, past all the recent building, first impressions are of a newish town.

The Büyük Menderes plain, with Aydın at its centre, is a region of intensive cultivation where, in addition to the main crop cotton, Turkey's best grapes (wine, raisins) and best figs are also grown. Emery, occuring locally in the crystalline rock to the west of Aydın, makes this the country's principal source of the mineral. Straddling a tectonic fault-line (Menderes trench), the town is subject to frequent earthquakes. As recently as 1895 a quake near Aydın threw up a ridge a metre high.

History

Though built on a site immediately below that of ancient Tralles, the town is actually of Turkish origin. It was the seat of the emirs of Aydın, the first of whom, Mehmet Aydınoğlu, established the beylik (principality) of Aydın in 1307 and founded the Aydın Oğulları dynasty. The town was named Aydın Güzelhisar by Mehmet's father. When in 1424 the area came under Ottoman control, Aydın continued as an important regional centre. From the 18th c. until 1822, with the Ottoman Empire already in decline, its rulers were the Karaosmanoğlu derebeys.

The name Güzel Hisar, meaning "handsome fortress", refers in fact to the ruined Tralles. As far as the old beylik capital is concerned, several earthquakes and a devasting fire at the time of the Greek retreat in 1922, have left virtually no historic buildings standing. Only the mosques are of any real interest today.

Sights

Ağaçarası Camii

The Ağaçarası (or Üveys Paşa) Camii in the Köprülü district is a splendidly baroque mosque dating from 1565. Also worth seeing is the domed 14th c. Alihan Kümbeti mausoleum in the Üveys Paşa quarter. Note the brick mosaic above the entrance, as well as the four tombs.

Cihanoğlu Camii

The Cihanoğlu (or Cihanzade) Camii, another exuberantly decorated building, square in plan, was erected in 1756. The sadirvan has a marble basin and twelve columns. The elaborate ornamentation of the mosque makes it one of the acknowledged masterpieces of the Turkish baroque style.

Museum

Aydın's museum is also worth visiting, situated just west of the town centre. While the majority of the exhibits come from Tralles it has, in addition, a section devoted to the ethnography of the area (open: 8.30am–noon; 1.30–5pm).

Osmanoğlu Külliyesi

The Osmanoğlu Hanı (Zinçirli Han), endowed by Nasuh Paşa, dates from between 1699 and 1707. As well as the caravanserai, a mosque, 20-roomed medrese and baths were all built at the same time. The Seljuk-style baths are now known as the Paşa Hamamı.

Süleiman Bey Camii

The Suleiman Bey Camii (1683), situated near the railway station, is one of the loveliest of all Aydın's mosques, another fine example of Turkish baroque. It has a şadırvan with a pyramidal domed roof.

★Tralles

The ruins of ancient Tralles stand encircled by olive groves 100m/328ft above Aydın on the steep mountain terrace known as Güzel Hisar (superb views). The site is in a restricted military zone and special permission is needed to visit it.

Originally founded by Argive colonists, at the time of its first mention (by Xenophon) Tralles was a fortified Persian military training area in the satrapy of the young Kyros. The town's surrender to Alexander the Great in 334 B.C. marked the start of a long period of prosperity and cultural vitality. It continued to flourish under Lysimachos, then under the Seleucids, when the town was known as Seleukia, and also under the kings of Pergamum, the Attalids, who maintained a palace here. Tralles figs were every bit as renowned then as they are today. The town was also famous for its school of philosophy. Having fallen to the Romans in 133 B.C., in 26 B.C. Tralles was devastated by an earthquake, being rebuilt largely through the beneficence of Augustus. The appreciative citizens renamed the city Caesarea, a name it retained until the late 1st c. In the 14th c. Güzelhisar (as it was then known) gave way to Aydın, newly established seat of the Aydın Oğulları built on the plain immediately below. Tralles's ancient buildings were pillaged for their stone.

The earliest excavations, undertaken in about 1888, bore little fruit, but in 1902/03 archaeologists from the Ottoman Museum in İstanbul uncovered the remains of baths and a stoá. The major find was a marble statue of a youth wearing a mantle (the Ephebe of Thalles, now in the Archaeological Museum in İstanbul).

Visiting the ruins

Stripped of nearly all its stone (some of it still found in buildings in the old part of Aydın) the remains of the huge stadium are not particularly impressive. Beyond the stadium, to the north, lie the ruins of the theatre – substantial walls of masonry with a mortar and rubble core – built up against the side of the acropolis. Note especially the unusual tunnel under the orchestra. At one time the 280m/920ft-high acropolis was supplied with water by means of a high-pressure conduit. Near the stadium are two ruined Early Byzantine churches with interesting ground plans.

A little to the right of the agora are three ruined arches which the Turks used to call "Üç Göz" (Three Eyes). These are now virtually the only remains of a large Late Roman gymnasium which had brick walls faced with marble.

The city walls, enclosing an oval area 1800m/1970yd long and 1000m/1094yd wide, have been reduced to just a few fragmentary remnants. On its east side Tralles was protected by the Tabakhne Çayı.

Bandırma C 3

Southern Sea of Marmara
Province: Balıkesir
Altitude: 10m/32ft
Population: 77,000

Situation and ★importance

This large port lies on a bay of the same name on the southern Sea of Marmara, facing the south-east side of the Kapıdağ peninsula. It has an airport and is the terminus of the İzmir to Balıkesir railway. A busy commercial and industrial centre, it has a regular ferry service to İstanbul (the first modern harbour was built in 1924). In 1943 a 2500ha/6180 acre farm was set up on the southern outskirts of town to rear merino sheep. It has a stock of about 5000 animals. Because of Bandirma's industries, its bay is not particularly attractive to holidaymakers. But there are still a number of sandy beaches e.g. at Karşıyakaköyü, and also near the Kyzikos ruins (see below).

History

Little is known of the early history of the town or its origins. It was Mysian to begin with, and later – probably in the guise of a small fishing village – part of the kingdom of Kyzikos. In 1076, at the time of Sultan Süleiman Kutulmuş, it came under the hegemony of the Seljuks of Rum. After their empire collapsed, it was part of the Karası beylik (see Balıkesir). Under Ottoman rule (until 1922) the population was predominantly Greek and Armenian. A substantial section of the town was destroyed in a fire in 1874 and today there is nothing much of interest to see.

Surroundings

Daskyleion

South-east of Kuş/Manyas Gölü, near the village of Ergili (formerly Eski Köy, i.e. "old village"), are the remains of ancient Daskylos, founded in the 7th c. B.C. by the father of the Lydian King Gyges. Later the Persian satraps of the small state of Phrygia made it into their capital. Pharnabazos built a palace and had a splendid garden laid (foundation walls can still be seen). Tomb reliefs and several imprints from Persian stone seals were also uncovered during excavation; they are now in the archaeological museums of İstanbul and Ankara.

Denizkent

About 26km/16 miles north-west of Gönen the Çanakkale road touches the Sea of Marmara coast at Denizkent. Here miles of sandy beaches and numerous holiday villages cater for mainly Turkish holidaymakers.

A short distance before Denizkent, on the left, is the Tahır Ovası model farm, founded jointly by the Turkish agricultural ministry and the Germano-Turkish Association. As well as breeding horses, sheep and plants it provides agricultural training.

★Erdek

Erdek, on the south-west corner of the Kapıdağ peninsula about 20km/14 miles north-west of Bandırma, not only enjoys a pleasantly equable climate but is blessed with an exceptionally attractive location as well. Since about 1950 it has proved more and more popular with the crowds of holiday-makers who come from the cities to the Sea of Marmara, and numerous apartment blocks have been built to accommodate them. Until 1921 the town was called Pithos and the population was mainly Greek. When the Greeks left large parts of Pithos were burned down. Erdek arose from the rubble, a new and to a large extent planned seaside town.

In antiquity Milesian settlers founded a colony called Artake on the site now occupied by Erdek. Destroyed by the Persians, it subsequently took on the modest role of a harbour for Kyzikos. Fishing for palamut, a short-finned variety of tuna, must have been of considerable importance at the time because the fish is featured on the kingdom's coinage.

Gönen

Intensive rice cultivation is the most striking feature of the wide Gönen plain, the cereal being grown in huge paddy fields along the length of the Gönen Çayı almost as far as its estuary near Denizkent. Gönen itself, a well-known thermal spa as well as the district town, is situated on the old Çannakale road, about 50km/30 miles south-west of Bandırma, right on the border of the Troas. Relics of the past include some remains from an ancient sacred spring dedicated to Artemis (Artemis Thermae; 5th c. mosaics in the Mosaic Museum in the spa area of the town). The hot springs (up to 82°C/179°F) assist the treatment of urinary, skin and nervous disorders. About 13km/8 miles south of Gönen, in the village of Eksidere in the Delical Dağ, there is another spa (Dağ Ilıcası) with hot springs (43°C/109°F) said to help cure rheumatism, gynaecological and gastric complaints.

Other places of interest around Gönen include: the Yarasa Mağları bat caves, a short distance to the north-west at Dereköy; the İskender Köprüsü, a very ancient – possibly 4th c.B.C. – bridge at Güvercinli, about 11km/7 miles north; and the remains of a granite block fort at Babayaka, 7km/4 miles from the town.

Kapidağ Yarımadası

The Kapıdağ peninsular north-west of Bandırma is linked to the mainland by a narrow isthmus. Mainly composed of granite (rock arch at ancient Dindymos), it is partly wooded, with mountains up to 782m/2566ft in height. When still an island in antiquity it was known as Arctonnesos, inhabited, according to legend, by Zeus's wetnurses transformed into bears.

Kyzikos

At the northern end of the isthmus between the Kapidağ peninsula and the mainland, beside the Bandırma road about 10km/6 miles south-west of Erdek, lie the remains of the ancient trading colony of Kyzikos (or Belkis), known by the poetic name of Dindymos. It was probably settled from Miletus in the 2nd millennium B.C. and was certainly inhabited by Miletian settlers by 756 B.C. It is mentioned in the story of Jason and the Argonauts which tells how in error they killed the hospitable king who had earlier made them welcome. In 334 Alexander the Great built two bridges joining the southern tip of the island to the mainland. After Kyzikos declined, sand continuously washing up against the piles of the bridges caused the channel slowly to silt up and the isthmus was formed. Following Lucullus's decisive victory over Mithridates, Kyzikos became a "free" city and capital of Mysia. Badly damaged on several occasions by earthquakes (particularly in 543 and 1063) and by Arab assault (673), and further ravaged in fighting between Byzantines, Seljuks and Crusaders, it was finally abandoned in 1224. Little now remains to be seen, only a section of the walls, the site of the theatre and some ruins of the amphitheatre and of Hadrian's Temple to Zeus from which in the 16th c. columns were removed to embellish İstanbul's mosques. Finds from Kyzikos are displayed in the museum in Erdek.

Soğuksu

Situated about 10km/6 miles south-east of Manyas, below a flat-topped hill called Keltepe, Soğuksu takes its name from the cold freshwater springs which gush out above the village. On Keltepe itself are ruins of a much older and larger town, thought to have been ancient Poemanios (Poemanenos). This, some experts believe, was the principal settlement of the Poemanens, a people who for a time were under the sway of their more powerful neighbour Kyzikos (see above). The site was still inhabited in 1832, but by 1902 it was already abandoned and falling into ruin. Relics from this period can be seen among the remains, including two almost completely destroyed mosques, two ruined türbes and a crumbling fort (possibly Byzantine) on the spur occupied by the acropolis. From the latter there are splendid views of Kuş Gölü and of the small village of Soğuksu below. The village was founded from nothing in the 19th c. by returning Circassian migrants.

National Park
★Kuşcenneti

This 52ha/128 acre nature reserve known as "Bird Paradise" was set up by the German hydrologist and zoologist Curt Crosswig in 1938. Frequented by some 250 different species of bird, the sanctuary has a small ornithological museum and an observation tower erected in 1952 by the Hydrology Department of the University of İstanbul. Occupying a largely unspoilt area of the lakeside near Siğircik in the north-east corner of Manyas Gölü (now renamed Kuş Gölü, "Bird Lake"), it was designated a National Park in 1959 and awarded the Europa Diploma in 1976. Specially built hides enable resident species and migrant visitors to be observed without causing them the least disturbance. Herons (common herons, night-herons, purple-herons, squacco herons and little egrets) and spoonbills crowd together in the trees. The two species of pelicans, Dalmatian and pink, and the cormorants, on the other hand, keep themselves to themselves.

Manyas

The story of Manyas, centre of its district and situated about 10km/6 miles south of Kuş Gölü, is typical of many a small Turkish town. The present community took root at the earliest towards the end of the 19th c. (probably around 1877), when 25 Tartar families, political returnees from Dobrudscha in Rumania, took over what was a fair ground and established Tatarköy (Tartar Village). Although new, the village stood on the site of ancient Miletopolis and so could justifiably claim a much longer if somewhat confused history. In fact the name Miletopolis was still in use in a contracted form ("Maltepe") for the spot where the present town stands. Today very little is known about Miletopolis, few finds having ever come to light. Rather more is known of Manyas's immediate predecessor, Eski Manyas (see Soğuksu). There are two spas in the vicinity of Manyas, Ilıca (Hamamlı) near Çingir, and Kum Ilıcası.

The Manyas (Kuş) Panayırı, mentioned as early as the 17th c. by Evliya Celebi in his travelogue, is held twice a year (June 3rd–6th and September 15th–17th).

Manyas Gölü (Kuş Gölü)

Lake Manyas (166sq.km/64sq. miles; maximum depth: 8m/26ft) nestles among hills about 20km/12½ miles south of Bandırma. The east side of the freshwater lake is now the Kuşcenneti bird sanctuary (see above), while in the south there are some tamarisk swamps with waterlilies and reed beds. The lake is fed mainly by the Kadiköyü Deresi and teems with plankton, fish and birdlife. Known to the ancients as Lake Miletopolis it drains across the Kara Dere into the Koca Çayı.

Marmara Adası

See the Sea of Marmara

Susurluk

The district town of Susurluk, on the Balıkesir road about 55km/33 miles south of Bandırma, has few sights of interest apart from the Deveci Hanı, a 16th c. Ottoman caravanserai, and an Ottoman medrese with a little mosque. The countryside around the town however is dotted with well-known spas including Gökçedere İlıcası (30km/20 miles south-west, the water being a warm 25°C/77°F) and Kepekler Kaplıcası (Göbel, 10km/6 miles north, on the road to Bandırma; hot springs 45°C/113°F; treatment for rheumatism and sciatica). The waters at Ömerköy İlıcası (about 30km/19 miles south-west, on the railway line to Balıkesir) are beneficial for general aches and nervous disorders, while at Yıldız Kaplıcası (about 15km/10 miles south, on the Simav Çayı) there are therapeutic hot springs (74°C/165°F) for treating rheumatism, sciatica and similar complaints.

Black Sea Coast C–R 1–3

Provinces (from west to east): Kırkareli, İstanbul, Kocaeli, Sakarya, Bolu, Zonguidak, Kastamonu, Sinop, Samsun, Ordu, Giresun, Tabzon, Rize, Artvin
Total length: about 2000km/1240 miles

★Scenery

★★Bathing beaches

The Turkish Black Sea coast, with its rich growth of vegetation, will come as a surprise to those who think of Turkey as a hot, dry land. the beautiful coastal regions, with their dense coniferous forests and gentle river valleys, their miles of bathing beaches, busy ports and sleepy fishing villages of typical wooden houses, and a mild and wet climate in which hazelnuts, tobacco, maize, rice and tea flourish, are in sharp contrast to the high plateaux of inland Anatolia.

Characteristics

These regions along the Turkish coasts of the Black Sea (in Turkish Kara Deniz), with their wealth of natural beauties, are bounded on the south by the Pontic Mountains, which rear up to almost 4000m/13,000ft. As a result of abrasion, however, the coast has fewer bays and inlets than any other part of the Turkish coastline. The climate in the western regions is cooler, so that even at the height of summer it never becomes too hot, while the eastern half is very warm and rainy (with annual precipitation of 2500mm/100in. at Rize), favouring the growth of the extensive forests in this area. These northern coastal regions of Turkey are well worth an extended visit for the sake of their many bathing resorts, most of them with good sandy beaches, as well as for their rich remains of the past.

Myth and history

The coastal strip along the Pontos Euxeinos, the "hospitable sea", features prominently in Greek mythology for example in the legends of Prometheus, the warlike Amazons or the Argonauts who sailed from Kolchis in the "Argo" in quest of the Golden Fleece.

From the 7th c. B.C. onwards flourishing Greek colonies were established all along the coast mostly founded by Miletus (Amisos, Kotyora, Kerasous, Trapezous, etc). In 281 B.C., after the death of Antigonos, Mithradates V founded the kingdom of Pontos, which reached its greatest extent in the reign of Mithradates Eupator, the Great (120–63 B.C.). This most dangerous of Rome's enemies was defeated by Pompey in 63 B.C. and the whole coastline then fell into Roman hands. In the 3rd c. A.D. the territory was

A tea plantation in the hinterland of Rize

A farmhouse near Rize

divided into two provinces, which were reunited in the reign of Justinian, with Neocaesarea (now Nıksar) as the chief town. After the capture of Constantinople by the Crusaders in 1204 the Byzantine dynasty of the Comneni ruled the empire of Trebizond (Trapezous) which extended from Thermodon to Phasis. Trapezous then became the leading commercial city of the Ancient World. In 1461, however, Sultan Mehnet II conquered these territories and incorporated them in the Ottoman Empire. On May 19th 1919 Kemal Paşa (Atatürk) landed at Samsun – an event of decisive importance in modern Turkish history, marking the beginning of the campaign to free Turkey of foreign occupation, which finally led to the abolition of the Sultanate and the establishment of the Turkish Republic.

Access

Although the western half of the Black Sea coast, between the Bulgarian frontier and Ince Burun, the most northerly point in Asia Minor, has no good modern road for its whole length, a beautiful coast road runs east from Sinop (in antiquity the most powerful of the Greek Black Sea colonies) to the Turkish–Georgian border. It passes through a series of interesting towns including Samsun, the most important port and commercial town on the north coast of Turkey, and Trabzon (ancient Trapezous and later Trebizond), to the tea-producing town of Rize, chief place in the mountainous territory of Lazistan, and the little Turkish port of Hopa, near the Georgian frontier.

A reasonable regular boat service runs from İstanbul to Zonguldak, Sinop, Samsun, Giresun and Trabzon, and air services connect İstanbul and Ankara to the regional airports of Sumsun and Trabzon.

The principal places along the Black Sea coast are listed below, going from west to east.

Western Black Sea coast

İğneada

A typical fishing village in a bay sheltered by İğneada Burun (lighthouse), 15km/9 miles south of the Bulgarian frontier. To the west are the wooded Istranca Hills.

Kilyos

A seaside resort with a beautiful sandy beach and accommodation for visitors; popular with the people of İstanbul. 40km/25 miles south.

Bosporus

See entry.

Sile

A bathing and holiday resort with a good beach; the sand has a healing effect on rheumatism and sciatica. There are a number of rocky offshore islets. The town is noted for the manufacture of Silebezi, a gauzy cotton fabric.

The best bathing places in the immediate vicinity are Ağlayan Kaya, Şile Feneri, Ocak Ada and Kumbaba.

Yesilçay

A small resort with a sandy beach and a camping site.

Karasu

A small town 2km/1¼ miles inland near the mouth of the River Sakarya, known to Homer and Hesiod as the Sangarious (the name of a Phrygian river god, son of Okeanos and Trthys).

On the coast are mile-long beaches of fine sand.

★Akçakoca
Diospolis

A beautifully situated little seaside town with a first-rate bathing beach; it occupies the site of the Greek city of Diospolis or Dia. To the west of the town is a ruined Genoese fortress (14th c.). Hazelnut plantations in the surrounding area.

Ereğli

See Zonguldak, surroundings.

Zonguldak

See entry.

Black Sea Coast

Hisarönü
Filyos

A coastal town, near which is the seaside resort of Filyos, with Roman remains (town walls and gate, theatre, citadel).

Bartın

A small town 10km/6 miles inland on the River Bartın, with typical wooden houses and a Roman road dating from the time of the Emperor Claudius.

İnkum

At the mouth of the river is the resort of İnkum, on the fringes of a hill forest.

Amasara

See Zonguldak, surroundings.

Çakraz
Kurucaşile
Cide

From Amasara a coast road (fine views) runs north-east by way of the fishing village of Çakraz (good sandy beach) and the little towns of Kurucaşile (boatyard) and Cide (good beach) and past Kerempe Burun (the ancient Carambis Promontorium) to İnebolu.

★İnebolu

★Wooden houses

The principal port on this stretch of slate-covered coast is situated at the mouth of a little river with the same name in a lush garden-like landscape. As well as a ruined castle, the traditional wooden houses are particularly interesting. İnebolu boasts several handsome Pontic-style town houses, some with slate-covered roofs in the traditional style. In antiquity the town was known as Abonouteichos, but was renamed Ionopolis (hence İnebolu) during the period of Roman Imperial rule. Some of the historically important buildings in the old town include Eski Cami, Yen Cami, Küçük Cami and the ruins of a church in the Christian quarter of Erkistos Mahalles. More fine beaches are to be found in the vicinity. Other excellent beaches enhance the neighbouring towns of Gemiciler (10km/6 miles to the east), Özlüce (14km/9 miles to the west), Kayran (24km/15 miles to the west) and Doğnyurt (32km/20 miles to the west) from where boat trips to the Fokkayazı caves leave.

Abonouteichos

This was the site of ancient Abonouteichos, renamed Ionopolis in the Roman Imperial period.

Abana

A holiday resort beautifully situated on the coast, here largely wooded, with a 5km/3 mile long bathing beach.

Ayancık

A coastal resort in wooded surroundings with long beaches.

İnce Burun

This cape (lighthouse), the ancient Syrias Promontorium, is the most northerly point in the whole of Turkey.

★Eastern Black Sea coast

Sinop

See entry.

★Bafra

Bafra lies some 25km/15 miles south of the wooded Bafra Burun, where the Kızılırmak (Red River), the ancient Halys (which from 301 to 183 B.C. marked the boundary between Paphlagonia and the kingdom of Pontos), flows into the sea. Bafra is noted for its thermal springs, its tobacco and its caviare. Notable features are a 13th c. bath-house and a 15th c. complex consisting of a mosque, a mausoleum and a medrese. East of the town is the coastal lagoon of Balık Gölü (Fish Lake). Farther east along the Gulf of Samsun are large tobacco plantations.

Samsun

See entry.

Çarşamba

Çarşamba lies some 30km/20 miles on the alluvial plain in the delta of the Yeşilırmak (Green River), known in antiquity as the Iris, which reaches the sea north-west of the town at Cliva Burun (ancient Ankon). To the east of the cape are numerous projecting spits of land (dunes) and coastal lagoons created by eastward movement of the beaches under the prevailing north-west winds, thus gradually producing a more regular coastline.

Terme

A little way south of Çaltı Burun (ancient Heracleum Promontorium, the Cape of Hercules) lies this small town on the river of the same name, which is probably the ancient Thermodon.

Themiskyra

At the mouth of the Thermodon was ancient Themiskyra, which may have been the town besieged by Lucullus in 73 B.C. during the Third Mithradatic War, captured after a stubborn resistance and plundered or destroyed. Themiskyra was also the name of the plain which according to Strabo began 60 stadia (11km/7 miles) beyond Amisos (Samsun) and extended to the River Thermodon and which was renowned for its fertility.

Amazons

Themiskyra was also believed to be the home of the Amazons, the warlike women, descended from the god Ares and the nymph Harmonia, who cut off their breasts lest these should interfere with the handling of the bow (Amazon = without breasts). According to Greek legend one of the Labours of Herakles was to go to Themiskyra and take back to Argos the girdle of the Amazon Queen Hippolyte. When the Greeks came to this area to establish their colonies and found no Amazons they concluded that Harakles had either killed them all or driven them away.

The Amazons were credited with the foundation of various cities (Myrine, Kyme, Mytilene, Smyrna, Ephesus, etc.). Fights with Amazons were a favourite theme of Greek art.

To the east, beyond the River Terme, the sandy beaches with their dunes are fringed by rice-fields, wells, fishermen's houses built on piles, and grain-stores with thatched walls and roofs.

Ünye

A pleasant little port town (ancient Oinoe) in the bay of the same name, with macchia-covered hills rising above the turquoise-coloured sea. The town has a fine 18th c. Town Hall. Nearby is the beautiful beach of Çamlık. Ünye lies at the beginning of the "Hazelnut Coast" (Fındıksahili).

Fatsa
Bolaman

The coast road runs east from Ünye to Fatsa (small harbour) and Bolaman, and continues above the steeply scarped shore, encircling a fairly large peninsula ending in Yasun Burun (ancient Iasonium Promontorium, referring to Jason and his Argonauts) and then Vona Burun, to Perşembe.

Perşembe

A little town near a bay which was formerly called Vona – probably from ancient Boon, described as a safe harbour and fortress 90 stadia (16km/10 miles) from Kotyora (Ordu).

★Ordu

Chief town of the province of the same name, a busy port (shipping timber and hazelnuts) and the market centre of a fertile agricultural area, situated in a large bay. Notable features are an 18th c. church and the beautiful beach of Güzelyalı.

Kotyora

Ordu occupies the site of ancient Kotyora, an Ionian colony in the territory of the Tibarenoi, on the coast of Pontos Polemoniakos. Here Xenophon and his Ten Thousand are said to have embarked for Sinope in 401 B.C. When King Pharnakes moved families from Kotyora to occupy the town of Pharnakeia (Giresun) Kotyora itself declined, and in the time of Strabo was a little place of no consequence. In the Middle Ages the area round Ordu belonged to the empire of Trebizond. It was incorporated in the Ottoman Empire by Mehmet II in 1462. In 1913 fire destroyed large areas.

★Giresun

Chief town of its province and a port exporting timber and hazelnuts, Giresun is beautifully situated on a small rocky peninsula which was once fortified. The coast in this area is covered with lush green vegetation.

Features of interest in Giresun are the tombs of Seyyidi Vakkas and Osman Ağa and an 18th c. church. From the town a wide depression leads up to a flat-topped conical hill crowned by a Byzantine fortress.

There is a pleasant walk up the hill above the town, which commands extensive views. On the slopes of the hill are large hazelnut plantations.

Just outside the harbour is the little island of Giresun Adası (ancient Aretia), where according to legend the Argonauts landed; the island, which was uninhabited, had a temple dedicated to the war god Ares. There are the ruins of a Byzantine monastery.

In the immediate vicinity of the town are long stretches of beach with bathing facilities and camping sites.

Kerasous

Pharnakeia

Giresun occupies the site of ancient Kerasous, founded by Miletus in the 7th c. B.C. Xenophon and his Ten Thousand halted here in 400 B.C. on their march to the sea. The place was later named Pharnakeia after King Pharnakes (grandfather of Mithradates the Great), who settled families from Kotyora (Ordu) in the town. During his war with the Romans Mithradates moved his harem to Pharnakeia.

The present name of Giresun is explained by a story that the Roman General Lucullus found a particularly good kind of cherry here (Greek kerasos; Latin cerasus; Turkish kiraz), which he took back to Rome.

In later times the town shared the destinies of the Pontos region. In the Byzantine period it belonged to Pontos Polemoniakos, later to Armenia Prima and in the 13th c. to Trebizond. In 1462 it fell into the hands of the Ottomans.

Keşap

20km/12½ miles east of Giresun the coast road passes through the little town of Keşap on to the promontory of Kel Dağ with Çam Burun, a cape known in antiquity as Zephyros.

Tirebolu

In medieval times this little port (ancient Tripolis), which Pliny refers to as a "castellum", was a place of some consequence in the empire of Trebizond, supplying copper, timber and fruit. In the bay containing the harbour are two crags with a ruined castle and a Byzantine fortress (lighthouse).

Görele

A small pot beside a headland reaching out into the sea, known as Koralla when it belonged to the empire of Trebizond. It has a monastery and a castle, with a squat tower, which were reported in the mid 19th c. to be already in a state of ruin.

Eynesil
Beşikdüzü
Vakfıkebir
İskefiye
Akçaabat

From Görele the coast road continues to the little towns of Eynesil, Beşikdüzü, Vakfıkebir (perhaps ancient Kerason, a colony of Sinope, three days' march from Trapezous) and İskefiye, past Fener Burun (lighthouse; probably the ancient Cape of Hieron Oros, one of the highest in the Black Sea), on to the port of Akçaabat, over the River Galanima (Kalanima, Kalenüma), on which the old port of Platana (once Hermonassa) lay, and so to the ancient port of Trabzon, picturesquely situated on three hill ridges. Just before reaching the town there is a view of the Church of Hagia Sophia on its western outskirts.

Trabzon

See entry.

Sürmene

40km/25 miles east of Trabzon lies the little town of Sürmene (ancient Susarmia), on the River Kora, where Xenophon and his Ten Thousand fell sick after eating wild honey.

★Rize

Chief town of Rize province, beautifully situated in a bay at the foot of a mountain (fine views from the Botanical Gardens above the town), producing tea, rice and fruit, linen and copper articles and shipping tea and timber from its port. Tea has been grown here since 1938, and the town has many factories preparing it both for domestic consumption and for the export market. A notable feature is the 16th c. Islam Paşa Mosque.

In antiquity the town was called Rhizion (Rhizous, Rhition, Rhitium) and was a port in the territory of the Kissioi. In medieval times it was known as Risso. In 1461, after Mehmet II's capture of Trebizond, it became part of the Ottoman Empire.

Lazistan

South-east of Rize extends the wild mountainous country of Lazistan (Tatos Dağları), where snow-covered peaks rise to a height of just under 4000m/13,000ft in Kaçkar Dağı.

Hopa

The most easterly Turkish Black Sea port, in a wooded setting 8km/5 miles from the Georgian border at Kemalpaşa.

Bodrum C 6

West coast (Aegean Sea)
Province: Muğla
Altitude: 0–50m/0–165ft
Population: 21,000

Situation

The modern town of Bodrum (formerly Budrum), in Caria, lies on the site of the important ancient city of **Halicarnassus** in a little bay (Bodrum Limanı) on the south-west coast of Asia Minor opposite the Greek island of Kos (Turkish İstanköy).

Rising in terraces above the bay, with its old walls, its whitewashed houses nestling amid gardens and vineyards within a semicircle of hills – a layout compared by Vitruvius in his "De Architectura" (II, 8) to an amphitheatre – it is an exceedingly picturesque little town. The harbour is sheltered by a tongue of land extending to the former island of Zephyrion, with the Crusader Castle of St Peter.

The name Bodrum (= cellar or casemate) may be a corruption of the name of the castle (Petronium), or it may refer to the arcading on the west side of the castle.

★★Holiday resort

In recent years Bodrum has developed into one of the leading holiday centres on the Aegean coast of Turkey. Its great attractions, in addition to its mild climate and picturesque situation, are the beautiful bathing beaches and diving grounds in the immediate vicinity, the sheltered harbour (port of call for regular shipping lines and cruise ships; local services to Kos, Knidos and Datça; boatyard for charter boats) and the friendly atmosphere of the town with its busy and colourful bazaar.

Bazaar quarter

The centre of modern Bodrum lies at the north end of the peninsula on which the castle stands. This is the lively bazaar quarter with its open-fronted craftsmen's workshops (tailors, cobblers, smiths, etc.), its fruit and vegetable market, its shops and boutiques (leather goods, textiles, sponges, gold and silver jewellery, souvenirs, etc.) and its restaurants. To the east extends the harbour bay with its berths for yachts and other pleasure-craft, while to the west is a wide open bay with a seafront promenade, various restaurants and the landing-stages for pleasure boats.

History of Halicarnassus

Halicarnassus was founded about 1200 B.C. by Dorian Greeks from Troezen in the eastern Argolid (the area associated with the legends of Theseus and his son Hippolytos), traditionally said to have been led by Anthes, a descendant of the founder of Troezen. The town was established beside an old Carian settlement round the Fortress of Salmakis, which remained independent until the 5th c. B.C. Thanks to its good harbour, its strong situation and the fertile surrounding country Halicarnassus quickly developed into an important commercial city. Originally belonging to the Dorian League of six cities, the Hexapolis – though by the 5th c. Ionian, the language which Herodotus wrote, was already the official language of the city – it came under Lydian rule in the reign of Kroisos (Croesus, 560–546). In 540 it passed, without resistance, to the Persians, under whose overlordship the city was ruled by Carian princely families, such as the Lygdamids in the early 5th c. Artemisia (the Elder), a daughter of Lygdamis, commanded a flotilla of five ships in Xerxes' fleet and distinguished herself in the Battle of Salamis (480 B.C.). After the Battle of Mykale (479) Halikarnassos became part of the Athenian Empire. Herodotus (484–425), the

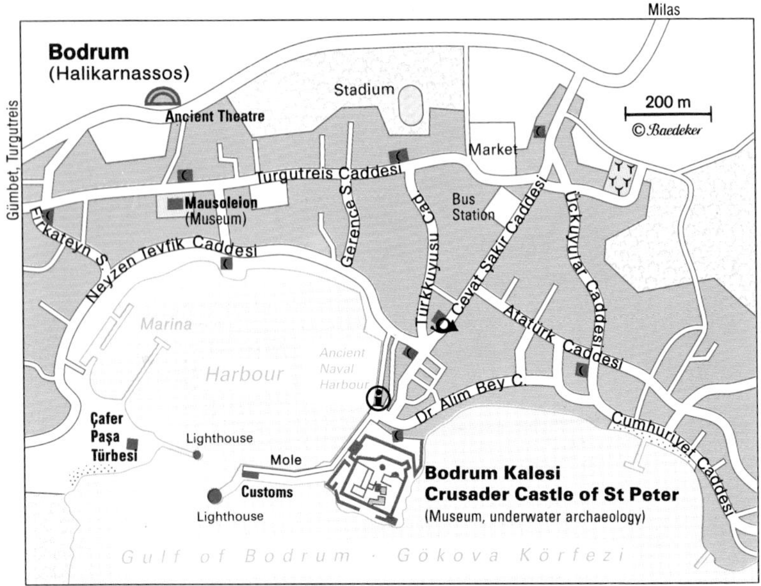

"Father of History" and the city's greatest son, was involved in the factional struggles which followed. In 413 Halicarnassus again fell into Persian hands and, after a brief period of autonomy (*c.* 394–377), remained under Persian rule until Alexander's campaign. During this period it enjoyed a time of great prosperity when Hekatomnos, Satrap of Mylasa (Milas), gained control of the town and in 387 made it the chief city of Caria in place of the remote Mylasa.

The successive rulers of Halicarnassus during the period of Persian control (when, under ancient Carian law, women enjoyed great authority, as wives of their brothers) were Hekatomnos (377), Mausolos and Artemesia II (377–353), Artemisia II on her own (353–351), Idrieus and Ada (brother and sister of their predecessors, 351–344), Ada by herself (344–340) and her brother Pixodaros (340–334), Hekatomnos' youngest son.

The most important of these rulers was Mausolus, who established a strong position by skilful statesmanship and war and, following Hellenistic models, equipped the city with walls, harbours, palaces and temples. He was succeeded by his sister and wife Artemisia II, who built the Mausoleion (Mausoleum), one of the Seven Wonders of the World, in his honour.

In 334 B.C., during Alexander's Persian campaign, the city withstood a long siege by his general Ptolemaios but was finally taken and destroyed. After Alexander's death it was involved in the struggles for his succession, falling to Lysimachos in 301 and Seleukos in 281, before finally passing into Roman hands in 129. In 88 B.C. it was taken by Mithradates. Between 62 and 58 it was several times plundered by pirates, but was later restored by Cicero. Under the Roman Empire the city enjoyed a new period of prosperity. In A.D. 395 it became part of the Byzantine Empire. In 1402 it was conquered by the Knights Hospitallers of St John, and the Castle of St Peter was built from the stones of the Mausoleum (1437). In 1523 Halicarnassus fell to the Ottomans, the castle surrendering without a fight.

The Ancient Remains

Mausoleion

The ancient city was traversed by a main street running from its east end to the fine Myndos Gate (Gümüslü Kapı) with its towers at the west end. In this street, in the centre of the town, stood the famous Mausoleion or Mausoleum, which from the time of Augustus became a general term for a large tomb. Built in 351 B.C., it survived in good condition until the 12th c. A.D. Thereafter it may have been damaged by earthquakes and was then gradually pulled down, being finally destroyed in 1522, when the remaining stone was used to strengthen the castle against Ottoman attack. Dressed stones from the Mausoleum can be seen in the castle and the town walls and at the bottom of an old well in the town. A reconstruction of the monument is planned.

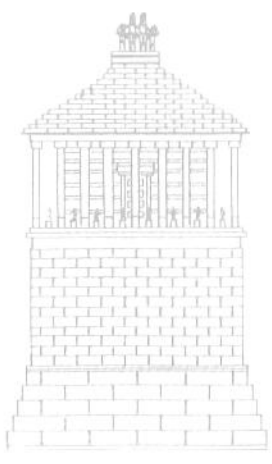

Planned reconstruction

Various scholars have put forward suggested reconstructions of the Mausoleion based on ancient accounts and the evidence of the remains. The rectangular funerary temple, surrounded by 36 Ionic columns, stood on a rectangular base 33m/108ft by 37m/121ft and had a stepped pyramidal roof of 24 courses, surmounted by a quadriga (four-horse chariot). The whole structure stood 46m/150ft high. Designed by Pytheos, who was also responsible for the Temple of Athena at Priene, it was built under the direction of Satyros and decorated with sculpture by the four greatest Greek sculptors of the day, each taking responsibility for one side of the monument. The Amazon frieze on the east side was the work of Skopas of Paros, one of the most celebrated marble sculptors of the 4th c. B.C., the north side was by the Attic sculptor Bryaxis, the west side by Leochares, famous for his figure of Ganymede, and the south side by Timotheos of Athens. The monument is believed to have been completed only in the time of Alexander the Great. The first reliefs from the Mausoleion reached London in 1846; then in 1862–63 C. T. (later Sir Charles) Newton identified the site of the monument and brought back much sculpture from the Mausoleion and the castle to the British Museum. Excavations were carried out by Danish archaeologists in 1966–67.

Theatre

Above the Mausoleion, to the north-west, is the ancient theatre, from which there are extensive views. To the north-east are remains of a Doric stoa (colonnade), and above this the remains of a Temple of Area (?). Still higher up, outside the town walls to east and west, are various tombs. At the entrance to the oval harbour, which measures some 620m/680yd from east to west, and probably had a small separate naval harbour at its east end, with an entrance to the north of the former islet now occupied by the castle, are remains of the ancient piers. The west pier extended from the little promontory along which now run the walls of the Arsenal the east pier from the islet of Zephyrion.

To the east of the naval harbour stood the palace of Mausolos, built in the early 4th c. B.C. with a lavish use of marble. Its stones were used to construct the strip of land linking the former island with the mainland and the glacis (sloping bank) of the Crusader castle.

Along the north side of the harbour was the agora, in which stood a colossal statue of the god Ares.

To the west of the city on the Hill of Kaplan Kalesi, the former acropolis, now crowned by a tower, was the Carian stronghold of Salmakis. The famous spring of that name must have been somewhere below the north side of the hill. From the acropolis the town walls (which can still be traced at some points) followed the contours round the city, mostly running along the crest of the hills.

★★Bodrum Kalesi (Crusader Castle of St Peter)

★Castle

Bodrum's principal sight, the Castle of St Peter, now known as Bodrum Kalesi, with its tall, well-preserved towers, was built by the Knights

Hospitallers of St John between 1402 and 1437 on the islet of Zephyrion, now joined to the mainland. It replaced an earlier castle built on the site of the first Greek settlement. The Turks erected other buildings within the precincts of the castle, and in the Late Ottoman period it was used as a place of exile. As with the defences of Rhodes, knights of the various nationalities in the Order were entrusted with the defence of particular sections of the walls. The English Tower, also known as the Lion Tower (Arslanı Kule), has a marble lion with the Plantagenet arms, a relief of St George and the Dragon and the names of English knights carved on the walls of the window recesses.

★Museum

The various buldings within the castle, together with the upper and lower wards, are now a very interesting museum. The Italian and French towers are not open to the public.

From the mosque (1723) in the Harbour Square a ramp leads up into the outer ward, on the far side of which an arched gateway gives access to the lower ward (ticket office). At the east end of this can be found the first part of the museum, a Gothic chapel, built by Spanish knights in 1519–20 and later converted into a mosque. It contains Bronze Age material and the only fragment of a frieze from the Mausoleion still preserved in Bodrum. In the towers of the castle are collections of objects of various kinds and different periods (architectural fragments, sculpture, jewellery, coins, etc.), and other items are displayed in the open, including some lively peacocks.

★★Underwater archaeology

The most interesting part of the museum is the section devoted to underwater archaeology, with originals and reconstructions of material recovered from wrecks at Yassı Ada (a short distance west of Bodrum) and Cape Gelidonya (at Finike), the equipment used by underwater archaeologists, displays illustrating their methods, and a great variety of objects recovered from the sea.

The harbour, with the Crusader castle Bodrum Kalesi

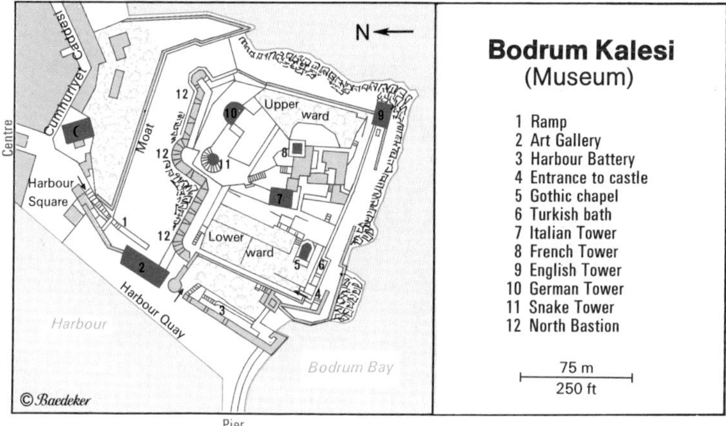

Bodrum is the Turkish base of the Institute of Nautical Archaeology of the University of Texas (College Station, TX).

Bosphorus — D/E 2/3

Strait between the Black Sea and the Sea of Marmara
Length: 32km/20 miles
Breadth: 0.66–3.3km/720–3600yd
Depth: 30–120m/100–395ft

The Bosphorus (from a Thracian word of unknown origin, interpreted in Greek as meaning "Ford of the Cow", from the legend of Io, who swam across the sea here as a cow), known in Turkish as Boğaziçi (the Strait), links the Black Sea with the Sea of Marmara and, with the Dardanelles, separates Europe from Asia.

It is a former river valley which was drowned by the sea at the end of the Tertiary period.

★★Scenery

With the shores rising to heights of up to 200m/650ft, lined with palaces, ruins, villages and gardens, this is one of the most beautiful stretches of scenery in Turkey.

By boat through the Bosphorus

The best way of seeing the Bosphorus in all its beauty is to take a trip from İstanbul on one of the coastal boats which ply along its length, calling in alternately at landing-stages on each side and thus affording a constantly changing panorama.

The point of departure is just south-east of the Galata Bridge; the ports of call can be seen in the timetables displayed in the waiting-room.

Not all boats go as far as Rumeli Kavağı, the last station on the European side (1¾–2 hours). At each station there is a ferry to the other side.

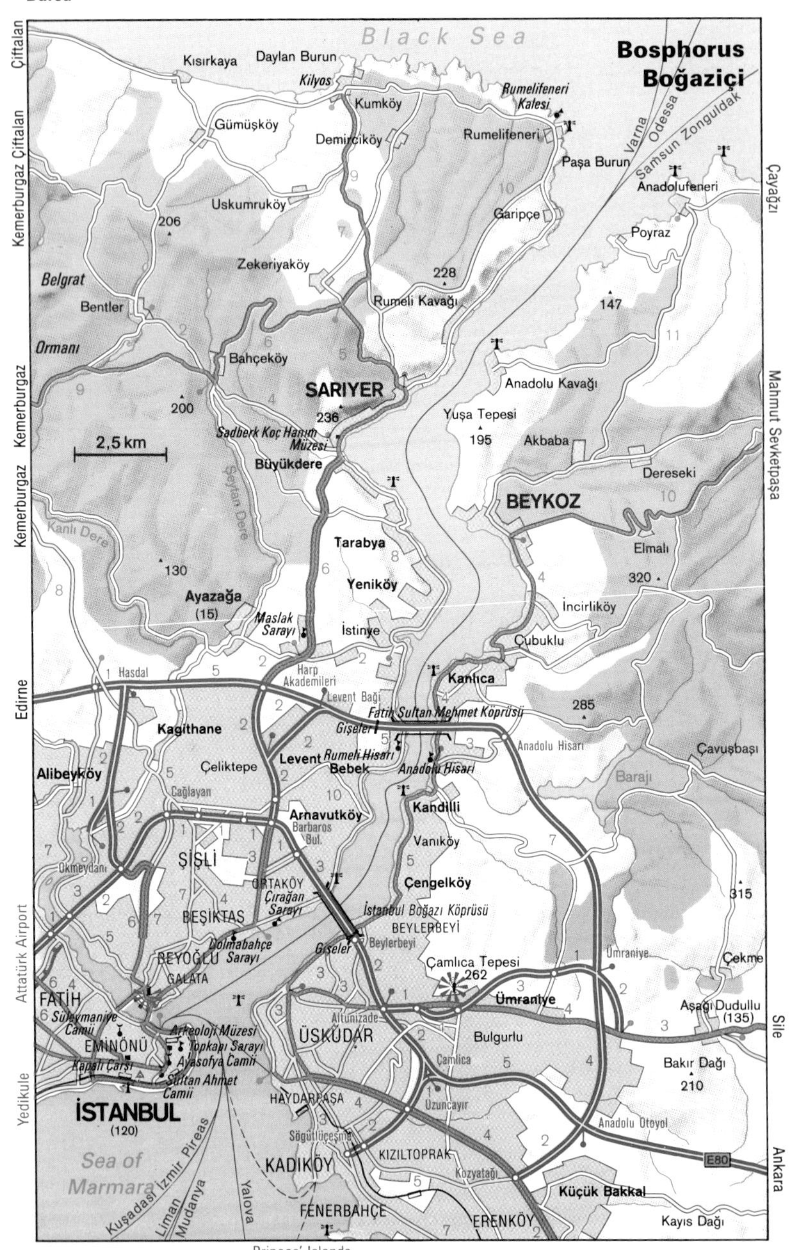
Black Sea
Bosphorus
Boğaziçi
Kısırkaya
Daylan Burun
Kilyos
Kumköy
Rumelifeneri Kalesi
Gümüşköy
Demirciköy
Rumelifeneri
Varna
Odessa
Samsun
Zonguldak
Paşa Burun
Anadolufeneri
Uskumruköy
Garipçe
Poyraz
206
Zekeriyaköy
228
Belgrat
Ormanı
Bentler
Rumeli Kavağı
147
Bahçeköy
Anadolu Kavağı
SARIYER
200
236
Yuşa Tepesi
195
Akbaba
Sadberk Koç Hanım Müzesi
2,5 km
Büyükdere
Dereseki
BEYKOZ
Kanlı Dere
Şeytan Dere
Tarabya
Elmalı
Yeniköy
320
130
Ayazağa
(15)
İncirliköy
Maslak Sarayı
İstinye
Çubuklu
Hasdal
Harp Akademileri
Kanlıca
Levent Bağı
Fatih Sultan Mehmet Köprüsü
285
Kagithane
Gişeleri
Anadolu Hisarı
Çavuşbaşı
Alibeyköy
Çeliktepe
Levent
Rumeli Hisarı
Bebek
Anadolu Hisarı
Barajı
Çağlayan
Kandilli
Arnavutköy
Barbaros Bul.
Vaniköy
Okmeydanı
ŞİŞLİ
ORTAKÖY
Çengelköy
Çırağan Sarayı
315
BEŞİKTAŞ
İstanbul Boğazı Köprüsü
BEYLERBEYİ
Dolmabahçe Sarayı
Gişeler
Beylerbeyi
Ümraniye
BEYOĞLU
Çekme
Çamlıca Tepesi
262
GALATA
FATİH
Ümraniye
Aşağı Dudullu
(135)
Süleymaniye Camii
Arkeoloji Müzesi
Altunizade
Topkapı Sarayı
ÜSKÜDAR
Bulgurlu
EMİNÖNÜ
Ayasofya Camii
Kapalı Çarşı
Çamlıca
Bakır Dağı
210
Sultan Ahmet Camii
Uzunçayır
HAYDARPAŞA
İSTANBUL
(120)
Anadolu Otoyol
Söğütlüçeşme
Sea of Marmara
İzmir Pireas
KIZILTOPRAK
E80
KADIKÖY
Kozyatağı
Kuşadası
Liman
Mudanya
Yalova
Küçük Bakkal
FENERBAHÇE
ERENKÖY
Kayıs Dağı
Princes' Islands
Çiftalan
Kemerburgaz Çiftalan
Kemerburgaz
Kemerburgaz Kemerburgaz
Edirne
Attatürk Airport
Yedikule
Çayağzı
Mahmut Sevketpaşa
Sile
Ankara

European side

İstanbul (*Galata Quay*); then, higher up, the massive square bulk of the Technological University.

★*Dolmabahçe*, with the large Dolmabahçe Palace.

Beşiktaş; opposite the landing-stage, the *Türbe of Kheireddin Barbarossa*. Beyond this, the massive ruins of the *Çıragan Sarayı*, a luxurious palace in the same style as the Dolmabahçe Palace (façade 950m/1040yd long), built by Abdul Aziz in 1874 and burned down in 1910. On the hill above it is the *Yıldız Köşkü* (Yıldız Sarayı), residence of the retiring Sultan Abdul Hamid II.

Suburb of *Ortaköy*, with beautiful gardens; handsome mosque (1870); last view of İstanbul to rear.

First bridge over the Bosphorus

Past the little promontory of *Defterdar Burun* and the *Duimi Bank* (navigational light) to the village of *Kuruçeşme* and the Albanian fishing village of *Arnavutköy* on Akıntı Point, where there is always a strong current.

Bebek, in a beautiful bay, with villas and waterside houses (yalıs).

Above the cypresses of an old cemetery rise the picturesque walls and towers of ★**Rumeli Hisarı** (European Castle). Above rises the second bridge over the Bosphorus.

Built by Mahmet II in 1452 (well worth a visit, open-air theatre in summer), it commands the narrowest part of the Bosphorus (660m/720yd), where the current is at its strongest (Şeytan Akıntısı (Satan's Stream)); fine ★view. Here Darius built a bridge of boats over the Bosphorus in 514 B.C.

On a low promontory beyond *Boyacıköyü Emirgan* are the palaces built by the Egyptian Khedive Ismail (d. 1895).

İstinye, with a shipyard.

Yeniköy (last station for most boats), with beautiful villas and gardens. In St George's Church is an old icon of the Mother of God Kamariotissa.

Asiatic side

Üsküdar; at the landing-stage, the Mihrimah Mosque.

Kuzguncuk, separated from Üsküdar by a low hill.

Beylerbey, with the ★*Beylerbey Sarayı*, the most elegant of the Sultans' palaces on the Bosphorus, built by Abdul Aziz in 1865; worth a visit.

★**First bridge** over the Bosphorus to Ortaköy (clear width 1074m/1175yd), height of piers 165m/540ft).

Past *Çengelköy*, *Kuleli*, *Vanıköy* and **Top Daği** (Cannon Hill; 130m/427ft), famed for its ★view over the whole of the Bosphorus, to *Kandilli*, on the promontory opposite Bebek Bay.

Between Kandilli and Anadolu Hisarı is the beautiful Valley of the *Sweet Waters of Asia*, at the mouth of the Göksu (Heavenly Water).

★**Second bridge over the Bosphorus** (*Fatih Sultan Mehmet Köprüsü; 1090m/1192yd long, 40m/131ft wide).*

Anadolu Hisarı (Anatolian Castle), also called *Güzel Hisar* (Beautiful Castle). The picturesque castle from which the place takes its name was built by Beyazit I in 1395 as an advanced post directed against Constantinople.

Kanlıca, on a small promontory. On the shore is the summer palace of Vizier Köprülü (17th c.), built on piles.

Çubuklu, in *Beykoz Bay*. In Byzantine times there was a monastery of the Akoimetoi (the "Unsleeping Ones") here, in which monks, in successive groups continued in prayer day and night.

European side

Tarabya (*Therapia*), a sizeable township in a little bay, known in antiquity as Pharmakeios (Poisoner, after the poison strewn here by Medsa in her pursuit of Jason). Pleasantly cool in summer owing to the wind blowing in from the Black Sea, Tarabya has numbers of elegant country houses, where some of the European diplomatic missions take up their summer quarters.

Asiatic side

At the head of the bay lies *Paşabahçe*, with beautiful gardens. Near the shore is a Persian-style palace built by Murat III.

Beyond this is **Beykoz**, at the north end of Beykoz Bay.

An hour away to the north is **Yuşa Tepesi** (Joshua's Hill; 195m/640ft), known to Europeans as the *Giant's Grave*, an important landmark for vessels coming from the Black Sea. The road passes behind the palace of Mohammed Ali Paşa along the wooded and well-watered Valley of *Hünkar İskelesi*, once a favoured estate of the Byzantine Emperors and the Sultans. On the summit of the hill is a mosque, with the "Giant's Grave" and a ★view extending over the whole of the Bosphorus (though İstanbul itself is concealed) and part of the Black Sea.

From the little promontory of *Cape Kireç* the Black Sea can be seen in the distance.

Büyükdere, a popular summer resort, with a large park. The bay of Büyükdere (Large Valley) forms the broadest part of the Bosphorus. Inland, 10km/6 miles north-west, is the *Belgrade Forest* (Belgrat Ormanı), with a number of reservoirs.

Sarıyer, at the mouth of the wooded and well-watered Valley of Roses. There is an interesting museum, *Sadberk Koç Hanım Müzesi* (tiles, porcelain, glass, crystal, silver, costumes, jewellery; documents relating to the Sadberk Koç family), in the old Azaryan Yalı. From here a bus or dolmus (communal taxi) can be taken to **Kilyos** (10km/6 miles north), a popular little resort on the Black Sea with a good sandy beach. Then on past the *Dikili* cliffs.

Beyond the conspicuous palace of Mohammed Ali Paşa and the mouth of the Hünkar İskelesi Valley are the promontory of *Selvi Burun* and the little Bay of *Umur Yeri*.

Rumeli Kavağı, the last station on the European side, below a castle built by Murat IV in 1628. On a hill to the north are the ruins of the Byzantine Castle of *İmroz Kalesi*, the walls of which once reached right down to the sea and were linked by a chain with the mole and the walls of Yoroz Kalesi on the Asiatic side (see opposite).

In summer the boats usually go on (5 minutes) to the resort of **Altınkum** (Golden Sand), with a restaurant on the plateau of an old fortification (view).

Anadolu Kavağı, the last station on the Asiatic side, an authentically Turkish village in *Macar Bay*, between two promontories with abandoned forts. On the northern promontory are the picturesque ruins of the Byzantine Castle of *Yoroz Kalesi*, known since the 14th c. as the *Genoese Castle*. In antiquity the promontory and the strait (one of the narrowest points in the Bosphorus) were called *Hieron* (Sacred Place, after the Altar of the Twelve Gods and a Temple of Zeus Ourios, granter of fair winds.

The tourist ships continue to the north end of the Bosphorus (4.7km/3 miles wide) and turn back when they reach the Black Sea. On both sides bare basalt cliffs rise almost vertically from the sea.

European side

Between Rumeli Kavağı and the promontory of *Garipçe Kalesi* is the little Bay of *Büyük Liman.*

Rumeli Feneri (European Lighthouse, at the northern entrance to the Bosphorus, with the village of the same name and an old fortress on the cliffs at the north end of the bay. The dark basalt cliffs to the east are the *Cyanaean Islands* or *Symplegades*, the "clashing rocks" of the Argonaut legend.

Asiatic side

Beyond Macar Bay lies the wide *Keçili Bay*, bounded on the north by the *Fil Burun* promontory.

Anadolu Feneri (Anatolian Lighthouse), on a low cape by the village of the same name, situated on the cliff-fringed coast, with an old fort

Then comes *Kabakos Bay*, with basalt cliffs in which countless sea-birds nest, and the steep-sided promontory of *Yum Burun*, at the northern entrance to the Bosphorus.

Bursa E 3

Marmara region
Province: Bursa. Altitude: 150–250m/490–820ft
Population: 838,000

Situation

The early Ottoman capital of Bursa, formerly called Broussa and known in antiquity as Prusa, lies some miles inland from the Sea of Marmara below the north-west side of Ulu Dağ, the Mysian or Bithynian Olympus, on a limestone terrace cut by two mountain streams, the Gök Dere and the Djilimbos, above a fertile plain traversed by the River Nilüfer. It is roughly 100km/60 miles south of İstanbul as the crow flies.

Towards Asia from the Dolmabahça Palace

The first bridge over the Bosphorus

★★The town

With its beautiful situation, good climate, picturesque old town and magnificent old buildings (mosques and türbes) Bursa is one of the highlights of a visit to Turkey. Its thermal springs, already frequented in Roman times, attract large numbers of visitors.

Characteristics

Bursa, capital of a province and a university town, is one of Turkey's most prosperous cities, thanks not only to the flourishing agriculture of the fertile surrounding country (fruit- and vegetable-growing, particularly peaches and apricots; several canning and preserving factories) but also to its large textile factories centred on an efficient and productive silk-spinning mill. In recent years many metal-working plants have been established.

A significant contribution to the city's economy is also made by the holiday and tourist trade, which is being promoted by the steady modernisation of the baths and treatment facilities in the suburb of Çekirge.

History

The town is said to have been founded by King Prusias I of Bithynia in 186 B.C. The first settlement was on the citadel hill, which was also the site of the Roman town. In the reign of Trajan the baths were rebuilt and a library was established by Pliny the Younger, then Governor of Bithynia. In Byzantine times the prosperity of the town continued to depend mainly on its thermal springs. About A.D. 950, after a number of unsuccessful attacks, Bursa was captured by the Arabs and destroyed. After being recovered by the Emperor Alexius Comnenus it fell into the hands of the Seljuks in 1097, but at the beginning of the Fourth Crusade it was again held by the Byzantines. In

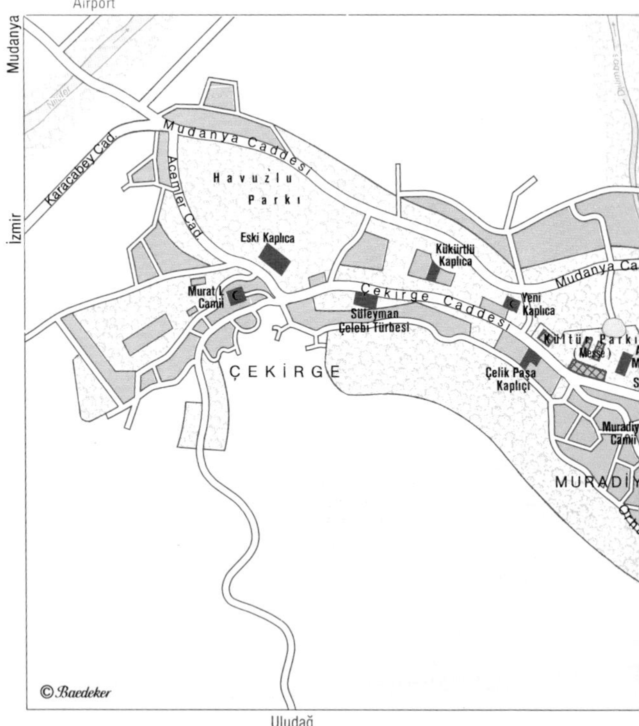

1326 Orsan, son of Osman I (the first Turkish Sultan), took the town, which became the first capital of the Sultans, a status it retained until 1361. Its great heyday was in the 15th c., which has left many monuments of art and architecture. During the 19th c. it suffered destruction by fire and earthquake. In 1920 it was taken by the Greeks but was recovered by the Turks two years later.

Sights

★Great Mosque

The Great Mosque (Ulu Cami) in the city centre was begun in 1379, during the reign of Sultan Murat I, and completed by Beyazit and Mehmet I. It is a typical pillared mosque, very much in the Seljuk tradition.

The entrance, on the north side with its two flanking minarets, leads directly into the main hall, its 20 domes supported on 12 pillars linked by pointed arches. The open central dome and the fountain basin below it give the hall something of the aspect of an inner courtyard. Round the fountain are the raised platforms of which worshippers pray. On the square pillars and the walls are calligraphic inscriptions in the angular Kufic script and the Neshi script. There is a fine cedarwood mimber (pulpit) of about 1400.

Bazaar quarter

The bazaar quarter (Atpazarı), in the city centre, was badly damaged by the 1855 earthquake and a fire in 1957, but has recently been restored. Notable features are the Bedesten (market hall) with its 14 domes, one of the earliest of its kind (*c.* 1400), and several hans (caravanserais).

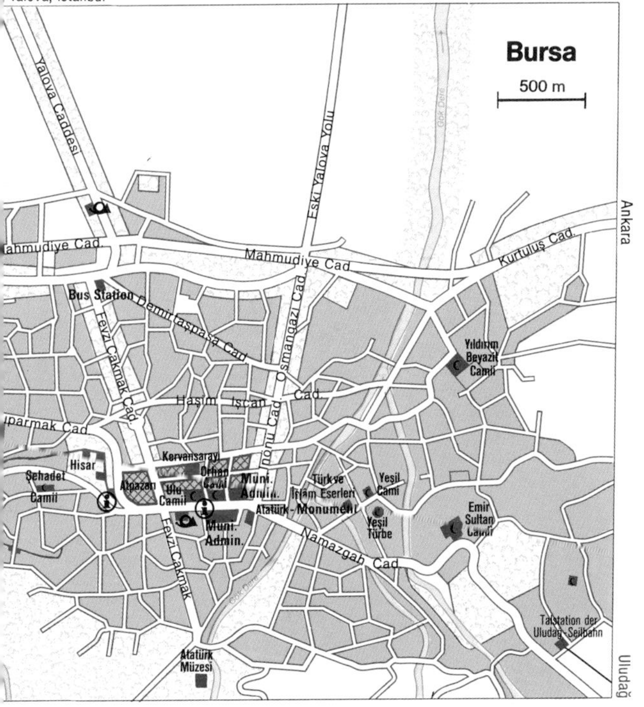

Osman caravanserai Koza Hanı in the bazaar quarter

Citadel

The Citadel (Hisar), to the west of the city centre, is strategically situated on a small plateau which falls steeply away on the north, east and west sides and on the south side is linked with the Ulu Dağ Massif by a lower-lying area with numerous springs. The citadel proper is surrounded by a wall, originally with four gates, which was built in Roman times and several times renovated during the Byzantine and Ottoman periods. Here, too, are the türbes of Sultans Orhan and Osman, which were badly damaged by the 1855 earthquake and rebuilt in the reign of Sultan Abdül Aziz.

★View

On the north side of the capital hill is a terrace (clock-tower) from which there are fine views of the city and surrounding area.

Art Gallery

Bursa's Art Gallery, housed in the Ahmed Vefik Paşa Theatre in Cumhuriyet Meydanı, displays works by numerous artists, most of them little known outside Turkey. There are a number of fine sculptures which have attracted particular attention.

★Green Mosque

It sumptuous decoration makes the Green Mosque (Yeşil Cami), 1km/¾ mile east of the city centre, one of the great master works of Ottoman religious architecture. It was built by Mehmet I between 1419 and 1423 on the site of an earlier Byzantine church. The original minarets, clad with green tiles, were destroyed in an earthquake in 1855, as was the marble vestibule. The doorway with its stalactitic niche, however, is well preserved. There is also a very beautiful marble fountain. The mosque consists of two main halls, one behind the other, and two rooms on each side, all domed. On either side of the entrance to the central hall and beautiful tiled niches, above which are the Sultan's loge and the women's loges, screened by grilles. In the main hall the bases of the walls are covered with the bluish-green tiles from which the mosque gets its name, and above this an inscription round the walls. The mihrab is one of the finest of its kind.

Green Mausoleum

Facing the Green Mosque, rather higher up, is the Green Mausoleum (Yeşil Türbe) of Mehmet I, a domed octagonal building originally clad externally with the green tiles with which parts of the interior walls are still faced. The missing tiles have been replaced by modern reproductions.

On an octagonal base is the Sarcophagus of Mehmet I, with superb tile decoration (floral motifs, calligraphic inscriptions). The beautiful mihrab is in the form of a doorway.

Three of Mehmet's sons are buried beside their father.

★Museum of Turkish and Islamic Art

The Museum of Turkish and Islamic Art, in the Green Medrese (Yeşil Medrese, 1414–24), 1km/¾ mile east of the city centre, was opened in 1974. It offers a comprehensive survey of the art of the Ottoman period: candlesticks, pearl and ivory articles, intarsia work, manuscripts, decorated book-covers, screens, sections of beautifully decorated wooden ceilings, weapons, copper ware, tiles from İznik and Kütahya, embroidery, ornaments, fine textiles, beautifully wrought articles from tekkes (dervish convents), calligraphy, tombstones.

Yıldırım Beyazit Mosque

The Yıldırım Beyazit Mosque, 2km/1¼ miles north-east of the city centre, was built by Sultan Beyazit I about 1400. It was badly damaged in the 1855 earthquake, and the interior, which is notable for its beautiful marble decoration, was considerably altered in the subsequent restoration. The vestibule has been preserved, however, in its original Early Ottoman form.

The Türbe of Beyazit I and the medrese have recently been restored. There were originally also an imaret (public kitchen) and a hamam associated with the mosque.

Atatürk Museum

On the south side of the town is the trim late 19th c. house in which the "Father of modern Turkey" stayed during his 13 visits to Bursa between 1923 and 1938. It contains furniture and personal effect belonging to Atatürk and a variety of documentation on his life.

Interior of the türbe of Murat I

Exterior of the türbe of Mehmet I

★Mosque of Murat II

The Mosque of Murat II (Muradiye Camii), 1.5km/1 mile west of the city centre, was built by Sultan Murat II in 1447, after Bursa had ceased to be the capital of the Ottoman Empire. A forecourt with cypresses and a beautiful fountain leads into an outer hall with four windows and a doorway, beyond which is an inner hall, its ceiling clad with rare and beautiful tiles.

Türbes

In the gardens of the mosque are ten polygonal domed türbes, their entrances sheltered under overhanging roofs, belonging to Murat II and members of his family. Of particular interest for their architecture and their tiled facing are the Mausoleum of Murat II (with a dome open in the middle so that, in accordance with the Sultan's wish, the rain from heaven should water his grave), the Tomb of Musa, son of Beyazit I (green wall tiles), the Türbe of Šehzade Mustafa (16th c. Persian tiles), the Türbe of Çem Beyazit II's brother (greenish-blue tiles), and the Türbe of Mahmut.

Archaeological Museum

The Archaeological Museum, originally housed in the Green Medrese, moved in 1972 to a new building in the Çekirge Park of Culture. The new museum has four exhibition halls, storerooms, a library and a laboratory.

★Baths (Çekirge)

In the western suburb of Çekirge are some of the most celebrated sulphurous and chalybeate thermal springs and baths in the East. Known in antiquity as the "royal" springs, they were undoubtedly in use before the Roman Imperial period, but both the Romans and the Byzantine buildings, which were visited by the Empress Theodora among others, have almost completely disappeared. The Old Bath (Eski Kaplıca) was built by Sultan Murat I, using the remains of an earlier building. Close by is his first mosque, Gazi Hunkiar Camii (1365), on a cruciform plan. On the terrace of the mosque is the Türbe of Murat I, who was murdered in 1389 after the Battle of Kosovo in Serbia.

The New Bath (Yeni Kaplıca), a master work of architecture with beautiful marble and tile decoration, was built by Grand Vizier Rüsten Paşa in the 16th c.

Other well-known baths are the Kara Mustafa Paşa Kaplıca (radioactive water) and the Armutlu Kaplıca (treatment of gynaecological conditions).

Almost all the larger hotels have piped thermal water.

Surroundings of Bursa

★Ulu Dağ (Mysian or Bithynian Olympus)

Cableway from Bursa to north-west plateau (1700m/5600ft). Scenic road (buses) to Büyük Ulu Dağ Oteli

The Ulu Dağ massif (highest point 2543m/8344ft), 17km/11 miles south of Bursa, is the most popular and best-equipped winter-sports area in Turkey and also, with its forests and Alpine meadows, an excellent holiday area for those seeking rest and relaxation.

The massif consists mainly of granites and gneisses, with some metamorphic rocks higher up, and shows signs of glacial action (corries, etc.). It has preserved a very varied flora and fauna.

Ulu Dağ offers numerous viewpoints (many reached only by a strenuous walk) from which in good weather the prospect extends to İstanbul and the Bosphorus or to the Black Sea.

Çanakkale B 3

Marmara region (Dardanelles)
Province: Çanakkale. Altitude: 0–5m/0–15ft. Population: 54,000

Situation and importance

The principal place on the Dardanelles (Çanakkale Boğazı) is the town of Çanakkale, situated at the narrowest point (1244m/1360yd) of this busy strait, the administrative centre of the province of Çanakkale, which broadly corresponds to the ancient Troad. It is the starting-point of a visit to Troy (see entry) and also to the scene of the fighting during the Dardanelles

Campaign of 1915 (see Dardanelles). Regular excursions to the battlefields and military cemeteries on the Gallipoli Peninsula are organised by the Troyanzac tourist agency (Yalı Cad. 2, by the clock-tower).

The town

Çanakkale (Pottery Castle), so called after the ceramics industry which formerly flourished here, is a relatively recent town with few buildings of any interest, particularly since an earthquake which caused heavy damage in 1912.

Ferry harbour

On the west side of the fairly cramped central area of the town is the harbour, from which there is a ferry service across the Dardanelles to Eceabat on the European side.

Sultaniye Kale

The fortress of Sultaniye Kale (Sultan's Castle; 1454) on the shores of the strait is the counterpart to the Fortress of Kilitbahir (Key of the Sea; built 1462–63, with three massive round towers) on the European side. Between them the two forts controlled the narrowest point on the Dardanelles.

Military Museum

The Sultaniye Kale now houses a Military Museum maintained by the Turkish Navy. In addition to guns and other military equipment it has an interesting collection of material concerning the battle for the Dardanelles in 1915. Here, too, is the minelayer "Nusrat", which mounted the successful attack leading finally to the Allied withdrawal.

Archaeological Museum

On the outskirts of the town, on the road to Troy and Edremit, is Çanakkale's new Archaeological Museum, with Hellenistic and Roman material and the rich grave-goods found in the Tumulus of Dardanos, 10km/6 miles south-west.

Surroundings of Çanakkale

★★Troy

See entry

Nara

8km/5 miles north of Çanakkale is Nara, on Nara Burun, which is believed to occupy the site of ancient Nagara. The cape is at the second narrowest point (1450m/1590yd) on the Dardanelles, which here turn south. In ancient times, when this was the narrowest part of the Dardanelles, some 1300m/1420yd wide, it was known as the Heptastadion (Seven Stadia) and was crossed by a ferry. It was here that Xerxes, Alexander the Great and the Turks (1356) crossed the straits into Europe.

Abydos

On a hill to the east was the ancient city of Abydos, which Homer tells us belonged to a Trojan prince named Asios. Later a colony of Miletus, it is best known as the place where Xerxes reviewed his troops and constructed his bridge of boats over the Hellespont in 480 B.C. in his expedition against Greece.

Hero and Leander

Abydos and Sestos, on the opposite side of the strait, are associated with the story of Hero and Leander, which was recounted by the Greek poet Musaeus (Mousaios; end of 6th c. A.D.?). The handsome youth Leander lived in Abydos and Hero was a priestess in the Temple of Aphrodite in Sestos. Meeting at a Festival of Aphrodite, they fell in love, and thereafter Leander swam across the Hellespont every night to be with his loved one, who lit a beacon on a tower to show him the way. One dark night, however, the beacon was extinguished by a storm and Leander was drowned. When his body was washed ashore on the following morning Hero cast herself into the sea to be united with her lover in death.

In early May 1810 Byron repeated Leander's feat in swimming from Abydos to Sestos in about 70 minutes, as he boasts in "Don Juan".

Lâpseki

40km/25 miles north-east of Çanakkale on the east side of the Dardanelles, near the entrance to the Sea of Marmara, lies the ancient little port of

Baedeker Special

Damn the Dardanelles! They will be our graveyard yet!

At dawn on April 25th 1915 50,000 Allied troops landed on seven sections of beach on the Gallipoli Peninsula (now known as Gelibolu). So far everything was going according to plan. There was no enemy resistance – apparently. But then the Turks prepared their welcome. At Cape Helles, in the south of the peninsula, they waited until the ships had almost reached land; then their bullets whistled across the water with telling accuracy, and the sea became red with blood. British troops who were clambering ashore in another bay were also met by a deadly hail of bullets. And the Turkish counter-attack, led by Colonel Mustafa Kemal, in the northern section of the landings, was as frenzied as a dervish dance, and the Allies were repelled with heavy losses.

In the end the Allies did succeed in landing. However, the real aim of this campaign, namely, to conquer the Dardanelles and then to take İstanbul, was foiled.

If the Allied attack had been carried out earlier, at the end of 1914 or the beginning of 1915, it would undoubtedly have been successful, for at that time the Turkish defences were very piecemeal indeed. It had long been recognised that control of the strait was of the utmost importance. However, as Turkey enjoyed a neutral status at that time little regard was paid to this. Then, however, the situation changed. Ever since the war began there had been indications that, if it did decide to join in, Turkey would be on the side of the Central Powers of Germany and Austria-Hungary.

German influence on the Turkish army was considerable, and very soon it was being re-organised under the leadership of the German General Otto Liman von Sanders. Their War Minister Enver Pasha showed himself to be a firm friend of the Germans, and ever-stronger economic ties bound the two nations together. However, the war was the last thing Turkey really wanted, having been seriously weakened by a series of earlier short conflicts. Now, as Great Britain – who for hundreds of years had intervened to prevent Russia from pushing through the Bosphorus and the Dardenelles to the Mediterranean – entered into an alliance with the Czar, Turkey was obliged to take sides. Seeking a new ally who would defend the strait, it provided the German cruisers "Goeben" and "Breslau" with shelter from the pursuing British ships. And that was not all! On October 28th 1914 these two ships, under Turkish command, attacked Russian ports on the Black Sea – without war having been declared. They did not have to wait long for retaliation; on November 5th Great Britain, France and Russia declared war on the Ottoman Empire. Gradually the Allies formulated a plan to attack Turkey. The aim was to provide Russia with assistance against the ever threatening pincer movements by Turkey, to encourage the neutral states to enter the war against the Central Powers, and to fight their way through to the Sea of Mármara and İstanbul.

In fact the Allies were also seeking a way to free the deadlock which was now prevailing on the Western Front; a military operation in the Mediterranean, where the Western Powers held sway, seemed to be called for. The idea behind this was that instead of waging war on the Western Front, with inevitable enormous losses, it could be won by following the maxim that "a chain is only as strong as its weakest link".

Baedeker Special

On February 19th 1915 the marine bombardment of the outermost ring of the Turkish defences began. Between February 26th and March 12th the central defence installations of Gallipoli were bombarded by British and French ships. After that there was little to fear from the Turkish batteries. On March 18th an Anglo-French naval squadron attacked the strait. After some initial resistance Turkish defence became weaker and weaker and the Allies appeared certain of victory. But then the unforeseeable happened. The French warship "Bouvet" which was leading the squadron suddenly exploded and sank with almost all its crew of 600 men. Other explosions soon followed; six of the total of nine Allied ships either sank or were put out of action. The Allied command, shocked by the enormous losses, called off the battle. This proved to be a fatal error of judgement, as the mine barrier laid by the Turks had also been detonated as a result of the explosion and İstanbul was in fact there for the taking.

Instead, the Allies planned a new attack on the Dardanelles – this time employing British, Australian, New Zealand and French troops. However, they took an unnecessarily long time over their preparations, and Liman von Sanders, with the consent of Enver Pasha granted on March 25th, was able to complete the Turkish defences and to bring in reinforcements. By April 25th all was ready.

At 5am the 29th (British) Division, led by Sir Ian Hamilton, landed in five small bays at the southern end of the Gallipoli Peninsula. The ANZACS (Australian and New Zealand Army Corps) were in position 15km/9½ miles north, near Kabatepe, on the west side of the peninsula; and the French landed temporarily near Kum Burum, on the Asiatic side of of the strait. However, the attack failed to have the required effect. For one thing, the Allied troops met with bitter Turkish resistance; above all, Colonel Mustafa Kemal, later known as the Atatürk, made a name for himself with his historical order "I do not order you to attack; I order you to die" (moreover, he only survived the Battle of Anafarta because a bullet richoteted off the watch in his breast pocket). Furthermore, some of the Allied troops who – as a result of a lack of orders or co-ordinated plans – failed to make contact with the enemy, spent the day sitting on the cliffs and "enjoying the view". The struggles lasted several days; as on the Western front, it became a matter of fierce and prolonged fighting simply to gain a few yards, with heavy casualties on both sides.

In London, opposition to the campaign grew by the day. Winston Churchill, who had been mainly responsible for the military operation, was obliged to resign. In August 1915 the Allies tried once more to gain the initiative by trying to land in Suvia Bay, 5km/3 miles north of the spot where the ANZACS had set foot on Turkish soil in the previous April. However, this attempt resulted in more trench warfare. By the end of the year an Allied evacuation became inevitable, partly because the Central Powers had recaptured the Berlin–Baghdad Railway and could provide their Turkish allies with reinforcements. Surprisingly, the retreat was accomplished without incident. Each side had suffered losses of a quarter of a million dead and wounded. Admiral Fisher's prophecy (see the heading above) in a letter of April 5th to Winston Churchill was thus fulfilled, but the Allies were able to learn lessons from the "Gallipoli catastrophe" which served them well in the Second World War.

Lâpseki, situated in the kuşova (Bird Plain) amid vineyards and olive groves. From here there is a ferry (cars carried) to Gelibolu on the Gallipoli Peninsula, on the European side.

Lampsakos

Lâpseki, occupies the site of ancient Lampsakos, where Aphrodite was said to have given birth to Priapos; and Lampsakos accordingly was the chief centre of the cult of Priapos. When the Phocaeans established a settlement here the place was known at Pityoussa, and according to Strabo was an important town with a good harbour. About 460 the Persian King Artaxerxes I presented the town to the Athenian General Themistokles in return for a supply of wine. In 482 B.C. the philospher Anaxagoras of Klazomenai (b. *c.* 500 B.C.) died in exile here. Lampsakos was also the birthplace of the 4th c. rhetor and historian Anaximenes, who accompanied Alexander the Great on his expedition and was able to save his native town from destruction when Alexander's army passed that way.

In Early christian times the town was the see of a bishop, and it was still a commercial town of some importance in the medieval period. In 1190 it was the starting-point of the arduous march of the Crusading army of the Emperor Frederick I Barbarossa.

Dardanelles — B 3

Straits between the Sea of Marmara and the Aegean
Length: 61km/38 miles
Width: 1.2–7.5km/¾–4¾ miles
Depth: 54–103m/117–338ft

Name and situation
★Scenery

The Dardanelles (the Hellespont of antiquity; in Turkish Çanakkale-Boğazi) take their name from the ancient Greek city of Dardanos. Situated about 10km/6 miles south-west of Çanakkale they are the straits between the peninsula of Gelibolu (Gallipoli) on the European side and the mainland of Asia Minor. The straits provide a link between the Aegean (and Mediterranean) and the Sea of Marmara (see entry) and also, by way of the Bosphorus (see entry), with the Black Sea.

Ferries

There are ferry services (cars carried) across the Dardanelles between Gelibolu and Lâpseki and between Çanakkale and Eceabat. Roads follow the coast on both sides.

Physical geography

The Dardanelles are a former river valley which was drowned as a result of the sinking of the land during the Pleistocene period. The Sea of Marmara came into being at the same time. Clearly visible raised beaches are evidence of temporary rises in sea-level at various times in the past.

During the warmer weather of the inter-Glacial phases the sea was swollen by water from the melting glaciers and rose above its present level, leaving its mark in the form of abrasions and deposits of gravel.

The surplus of water from the Black Sea flows through the Bosphorus and the Sea of Marmara into the Dardanelles and thence into the Mediterranean. The difference in density between the water of the Black Sea and the Mediterranean resulting from the inflow of great quantities of fresh water into the Black Sea has the effect of producing a strong surface current flowing at a rate of up to 8.3km/5¼ miles an hour from the Sea of Marmara into the Aegean – which makes it difficult for small vessels to enter the Dardanelles. This applies particularly when the so-called Dardanelles Wind is blowing from the east-north-east – while at the same time heavier water with a high salt content is flowing back along the bottom into the Sea of Marmara at a slower rate.

The hills of Tertiary limestone and marls which rise to heights of 250–375m/820–1230ft along the shore of the Dardanelles have a certain amount of tree cover. The mild and rainy winter climate favours the growing of olives, which constitute the main source of income for the rural population.

The Dardenelles, the strait between Europe and Asia

History

These straits between Europe and Asia have been an important waterway from time immemorial. The excavations at Troy have shown that the Hellespont area (the "sea-coast of Helle", the mythical daughter of Athamas, who fell into the sea here when fleeing from her stepmother) was already settled by man about 3000 B.C. In the 13th c. B.C. the territory was conquered by Achaeans from Greece. The siege of Troy described in the "Iliad" probably took place during this period.

In a second wave of immigration the area was occupied by Ionian Greeks.

In 480 B.C. Xerxes' Persian army crossed the straits on a bridge of boats, but only a year later, after the Greek naval victory at Mykale, the Hellespont fell to the Athenians. During the Peloponnesian War the Spartans sought to gain control of the straits. In 334 B.C. they were crossed by Alexander the Great.

The Byzantines, for whom free access to the Aegean was vital, fortified both sides of the Hellespont. Thereafter Arab fleets managed on three occasions (in 668, 672 and 717) to force a passage into the Sea of Marmara. On Easter Day in 1190 the Emperor Frederick I Barbarossa crossed the Dardanelles with his Crusading army.

During the Middle Ages it was the Venetians and Genoese who were principally concerned to maintain freedom of passage through the straits.

In 1356 the Dardanelles fell into the hands of the Ottomans, and Constantinople was thus cut off from the Mediterranean. In 1462 Sultan Mehmet II built two castles at the narrowest point of the straits (1244m/1360yd), Kilitbahir (Key of the Sea) on the European side and Sultaniye Kale (Sultan's Castle) at Çanakkale on the Asiatic side. In 1499, and again in 1657, the Venetians defeated the Turkish fleet at the entrance to the Dardanelles. The Venetians were mainly concerned to secure unrestricted access to the Black Sea, where the Genoese had hitherto enjoyed an almost complete monopoly of trade. Only after the Turkish fleet had inflicted a decisive defeat on the Venetians in 1694 did Venice abandon her attacks.

In 1699 Peter the Great demanded free passage for Russian ships. In 1770 the Russian fleet tried, without success, to push into the Dardanelles. Later it defeated the Turkish fleet at Çesme; and under the Treaty of Küçük Kainarce (1774) Russia secured free passage for its merchant ships. In 1807 a British squadron sailed through the straits to Constantinople; but under a treaty of 1809 between Russia and Britain, confirmed by the Dardanelles Treaty signed by the five Great Powers in 1841 and by the Peace of Paris in 1856, all non-Turkish warships were prohibited from passing through the straits. During the Crimean War (1853–56) British and French warships made their way into the Black Sea. In 1892 and 1893, under British pressure, the Turkish fortifications on the Dardanelles were considerably strengthened.

Didyma C 6

West coast (Aegean Sea)
Province: Aydın
Altitude: 52m/170ft
Place: Didim (Yeni Hisar)

Situation of the ★★ruins

The site of Didyma, once the greatest Greek oracular sanctuary in Asia Minor, with the ruins of a mighty Temple of Apollo, lies some 170km/105 miles south of İzmir in ancient Caria. It is situated on the Miletus Peninsula 4km/2½ miles from the Aegean coast.

Didyma is linked with Miletus, 20km/12 miles north, by a Sacred Way, still partly traceable, which according to an inscription on the last milestone was built in A.D. 101, in the reign of Trajan. 16km/10 miles long and 5–7m/16–23ft wide, it ran past the ancient pilgrim port of Panormos (now Kovela Burun) to the sanctuary 2km/1¼ miles farther on. The last section, which has been excavated, was lined with Archaic seated figures and recumbent lions (remains in the British Museum) and with later tombs.

Within the area of the site is the village of Yeni Hisar (New Castle), which was partly abandoned after the Greek withdrawal in 1923. The remaining inhabitants were later moved to Altınkum in order to leave the site clear for large-scale excavation.

7km/4½ miles south-west of Didyma, at the tip of the picturesque Miletus Peninsula, is Tekağaç Burun, a cape known in antiquity as Poseidonion.

Myth and history

Even before the coming of the Greeks and the foundation of Miletus there was a Carian oracular shrine here under the name of Didyma. The Ionians who settled in this area in the 10th c. B.C. dedicated the shrine to Apollo Philesios, and thereafter the oracle enjoyed great prestige, even rivalling Delphi. The last King of Lydia, Kroisos (Croesus), consulted it and made rich offerings to the shrine, as did the Egyptian Pharaoh Necho.

The original sanctuary was destroyed in 494 B.C. by Darius' Persians after members of the local priestly family, the Branchids (after whom the temple was also called Branchida), had surrendered the cult image and the temple treasure to the Persians. Only a few fragments of masonry from the first temple have been found.

After Alexander the Great's victory over the Persians the temple, the Didymaion, was rebuilt on a considerably larger scale. It was begun about 300 B.C. by Paionios of Ephesus and Daphnes of Miletus after the completion of the Temple of Artemis in Ephesus. The new temple was planned on such a grandiose scale, however, that in spite of financial support from the Roman emperors and other sources it was never finished. By 280 B.C. the shell of the building was completed, but Strabo tells us that because of its size it was never roofed.

In thanksgiving for a favourable oracular pronouncement in 312 B.C. Seleukos I Nikator caused the statue of Apollo, which had been stolen and carried off to Persia, to be returned to the temple. From 290 B.C. games were held at Didyma, and from an early period it enjoyed the right of sanctuary.

In the Early Byzantine period the temple, still perfectly preserved, was converted into a Christian basilica, with a holy well. Later, after the building had suffered severe damage in a fire, a fortress was constructed in the ruins. The destruction of the temple was completed by another fire and a severe earthquake in 1446. During the 15th c. it was used to provide makeshift accommodation for harvest workers from Samos.

The excavation of the site was begun by British archaeologists in 1858 and continued on a larger scale by French expeditions in 1872 and 1895–96. Further work has been done since 1962; in 1985 a sacred area (Temeros) was uncovered.

★★Temple of Apollo (Didymaion)

Layout

The huge Temple of Apollo or Didymaion (well excavated and partly restored), was oriented from north-east to south-west and was originally surrounded by a sacred grove. At the north-east end was a semicircular terrace (partly built up) dating from the Archaic period, on which were a portico, other buildings and various votive gifts. Four flights of steps 2.50m/8 ft wide led down to the cella of the temple.

Outside the north-east end of the temple is the main altar, which was similar to the one at Olympia in the Peloponnese. Within a low parapet was a conical structure built up from ashes mixed with the blood of sacrificial animals. To the north of the altar are bases for votive statues and a well of the Hellenistic period.

Along the south-east side of the temple, 15m/50ft away, were seven tiers of seating for spectators at the games.

Temple buildings

The temple itself was 108.5m/356ft long by almost 50m/165ft across. It stood on a seven-stepped base, with five additional steps at the north-east end, the main front. It was of the type technically known as dipteral decastyle, surrounded by a double row of columns, with 10 at each end and 21 along the sides. Three of the columns at the ends, 19.40m/64ft high, are still standing. The unusual bases, dating from the time of Caligula (A.D. 37–41), are in similar pairs. The corner columns on the east front had figural capitals of the 2nd c. A.D., each

Head of Medusa

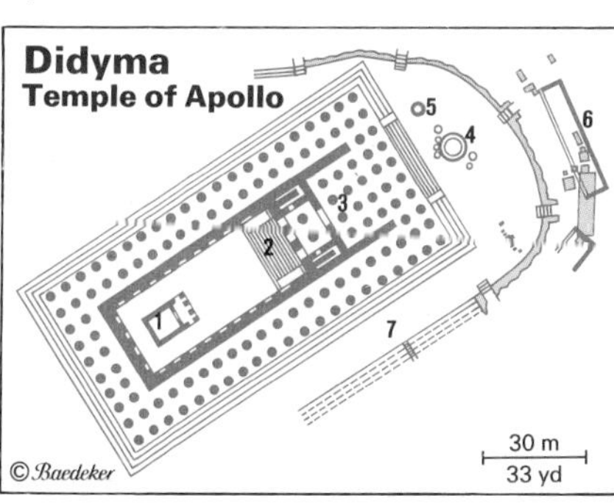

Didymaion
in the Hellenistic period

1 Sacred spring
2 Steps down to cella
3 Pronaos forecourt
4 Main altar
5 Well
6 Stoa
7 Tiers of seating

with two bulls' heads, a bust of a god and a griffin. The frieze had an alternation of foliage ornament and Medusa heads.

Pronaos (forecourt)

The temple consisted of a pronaos or forecourt, a small antechamber and the cella or main chamber. In the pronaos, the walls of which still stand 11m/36ft high, were four rows of three columns. Including the double row of columns of the portico, therefore, the entrance to the temple had four rows of five columns.

From the pronaos, which had a magnificent coffered ceiling, the cella was reached either through two small doors flanking the main doorway and then down two vaulted tunnels, or through the main doorway (8m/26ft wide) and a small antechamber on a slightly higher level. This antechamber was the chresmographeion, in which the priests revealed and interpreted the pronouncements of the oracle. The ceiling of this room was borne on two Ionic columns (making the total number of columns in the temple 122).

Cella

From the antechamber three doors opened on to a flight of steps 16m/52ft wide leading into the cella 5.5m/18ft lower down, which was roofless. Round the walls were pilasters with griffin capitals; originally of the same height as the columns on the outside of the temple; the pilasters have been re-erected to a height of 6m/20ft. In the cella were the sacred spring, at which the priestess put questions to the oracle, and a sacred olive tree. On the end wall, in a special room, was the cult statue of Apollo.

Surrounding the temple were gymnasia, baths and hostels for pilgrims. Further excavation is required to determine their nature.

★View

From the site there are magnificent views, extending northward to Karakuyu Bay, in which lay the Milesian port of Teichioussa, eastwards to the hills of Caria and southward to the Bodrum Peninsula and the Greek island of Kos.

Surroundings of Didyma

Didim Plaji

This lively resort with numerous hotels, guest houses and apartment blocks lies about 4km/2½ miles to the south. More holiday accommodation can be found further to the east in the Akbük Limani Bay.

Edirne B 2

Thrace
Province: Edirne
Altitude: 49m/160ft
Population: 102,000

Situation and ★Importance

Once known as Adrianopolis, Edirne, capital of its province, is situated 245km/152 miles north-west of İstanbul at the confluence of the Tunca and Arda with the Meriç (Maritza). It is the second largest city in European Turkey, benefiting from its position as a major road and rail junction close to the Greek and Bulgarian frontiers. It is surrounded by fertile farming country and has recently emerged as an increasingly prosperous industrial town (textiles, leather goods, staple and luxury foods, perfume).

With its endowment of mosques, including the magnificent Selimiye Camii, its caravanserais, low timber houses and narrow alleyways, this historic Thracian border town still retains its Old Turkish air.

History

Edirne was founded around A.D. 125 by the Roman emperor Hadrian (hence Hadrianopolis/Adrianopolis), afterwards being continually fought over on account of its strategic position. From the time of its capture by the Turkish Sultan Murat I, to the fall of Constantinople in 1453, Edirne was the seat of

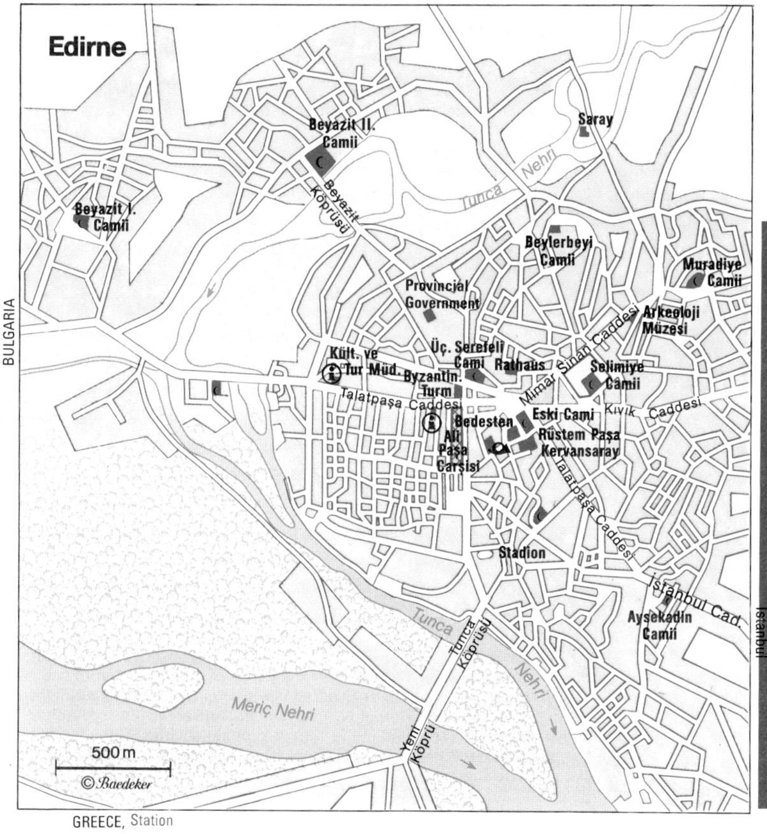

the Turkish rulers. At the end of the 19th c. it became a frontier stronghold and played an important role during the Balkan Wars. In 1989 hundreds of thousands of Bulgarian Turks, fleeing across the Turkish-Bulgarian border, settled in the Edirne-İstanbul area.

Sights

Ali Paşa Çarşısı

This covered bazaar in the Saraçılar Caddesi was built by the famous architect Sinan for Hersekli Ali Paşa, one of Süleiman the Magnificent's viziers. It is constructed on the traditional pattern: a roofed-over street, with rows of shops running parallel, and entrances at the front and sides.

Arkeoloji Müzesi

The archaeological museum, originally housed in the Selimiye Camii medrese but since 1971 in a modern building, has collections of pottery, bronze-work, Thracian capitals (8th c. B.C.), glass, and coins from a number of periods. The ethnographic section includes a variety of textiles, rose-water bottles, sewing boxes, cutlery, writing materials, weapons (some with especially fine inlay) and kitchen utensils. Also on display are Anatolian carpets, prayer rugs from Gördes, Bergama and Kırşehir, and kilims, including Sarkoy and Turkmen kilims.

Bedesten

Now in less exalted use as an antique emporium, the old bedesten in the city centre was built by the Sultan Mehmet I. Fourteen small cupolas adorn the roof of the two-aisle, pillared hall and cluster of little shops.

Bayazit I Camii

The 14th c. Bayazit I Camii stands in what is now the suburb of Yıldırım on the western edge of the town. It is built in the early Bursa style, laid out in the shape of an inverted "T". A relatively narrow corridor, with domed chambers either side, leads from a narthex-like portico to the domed central space, square in plan, from which barrel-vaulted rooms radiate in the manner of a church.

★Bayazit II Camii

Also situated well outside the centre, on the north-west edge of the town, is a mosque considered one of the finest to be built by the great Ottoman architect Hayrettin. The Bayazit II Camii and the other buildings in the complex were erected between 1484 and 1488, loosely modelled on the Sultan Mehmet Fâtih Külliye in İstanbul. The mosque itself has a tall central dome, its loftiness accentuated by the modest height of the nine-domed tabhanes either side and the low porch. The lovely interior is further enhanced by the effect of light from the four-tier arrangement of the windows.

Adjacent to the mosque on its south-west side stands a complex of three buildings, the first being a hospital, hexagonal in plan, with a central dome. This is linked by a hall and courtyard to a medrese, the latter entirely classical in conception. North-east of the mosque are two domestic blocks comprising a kitchen for the poor and bakery with storerooms.

Rüstem Paşa Kervanserayı

The Rüstem Paşa Caravanserai in the south-east corner of the city centre was built by the great Sinan for Rüstem Paşa, Grand Vizier to Süleiman the Magnificent. Completed around 1560 the imposing rectangular, two-storeyed building, with its large inner courtyard and hamam, was restored some years ago and is now a hotel.

Saray

The turmoil of the 1878 Turko-Russian War left this once magnificent sultan's palace and fortifications on the banks of the Tunca almost completely destroyed, apart from a few fragmentary remains. The first building to occupy the site was a Roman fortress constructed at the time of Hadrian. A pavilion was then erected in the 15th c., probably by the Sultan Murat II. His son, Mehmet II Fâtih, added further buildings until a complete palace precinct took shape.

★★Selimiye Camii

The Selimiye Camii, on a hill on the east side of the Old City, was commissioned by the Sultan Selim II and built between 1567 and 1574. It is among the most beautiful buildings of its kind, designed by the great architect Sinan (see Famous People) late in his career when at the pinnacle of his powers. The lesser elements of the complex (arasta, medrese, Koranic school and timekeepers' room) seem to strive upwards towards the mosque itself with its four minarets, each of which has three balconies. The 45m/148ft-high dome, 31.3m/102ft in diameter, rests on a circle of eight enormous marble and granite pillars linked by arches.

The interior of the mosque is magnificent. Granite, porphyry and marble columns support the galleries while the subtle play of light from the skilfully positioned windows creates extraordinary effects as it falls on the stalactitic vaulting and tiled panels. Fine marble plaques, exquisite tiling, gilt calligraphic decoration and generally rich ornamentation add to the splendour of the mihrab, mimber and royal loge in particular. Even the location of the muezzin's tribune is unusual. Raised on twelve small pillars it is placed centrally beneath the dome, enclosing an attractive fountain.

Museum of Turkish and Islamic Art

In 1925 the first Museum of Turkish and Islamic Art was established in the former medrese of the Selimiye Camii. The exhibition comprises Ottoman inscriptions, Koranic manuscripts, tiles, embroidery, glass and weapons. A

Selimiye Camii, masterpiece of the famous architect Sinan

magnificent satin tent in which the Ottoman viziers conducted state affairs has been erected in the main hall. Side rooms contain antique furnishings and household items, also medallions, calligraphy and goblets. In the garden are a number of tombs (15th c. onwards) including that of Siddi Şah Sultan, the wife of Sultan Mehmet the Conqueror.

★Üç Serefeli Cami

The "Three Galleried Mosque" on Cumhuriyet Meydanı takes its name from the three (Turkish "uç") galleries (Turkish "şerefe") of its tall south minaret. Founded by Murat II, the 15th c. mosque is transitional from an architectural point of view between the Bursa and later Classical styles.

It is rectangular in plan, crowned by a vast vaulted central dome on a hexagonal base augmented by four large and three smaller cupolas. The Üç Şerefeli was the first mosque to have an inner courtyard the arcades of which were domed.

The four minarets at the corners of the inner court are all different in design. The tallest, to the south, has three galleries. The "baklavalı minare" (Rhomboid Minaret) has two galleries. The others, one of which is known as the "burmalı minare" (Spiral Minaret), have just one gallery.

Surroundings

Kırklareli

About 60km/37 miles east of Edirne lies the provincial town of Kırklareli (pop. 45,000), tucked away at the south-west foot of the Yıldız Dağları (İstranca uplands; about 1000m/3280ft). As well as sunflowers grown for their seeds, livestock are reared in the steppe-like countryside around. In the Byzantine era the town, presumably Roman in origin, achieved a modest degree of prosperity, to which its many Christian churches testify. When the Turks captured the town in 1363 they called it Kırk Kilise (Town of 40 Churches), from which the present name derives.

The Bayazıt Paşa Camii in the Hatice Hatun district was built by the town's governor Güllâbi Ahmet Paşa at the end of the 16th c. His tomb is found in the mosque garden. The much-restored Büyük Hızır Bey Cami, commissioned by Kösenihalzade Hızır Bey for his son Abdullah Bey and built in 1383, is the oldest mosque in Thrace. Opposite the Ahmet Midhat primary school (İlkokul) stands the Kadi Camii, endowed by Emin Ali Çelebi in 1577.

Several villages in the vicinity of Kırklareli contain rather unusual domed tombs. Examples can be seen in the ancient cemeteries (2nd–4th c. B.C.) near Eriklice, 3km/2 miles north-west of Kırklareli, and at Çadırahlar Tepesi, 3km/2 miles south-east.

Lüleburgaz

The centre of Lüleburgaz (ancient Arcadiopolis), a town in the Karaağaç Deresi, about 60km/37 miles south-east of Edirne, on the İstanbul road, is graced by the Sokullu Mehmet Paşa Külliyesi, endowed by Sokullu Mehmet Paşa in 1549 and constructed by the Ottoman master builder Sinan. In addition to a mosque the complex comprises a medrese, baths (Çifte Hamam), library and caravanserai (Mimar Sinan Kervansarayı; now just remains). The garden of the mosque contains the 14th c. mausoleum of Zindan Babas, standard bearer to Gazi Evrenos Bey. The name Lüleburgaz derives from the Turkish word "lule" meaning pipe-bowl, for the manufacture of which the town is famous.

Edremit Körfezi B 4

North-east Aegean
Province: Balıkesir
Length (W–E): 50km/31 miles
Width (N–S): 25km/15½ miles

Situation and Characteristics

The southern part of the Troas, in the guise of the Kaz Dağı massif (the ancient Mt Ida; Kırkler Tepesi 1774m/5822ft fringes the Gulf of Edremit to the south. Towering wall-like above its north shore, the mountains act as a barrier, preventing influxes of cold northern air.

Sheltered to the south-east by the Madra Dağı (1338m/4391ft) and to the west by the Greek island of Lesbos (Turkish Midilli), the Gulf, named after Edremit, the principal town, enjoys higher spring temperatures and lower rainfall than the windswept Troas, temperatures in summer being every bit as hot. This favourable climate, together with more than 100km/62 miles of equally fine coastline, combine to make the Gulf one of the premier tourist areas in Turkey. Today its character is dominated by the resorts strung like beads along its shores, the main centres being Altınoluk, Edremit–Akçay, Burhaniye–Ören and Ayvalık–Sarmısaklı. Countless hotels of every category cater for holidymakers from the cities of the Anatolian hinterland – Ankara, Eskişehir, Konya.

Sights

★Akçay

Akçay is an offshoot of Edremit, about 12km/7½ miles further west. It is one of the most popular resorts, recently attracting an increasing number of European holidaymakers. On its west side, beyond the thermal baths (ruins of a Roman bath) are the rather scant remains of ancient Astyra in the Troas, a colony of ancient Adramittium (Edremit) with a Temple of Artemis Astyrene. Akçay's natural springs (Artemis Sofbanları) offer treatment for gynaecological and other complaints.

Altınoluk

About 26km/16 miles west of Edremit, near Altınoluk, are the sites of two more ancient settlements, Gargara at the resort itself and, 215m/700ft above it, the overgrown ruins of Antandros. It was here on Mt Alexandreia (Kaz Dağı/Mt Ida) that Paris, a shepherd on Mount Ida, son of Priam, King of Troy, was judge in the beauty contest between the goddesses Athene, Aphrodite and Hera. Although its origin remains uncertain, the town was probably founded by the Pelasgi. The necropolis, a fortress (Sahinkale) and a few other fragments survive.

★Assos

See entry

Ayvalık

Near the busy port of Ayvalık, about 50km/31 miles south-west of Edremit, the coastline curves around a series of bays backed by pine woods and olive groves, an area of much-frequented beaches and good holiday accommodation. There are also more than 20 offshore islands and islets, the largest of which, Alibey Adası, named after a Turkish general in the War of Liberation, was already settled in antiquity and experienced a golden age under the Romans. Ayvalık itself, which contrary to the Turkish custom faces the sea, was until 1922 a purely Christian (Greek) community. Even today the neo-classical façades of its older houses and the alleys of the Old Town give it a distinctive air. It grew up between the 16th and 18th centuries, becoming a kind of sanctuary for its small Greek population. In 1773 Muslims were actually banned from living there by the Ottoman Sultan Mustafa III. By the beginning of the 19th c. the town had attained a peak of prosperity. In 1821 however the Kydonians siezed two Turkish ships, as a result of which they found themselves expelled, setting fire to the town as they went. In 1827 the Sultan Mahmut II allowed some 18,000 Greeks to return, though without restoring their earlier privileges. The town quickly resumed its role as an important port, reflected in its having as many as five consulates. Its citizens are said to have been accomplished smugglers. Less than a hundred years later the inhabitants again found themselves forced to leave, this time as part of the exchanges of population following the abortive Greek occupation (1919–22). The Greek Christians left behind a great many churches which the Muslims put to use as mosques. The Taksiyarhis Kilisesi, a 19th c. building with a lovely interior, on the northern outskirts of the town, is well worth seeing.

Be sure also to visit two nearby viewpoints at Şeytab Sofrası (Devil's Table) and Tavsankuları (Rabbit's Ear Hill). Both are on the Timerhane peninsula and offer magnificent views across a sea dotted with islets and islands and the picturesquely indented coastline. There is also a small national park with red and roe deer and partridges. Timarhane was at one time known as "Madhouse Peninsula", the mentally ill being banished there in chains. They are said to have returned completely cured.

Edremit

Edremit (pop. 30,000), the district town, is situated about 10km (6 miles) from the coast at the eastern end of the gulf which bears its name. A short distance to the south, near the village of Kalabak Köyü, are the remains of the earlier Adramittium (Adramittium Thebe; see Ören). Edremit's Seljuk Kurşunlu Cami dates from around 1231 and, together with its türbe (1241), was built by Yusuf Sinan. In the early 14th c. thoro was a Genoese fortress in the town. The Esnef Rumi Camii was built during the Ottoman period. Today Edremit–Akçay is a popular seaside resort. As well as archaeological finds the town museum has a splendid collection of weapons.

★Ören

Situated on the coast about 10km (6 miles) south-west of Edremit, Ören is a suburb of Burhaniye which lies just inland. It is one of those well-patronised resorts usually crowded with Turks enjoying their holidays. The long beach has fine sand and is well maintained.

A few kilometres south of Ören (which means "ruined place") is a mound marking the site of the ancient (Lydian) town of Adramyteion, in Strabo's time the Roman port of Pedasus. First settled in 1443 B.C., the town was later destroyed by pirates and between 1093 and 1109 was rebuilt further inland (as Adramittium).

Adramyteion (or Adramittium Thebe further east) is also identified with the Thebe of Homeric legend. According to Homer it was founded by Hercules in honour of his wife Thebe, daughter of Adramys (brother of the Lydian king Croesus). The town, where Hector's wife Andromache had her palace, was sacked by Achilles in the ninth year of the Trojan War. In reality Thebe was probably founded by the Milesians about 600 B.C., growing to be an important trading town on the route between Troy and Pergamum (Bergama). It was already in ruins in Strabo's day.

Ephesus C 6

West coast (Aegean Sea)
Province: İzmir
Altitude: 20–358m/65–1175ft
Place: Selçuk (pop. 20,000)

Situation and ★★importance

The remains of the ancient Greek city of Ephesus (Greek Ephesos, Turkish Efes), one of the outstanding ancient sites and tourist attractions in Turkey, lies near the little town of Selçuk in the coastal plain of the Küçük Menderes (Little Maeander), the ancient River Kaystros (Cayster), some 75km/47 miles south of İsmir and 17km/10½ miles north-east of the port and holiday resort of Kuşadası. Like Miletus, ancient Ephesus lay directly on the sea and had an important harbour, the main source of its wealth, but the Little Maeander, heavily laden with sediment and frequently changing its course, pushed the coastline ever farther away, while the marine currents off the bay built up a spit of land behind which the ground degenerated into marsh. By Roman times only a tongue-shaped harbour basin could be kept open for shipping. To maintain the city's contact with the sea would have involved a major effort which could not be contemplated in the troubled times after the Hellenistic period, still less in the changed political and economic circumstances of the Byzantine and Ottoman periods. Ephesus was deserted and gradually disappeared under the silt brought down by the river. Any structures remaining above ground were used as a quarry of building materials or were burned to provide lime. Excavation of the site began only in the second half of the 19th c., revealing the impressive remains to be seen today.

History

The earliest inhabitants of this region, the Carians and Lydians, no doubt had a fortified settlement on the hill immediately north of Selçuk (some 2km/1¼ miles north-east of the Hellenistic city), which was once directly on the sea (Sacred Harbour). On the west side of the hill stood the very ancient shrine of the great nature goddess of Asia Minor whom the Greeks later equated with Artemis.

From the 11th c. B.C. onwards this settlement was occupied and Hellenised, after much fighting, by Ionian Greeks from Samos, whose leader, according to the legend, was Androklos, son of Kodros. Then incomers and natives came together in the service of the great nature goddess and called themselves Ephesians. Thanks to its excellent situation on an inlet cutting deep into the land, at the end of a major trade route from the interior, and in a fertile plain, Ephesus developed into a flourishing commercial city, a member of the Panionic league of twelve cities.

About 550 B.C. Ephesus was captured by the Lydians under their King Kroisos (Croesus), who treated the inhabitants well but moved them to a new site in the plain round the Temple of Artemis. After the fall of the Lydian kingdom (545) the city came under Persian rule and was linked with the Persian "royal road" by a branch from Sardis. The philosopher Herakleitos

(Heraclitus) lived in Ephesus between 540 and 480. As an unfortified town Ephesus played no part in the Ionian rising against the Persians, and remained Persian longer than neighbouring cities (until about 466). In 412 it broke away from the Athenian Empire and became the headquarters of the Spartan General Lysander (d. 395). Thereafter it again fell into Persian hands until liberated by Alexander the Great (334 B.C.). In order to re-establish the city's link with the sea King Lysimachos had it moved (*c.* 287) to the low-lying ground between Mounts Pion and Koressos (now Panayır Dağı and Bülbül Dağı), which were both brought within the walls of the city, though the walled area was never fully built up; the Temple of Artemis (Artemiseion), however, now lay outside the city. The older settlement was then demolished. Lysimachos named the new foundation Arsinoeia after his wife, but after his death it reverted to its old name of Ephesus.

After belonging to the kingdom of Pergamon for some time Ephesus came under Roman rule in 133 B.C. From 88 to 84 B.C. it was held by King Mithradates of Pontos, who issued from Ephesus his notorious order for the killing of all Romans in western Asia Minor. Under the Roman Empire (1st and 2nd c. A.D.) it enjoyed a fresh period of prosperity as capital of the Roman province of Asia and became the largest city in the East after Alexandria, with a population of over 200,000. In the reign of Tiberius it was devastated by an earthquake (A.D. 29). Hadrian initiated major engineering works to protect the harbour and perhaps also constructed the canal which can still be traced.

Ephesus played an important part in the early days of Christianity. Paul preached here on his second missionary journey, and later spent three years (55–58) in Ephesus (Acts 18: 19; 19). The city's principal church was later dedicated to St John and became one of the great pilgrimage centres of Asia Minor.

In A.D. 263 the Goths destroyed the city and the Artemiseion on one of their raiding expeditions. Under the Eastern Empire, mainly as a result of the steady silting up of its harbour, Ephesus declined in importance and in size. Its circuit of walls was reduced in extent, excluding the Hellenistic agora and giving little protection to the harbour area – though the city was still sufficiently important to be the venue of the Third Ecumenical Council

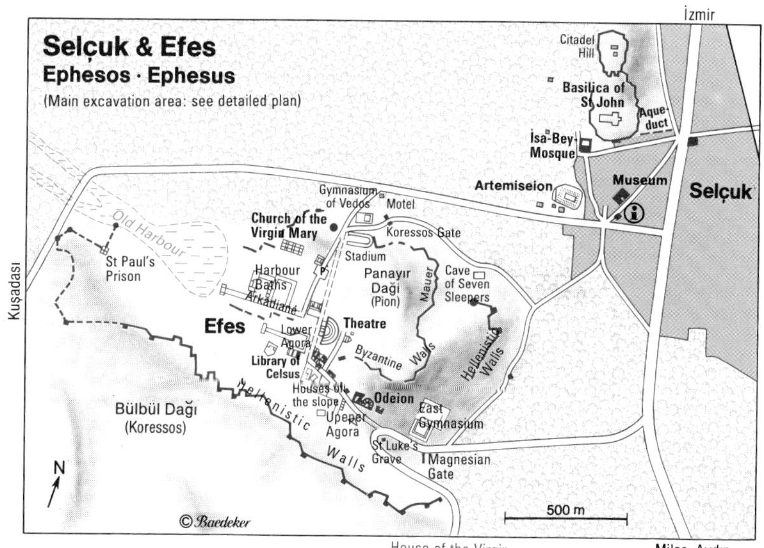

in 431. In the reign of Justinian the population withdrew to the original settlement site on the hill above the Artemiseion.

From the late 11th c. onwards the Seljuks several times captured and then lost the town, which was known to the Venetians as Atoluogo. Together with Palatia on the Sea of Marmara, however, it long remained an important trading centre with a large bazaar on the castle hill. In a nearby port town, probably the place later known as New Ephesus (now Kuşadası), were the residences of wealthy Christian merchants and an Italian Consul.

After a brief period of Ottoman rule (1426), during which the castle was enlarged and strengthened, Ephesus was captured and plundered by the Mongols of Tamerlane (Timur-Leng). Thereafter the last surviving remains of the town were reduced to ruins during the bitter conflicts between the Seljuks and the Ottomans.

Excavations

The excavation of the site began in 1866, when an English engineer, J. T. Wood, rediscovered the Artemiseion, which like most of the other ancient buildings was buried underground, and subsequently (1871–74) excavated it. Excavations were continued between 1896 and 1913 by the Austrian Archaeological Institute, when much of the Lysimachean town was laid bare. Green archaeologists investigated the site of the Basilica of St John in 1919–22. Further excavations by Austrian archaeologists under Turkish direction followed by the excavations which have been carried on continuously since 1954 by the Austrian Archaeological Institute have brought to light the extensive remains of the city as we see it today.

Visiting the ruins of ★★Ephesus

Gymnasium of Vedius

On the slope of the hill to the left is the Gymnasium of Vedius (2nd c. A.D.), the remains of a large rectangular building divided into numerous rooms with an arcaded courtyard, the palaestra (hall for wrestling), on the east side. The eastern half of the structure, built of brick faced with marble, is better preserved and shows interesting details of the internal arrangement.

Stadium

Some 100m/110yd south of the Gymnasium of Vedius is the Stadium, which dates from the time of Nero (A.D. 54–68). On the south side the tiers of seating for spectators were hewn out of the hillside; the stone benches are missing. At the semicircular east end was an arena which could be shut off from the main part of the stadium and used, in the absence of a circus, for gladiatorial contests and fights between wild beasts. Between the Gymnasium of Vedius and the Stadium a marble-paved way ran east to the Koressos Gate, of which some remains survive. From the gate a road leads south to Mount Koressos (Bülbül Dağı).

On a mound, the so-called Acropolis, at the point where the marble road turns west (500m/550yd west of the Stadium), there once stood within a square arcaded courtyard a circular building of unknown function, of which there remain only part of the base and a few stones from a cornice. Tradition and finds of potsherds on the hill make it probable that there was a settlement here in the Early Ionian period.

200m/220yd along the modern road which runs south from the Gymnasium of Vedius, on the left, are the ruins of a Byzantine building. Notable features are the large room with semicircular niches on the south side and the 50m/165ft long apsed hall on the west side.

Church of the Virgin Mary

To the right of the car park can be seen a 260m/295yd long complex of remains known as the Church of the Virgin Mary, or the Double Church, or the Council Church. This was the meeting-place of the Third Ecumenical Council in 431 A.D. It was originally the Mouseion (Museum: a centre of research and teaching), a three-aisled hall of the 2nd c. A.D., in which a pillared basilica was inserted in the 4th c. At the west end was a long rectangular courtyard. The eastern part of the original hall seems to have been the residence of a bishop. In the 7th c. the basilica was replaced by a

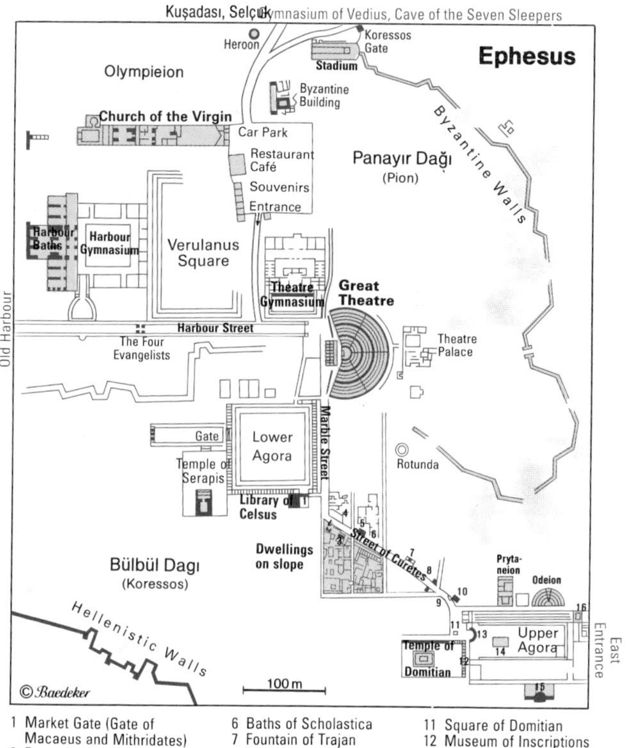

domed church, and later, when this collapsed, a pillared basilica was built on to one end of it.

Theatre Gymnasium

The new road continues south for another 300m/330yd to the Theatre Gymnasium, a large rectangular structure of the Roman Imperial period with an arcaded courtyard measuring 70m/230ft by 30m/100ft on its north side.

Square of Verulanus

Harbour Gymnasium

Immediately west of the Theatre Gymnasium is a large complex of buildings, the plan of which is not easy to distinguish. Nearest the gymnasium is the Square of Verulanus, a spacious arcaded courtyard, 200m/220yd by 240m/263yd, for the training of athletes, and beyond this is the Harbour Gymnasium, which dates from the Early Empire.

Harbour Baths

This consisted of a number of buildings grouped round a central courtyard. On the north and south sides of the courtyard were two magnificent marble halls measuring 16m/52ft by 32m/104ft, with columns and niches for statues. Immediately beyond this were the Great Baths or Harbour Baths, built in the 2nd c. A.D. and sumptuously rebuilt in the reign of Constantine the Great (4th c.), which have not been completely excavated.

Old Harbour

To the west of the baths lay the Old Harbour of Ephesus, now an area of marshy ground.

Arkadiane

Immediately south of this group of buildings, which lay in the centre of the ancient city, is the Arkadiane, a fine arcaded street running east from the harbour. The effect of this magnificent avenue, which was built by Arcadius, the first Eastern Emperor, about 400 A.D. and which is lit at night, was still further enhanced by an elaborately decorated gate at each end. At the east end of the Arkadiane, was a long square running north–south, with the Theatre Gymnasium at its north end, the Great Theatre built into the slopes of Panayır Dağı on its east side and the Lower Agora at its south end.

★★Great Theatre

The Great Theatre, begun in the reign of Claudius (41–54) and completed in the reign of Trajan (98–117), is particularly impressive, both for its great size and for the excellent state of preservation of the orchestra and the stage buildings. Its 3 by 22 tiers of seating, divided into sections by 12 stairways, with another 11 intermediate stairways in the top range of seating, could accommodate an audience of some 25,000. From the top there is a fine view extending down to the Old Harbour. There were also staircase tunnels leading up to the upper tiers. The stage wall, originally three-storeyed and 18m/60ft high but now preserved only to the height of the lowest storey, was elaborately articulated, with columns, niches for statues and richly decorated cornices. In the west terrace wall is a Hellenistic fountain-house in the form of a temple *in antis*, which in spite of its ruinous state is notable for the clarity and simplicity of its structure.

The Great Theatre may have been the scene of the riot incited by Demetrius, the silversmith of Ephesus whose silver shrines of Diana were not selling because of Paul's preaching of Christianity (Acts 19: 23–40).

★Lower Agora

South-west of the Great Theatre is the Lower Agora, a spacious square, 116m/127yd each way, from which a colonnaded street leads west. The agora (market square), which has been only partly excavated, was a 3rd c. rebuilding of an earlier structure, to which the use of stone from earlier buildings gives an interesting variety of detail. It was surrounded by a double colonnade housing shops and offices, with a set-back upper storey on the east side.

Colonnaded street

Serapeion

On the south side of the colonnaded street, which runs west for some 160m/175yd and has an elaborate gate at each end, steps lead up to a colonnaded square, on the south side of which is the colossal Serapeion, the temple of the Egyptian god Serapis. Along the 29m/95ft long façade of the temple were monolithic columns 15m/50ft high with Corinthian capitals. The cella was entered through a massive doorway, with doors moving on wheels. In Byzantine times the Serapeion was converted into a Christian basilica.

Marble Street

Along the east side of the Lower Agora the Marble Street leads from the Koressos Gate but has been excavated only from the Great Theatre southward. This fine marble-paved street, once lined with arcades and decorated with statues, continues south to the Library of Celsus. Along the middle can be seen a series of holes through which surface water flowed into the drains.

★★Library of Celsus

In a small square lying below street-level is the imposing two-storey façade, with its rather crowded columns and prominent cornices (re-erected 1970–78 by Austrian archaeologists), of the Library of Celsus. The library itself, which was entirely faced with coloured marble, was of three storeys, with colonnades round the two lower storeys. Along the rear wall was a series of rectangular niches for holding parchment books and scrolls. Below the central niche is a grave-chamber with the Sarcophagus of Titus Julius Celsus Polemaenus, Governor of the province of Asia, in whose honour his son built the library in the early 2nd c. A.D.; it was completed in A.D. 135.

Ephesus: façade of the Library of Celsus and the Market Gate

The Marble Street leads from the Great Theatre to the Celsus Library

Market Gate

Immediately adjoining the Library of Celsus, at the south-east corner of the Lower Agora is the Market Gate or Gate of Macaeus and Mithridates, so named in an inscription. It has recently been restored.

★Street of the Curetes

South-east of the Lower Agora the plain narrows into a valley Beır Dağı (Mount Pion) and Bülbül Dağı (Mount Koressos), through which the Street of the Curetes (a college of priests), flanked by numerous public buildings, runs up from the end of the Marble Street to the Upper Agora and the Magnesian Gate. At the point where the Street of the Curetes bends south-east are the bases of the Propylaion, a gate of the 2nd c. A.D. from which a street, continued by a stepped lane, led south up Mount Koressos.

On the east side of the Propylaion is the Octagon, a momumental heroon (tomb of a hero) with an eight-sided superstructure, surrounded by a Corinthian colonnade with a stone bench, on a square marble base.

Higher up the slope of the hill a group of terraced buildings are in course of excavation.

★Temple of Hadrian

Baths of Scholastica

On the opposite side of the street is a house which is assumed to have been a brothel. Beyond this is a small temple, much restored, which an inscription shows was dedicated to the Emperor Hadrian (117–38). Beyond this are the remains of the Baths of Scholastica, once of several storeys, which were originally built in the 2nd c. and were rebuilt about A.D. 400 by a Christian woman named Scholastica.

Higher up, on the south-western slopes of Mount Pion, we come to a two-storey rotunda on a square base, with Doric columns round the lower storey and free-standing Ionic columns round the upper storey. Probably this, like the Octagon, was a hero's tomb.

Fountain of Trajan
Gate of Hercules
Monument of Memmius
Fountain of Pollio
Temple of Domitian
★Museum of Inscriptions

Next we come to the Fountain of Trajan (a nymphaeum), the Gate of Hercules and the Monument of Gaius Memmius (1st c. B.C.). The Street then bears right to enter the so-called Square of Domitian, with the Fountain of Pollio in a niche on the east side. Above the square rises the massive substructure of the Temple of Domitian, erected by the province of Asia in honour of the Emperor (A.D. 81–96). In the basement of the temple is the Museum of Inscriptions.

Upper Agora

To the east of the Temple of Domitian is the Upper Agora, with a Temple of Isis and a hydreion (water-tower) which collected spring water flowing down from the hill.

Prytaneion

On the north side of the Upper Agora is the site of the Prytaneion (council chamber, town hall), located after a long search. The figures of Artemis which were found here are now in the Archaeological Museum in Selçuk.

★Odeion

Farther east is the semicircular structure of the Odeion, built by Publius Vedius Antonius in the 2nd c. A.D. The lower tiers of marble benches are original, the rest are reconstructions. The auditorium of this little theatre or concert hall, with seating for an audience of 1400, was divided by an intermediate gangway into a lower block with 13 tiers of seating and 6 stairways and an upper block with 10 tiers and 7 stairways. Since there is no provision for the drainage of rainwater it is assumed that the Odeion was roofed, probably by a wooden structure spanning the 25m/80ft width of the auditorium.

Magnesian Gate

Tomb of St Luke

From the Upper Agora the old main street continues east to the eastern gate of the excavations (on the road to the House of the Virgin Mary), ending outside the enclosure at the three-arched Magnesian Gate, the starting-point of the road to Magnesia on the Maeander. At a bend in the road is the base of a circular Roman structure, the so-called Tomb of St Luke, which was converted into a church in Byzantine times by the addition of an apse and a porch.

Eastern Gymnasium

Immediately north of the Magnesian Gate are the imposing ruins of the Eastern Gymnasium (1st–2nd c. A.D.). Like the other three gymnasia in

Reconstruction of Hadrian's Temple in the Street of the Curetes

Ephesus, this is a large rectangular building with several magnificent halls and a palaestra. Since many statues of girls were found on the site it is also known as the Girls' Gymnasium. Its most notable feature is the caldarium (warm room of the baths), which measures 25m/80ft by 30m/100ft. There were large halls on the east and west sides of the palaestra, which lies to the south of the gymnasium. The remains of tiers of seating in the east hall suggest that this may have been a lecture-room.

Surroundings

Panayır Dağı (Pion)

★View

From the Eastern Gymnasium a good road runs north-east up Panayır Dağı (Mount Pion, 155m/510ft), from which there is a fine view of the ancient site set in a semicircle round the hill. A Byzantine wall, some stretches of it well preserved, leads north along the crest of the hill to the Koressos Gate.

Cave of the Seven Sleepers

Under the north-east side of the hills is the so-called Cave of the Seven Sleepers of Ephesus. According to the legend seven young men of Ephesus were walled up in a cave during the persecution of Christians in the middle of the 2nd c., fell into a deep sleep and were discovered, alive and well, in the reign of Theodosius II (414–50). After their death, it is said, the Emperor had them buried in the cave and built a pilgrimage church in their honour. During the Turkish period the shrine fell into disrepair and was completely buried under soil washed down from the hill. Excavations in 1926–28 brought to light and intricate complex of rooms containing hundreds of burials in wall niches and under the ground. In the centre of the area was a church, under which was a catacomb-like vault containing ten grave-chambers. The walls of these chambers were covered with scratched or painted inscriptions in Greek, Armenian and Latin invoking the Seven Sleepers. This was probably a much-venerated Early Byzantine burial-place to which the story of the Seven Sleepers, originally an Oriental legend, was later attached.

Bülbül Dağı (Koressos)

Nightingale Hill

To the south-west of the excavated area is the long ridge of Bülbül Dağı (Nightingale Hill, 358m/1175ft), known in antiquity as Mount Koressos, which can be climbed either from the east side or on a road climbing from the ancient harbour to the west end of the ridge. Along the ridge extends the Hellenistic town wall of the time of Lysimachos, still retaining some of its battlements. A bridle-path follows the line of the wall.

St Paul's Prison

On a hill above the harbour canal, known in Hellenistic times as Pagos Astyagou, stands a ruined watch-tower, originally on the Hellenistic town walls, which for some unexplained reason is known as St Paul's Prison.

★House of the Virgin Mary

South-east of Bülbül Dağı, on Ala Dağı (the ancient Mount Solmissos, 420m/1378ft), is a building known as the House of the Virgin Mary (Panaya Kapulu), in which the Virgin is said to have lived and died. The building, the foundations of which date from the 1st c. A.D., was restored in Byzantine times but thereafter was abandoned and fell into disrepair. Its association with the Virgin dates only from the 19th c., following the visions of a German nun, Katharina Emmerich (1774–1824), who gave an exact description of the situation and appearance of a house at Ephesus in which the Virgin had lived and died. In 1891, on the basis of her account, Lazarists from Smyrna (İzmir) discovered on the south side of Bülbül Dağı the ruins of a small church which had evidently belonged to a monastery, and this is now revered as the Virgin's house.

Pilgrimages

The pilgrimages which began after the finding of the house continued on an increased scale after the Second World War, and the Feast of the Assumption (August 15th) is celebrated here with particular ceremony. The house, beautifully situated and commanding an extensive view, has also become a major tourist attraction.

The road to the House of the Virign branches off the main Selçuk–Aydın road. In 4.5km/3 miles it passes close to the Eastern gymnasium and the Magnesian Gate and then continues for another 3.5km/2 miles round the east side of Bülbül Dağı to the site.

Selçuk

Citadel hill

Aqueduct

Byzantine Gate

Entrance gateway

★View

From the main square of Selçuk, through which runs the road from İzmir to Aydın (on the south-east side of the square a Seljuk mosque), a side road leads south-west, passing a Byzantine aqueduct (recently restored). 200m/220yd beyond this, on the right, is the entrance to the citadel. The lower ward is entered by the Byzantine Gate, built in the 7th c. from fragments of earlier masonry; it is also known as the Gate of Persecution, from a relief showing Achilles dragging the body of the dead Hector. The entrance gateway of the fortress proper, flanked by two rectangular towers, also has two arched openings, one behind the other. Beyond the gate there is a fine view, to the left, of the Küçük Menderes Plain.

★Basilica of St John

A few paces beyond this are the remains of the Basilica of St John, which occupied almost the whole breadth of the hill and ranked with Hagia Sophia and the Church of the Holy Apostles (destroyed) in Constantinople as one of the largest Byzantine churches. According to tradition the grave of St John the Divine is under the church. Originally a mausoleum with a domed roof borne on four columns was built over the grave, later converted into a basilican church by the addition of an aisled nave, transept and five-aisled choir, with a timber roof. The Emperor Justinian (527–65) replaced this church by a monumental aisled basilica on a Latin-cross plan, with six domes (four over the nave and two over the arms of the transept). Including the narthex at the west end and the arcaded courtyard the new church was 130m/427ft long and 40m/130ft wide. Over the aisles were galleries which continued across the transept into the apse. The position of the Saint's tomb was marked by a stepped marbled platform, on the east

Basilica of St John in Selçuk

side of which was an apse with benches for the presbyters, from which steps led down to the tomb.

After the Seljuks captured Ephesus they converted the church into a mosque (1130). Later it served as a bazaar until it was finally destroyed in an earthquake; in recent times it has been partly restored.

A tablet commemorates a visit by Pope Paul VI on June 26th 1967.

Citadel

To the north of the basilica, on the highest point of the hill, stands the Citadel, in an excellent state of preservation. There is no written evidence on its date, but the style of masonry indicates that it was built in Byzantine times and extended by the Seljuks. The mighty enclosure wall had 15 towers, mostly rectangular, and both walls and towers are topped by a continuous ring of battlements. Probably there was only one entrance. Within the walls are several cisterns, a small Seljuk mosque and a Byzantine church.

★İsa Bey Mosque

On the south-west side of the citadel hill is the Great Mosque (also known as the İsa Bey Mosque or Selim Mosque; in course of restoration), which dates from Seljuk times. The tall outer walls, 57m/187ft long by 51m/167ft wide, enclose a large arcaded courtyard with the fountain for ritual ablutions and the prayer-hall, the central area of which had two domes borne on columns, while the two side wings had flat timber roofs. The large columns of black granite came from the Roman baths at the harbour. The prayer-hall was entered from the courtyard by a main doorway with three arches and two side doorways. Above the marble-clad west wall of the mosque rises a round minaret, complete up to the gallery for the muezzin; the corresponding minaret on the east side has been completely destroyed. The tall rectangular windows have decorated frames in different styles of ornamentation. Above the doorway, which is richly decorated with inlay work, is an elaborate calligraphic inscription: "In the name of God, the merciful, the compassionate! The building of this blessed mosque was ordered by

İsa Bey Mosque

the glorious Sultan, the ruler over the peoples and the faithful, the hero of the faith Isa, son of Mohammed, son of Aydın, whose reign God may grant to be long. Built by the master builder Ali, son of Mushimish al-damishki, and written by him on the 9th day of the month of Shaban at new moon in the year 776" [January 30th 1375].

Other mosques

In the vicinity of the Great Mosque there were in Seljuk times 14 other small mosques. Some, usually square domed structures, have survived in varying states of preservation.

Artemiseion

Some 300m/330yd south of the Great Mosque, reached from the main square of Selçuk by a narrow street bearing right, are the scanty remains of the Artemiseion or Temple of Artemis, once one of the Seven Wonders of the World, in a low-lying marshy area to the right of the road.

Building history

The excavations carried out by J. R. Wood and an expedition from the British Museum showed that the site was originally occupied by a stone-platform on which stood the cult image of the goddess, while under the platform were rooms in which votive gifts were preserved; to the west was another platform. In a later building phase the two platforms were linked with one another, and later still a cella measuring 16m/52ft by 31m/102ft was built over them. It is not known whether the cella was surrounded by columns. Finally, in the 6th c. B.C., a gigantic marble temple was built. Dipteral in type (i.e. surrounded by two rows of columns), it was 109m/360ft long by 55m/180ft wide. In the inner row of columns there were 6 at each end and 18 along the sides, in the outer rows 8 and 20. In addition there were 2 rows of 4 columns in the pronaos (antechamber), 2 rows of 2 in the opisthodomos, the corresponding chamber at the rear end, and 2 rows of 9 plus one in the cella, making a total of 127 columns in all. On 36 of the columns the lowest drum of the shaft had relief decoration. In 356 B.C. the temple was set on fire and destroyed by one Herostratos, who sought by

this means to immortalise his name. In the rebuilding that followed the foundation platform was raised by 2.7m/9ft, but otherwise the original form and dimensions of the temple were preserved.

The second destruction of the temple began with a raid on Ephesus by the Goths about A.D. 260. In Byzantine times it fell into a state of complete dilapidation and was used as a quarry of building material. Columns and marble slabs from the temple can be seen in Hagia Sophia (Ayasofya) in İstanbul and elsewhere. The foundations of the altar, measuring 30m/100ft by 40m/130ft, were discovered in 1965.

In the western part of Selçuk, some 500m/550yd south of the citadel hill, is the recently reorganised Archaeological Museum, with finds from the site of ancient Ephesus, including several statues of Artemis. Diagonally opposite is a small tourist bazaar with an information bureau.

Going west from here on the Kuşadası road and turning left in 1.5km/1 mile at the Tusan Motel, we come in another 200m/220yd to one of the most magnificent ancient sites in Turkey, the new city of Ephesus founded by Lysimachos in the 3rd c. B.C.

Fethiye E 7

south-west coast (Mediterranean)
Province: Muğla
Altitude: 0–50m/0–165ft
Population: 20,000

Situation and importance

The port of Fethiye, chief town of a district, lies on the Lycian coast some 150km/95 miles south-east of the provincial capital of Muğla, at the innermost tip of the Gulf of Fethiye (previously called Makri Bay, in antiquity Sinus Glaucus). The gulf, dotted with numerous islets, is closed by the little island known in antiquity as Makris, in the Middle Ages as Isola Longa and since 1936 as Cavaliere, the Island of the Knights. The town, previously called Megri or Makri, was renamed Fethiye in 1957 in honour of a pilot who crashed here, Fethi Bey. it was devastated by an earthquake in 1856, and after a further earthquake in 1957 much of it had to be rebuilt again. As a result it is now a modern town with a long seafront promenade and a lively bazaar. In recent years, thanks to its sheltered boating harbour and the many beautiful bathing beaches on the shores of the gulf and on the islands (boat services), Fethiye has developed into a flourishing holiday resort served by the regional airport of Dalaman (50km/30 miles north-west).

Telmessos

Fethiye occupies the site of ancient Telmessos, an important Lycian city which was already famed in the time of Kroisos (Croesus) for its soothsayers. The acropolis was on a crag detached from the steeply scarped hill which rises above the town. In Byzantine times it was called Anastasiopolis. It is now difficult, after two earthquakes and the subsequent rebuilding, to find any traces of ancient Telmessos in the modern town. The

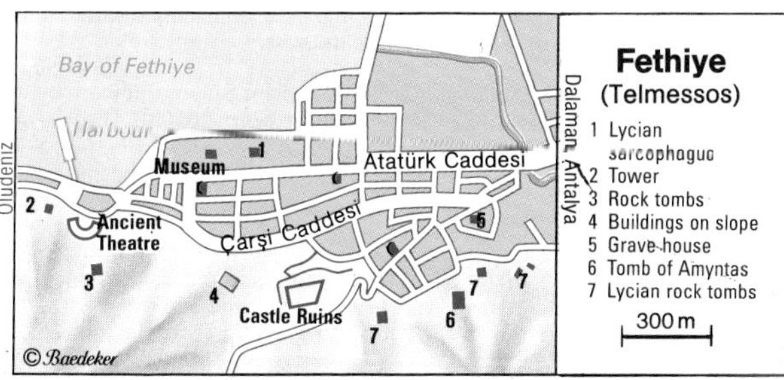

boundaries of the Hellenistic and Roman town are no doubt marked out by the almost vertical rock face to the west, the Roman tombs on the east side of the town and the Lycian necropolis to the south. The finding of sarcophagi near the edge of the modern town indicates the course of the ancient coastline.

On the castle hill, occupied in the Middle Ages by the Knights of St John, then based on Rhodes, and the Genoese, there are remains of much earlier buildings. The remains of houses on the north-west side of the hill, with a number of cisterns and water-supply channels suggest that there was an unwalled Lycian settlement here, though in a later period the focus of urban life moved down to the coastal plain. Of the ancient theatre, which was located and described by the French traveller Charles Texier before the 1856 earthquake, nothing can now be seen but the outline of the cavea (auditorium). The most striking ancient remains are a number of fine rock tombs of characteristic type, modelled on Lycian timber-built architecture and later Ionian temple architecture. The main group is in the rock face to the east of the present built-up area. Particularly notable is the Tomb of Amyntas, which is dated to the 4th c. B.C.

★Rock tombs

Museum

The little museum in the Town hall (Belediye) of Fethiye displays material from all the main periods of the town's eventful history.

Surroundings of Fethiye

★Kaya (Levissi)

Although now almost completely abandoned, in the 19th c. Levissi (Kaya), 8km/5 miles south of Fethiye, was a town of more than 3000 inhabitants. No more than 200 to 300 years old, it stands on the site of ancient Carmylessus. There was also a settlement here in the Middle Ages (1106), known for its good harbour. In the 19th c., after neighbouring Makri (Fethiye) had been devastated, first by the earthquake of 1856 and then by a disasterous fire in 1885, its predominantly Greek inhabitants moved to Levissi where many of them had summer homes. At the beginning of this century most returned to Makri. Of those who remained, some left Levissi in 1922 during the population exchanges and the rest after the 1957 earthquake. The terraces of large, stone-built, turn-of-the-century European-style houses on the hillside have a sorry, abandoned air.

★★Ölüdeniz

Of the many charming bathing-places in the surrounding area the sheltered coastal lagoon of Ölüdeniz (Dead Sea) in Belceğiz Bay (15km/9 miles south of Fethiye as the crow flies) is undoubtedly the finest, with beaches of fine sand in an idyllic setting of coastal hills. Ölüdeniz has developed into a very popular holiday centre, with hotels, pensions and inns.

Pinara

Pinara, in the hills above the Eşen Ovası south-east of Fethiye, is the site of an exceptionally interesting Lycian necropolis, a honeycomb of more than 900 rock tombs and monolithic house tombs. So inaccessible was the site that the tomb-builders had to be lowered on stages secured with ropes. The monolithic Royal Tomb (with an urban scene in relief inside) is particularly noteworthy, this type of tomb being rare in Lycia.

Sidyma

More tombs, also interesting, are found at ancient Sidyma (lower city at 500m/1641ft, acropolis, with small theatre, at 820m/2690ft). The site is about 15km/9 miles south-west of Eşen, near the village of Hisar (gravel road).

★Tlos

The ruins of the ancient city of Tlos are situated in the hills above the Eşen Ovası, about 36km/22 miles east of Fethiye (via Kemer and Yakaköy). Crowning the rounded acropolis hill are the ruins of a Turkish castle, erected over a Lycian fortress. On the east side of the acropolis are remnants of Lycian and Roman walls, with a gate dating from the 2nd c. B.C.. Beyond lie the remains of a number of houses, public buildings and other

Rock tombs in Pinara resembling honeycombs

structures from the Lycian, Roman and Byzantine periods. They include cisterns, a stadium, a hall-like edifice which was possibly an indoor market, two large baths, an agora, churches, a theatre and a necropolis (Lycian). The Roman town centre (2nd c. B.C.) testifies to the considerable importance of the city in Imperial times. Being tucked away in the mountains the Turkish castle was, until the late 19th c., the stronghold of various "valley princes" (derebeys) and brigands, of whom Kanlı Ali, known as "Bloodthirsty Ali", was the most notorious.

Saklıkent

About 10km/6 miles south of Tlos, a large tributary stream of the Koca Cay emerges from a narrow ravine cut deeply into the karst mountains of the Ak Dağları (karst springs, fish restaurants).

Finike — E 6

South-west coast (Mediterranean)
Province: Antalya
Altitude: 0–15m/0–50ft
Population: 20,000

Situation and characteristics

The port of Finike (formerly Phoinika) lies in a coastal plain on the west side of the wide Gulf of Finike, in Lycia. It is some 120km/75 miles south-west of the provincial capital of Antalya. The town is not particularly attractive and has no sights of any interest, but has many miles of beautiful beaches of fine sand on the shores of the bay, particularly along the coast road (in course of improvement to motorway standard) to the busy industrial town of Kumluca.

Surroundings of Finike

Limyra

10km/6 miles north-east of Finike at the village of Zengerler (between Turunçova and Kumluca), at the foot of Mount Tocat, is the site of ancient Limyra (Lycian Zemu), the origins of which can be traced back to the 5th c. B.C., making it one of the oldest cities in Lycia. Excavations have been carried out here since 1969 by a German archaeologist, J. Borchhardt.

On the hill to the north of the sight are an upper and a lower acropolis (the latter with the remains of a Byzantine church). On the crag to the south can be found the so-called Heroon of Perikles (*c.* 370 B.C.), hewn from the rock in the form of a temple. In the plain below the acropolis hill is the theatre (A.D. 141), built at the expense of a wealthy citizen called Opramoas, and near by are remains of Roman and Byzantine fortifications. Other notable features are the Tomb of Gaius Caesar (d. A.D. 4), the tall Sarcophagus of Katabura and the Tomb of Tebersele, both dating from the 4th c. B.C., and three large groups of Lycian rock tombs.

★Myra

30km/20 miles south-west of Finike, round the mouth of the Demre Dere (the ancient Myros), is a wide coastal plain, now occupied by large numbers of hothouses (mostly with plastic sheeting) for the cultivation of vegetables, particularly aubergines and tomatoes. The little town of Kale (Demre) occupies the site of the important Lycian city of Myra, which was visited by the Apostle Paul on his first journey to Rome in A.D. 61. In the 3rd c. St Nicholas was Bishop of Myra. Theodosius II made the city capital of Lycia.

There are some impressive ancient remains at the foot of the acropolis hill, mostly hewn from the rock, including a large theatre and many Lycian rock tombs (some of them dating from the 4th c. B.C.).

★Basilica of St Nicholas

In Kale (Demre) is the interesting early medieval Basilica of St Nicholas, which apart from some minor restoration has been preserved in its original

Rock tombs in Myra

11th c. form. Built into the sides of the nave are 2nd and 3rd c. sarcophagi. There are remains of frescos in the apse and at certain points on the walls.

★Mediterranean coast

The coast road between Finike and Kale runs close to the sea at some points, passing picturesque rocky coves with crystal-clear water which are tempting places for bathing. There are also beautiful sandy beaches (including a large sandbank) and flat stretches of coast in the immediate vicinity of Kale.

Herakleia (Latmos) C 6

West coast (Aegean Sea)
Province: 10–500m/35–1640ft
Altitude: Muğla
Place: Kapıkırı

Situation on Lake Bafa

The site of ancient Herakleia lies on the north-east shore of the beautiful Lake of Bafa (Bafa Gölü), which was once the innermost southern tip of the Latmian Gulf but was then cut off from the sea by sediment brought down by the Maeander (Büyük Menderes) to become a "bastard sea" (Bastarda Thalassa). As a result it has slightly salty water and an abundance of fish.

Herakleia can be reached on an unmetlled road (11km/7 miles) which branches off the trunk road from İzmir to Muğla at the village of Mersinet (some 50km/30 miles south-east of Söke) and runs north to Kapıkırı.

History

The city of Herakleia, with its extensive remains below the rugged height of Mount Latmos, is one of the most picturesque places in Western Asia Minor. Once reaching to the sea it enjoyed only a brief period of prosperity in Hellenistic times. In the Early Christian period the town, like the islands, the shores of the lake and Mount Latmos, was a favourite haunt of monks and hermits. The Seljuks, however, drove the Christians out of the area, beginning about 1080 and completing the process about 1300. Excavations were carried out on the site before the First World War.

Visiting the ★ruins

East Gate
Castle

The city area is entered through the East Gate, with a well-preserved arch in cut stone (one of the earliest of the kind). To the south extends a peninsula with a Byzantine castle, the bishop's residence (fine view), and numerous tombs.

Rock shrine
Agora

Farther west we come to a rock shrine with a four-columned porch dedicated to Endymion, who lived on Latmos and was revered by the people of Herakleia as a local hero; facing it, to the south, is another temple. To the north lies the agora, partly overlaid with soil; on its east side is the bouleuterion (council chamber), at its south end a market building.

Temple of Athena

To the west of the agora stands the Temple of Athena, a tall structure preserved up to roof-level, with a pronaos (antechamber). Still farther west, over rough and rocky ground, are the West Gate, remains of the town walls and the defences of the harbour.

Baths
North Gate
Theatre

To the north of the Council Chamber are the ruins of Roman baths, and to the east of these are a gate and a sallyport, beside a massive corner tower. North of the tower the town walls enclose an older shrine which consisted of a ring of stelae. Farther north stands the best preserved of the town gates, the North Gate; to the west of this is the theatre, to the north a nymphaeum and a temple.

★Town walls

The town walls, some 6m/20ft high, with an average thickness of 2.25m/7½ft, but in places up to 3.20m/10½ft thick, are preserved at some points up to the height of the parapet and are one of the best surviving examples of ancient fortifications. The two stretches of wall, which originally had a total of 65 towers, meet high up on the hill, with a total extent of 4.5km/2¾ miles. At one time the upper section of walls enclosed a second acropolis. From the highest point, however, the walls continued farther, enclosing a third acropolis (alt. 350m/1150ft), for the city originally extended farther east, with a total circumference of 6.5km/4 miles. Remains of walls high up to the north-east (500m/1640ft) and other remains to the east were outworks. Still other remains belong to the little hill town of Latmos, which controlled this area before the foundation of Herakleia about 300 B.C.

Surroundings of Herakleia

Mount Latmos

A visit to the monasteries and caves on Mount Latmos (in Turkish Beş Parmak Dağı, "Five Finger Mountain", 1367m/4485ft is an exceedingly strenuous expedition. The principal monastery, Stylos (10th c.; now Arabavli), which is dedicated to the Apostle Paul, is a 12-hour walk from Herakleia, through country of extreme wildness. In 1079 St Christodoulos left this monastery, and in 1088 founded the well-known Monastery of St John on the Greek island of Patmos. The Latmos caves have some notable wall-paintings of the 12th and 13th c.

In a cave south-west of Herakleia, according to Strabo, was the Tomb of Endymion, the handsome youth who won the love of the moon goddess Selene and was condemned to eternal sleep.

İskenderun M 7

South coast (eastern Mediterranean)
Province: Hatay
Altitude: 0–5m/0–15ft
Population: 156,000

Situation and importance

İskenderun (formerly known as Alexandretta), the most important Turkish Mediterranean port after İzmir, lies on the south side of the Gulf of İskenderun within the wooded foothills of the Amanus range, perhaps on the site of ancient Alexandria Scabiosa. The present-day town has little to offer the visitor and is very hot in summer. The harbour, the largest and the best on this stretch of coast, and sheltered by the surrounding hills, handles considerable shipping traffic. Round the harbour, which has a large jetty, are various modern installations (grain-stores, etc.).

History

The city of Alexandria, on the Issicus Sinus (Gulf of Issos), was probably founded some time after Alexander the Great's victory in the Battle of Issos (333). The town was intended to be the starting-point of the great caravan routes into Mesopotamia, but after Alexander's death the Seleucids preferred Antiocheia (Antakya) and Seleukeia Piereia. In the 3rd c. A.D. the town was destroyed by the Persians. In the 4th c. it was known as Little Alexandria; the epithet Scabiosa reflects the fact that leprosy was prevalent in this area. After a period of decline under the Ottomans at the end of the 19th c., İskenderun expanded from an insignificant harbour into the present town.

Surroundings

South-east of İskenderun

Belen

Belen (pop. 15,000; alt. 500m/1641ft), 14km/9 miles south-east of İskenderun and situated some way up the Topboğazı pass (750m/2461ft), is a summer resort popular with people from İskenderun. Evilya Çelebi's record (1640) shows that even in the 17th c. Arabs and Turks, some of them citizens of Aleppo, used to spend the summer months here. Having been from antiquity a staging post on an old trade route, the town boasts the remains of an aqueduct as well a mosque and caravanserai dating from the 16th c.

Güzelyala

The houses of Soğukoluk (now Güzelyala) can be seen across the valley to the south-west of Belen. This elegant summer village with its lovely view over the Gulf of İskenderun, was built in the early 20th c. as a holiday retreat for the rich burghers of Aleppo, Antakya, Reyhanlı, Kırıkhan and İskenderun. Now it enjoys a less salubrious reputation, frequented by the crews of ships lying in the port of İskenderun.

North of İskenderun

Jonah's Pillar

About 10km/6 miles north of the town is Arrian's Pass (Derbent), a narrow passage between the sea and the hills. In medieval times the pass, then probably a frontier and customs post of Little Armenia, was known as Passus Portellae or Portella. On the pass can be seen Jonah's Pillar, a remnant of a Roman building which is variously interpreted as a Seleucid triumphal arch, an obelisk, the remains of a fort and a triumphal arch erected by Pescenius. The 13th c. writer Willebrand of Oldenburg records a legend that Alexander's remains were deposited on this "gate of liberation" so that the kings and princes who had been compelled by Alexander to bow their heads before him should still have him above them in death. According to local seamen the pillar marks the spot where Jonah was cast ashore by the whale.

Sakal Tutan

600m/660yd north-east, higher up (alt. 91m/300ft), are the remains of an Armenian castle which in medieval times protected the pass and provided accommodation for travellers. Its name of Sakal Tutan (Tearer out of beards) refers to the bandits who lay in wait here to attack and plunder caravans. It has also been known, at different times, as Nigrinum, Neghertz (Middle Castle) and Kalatissia.

Xenophon's Pass

Beyond this, in the narrow coastal plain of the River Sarısekisu, is Xenophon's Pass (which Xenophon himself calls Karsos), with remains of walls, probably serving some defensive purpose, some 600m/660yd apart.

Payas

20km/12½ miles north of İskenderun is Payas (Yakacık), a beautifully situated little town on a bay north of the promontory of Ras Payas. Its name comes from Arabic bayas (white) – no doubt a reference to the snow-covered peaks of the Amanus range. It occupies the site of ancient Baiae, on the Issicus Sinus, a bathing resort much frequented by the Romans; there are remains of baths on the beach. In the Middle Ages it was an important commercial town and was still a place of some consequence in the mid 18th c. At the end of the 18th c., however, it fell into the hands of a Turkoman chieftain named Küçük Ali, under whose rule it was ruined and depopulated. Küçük Ali levied tribute on passing caravans and robbed travellers; in 1801 he held the Dutch Consul in Aleppo prisoner for eight months, releasing him only on payment of a ransom of 17,500 piastres. After his death in 1808 his son Dada Bey persisted in the same practices, but was finally betrayed to the authorities and beheaded at Adana in 1817.

First comes a complex of buildings – a han (caravanserai), a bazaar, a mosque, a medrese and a bath-house – erected in 1574 by Sokollu Mehmet Paşa, one of the most celebrated Grand Viziers of the Ottoman period, during the town's heyday in the reign of Sultan Selim II, son of Süleiman the Great. The han has a large courtyard surrounded by pointed-arched arcading. In front of it is the bazaar, a single-aisled building with a barrel-vaulted roof and a dome. To the south is the mosque, also with a large arcaded court, to the north the bath-house (ruined), with a domed camken (apodyterium) linking the soğukluk (tepidarium) and the domed harara (caldarium). To the west of this complex, 800m/½ mile from the sea, is a large medieval castle (14th c.) on a polygonal plan. From the interior it is possible to climb up on to the massive walls and towers (fine views).

Issos

The road continues north over the plain. This area close to the coast, extending to the Deli Çayı, is believed to be the scene of the Battle of Issos (333), in which Alexander the Great defeated the Persian King Darius III in a decisive cavalry encounter.

The exact site of the ancient town of Issos has not been established with certainty. It lay at the innermost tip of the Gulf of Issos and in Xenophon's time was a large and flourishing city. It is said to have been renamed Nikopolis (City of Victory) after Alexander's victory.

Epiphaneia

At Yeşilkent (Erzin), to the right of the main road, lies an extensive area of ruins, formerly thought to be the site of Issos but identified by the Austrian archaeologist Rudolf Heberdey (1864–1936) as the town of Epiphaneia, mentioned by Cicero as the place where he established his camp. According to Appianus Pompey resettled pirates here, and according to Ammianus Marcellinus this was the birthplace of St George, murdered in 361 as Archbishop of Alexandria.

From the main road can be seen the 116 surviving arches of a large late Roman acqueduct crossing the plain in a gentle curve. The acropolis of the ancient city was probably on the nearby hill. To the south of the hill extends the main part of the city, with the remains of walls (probably belonging to a temple) and a colonnaded street.

The main road then continues over the pass of Toprakkale (see Adana – Surroundings) and joins the road from Adana to Osmaniye.

İstanbul D/E 2/3

Marmara region (Bosphorus)
Province: İstanbul
Altitude: 0–125m/0–410ft
Population: 7.4 million (conurbation)

This description of İstanbul has deliberately been kept short, since there is a separate guide to the city in this series.

Situation and ★★importance

The great city of İstanbul, long known as Constantinople or, in the familiar European form of its Turkish name, as Stamboul, is picturesquely situated on the hills which flank the Bosphorus at its junction with the Sea of Marmara. Although it was superseded by Ankara as capital of Turkey in 1923, it still has the largest concentration of population in the country, with a university, a technological university and an academy of art. It is the seat of a Muslim Mufti, Greek and Armenian Patriarchs and a Roman Catholic Archbishop. Thanks to its favourable geographical situation, with a magnificent natural harbour – the largest in Turkey – in the golden Horn, and to its position at the intersection of the land route from the Balkans to the Near Eastern countries with the sea route from the Mediterranean to the Black Sea, İstanbul has been throughout history an important international commercial centre.

Enviromental Measures

Relentless migration to the city from the countryside keeps the İstanbul conurbation in a perpetual state of rapid growth. To counteract the threat of water, air and soil pollution, the city authorities have drawn up a redevelopment programme, due to be completed by the year 2000 (in association with İstanbul's bid for the Turn-of-the-Century Summer Olympic Games). To ease traffic congestion there are plans to build a metro under the Bosphorus and to extend the urban rail network (the Topkapı–Sirkeci line was recently opened) to include more of the outlying districts. Other measures involve the conversion of heating systems from toxic lignite to natural gas and the construction of three sewage treatment plants. (Visitors should be cautious about drinking-water.)

The city consists of three separate elements – the old Turkish town, in the form of an almost exactly equilateral triangle, which extends from the right bank of the Golden Horn to the Sea of Marmara; linked with the old town by the Galata and Atatürk Bridges, the district of Beyoğlu with its suburbs of Galata and Harbiye, largely inhabited by foreigners, on the slopes between the Golden Horn and the Bosphorus; and the district of Üsküdar, with its suburbs, on the Asiatic side of the Bosphorus. İstanbul is a unique and unforgettable sight with its towers and its palaces and the numerous domes and minarets of the 35 large and over a hundred smaller mosques rising above the water. Little is left of the bust and colourful Oriental life of the old capital of the Sultans, and the people of İstanbul now wear European dress; street names and shop signs are in the Latin alphabet; and the old rows of brown timber houses with red roofs and latticed *kafes* (bow-windows) have given place in the central areas to stone and reinforced-concrete blocks.

The climate of İstanbul is marked by sharp contrasts. In the evening it is frequently cool, even in summer. Among the city's numerous birds, visitors will be struck particularly by the black kites and, on the Bosphorus, the black cormorants. Dolphins are often seen playing in the Bosphorus and Sea of Marmara.

History

About 660 B.C. Dorian Greeks founded on what is now Seraglio Point the city of Byzantion (in latin Byzantium), which controlled access to the Black Sea at the entrance to the Bosphorus. In 513 B.C. the town was captured by the Persian King Darius I. During the 6th and 5th c. it was a member of the first and second Attic Leagues. In 148 B.C. the free city of Byzantion entered into an alliance with Rome, and thereafter it lost and then regained its freedom several times. In A.D. 196 the city was captured and harshly treated by Septimius Severus, but soon recovered. In 324, after his victory over Licinius, Constantine I (306–37) resolved to make it a second capital of the Empire.

In the autumn of 326 the construction of a line of town walls was begun, taking in an area which extended far to the west, and on May 11th 330 the new city was solemnly inaugurated, under the name of Nova Roma or New Rome, soon to be changed to Constantinopolis. Like Rome, the new city was divided into 14 regions, and it even had its seven hills. After the division of the Empire in 395 Constantinople became capital of the Eastern Roman Empire. In the reign of Justinian (527–565), who rebuilt the city in greater magnificence after much of it had been reduced to ashes during the Nika Insurrection, it enjoyed its period of greatest splendour. Late Greek and Roman culture developed into the distinctive Byzantine culture, which found expression in the Greek language.

Soon afterwards, however, the Empire was torn by domestic and external conflicts. The city was harried by the Avars and Persians (627) and by the Arabs under the Omayyad caliphs; in 813 and again in 924 it was besieged by the Bulgars; and in 907 and 1048 Russian fleets appeared off Constantinople. Finally came the catastrophe of 1204, when, following disputes over the succession to the Imperial throne, the Crusaders captured the city and founded a Latin Empire.

After the Ottoman conquest of Asia Minor in the 13th c. and the transfer in 1361 of the Sultan's capital from Bursa to Edirne (Adrianople) Constantinople was increasingly encircled by the Turks. In 1453 Mehmet II Fatih (the Conqueror) took the city, which now became the Ottoman capital under the name of İstanbul. There was a great wave of building by the Sultans and Turkish grandees, particularly by Selim I (1512–20) and Süleiman the Magnificent (1520–66). Many major buildings were also erected in the 17th and 18th c. During the 19th c. Western influences began to make themselves felt in the city's architecture.

After the First World War, in which Turkey had been allied with the Central Powers, İstanbul was occupied by the Allies. In 1922, following Turkey's victory in the war of independence, Turkish troops re-entered the city. In 1923 the Sultanate and Caliphate were abolished and Turkey became a Republic. Its first President, Mustafa Kemal Atatürk, moved the capital to Ankara and in a drastic programme of reform he banned the fez,

Eyüp Camii
First Bosporus Bridge

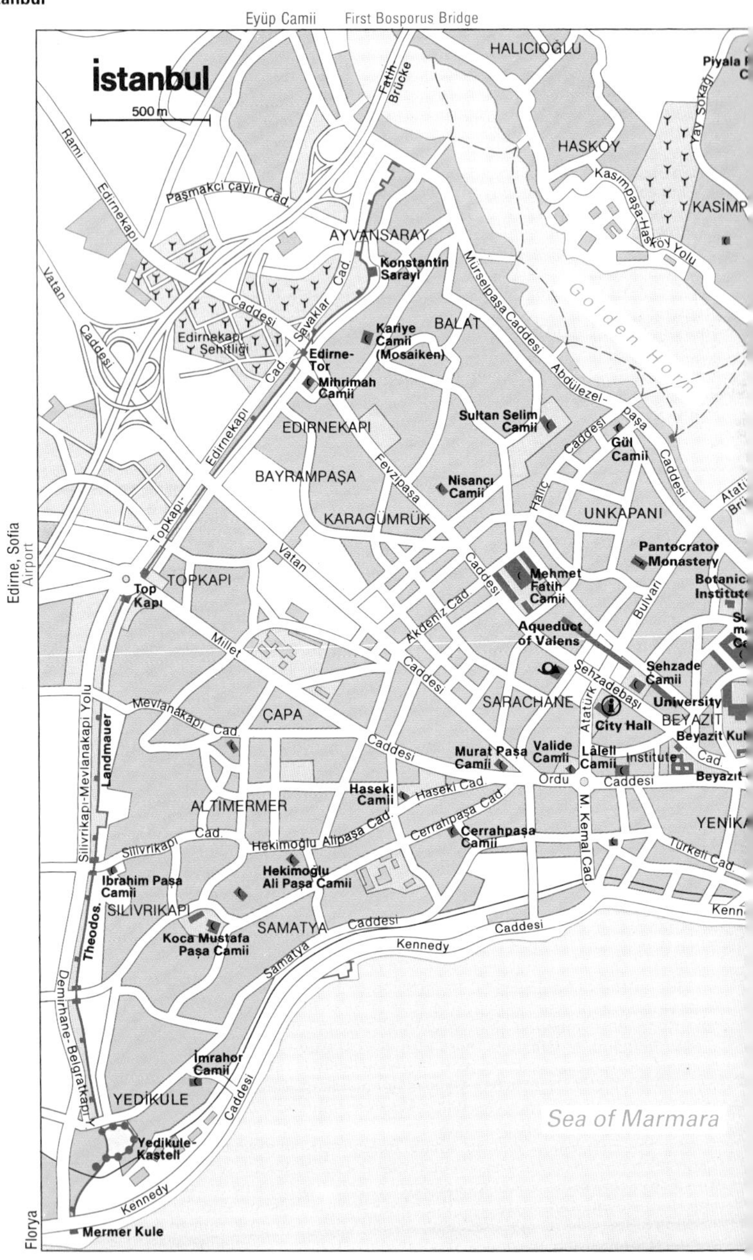

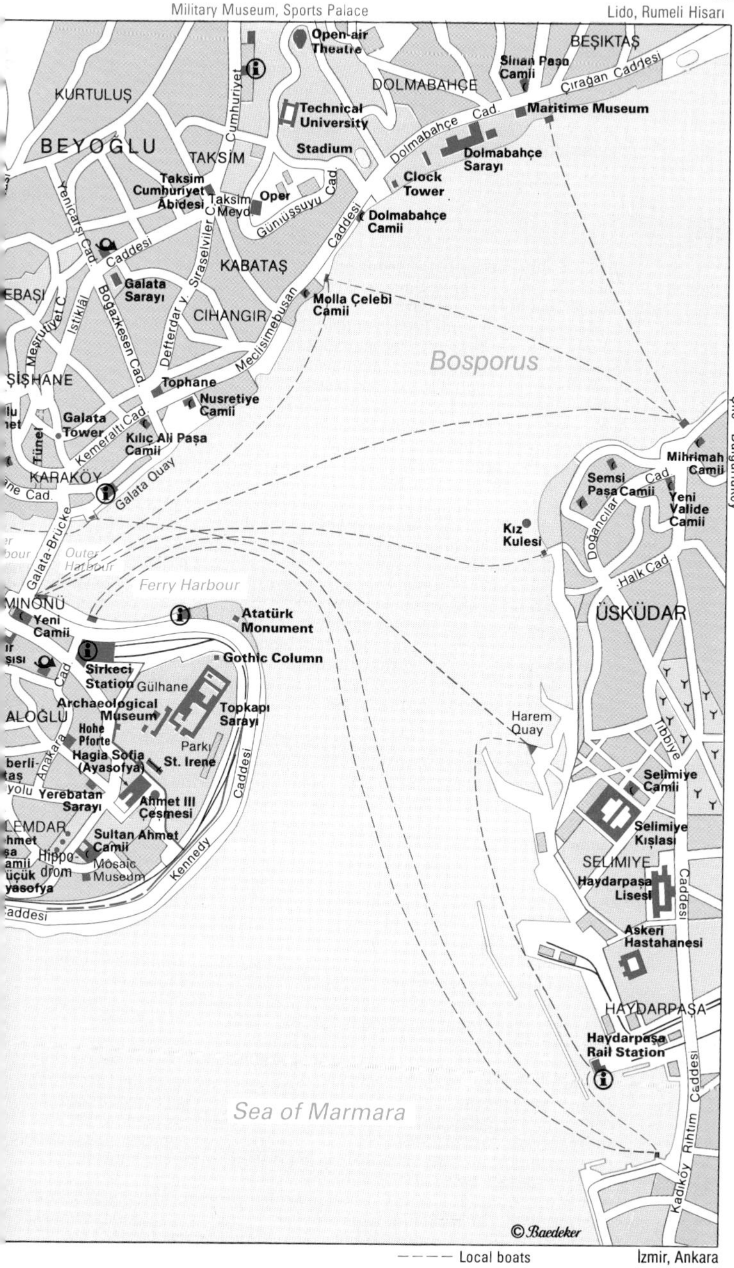

Military Museum, Sports Palace

Lido, Rumeli Hisarı

Open-air Theatre
BEŞIKTAŞ
Sinan Paşa Camii
KURTULUŞ
Cumhuriyet
DOLMABAHÇE
Çırağan Caddesi
Technical University
Maritime Museum
BEYOĞLU
TAKSİM
Stadium
Dolmabahçe Cad.
Dolmabahçe Sarayı
Taksim Cumhuriyet Abidesi
Taksim Meyd.
Oper
Clock Tower
Yeniçarşı Cad.
Günüşsuyu Cad.
Dolmabahçe Camii
Caddesi
Sıraselviler C.
KABATAŞ
Galata Sarayı
Meşrutiyet C.
İstiklâl
Boğazkesen Cad.
Defterdar Y.
CİHANGİR
Meclisimebusan
Molla Çelebi Camii
Bosporus
ŞİŞHANE
Tophane
Nusretiye Camii
Galata Tower
Kemeraltı Cad.
Kılıç Ali Paşa Camii
Tünel
KARAKÖY
Galata Quay
Şile
Bulgurluköy
Mihrimah Camii
Semsi Paşa Camii
Cad.
Yeni Valide Camii
Doğancılar
Kız Kulesi
Galata-Brücke
Outer Harbour
Ferry Harbour
Halk Cad.
ÜSKÜDAR
Yeni Camii
Atatürk Monument
Sirkeci Station
Gothic Column
Gülhane
Archaeological Museum
Topkapı Sarayı
Parkı
Hohe Pforte
Hagia Sofia (Ayasofya)
St. Irene
Ankara
Caddesi
Harem Quay
Yerebatan Sarayı
Ahmet III Çeşmesi
Tıbbiye
Selimiye Camii
Selimiye Kışlası
Sultan Ahmet Camii
Hippodrom
Mosaic Museum
Kennedy
SELİMİYE
Haydarpaşa Lisesi
Caddesi
Askeri Hastahanesi
HAYDARPAŞA
Haydarpaşa Rail Station
Sea of Marmara
Rıhtım Caddesi
Kadıköy

© Baedeker

– – – – Local boats

İzmir, Ankara

the wearing of veils by women, the Order of Dervishes and polygamy and introduced the Latin alphabet, the metric system and regular surnames. İstanbul has, since then, been increasingly Europeanised by constructing wide modern streets through the old town, pulling down old wooden houses and replacing them by new blocks of flats and offices, the establishment of a new commercial and business centre north of Taksim Square and the development of whole new districts of the city.

Beyoğlu

Karaköy Square
Galata Quay

On the southern edge of the district of Galata, at the north end of the Galata Bridge, is busy Karaköy Square. From the south side of the square the Galata Quay runs north-east along the Bosphorus. This is the arrival and departure point for both Turkish and foreign shipping lines (Yolcu Salonu).

Grande Rue de Galata

From Karaköy Square, Meclisimebusan Cad. formerly known as the Grande Rue de Galata is parallel to the Galata Quay but at some distance from the sea through the Tophane district to the Dolmabahçe Palace.

Galata Tower

★★ View

İstiklâl Caddesi

From the north end of the square Yüksek Kaldırım, a steep street lined with shops and with 113 steps on each side, goes up to the Galata Tower (Galata Kulesi), off the street to the left. (The tower can also be reached by following Voyvoda Caddesi and bearing right.) The Galata Tower (68m/223ft high), originally built in Byzantine times, was restored in 1423 by the Genoese and again in 1875; it now contains a restaurant, night-club and bar and affords the best panorama of the Bosphorus and the Golden Horn. The street continues up to Tunnel Square, with the upper station of the Tünel, an underground funicular, in the main part of Beyoğlu (Lord's son), the old district formerly known as Pera. The upper part of Beyoğlu, round Taksim Square, was developed only in the 19th c. in European style; in this area there are numerous hotels, foreign consulates, churches, schools and hospitals. The main artery of Beyoğlu is İstiklâl Caddesi (Independence Street), formerly known as the Grande Rue de Péra, which leads north-east from Tunnel Square, with numerous shops and offices and the Galata Sarayı School. Farther west is another busy street, Meşrutiyet Caddesi.

Taksim Square

İstiklâl Caddesi ends in Taksim Square (Taksim Meydanı), with the Monument to the Republic (1928) and the Opera House. On the north side of the square are the gardens of Republic Square (Cumhuriyet Meydanı).

Cumhuriyet Caddesi

From Taksim Square İstanbul's most elegant street, Cumhuriyet Caddesi, lined with hotels, shops and offices, goes past the gardens of Republic Square to the northern residential districts of Harbiye and Şişli, with numerous handsome villas belonging to the wealthier citizens of İstanbul. On the east side of Cumhuriyet Caddesi the Republic Square gardens are continued by Maçka Park, in which are the İstanbul Technical University, the Hilton Hotel, an open-air theatre, the Palace of Sport and Exhibitions and the Military Museum with its display of Ottoman weapons and a battle tent used by sultans. A marching band performs outside each afternoon. The museum is open from 3–4pm.

★★ Dolmabahçe Palace

Maritime Museum

From the south-east corner of Taksim Square Gümüşsuyu Caddesi runs south and then turns north-east, passing institutes belonging to the University of Technology (on the left) and the Stadium (also on the left) to the Dolmabahçe district, with the Dolmabahçe Palace, a huge edifice in what is called Turkish Renaissance style built by Abdul Mecid in 1854, which was the main residence of the Sultans until 1918 and is now a museum; it is also used for important State visits. Also in this district are the clock-tower of the old Dolmabahçe Mosque (1853) and the Maritime Museum (Deniz Müzesi), a little way north-east of the Dolmabahçe Palace at the landing-stage for Beşiktaş with a collection of large wooden figureheads, Imperial caiques and exhibits about Barbarossa, once First Admiral of the Turkish Fleet.

Gardens outside the Dolmabahçe Palace

A street in the Beyoğlu district

Galata Bridge

From Karaköy Square the Galata Bridge, busy all day with pedestrians and traffic, crosses the Golden Horn (magnificent views) to the old town of İstanbul. The present bridge (484m/512ft long and 42m/138ft wide; landing-stage used by local steamers) was built in 1992 with German assistance, replacing the old Galata Bridge which burnt down in 1991. The old bridge erected by a German firm between 1909 and 1912, rested on 22 pontoons, and the middle section swung open to allow the passage of large vessels. There are plans to reconstruct the historic Galata Bridge, but no decision has yet been made about its new location.

★Golden Horn

The Golden Horn (in Turkish Haliç; boat trip up the Horn recommended), a curving inlet 7km/4½ miles long and up to 40m/130ft deep opening off the Bosphorus, is one of the finest natural harbours in the world. It is in fact a drowned river valley, a tributary of the river which once flowed through the Bosporus. The lowest part, below the Galata Bridge, is the Outer Commercial Harbour, with the Galata Quay on the north side and other quays along the south side. Between the Galata Bridge and the Atatürk Bridge (1km/¾ mile west) is the Inner Commercial Harbour, to the north is the old Naval Harbour. In the Middle Ages the Golden Horn, like the Bosphorus, could be closed to shipping by a chain across the mouth.

The Old Town

At the south end of the Galata Bridge is Eminönü Square, at the start of the oldest part of İstanbul. From here a beautiful seafront road, Florya Sahil Yolu, encircles Seraglio Point and along the Sea of Marmara to Yeşilköy.

★Yeni Cami

On the south side of the square stands the large Yeni Cami, the New Mosque of the Sultan's mother, which was begun in 1615, on the model of the Ahmet I Mosque, for Ahmet's mother but completed only in 1663. The

Dolmabahçe Palace: decorative fountain and fine staircase

A room in the harem

Festival hall in the Padidsha

interior of the mosque and the adjoining royal apartments have rich decoration.

★Egyptian Bazar

Immediately west of the Yeni Cami is the Egyptian Bazaar (Mısır Çarşısı), originally intended only for goods from Egypt but now the most important market in the old town after the Great Bazaar.

Sublime Porte

From the Yeni Cami a street runs south-east, passing close to Sirkeci Station (İstanbul's main station), to the Sublime Porte, once the seat of the Grand Vizier, later the Foreign Ministry and now the office of the Governor (Valı) of İstanbul province. Opposite it, at the corner of the Seraglio wall, is the Alay Köşkü, from which the Sultan could watch, unobserved, the comings and goings at the Sublime Porte.

A little way south-east is the Soğuk Çeşme Gate, the main entrance to the Seraglio, reached on the street which runs up to the right.

The street straight ahead passes through Gülhane Park (admission charge) to a lookout terrace, with views of the Bosphorus and the Sea of Marmara. To the south, below the Tulip Garden, is the Gothic Column (2nd c. A.D.). Outside the park, near the tip of Seraglio Point, can be seen a bronze statue of Mustafa Kemal Atatürk.

★★Topkapı Sarayı

From the Soğuk Çeşme Gate we bear half right to the Topkapı Sarayı (Cannon Gate Palace) or Eski Saray (Old Palace), the old palace-city of the Sultans, built on the Seraglio Point hill, one of the seven hills of New Rome, on the site of the acropolis and the earliest settlement of Byzantion. This great complex of buildings set in gardens (now open to the public) bounded by battlemented walls and towers, consists of a number of buildings outside the main precincts (the Archaeological Museum, the Mint, the Church of Hagia Eirene, etc.) and, beyond these, the Inner Seraglio. Mehmet II built a summer palace here in 1468, and this was enlarged by Süleiman the Magnificent into the Sultan's principal residence, occupied by successive Sultans until Abdul Mecid moved to the Dolmabahçe Palace in 1855.

★★Archaeological Museum

On the west side of the Seraglio hill stands the Archaeological Museum (Arkeoloji Müzesi), which contains an important collection of prehistoric, Greek, Roman and Byzantine antiquities. Among its principal treasures are sarcophagi of the kings of Sidon from the Royal Necropolis of Saida (Sidon, in the Lebanon), including in particular the magnificent Alexander Sarcophagus and the Sarcophagus of the Mourners (with 18 figures of mourning women), both of the 4th c. B.C.; the Sarcophagus of the Satrap (5th c, B.C.); the Lycian Sarcophagus (*c.* 400 B.C.); the Sidamara Sarcophagus from Konya (3rd c. A.D.); and some fine funerary stelae and stones with inscriptions.

Opposite the south-west wing of the Archaeological Museum is the Museum of Ancient Oriental Art (Eski Şark Eserleri Müzesi) displaying items from earlier – Babylonian, Hittite and Assyrian – civilisations.

★Çinili Köşk

In the courtyard of the Archaeological Museum is the graceful Çinili Köşk (Tiled Pavilion), one of the oldest surviving Turkish buildings in İstanbul (1472), in a style which shows Persian influences. It has Turkish ceramic, tile (mainly from İznik, 16th c.) and faience (12th–19th c.) decoration.

Above the Archaeological Museum is the Outer Court of the Seraglio, with the Janissaries' Plane Tree.

Hagia Eirene

On the south-west side of the courtyard stands the reddish domed Church of Hagia Eirene (Divine Peace), one of the best-preserved Early Byzantine buildings in İstanbul, now a museum (Aya Irini Müzesi) St Irene Museum. In 318 it was the meeting-place of the Second Ecumenical Council. During the Turkish period it became an arsenal, and more recently housed an artillery museum.

On the north side of the Outer Court (to the right, the Executioner's Fountain, in front of which dignitaries who had fallen from favour were executed) is the Orta Kapı (Middle Gate; 1524), the entrance to the Inner

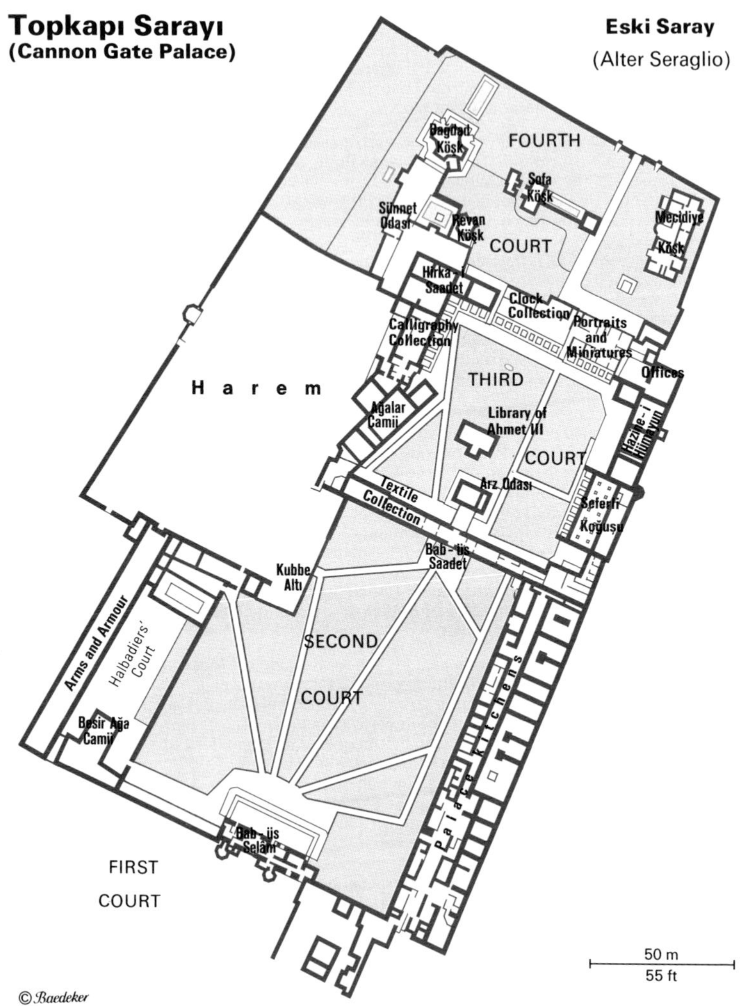

Seraglio, the palace-city of the Sultans, which consists of a series of buildings, large and small, laid out round three courtyards.

The first of the inner courtyards, the Court of the Divan, surrounded by colonnades, is the largest (150m/165yd long) and most impressive. On the right-hand side are the palace kitchens, topped by 30 dome-like chimneys.

★★Porcelain Collection

With their 24 fireplaces, the kitchens were said to serve up to 20,000 meals a day. They now house the Porcelain Collection, predominantly consisting of Chinese porcelain and faience (mostly 10th–18th c.), which includes many items of outstanding quality. On the left-hand side of the courtyard is the Kubbe Altı, built by Mehmet II, with a tall tower (41.5m/135ft; 16th c. upper

Chinese porcelain in the former harem kitchen

part 1819). This housed the Divan, the council chamber in which the Sultan's Council of Viziers met, and the audience chamber in which the Grand Vizier received foreign envoys. Adjoining the Kubbe Altı is a collection of Turkish faience, and beyond this is the interesting Collection of Arms and Armour.

★Collection of Arms and Armour

The Bab-üs Saadet, the Gate of Felicity (to the left, a collection of textiles), leads into the second of the inner courts. Immediately in front of the gate is the Audience Chamber (Arz Odası), a pavilion dating from the time of Süleiman the Magnificent, with a magnificent throne in a colonnaded hall. Beyond this is the Library of Ahmet III. On the right-hand side of the court we come to the Treasury (Hazine), with three rooms containing treasures of inestimable value (thrones, rich garments and weapons, precious stones, pearls, vases, clocks, candelabras, writing materials, etc.). Adjoining the Treasury is a collection of splendid costumes worn by the Sultans.

Treasury

On the left-hand side of the court stands the Eunuchs' Mosque (Ağalar Camii), now housing a library (12,000 manuscripts). Beyond this is the Harem (an Arabic word meaning "That which is forbidden"), the women's apartments to which only the Sultan, his blood relatives and the eunuchs had access. Part of the Harem is now open to the public (admission charge). Apart from a few larger rooms, richly appointed, the Harem is a maze of narrow corridors and small – sometimes tiny – rooms, which have preserved little in the way of Oriental splendour. (In imperial Turkey men might have up to four legitimate wives at a time; the Sultan was allowed seven. There was no limit on the number of subsidiary wives. Since 1926 monogamy has been enforced by law.)

Beyond the second inner court lies the terraced Tulip Garden. On the uppermost terrace (view) is the Bağdat Köşkü (Baghdad Pavilion), a domed building with magnificent tile decoration erected by Murat IV to commemorate the taking of Baghdad. Adjoining it are the Revan Köşkü (Erevan Pavilion) and the Circumcision Room (Sünnet Odası). Lower down are the

★Bağdat Köşkü

Baedeker Special

The Golden Cage

The five young girls were led into the "reception room" and made to stand against the wall. They were dressed in baggy Turkish trousers and shawls of sheer silk. On their heads were satin caps embroidered with gold, and they wore pearl necklaces and ear-rings. Their flowing hair was adorned with small chains and glittering jewels, and even their pointed shoes were decorated with precious stones. Then Sultan Mahmud appeared. But his attention was directed initially not at the young maidens but at his mother, who was also in the room. He greeted her in a kindly manner and chatted to her for a while. Then the Valide Sultan, the Sultan's mother and the most important woman in the *topkapı sarayı*, introduced the girls to her son in a low voice. Mahmud signalled briefly to one of the ladies of his harem and left the room. The "chosen one" would now spend the next night with the Sultan.

After all the girls had left the "reception room" the Valide Sultan, the "Crown of the Veiled Heads", as she was officially known, leaned back and closed her eyes. Once she, too, had been obliged to stand against the wall and be judged by the then mother of the Sultan and her son. If anybody had told her then what career lay before her . . . she began to think back over the years; her real name was Aimée Dubucq de Rivery, and as a young girl she had been a novice in a convent in France. When, in 1782, she voyaged to the island of Martinique to visit her parents, her ship was captured by Algerian pirates. They sold Aimée to the Bey of Algeria, who then presented her as a gift to Sultan Abdul Hamid of İstanbul. First she was taken before a large black man who introduced himself as the *kislar ağası*, the "Master of the Maidens", and gave her to understand that she must obey his orders implicitly, otherwise she would be severely punished. As she did not understand the language of the country he gave her another European girl as a companion, who would instruct her regarding life in the serail. This girl then led Aimée through the harem (Arabic for "forbidden") – a confusing labyrinth of more than 300 small chambers joined by stairways, small courtyards and corridors – and explained to her the special features of this "city within a city" established by Suleiman the Magnificent (1520–1566).

All the women might move about freely in the harem, but could not leave it – except when the Sultan went on a journey, although even then they were not allowed to be seen in public. There was a clearly-defined hierarchy among the members of the harem. Normally the Sultan had four chief wives and several concubines (*gözdeler*, from *gözde* = in the eye), who were kept apart from the others and were treated very specially and had their own rooms and entourage. The wife who was the first to

Baedeker Special

present the Sultan with a son would be raised to the status of *kadin*. For the majority of the several hundred or so ladies of the harem (as many as 1200 under Murat III), however, life was for the most part monotonous, sometimes even wretched. Many of them seldom or even never actually saw the Sultan. They passed their time with embroidery, beauty care and gossip, interspersed with outbreaks of quarrelling and displays of jealousy. They also sought affection and tenderness from one another and from the eunuchs, the castrated guardians of the harem. Any women who failed to please the mother of the Sultan came off worst – they would be given the least pleasant jobs to do in the harem.

Very often the women would find themselves completely at the mercy of a sadistic Sultan – in about 1640, for example, the insane Ottoman ruler Ibrahim had the 280 members of his harem sewn into sacks weighed down with stones and then thrown into the sea! Nevertheless, many young Turkish women, desperate to escape the slave-like conditions of life in the world outside, entered harems of their own free will. Apart from the odalisques – female slaves of Christian origin who came into the possession of their master as prisoners either purchased or received as gifts and who were not allowed to leave the harem until the day they died – they could leave again after a minimum of nine years, usually richly endowed with gifts.

In theory, any Muslim could keep a harem, and the number of concubines was unlimited and dependent only on how rich he was; apart from the Sultan himself, however, only a few, such as high officials, rich businessmen, etc., could in practice afford to maintain a permanent harem.

The Valide Sultan, the mother of the Sultan, enjoyed a unique position. Not only did she have a part to play in selecting the Sultan's bed partners, she was also a powerful figure in the political arena. Each of the chief concubines and other favourites naturally competed to become the most powerful woman in the harem, and in order to achieve this aim many of them even resorted to murder.

Aimée Dubucq de Rivery also had to face plots and intrigues. She bore Sultan Abdul Hamid a son and quickly became his favourite wife – much to the displeasure of his previous chief wife. She also became friendly with Selim III, the nephew and successor of Abdul Hamid, and advised him in political matters. Above all, she did much to improve relations between the Ottoman Empire and France, and in so doing received much support from her cousin, Napoleon's first wife, the Empress Josephine. On several occasions she had to protect her son Mahmud, who was second in line to the throne, from assassination attempts instigated by the mother of the Sultan's first-born son. After his accession to the throne, the latter also tried to put Mahmud out of the way for fear of being deposed by him. However, his would-be murderers were unable to accomplish their task because Aimée and her maidservants helped Mahmud to hide. Shortly afterwards Mahmud himself became Sultan of the Ottoman Empire, and his reign, from 1808 to 1839, was a period of reforms. Until the day she died his mother Aimée, now Valide Sultan, was always there to act as his adviser. Yet in all the 33 years since she had first arrived in İstanbul she was never allowed to leave the harem.

On a day in 1909, after the Sultan Abdul Hamid had been defeated by the Young Turks, 200 ladies of the harem, aged between 15 and 50, climbed into 31 elegant coaches and left the *topkapı sarayı* for ever. The centuries-old institution of the Turkish harem was at an end.

Sofa Köşkü (1704), a fine timber building, the Hekim Bası (Surgeon's Tower) and the Mecidiye Köşkü (19th c.), now a restaurant.

Sultan's Gate

On the south-west side of the Seraglio walls stands the magnificent Sultan's Gate (Bab-ı Hümayun), facing Hagia Sophia. Outside the gate is the Fountain of Ahmet III (1728).

★Fountain of Ahmet III

★★Hagia Sophia (Ayasofya)

The former Church of Hagia Sophia (Holy Wisdom), in Turkish Ayasofya, from the Turkish Conquest until 1935 İstanbul's principal mosque and now a museum, is the supreme achievement of Byzantine architecture and the city's most celebrated monument. The first church on this site, built by Constantine the Great in 326, was burned down and a later church was destroyed during the Nika Insurrection, It was rebuilt on a larger scale in 532–37, during the reign of Justinian, by Anthemios of Tralleis (Aydın) and Isidoros of Miletus, with the avowed intention of surpassing in splendour all the buildings of antiquity. Large numbers of columns were brought to Constantinople from temples in Asia Minor, the Lebanon, Greece and Italy, and the finest marbles and noblest metals were used. It is said that the total cost of the building was 360 hundredweight of gold and that 10,000 workmen were employed in its construction.

Hagia Sophia (entrance on south side) is 75m/245ft long, 70m/230ft wide and 58m/190ft high to the top of the dome. In the exonarthex and narthex (outer and inner porches) are fine Early Christian mosaics, which were formerly concealed under whitewash but have mostly been exposed since 1931. Particularly fine is the figure of Christ enthroned (9th c.) over the main entrance into the church, the Imperial Doorway. The interior, dominated by the magnificent central dome (diameter 32m/105ft and lit by countless windows, is of overpowering effect, though its harmonious proportions are somewhat disturbed by the huge circular wooden plaques on the main piers inscribed in gold script with the names of the first four Caliphs and by the mihrab (the niche indicating the direction of Mecca) in the apse.

Türbes

Outside the south side of the church are five türbes (tombs) of Sultans. To the south-west lies the busy Ayasofya Meydanı (Hagia Sophia Square), on the site of the old Augusteion (Agora), from which there is a fine view of the Blue Mosque.

★Cisterns

North-west of the square in Yerebatan Street is the entrance to the Yerebatan Sarayı (Underground Palace), a huge underground cistern (now electrically lighted) built in the time of Justinian (6th c.). It is the largest of İstanbul's cisterns, 140m/150yd long by 70m/75yd across, with 336 columns set in 12 rows supporting small domes and impressive brick vaulting.

★Atmeydanı

Adjoining the south-west side of Ayasofya Meydanı extends Atmeydanı (Horse Square), an open space more than 300m/330yd long which occupies part of the site of the ancient Hippodrome, begun by Septimus Severus in 203 and completed by Constantine the Great in 330. This was the centre of Byzantine Court and public life, the scene of games and chariot races and also of factional conflicts (Nika Insurrection). Between here and the sea-walls on the Sea of Marmara (still largely preserved) were the Roman and Byzantine Imperial palaces with their churches and associated buildings.

Emperor William's fountain

Egyptian Obelisk

Serpentine Column

Columns of Constantine

In the gardens on the north-west side of Atmeydanı can be seen a fountain, rather inappropriate to its surroundings, presented by the German Emperor, William II. Then follow, to the south-west, three ancient monuments: a 30m/100ft high Egyptian obelisk (from Heliopolis; reign of Thutmos III, 1501–1448 B.C.), with Roman reliefs of the time of Theodosius I on the base; the Serpentine Column, the stump (5m/16ft high) of a bronze column bearing a golden tripod on three snakes' heads which was set up at Delphi to commemorate the Greek victory over the Persians in the Battle of Plataea (479 B.C.); and the so-called Columns of Constantine, a masonry column of uncertain age with a Greek inscription in the name of Constantine VII Porphyrogenitus.

Hagia Sophia, the most celebrated building in İstanbul

★★Blue Mosque (Sultan Ahmet Mosque)

The south-east side of Atmeydanı is dominated by the Sultan Ahmet Mosque or Blue Mosque with its mighty dome (43m/141ft high, 23.5m/77ft in diameter) and six minarets, built by Sultan Ahmet I in 1609–16. The forecourt, with a beautiful fountain in the centre, is surrounded by colonnades roofed with a series of small domes. The interior (72m/235ft by 64m/210ft), in its lightness, spatial effect and colour, is one of the finest creations of Turkish architecture.

Mosaic Museum

On the south-east side of the Blue Mosque is the very fine Mosaic Museum displaying mosaic pavements from 5th and 6th c.

Küçük Ayasofya

South of Atmeydanı, near the Sea of Marmara, stands the Küçük Ayasofya Mosque, the Little Ayasofya. It was originally the Church of SS Sergius and Bacchus, built in the reign of Justinian (between A.D. 527 and 536). From the north end of Atmeydanı Divan Street (Divanyolu) runs west, following the line of the old main street of the Byzantine city. The second street on the left leads to the Binbirdirek (1001 Columns) Cistern, which dates from the 6th c. (64m/188ft by 56m/185ft; 212 columns). Since 1966 it has been dry.

Binbirdirek Cistern

★Burned Column

Farther along Divanyolu, on the second of the seven hills of New Rome (on the right), rises the co-called Burned Column (Çemberlitaş, Hooped Stone), the stump (still 40m/130ft high) of a porphyry column, originally 57m/185ft high, set up by Constantine the Great in his Forum. Until 1105 it bore a bronze statue of Constantine.

Nuru Osmaniye Mosque

North of the Burned Column, on the east side of the Great Bazaar, we come to the Nuru Osmaniye Mosque, constructed entirely in marble (1748–55).

★Great Bazaar

The Great Bazaar (Kapalı Çarşi, covered market), in the depression between the Nuru Osmaniye and Beyazit Mosques, is a whole quarter on its own, surrounded by a wall and entered through 11 gates, a maze of vaulted and dimly lit streets and lanes which even after a major fire in 1954 remains one

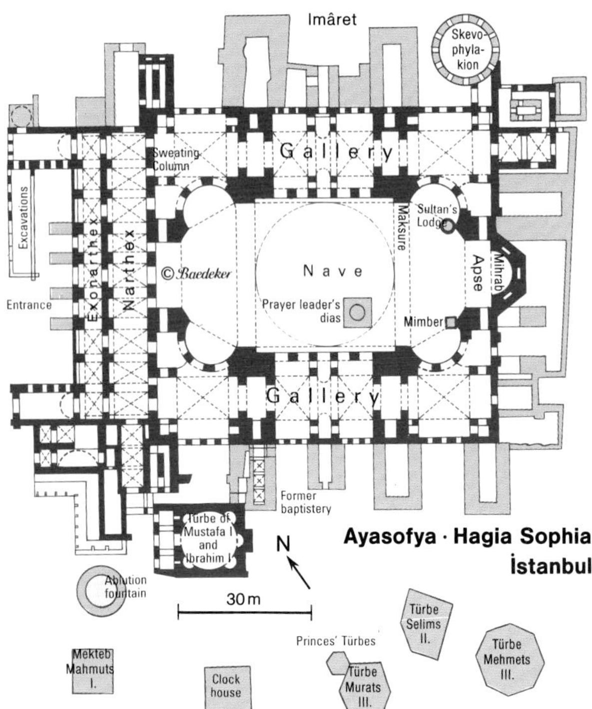

of the great sights of İstanbul. The various trades are still mostly segregated into particular streets or sections of the bazaar.

★Beyazit Mosque

To the west of the Great Bazaar, on the third of the city's seven hills, Beyazit Square occupies the site of Theodosius I's Forum. On the east side of the square is the Beyazit Mosque or Pigeon Mosque, built in 1498–1505, during the reign of Mehmet II's son Beyazit. The interior, painted in Turkish Rococo style in the 18th c., is a simplified imitation of the Hagia Sophia.

From the south side of the square Ordu Caddesi leads west in the direction of the land walls.

University

On the north side of Beyazit Square stands a large gate, the entrance to the University (İstanbul Üniversitesi; previously the War Ministry, Seras Kerat), on the site of the earliest palace of the Sultans. To the right of the University is the 60m/200ft high Beyazit Tower (Beyazit Kulesi, 1823), now a fire-watching tower; from the top (180 steps) there are superb views of İstanbul, finest at sunset or early in the morning.

★★Süleiman Mosque

Below the University to the north, situated on a terrace surrounded by schools, baths, etc., is the Süleiman Mosque (1549–57), built for Süleiman the Magnificent by the great architect Sinan, who, under the influence of Hagia Sophia, carried mosque architecture to its greatest development; after the Selim Mosque in Edirne the Süleimaniye is the greatest achievement. The interior, dominated by its great dome (53m/175ft high, 26.5m/85ft in diameter), is notable for its harmonious proportions and unity of design (on mihrab wall, beautiful tiles and stained glass). Behind the

Blue Mosque İstanbul

Sultan Ahmet Camii

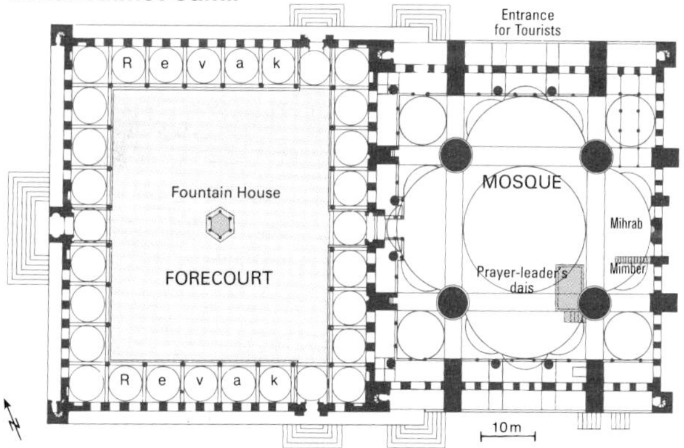

mosque is the burial-ground, with fine türbes (tomb chapels), in particular those of Süleiman and his favourite wife Roxolana.

Museum of Turkish and Islamic Art

To the west of the mosque, in the street along its outer court, is the Museum of Turkish and Islamic Art (Türk ve İslam Eserleri Müzesi), with both sacred and secular works of art including ceramics, miniatures and carpets.

★Şehzade Mosque

A road north-west under Beyazit Square in a 300m/330yd long tunnel leads into Vezneciler Caddesi (on the left, university buildings) and Şehzadebaşı Caddesi, on the right-hand side of which is the Şehzade Mosque (Prince's Mosque), an early master work by the great architect Sinan, built in 1543–47 during the reign of Süleiman and Roxolana in memory of their favourite son Mohammed; it has a charmingly decorated interior.

★Aqueduct of Valens

A little way north of the Şehzade Mosque, between the University and the Sultan Mehmet Mosque, can be seen the imposing bulk of the Aqueduct of Valens, built in the reign of Valens (A.D. 368), frequently restored and still in use. The two-storey aqueduct spans the lower ground between the third and fourth of the city's hills, and at its highest point, half-way along its

City panorama with the Blue Mosque and Hagia Sophia

course, crosses the Atatürk Boulevard, a modern street driven through the centre of the old town, including an area devastated by fire.

Municipal Museum

Near by is the Municipal Museum.

Fatih Mosque

West of the aqueduct, on the city's fourth hill, is the Fatih Mosque (Fatih Camii, Sultan Mehmet Camii), built in 1463–71 on the site of the Church of the Holy Apostles (founded by Constantine the Great and rebuilt by Justinian) and almost completely rebuilt after an earthquake in 1765. It is the holiest mosque in İstanbul after the Eyüp Mosque. In the first türbe behind the mosque is the Tomb of Sultan Mehmet.

Sultan Selim Mosque

To the north of the Fatih Mosque, on the city's fifth hill, stands the Sultan Selim Mosque (Selimiye; 1520–26), the plainest of İstanbul's royal mosques, built by Süleiman the Magnificent in memory of his warlike father Selim I. From the terrace there is a fine view of the Golden Horn.

Edirne Gate

Mihrimah Mosque

At the end of Fevzipaşa Caddesi, in the land walls, is the Edirne Gate (Edirnekapı), which was almost completely destroyed by an earthquake in 1894. Just before the gate, on the sixth and highest of the city's hills (to the left), is the Mihrimah Mosque, built by Sinan in 1556 for the daughter of Süleiman I (numerous windows).

★Katiye Camii

Some 300m/330yd north-east stands the beautiful Kariye Camii, originally the Church of St Saviour in Chora (in the country), belonging to a monastery which seems to have been in existence before the time of Theodosius II. It is world-famous for its mosaics and frescos of the period of the Palaeologue Renaissance (13th–14th c.). The date of the church and monastery has not been established with certainty. Some authorities believe that the foundation of the church may go back to the 5th c.; but much of the present church was built in the late 11th c. by Maria Dukaina, mother-in-law of the Emperor Alexius Comnenus. Her grandson Isaac Comnenus repaired the church after it had been severely damaged in an earthquake about 1120. The magnificent decoration of the interior dates from the 13th–14th c. The mosaics, preserved almost intact in the two narthexes and fragmentarily in the katholikon (nave), cover a wide range of themes, from the ancestors of Christ to the Last Judgment. In the parekklesion (side aisles), which served as a burial chapel, are a unique series of frescos on the theme of death, resurrection and the life after death.

★★Mosaics

From outside the Edirne Gate, where is situated İstanbul's largest Muslim cemetery, there is a good general view of the land walls of Constantinople, which extend, excellently preserved for much of the way, for a distance of 6670m/7300yd from the Golden Horn to the Sea of Marmara. With their numerous towers, large and small, they are a superbly impressive sight.

★★Land walls

The Theodosian walls, which form the main section of the circuit, were built between 413 and 439, and after an earthquake in 447 were developed into a threefold ring of defences some 60m/200ft wide, with a height, from the bottom of the moat, of 30m/100ft. There are superb views from the top of the walls.

A little way north of the Edirne Gate the line of the Theodosian walls is continued by the walls of the Blachernae quarter, originally built between the 7th and 12th c. Opposite the little Kerkoporta Gate are the ruins of a Byzantine palace, the Tekfur Sarayı (10th c.).

Tekfur Sarayı

For a good view of the land walls it is well worth while to drive down the road which runs outside the walls from the Edirne Gate, passing the Top Kapı (Cannon Gate) and the Silivri Gate, to the Fortress of Yedikule (Seven Towers) on the Sea of Marmara. This battlemented stronghold on a pentagonal plan was built by Mahmet II from 1455 onwards and served successively as a fortress, a treasury and a State prison. From the tower at the east corner there is a magnificent prospect of the whole of the land walls and other beautiful panoramic views.

★Yedikule

Eyüp

Outside the land walls, at the north end of the Golden Horn, lies the suburb of Eyüp, with İstanbul's holiest shrine, the Eyüp Mosque, built in 1459 and subsequently much altered. Here a new Sultan was girded with his sword. Facing the entrance to the mosque is the Türbe of Eyüp, the Prophet's Standard-bearer, who was killed during the first Arab siege of Constantinople (678).

★Eyüp Mosque

On the hill above the mosque, to the north-east, is a picturesque cemetery. Each grave has two gravestones, and until 1926 the headstone of a man's grave bore a fez or turban. From higher up, above the old Convent of the Whirling Dervishes, there is a magnificent view of both sides of the Golden Horn.

★Cemetery

★View

2km/1¼ miles east of Eyüp the Sweet Waters of Europe flow into the Golden Horn. This is still a favourite resort of the people of İstanbul.

Üsküdar

The best way to get to Üsküdar is to take the car ferry which plies regularly across the Bosphorus, here 2km/1¼ miles wide, from the Kabataş landing-stage (2km/1¼ miles north-east of the Galata Bridge). On an islet just off the Asiatic shore stands Leander's Tower (in Turkish Kız Kulesi, "Maiden's Tower"), 30m/100ft high, with a signal station and a lighthouse.

Leander's Tower

İstanbul's outlying district of Üsküdar, traditionally known as Scutari, on the Asiatic side of the Bosphorus, is the city's largest suburb. With its handsome old mosques, winding lanes and weathered brown timber houses (particularly between the landing-stage and the large cemetery) it has preserved more of its traditional Oriental character than the old town of İstanbul. The town, known in antiquity as Chrysopolis, was one of the earliest Greek settlements on the Bosphorus. It was much more exposed to attack by foreign conquerors than Constantinople, with its defensible situation and strong walls, but it was able to draw economic advantage from its exposed situation: until 1800 it was the terminus of the caravan routes which brought the treasures of the East to Constantinople, from which they were sent on to Europe.

Büyük Cami

At the landing-stage (on the left) is the Büyük Cami (Great Mosque), also known as the İskele Camii or Mihrimah Camii, which was built by Süleiman the Magnificent in 1547 for his daughter Mihrimah. A little way south is the Yeni Valide Camii, built by Sultan Ahmet III in 1707–10.

★Views

Between the two mosques a road branches off on the left to Bağlarbaşı, Kısıklı and the suburb of Bulgurluköy, 5km/3 miles away. 1km/¾ mile north rises the Hill of Büyük Çamıca (268m/879ft), from which there are superb views of İstanbul, the Bosphorus and the Sea of Marmara; the views are no less impressive at night.

★Cemetery

Selimiye Camii

The cemetery (Karacaahmet Mezarlığı) on the hill south-east of Üsküdar (1.5km/1 mile from landing-stage; buses) is the largest in the East, with ancient cypresses and large numbers of marble tombstones. At its north end is an old Convent of the Howling Dervishes. West of the cemetery, near the sea, is the Selimiye Camii, built by Selim III; to the south-west are the Selimiye Barracks, a huge complex with four corner towers in which Florence Nightingale established her hospital during the Crimean War.

Haydarpaşa

Kadıköy (Chalcedon)

Eastward from here, reached by turning right along Tibbiye Caddesi, passing a large school (1934), we reach the large suburb of Haydarpaşa, with port installatiions and, directly on the Sea of Marmara, the handsome terminus of the Anatolian Railway. To the south of the railway lines lies the suburb of Kadıköy, on the site of the ancient Greek city of Kalchedon (Chalcedon), founded about 675 B.C., which in Roman times was capital of the province of Bithynia and later the see of an archbishop. The Fourth Ecumenical Council met here in 451.

★★Bosphorus

See entry.

★Princes' Islands

See entry.

İzmir C 5

West coast (Aegean Sea)
Province: İzmir. Altitude: 0–185m/0–605ft
Population: 2.7 million (conurbation)

Situation and characteristics

The provincial capital of İzmir (formerly Smyrna), Turkey's third largest city and its most important port and commercial city after İstanbul, lies halfway down the west coast of Aisa Minor in the beautiful Gulf of İzmir (İzmir Körfezi; 8–24km/5–15 miles wide, 54km/33½ miles long), one of the finest bays in the Aegean. The rapidly growing city extends round the head of the gulf for a distance of over 30km/20 miles like some huge amphitheatre, climbing up the slopes of Mount Pagos, with the peaks of Manisa Dağı (Mount Sipylos; 1517m/4977ft) and Nif Dağı (1510m/4954ft) rearing up behind.

Although İzmir itself, after repeated destructions and its rebuilding in modern style after a great fire in 1922 started by the Turkish army plundering the city after it was mandated to Greece after the First World War, has preserved few ancient remains apart from its Agora, it attracts many visitors as a port of call on cruises in the eastern Mediterranean, as a take-off point for visits to Ephesus, Miletus and many other famous ancient sites in

Asia Minor and also as an important road and rail junction linking the north of Asia Minor with the south and the coast with the interior.

The city's economic importance (annual trade fairs) is based principally on its well-situated harbour, which is largely engaged in shipping the produce of western Anatolia. In recent years there has been a considerable development of industry (textiles, tobacco, foodstuffs, paper, chemicals, tanning and the famous Smyrna carpets). The principal exports are tobacco, cotton, raisins, figs, olives and olive oil.

İzmir has a university and a NATO command headquarters. Today the tallest building is the 31-storey Hilton Hotel.

History

About 3000 B.C., on the hill of Tepe Kule some 3.5km/2 miles north of the present city, there was a walled settlement of the Trojan Yortan culture, with a harbour. Excavation by the Archaeological Institute of Ankara showed that it was a considerable cultural centre. The excavations also indicated that towards the end of the 11th c. B.C. Aeolian Greeks established a colony here, naming it Smyrna after the myrrh which grew in abundance in the area. The 11th c. walls are the oldest known Greek town walls. In the same century a colony was founded by Ionian Greeks, who according to Herodotus came from Kolophon. Between 750 and 725 B.C. Homer, of whom many Greek cities claimed to be the birthplace, is said to have composed the "Iliad" here.

The first firm fact in the history of the city is given by Pausanias of Magnesia on Sipylos (2nd c. A.D.), who tells us that it was a member of the Panionic League. About 575 B.C. the city was destroyed by King Alyattes III of Lydia. Later in the 6th c. it was taken by the Medes, and later still by the Persians. In the second half of the 4th c. B.C. Alexander the Great ordered his General Lysimachos to build a stronghold on Mount Pagos, 5km/3 miles south of the town as it then was, and the new Hellenistic city grew up on the north-west side of the hill. The older settlement in the plain now decayed as a result of the silting up of the harbour. The city had a period of great prosperity in the 3rd and 2nd c. B.C.

Under Roman rule (from 27 B.C. onwards) Smyrna continued to prosper, and in the 2nd c. A.D. it enjoyed a second heyday. The Golden Road, still partly preserved, dates from this period. On the northern slope of Mount Pagos (on which remains of the fortress wall can still be seen) was the stadium. Farther west, probably in the southern district of Karatas, stood the Temple of Zeus. The agora was decked with columns and porticoes, and the streets were laid out at right angles in accordance with the principles of Hippodamos of Miletus (5th c. B.C.). The commercial market was down by the harbour. The city, which then had a population of over 100,000, was supplied with water by an extensive system of aqueducts.

Smyrna continued to be a place of importance after the coming of Christianity. The city was destroyed by severe earthquakes in A.D. 178 and 180 but was quickly rebuilt during the reign of Marcus Aurelius (161–180).

In the 4th c, Smyrna passed into Byzantine hands, and in the 7th c., thanks to energetic assistance from the Byzantines, held out against the Arab onslaught. In the 11th c., however, it fell to the Seljuks, who established large shipyards here. During the First Crusade, in 1097, a Byzantine fleet compelled the city, then still under Seljuk rule, to surrender. In recognition of the help given by Genoa in the recovery of Constantinople from the Franks the Byzantine emperors granted the Genoese extensive rights over Smyrna.

In 1320 the city was taken by the Seljuk Sultan of Aydın, but in 1344, on the urging of the Pope, the Crusaders (Knights of St John) assembled a large fleet and recaptured the town and fortress after bitter fighting. In 1403 Tamerlane (Timur-Leng) and his Mongols, however, took the town from the Crusaders. Between 1405 and 1415 Smyrna was incorporated in the Ottoman Empire by Mehmet I and defended against repeated attacks by the Venetians.

Although in subsequent centuries the town was not involved in any further military action it suffered severely from two major earthquakes

(1688 and 1788), plague and great fires (1840 and 1845). Its spirit, however, remained unbroken, and in the 19th c. it was one of the most flourishing cities in the Ottoman Empire. In 1886 the River Gediz was diverted to flow into the sea farther to the west, thus obviating any further silting up of the harbour.

During the war between Turkey and Greece, in 1919, Smyrna was occupied by Greek forces, and under the Treaty of Sèvres (1920) it passed temporarily under Greek sovereignty. After its recovery by Kemal Paşa on September 9th 1922 the wealthy northern part of the city (comprising the Frankish, Greek and Armenian quarters) was destroyed by fire, and the subsequent rebuilding, together with the removal of the Greek population, raised major problems. Wide new avenues, with gardens, were laid out and lined with modern buildings, and part of the area destroyed by fire is now occupied by the Culture Park and the Trade Fair Grounds. New industrial suburbs were built on the north side of the town, and large new residential districts grew up on the gulf to the south-west and on its northern shores.

Sights

★Atatürk Caddesi

The most important street for tourists in the long Atatürk Caddesi, which runs south from the northern tip of the city, in the district of Alsancak (landing-stage for passenger ships), for a distance some 3.5km/2 miles as a broad seafront promenade, passing alongside the harbour to the old district of Konak. To the right it affords fine views of the Gulf of İzmir, while the left-hand side is lined with handsome modern buildings (restaurants). At No. 248 is the Atatürk Museum, with mementoes of Atatürk's stay in İzmir. Farther down, standing by itself, is NATO's command headquarters.

Atatürk Museum

Republic Square

About half-way along Atatük Caddesi is Republic Square (Cumhuriyet Meydanı), with the Independence Monument (İstiklâl Anıtı), an equestrian

Konak Mosque

A shoeshine boy in İzmir

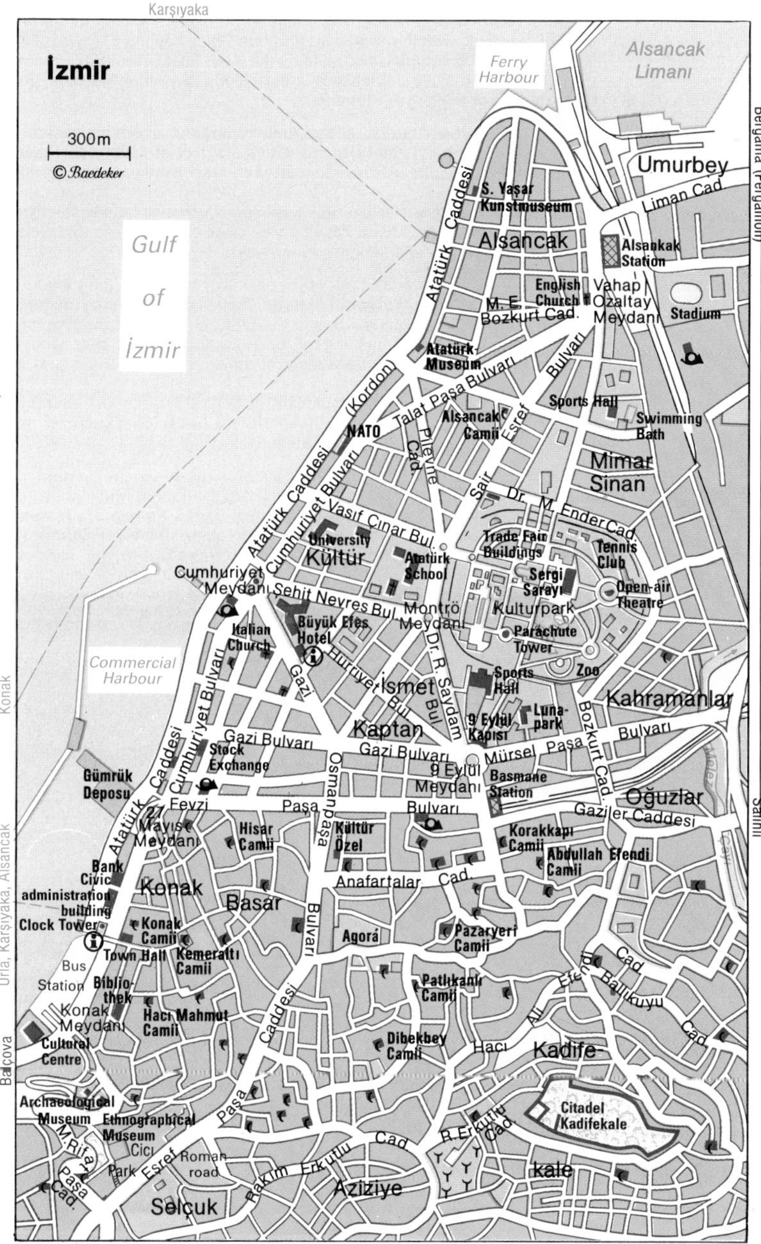
Karşıyaka
İzmir
300 m
© Baedeker
Gulf of İzmir
Ferry Harbour
Alsancak Limanı
Umurbey
Liman Cad.
Bergama (Pergamon)
Çanakkale
S. Yaşar Kunstmuseum
Alsancak
Alsankak Station
English Church
Vahap Özaltay Meydanı
Stadium
M. E. Bozkurt Cad.
Atatürk Caddesi
Atatürk-Museum
Talat Paşa Bulvarı
Bulvarı
Sports Hall
Swimming Bath
(Kordon)
NATO
Alsancak Camii
Pilevne Cad.
Eşref
Mimar Sinan
Şair
Dr. M. Ender Cad.
Cumhuriyet Bulvarı
Vasıf Çınar Bul.
University
Kültür
Atatürk School
Trade Fair Buildings
Tennis Club
Sergi Sarayı
Open-air Theatre
Cumhuriyet Meydanı
Şehit Nevres Bul.
Montrö Meydanı
Kulturpark
Büyük Efes Hotel
Italian Church
Parachute Tower
Zoo
Commercial Harbour
Gazi
Hürriyet Bul.
Dr. R. Saydam Bul.
İsmet Kaptan
Sports Hall
Kahramanlar
Konak
Luna-park
9 Eylül Kapısı
Bozkurt Cad.
Gazi Bulvarı
Mürsel Paşa Bulvarı
Stock Exchange
Osman Paşa
9 Eylül Meydanı
Basmane Station
Gümrük Deposu
Feyzi Paşa Bulvarı
Oğuzlar
Gaziler Caddesi
Salihli
27 Mayıs Meydanı
Hisar Camii
Kültür Özel
Korakkapı Camii
Abdullah Efendi Camii
Bank
Civic administration building
Clock Tower
Konak
Basar
Anafartalar Cad.
Konak Camii
Bulvarı
Agora
Pazaryeri Camii
Town Hall
Kemeraltı Camii
Urla, Karşıyaka, Alsancak
Bus Station
Biblio-thek
Patlıkanlı Camii
Ali Efendi Cad.
Ballıkuyu Cad.
Konak Meydanı
Hacı Mahmut Camii
Caddesi
Dibekbey Camii
Hacı
Kadife-kale
Cultural Centre
Çeşme, Karaburun
Balçova
Archaeological Museum
Ethnographical Museum
Citadel Kadifekale
Paşa
M. Rifat Paşa Cad.
Cici Park
Eşref
Roman road
R. Erkutlu Cad.
Cad.
Rakım Erkutlu
Aziziye
Selçuk
Airport
Kuşadası, Selçuk (Ephesus), Pamukkale

statue of Atatürk. On the south-east side of the square stands the large Büyük Efes Hotel, with the Tourist Information Office beyond it. The south-west corner of the square is occupied by the Head Post Office (PTT). From the east side of the square Şehitler Caddesi leads to Montrö Meydanı, on the west side of the large Culture Park.

Commercial Harbour

The southern part of Atatürk Caddesi runs from Republic Square past the Commercial Harbour (Ticaret Limanı), with the offices of various shipping lines and many banks. At the junction with Gazi Bulvarı is the Stock Exchange.

At the large Customs Hall Gümrük Deposu), which also houses the fish market, a broad avenue, Fevzi Paşa Bulvarı, goes off on the left and runs east to Basmahane Station (1km/¾ mile away).

Konak Square

At the south end of Atatürk Caddesi lies Konak Maydanı, a long square looking out on to the Gulf of İzmir. At its north end is the imposing modern Town Hall (Belediye), at its south end the Cultural Centre of the Aegean University, a complex of buildings in unusual architectural style which includes an opera house, an academy of music, exhibition halls and a museum of modern art.

Most of this busy square is occupied by the Central Bus Station. Near the Town Hall, at a pedestrian overpass, are the Clock Tower (Saat Kule), an old city landmark, and the little Konak Mosque.

★Archaeological Museum

A little way south-east, above Konak Square (on the curving main road to the south), we come to the interesting new Archaeological Museum, with finds from ancient Smyrna, Ephesus, Miletus, Sardis, Pergamon, Tralleis (Aydın) and other sites. Among particularly notable exhibits are figures of Poseidon and Demeter (2nd c. A.D.) from the Agora of Smyrna, various sarcophagi, a colossal Roman head, a mosaic pavement, fine collections of glass, coins and jewellery and a bronze figure of Demeter from Halikarnassos (Bodrum; 4th c. B.C.).

Exhibit in the Archaeological Museum in İzmir

Ethnographic Museum

On the opposite side of the street is the Ethnographic Museum, recently installed it contains a colourful collection of costumes, carpets and crafts and several traditional room settings.

Bazaar Quarter

To the north-east of Konak Square extends the Bazaar, a maze of narrow streets and lanes, with innumerable workshops, little shops and stalls, several 18th c. caravanserais (some of them restored) and a number of small mosques of the Ottoman period. Of particular interest is the well-restored Hisar Mosque (1597) İzmir's oldest and largest.

Agora

A little way south of Fevzi Paşa Bulvarı in the Basmahane district, some 150m/164yd east of Esrefpaşa Caddesi, are the partly excavated remains of the Agora (Market), which originally dated from the Greek period but was rebuilt in the 2nd c. A.D., in the reign of Marcus Aurelius, after an earthquake. Along the west end of the square, which is laid out in gardens, are 13 columns with fine capitals, still standing. On the north side is a three-aisled basilica 160m/175yd long with a vaulted roof borne on pillars. The marble figures which were found here are now in the new Archaeological Museum (above). The best impression of the situation and extent of the Agora is to be had in a distant view from Kadifekale Citadel.

Roman road

Continuing south along Esrefpaşa Caddesi, we come in some 900m/1000yd to a stretch of Roman road (Roma Yolu), part of the old Golden Road (Altın Yol).

To the west of the Roman road is Cici Park, on the slopes of Değirmen Tepe (Mill Hill, 75m/245ft). On the hill there were temples of Vesta and Asklepios., of which no trace is left, and this was also the terminal point of an aqueduct 17km/10½ miles long.

★Kadifekale

On the east side of the city (access road signposted) rises the Hill of Kadifekale (Velvet Castle), the ancient Mount Pagos (185m/607ft), on which was the acropolis of Lysimachos's city. From the summit, crowned by the

A shady corner on the Kadifekale

★★View

remains of a medieval citadel, there is an incomparable panoramic view of the whole city, the Gulf of İzmir and the hills.

The massive and well-preserved walls of the medieval citadel, which originally had 40 towers, incorporate foundations and other masonry from the Lysimachean acropolis as well as work dating from the Roman, Byzantine, Genoese and Ottoman periods.

On the slopes of the hill were the Roman theatre and the stadium (with seating for 20,000 spectators), of which practically no remains survive, though the outline of the stadium can still be traced. According to tradition the Tomb of St Polycarp, Bishop of Smyrna, who was martyred in A.D. 156 during the persecution of Christians, lay above the north side of the stadium.

Culture Park

In the north-east of the city (area razed to the ground in 1922), just beyond 9 Eylül Meydanı and east of Montrö Meydanı, lies the Culture Park with gardens and a lake, the Trade Fair exhibition halls, a zoo, an amusement park, an artificial lake and an open-air theatre.

Alsancak Stadium

To the north-east of the Culture Park, beyond the railway lines, is the large Alsancak Stadium.

Caravan Bridge

South-east of the Culture Park, to the east of Basmahane Station, the Kemer Bridge crosses the little River Melez (the ancient Meles), a modern structure on Greek and Roman foundations. It was formerly known as the Caravan Bridge, from the heavy caravan traffic which passed over it on the way into the interior (Manisa, Balıkesir, Sardis).

Diana's Bath

2km/1¼ miles east, outside the suburb of Tepecik, is Diana's Bath (Diana Hamamaları), a little lake with eight springs which supply İzmir with water.

Surroundings of İzmir

Balçova (Baths of Agamemnon)

İnciraltı

Barely 9km/5½ miles SW of İzmir after passing through extensive residential suburbs we reach a crossroads. To the left, in 700m/765yd we come to the spa centre of Balçova (radio-active Baths of Agamemnon; 35–40°C/95–105°F; a cable car takes the visitor to a panoramic restaurant). By turning right at the crossroads we come to the resort of İnciraltı.

13km/8 miles beyond the crossroads the main road, running west towards Urla and Çeşme, comes to another junction, where a road goes off on the left to the little town of Seferihisar, 22km/14 miles south. 2km/1¼ miles west of Seferihisar is Siğacık (tourist village; marina), on the bay of the same name.

Teos

In the plain to the south of Siğacık are the remains of ancient Teos, a member of the Panionic League of cities which was noted as a centre of the cult of Dionysos and the birthplace of the lyric poet Anakreon (*c.* 540 B.C.). No trace is left of the once-famous temple built by hermogenes of Alabanda.

Urla

Klazomenai

Continuing on the main road, we come in another 11km/7 miles to the town of Urla (baths, with water containing magnesium). 4km/2½ miles north, on an islet linked with the mainland by a causeway, near the little township of Urla İskelesi, are the remains of ancient Klazomenai, birthplace of the philosopher Anaxagoras (*c.* 500 B.C.). Numbers of Archaic painted clay sarcophagi were found in the grounds of the hospital here.

Çeşme

At the tip of the peninsula, 45km/28 miles west of Urla, lies the holiday centre of Çeşme, rising above the sea under the frowning walls of a Genoese fortress. It takes its name from its thermal springs (çeşme= spring; sulphurous water, temperature 35–50°C/95–122°F, recommended for the treatment of rheumatism). From here there is a ferry service (cars carried) to the Greek island of Chios (Turkish Sakız).

★Ilıca Beach

5km/3 miles east of Çeşme, on a bay with a beautiful sandy beach, is the seaside resort of Ilıca (hotels, holiday facilities).

Erythrai

North of Çeşme, on the Bay of Lytri (Ildır), is the site of ancient Erythrai, a member of the Panionic League of cities, with remains of the town walls, theatre, etc. Fine views of the bay may be seen from the top of the hill.

Airport

South of İzmir is Cumanovası, where the city's new civil airport of "Adnan Menderes" was completed in 1987. The road which branches off the main road and passes through the little town continues south to Değirmendere, near which is the site of ancient Kolophon.

Kolophon

Kolophon was one of the principal cities of the Panionic league, famed for its wealth and luxury and also noted for the breeding of horses and for the production of colophonium, a purified resin harvested from the pine trees on the hills surrounding the town. About 665 B.C. Kolophon was captured by King Gyges of Lydia and thereafter shared the destinies of the other Ionian cities. After a war fought about 287 B.C. King Lysimachos resettled the inhabitants of Kolophon and the neighbouring town of Lebedos, on the coast to the south-west, in the newly founded city of Ephesus. The surviving remains probably date from the rebuilding of the city after Lysimachos' death. In Roman times Kolophon was a little country town of no consequence.

The site is traversed by the Avcı Çayı (ancient Ales). To the south, above Değirmendere, is the site of the ancient acropolis, a hill surrounded by a wall which falls down to the valley in three artificial terraces, with numerous foundations of buildings. The wall, 2.25m/7½ft thick, enclosed a larger area than that of Pergamon. It still preserves numerous semicircular towers; excavations by Schuchardt and Wolters in 1886 found remains of 12 other towers, as on the Lysimachean walls of Ephesus. The main gate faced Değirmendere; the east gate led into the Kaystros Valley, the south gate to Notion. The theatre was in the hollow below the hill.

Notion

At the south end of the Ales Valley, 12km/7½ miles from Kolophon on a little bay which is now silted up, was the city's port, Notion. The remains of the ancient town are on a hill surrounded by walls and towers, from which two promontories project into the sea. On the east side of the site is a theatre which preserves more than 20 tiers of seating, and near by are remains of a temple, 12m/40ft long. To the north lies the town's necropolis.

Klaros

In a side valley to the east we come to the site of ancient Klaros, which was celebrated for its cave oracle of Apollo. The site was identified in 1907.

Lebedos

North-west of Notion, in the Bay of Lebedos, was the city of Lebedos. The site is on the former island of Xingi, now connected with the mainland by a sand spit. The walls and gate are reasonably well preserved. The city's thermal springs (sulphurous water) still attract many visitors.

Larissa

The road which runs north-west from İzmir, first skirting the beautiful Gulf of İzmir, comes in 40km/25 miles to the remains (to right of road) of ancient Larissa, with an acropolis built by Aeolian Greeks in the 6th c. B.C. On a hill to the east is the site of Neon Teichos, a stronghol directed against Larissa which was founded by Kyme in the 8th c. B.C. The lower town, with polygonal walls, lay under the acropolis.

Foça

Some 2km/1¼ miles farther north a side road branches off the main road on the left to the pleasant little port town of Foça (founded 1576), situated on the site of ancient Phokaia (Phocaea) at the northern entrance to the Gulf of İzmir.

Phokaia

Phokaia, the most northerly of the Ionian cities, was founded in the 8th c., probably from Teos. Situated on a promontory projecting into the gulf, the city had two harbours. The Phocaeans were daring seamen who by the

7th c. B.C. were familiar with the coasts of the western Mediterranean, founding Massalia (Marseilles) about 600 B.C. and Alalia (Aleria), on the east coast of Corsica, about 565 B.C. Many wealthy citizens of Phokaia moved to these new foundations when the city fell to the Persians about 540 B.C. From 478 it was a member of the confederacy of Delos. It became Persian again in 412, but remained for centuries a city of considerable consequence, yielding rich booty to looting Romans in 189 B.C. After a plundering Catalan raid in 1307 Focia Nuova (Yenifoça) was founded. The old town fell to the Turks in 1455. The only surviving ancient structures are the foundations of walls. There is also a ruined 15th c. Genoese castle.

Yenifoça

To the north-east, on the far side of the promontory (road via Bağlararası), is the little town of Yenifoça, with a beach, a small harbour and modern tourist developments. Founded at the beginning of the 14th c., it fell to the Turks at the same time as its twin town of Foça, in 1455. In the lonely surrounding area are several beautiful bathing beaches.

★Bathing beaches

Çandarlı

On a promontory on the north side of the Gulf of Çandarlı is the little grain port of Çandarlı, dominated by a 13th c. Venetian castle (restored). In antiquity the gulf was known as Sinus Elaiticus, after the city of Elaia, the port for Pergamon. There are still remains of the ancient town walls built by Attalos I. The acropolis was on an egg-shaped hill.

Çandarlı was traditionally believed to be the site of the Aeolian port of Pitane, founded by the Amazons, which had two harbours, one on each side of the promontory.

İzmit (Kocaeli) E 3

North-west Anatolia (Marmara region)
Province: Kocaeli
Altitude: 10–110m/32–360ft
Population: 255,000

Situation and Importance

This busy provincial town at the eastern end of the Gulf of İzmit, formerly known as the Gulf of Astakos, is a major industrial centre with factories not only in the immediate vicinity but also in the nearby towns around the Gulf (automobiles, metal-processing, chemicals; Yarımca: ironworks, Ipraz oil refinery). The dockyards of Gölcük on the opposite side of the gulf combine with İzmit to create a military base and garrison of considerable importance. As the town lies on one of Turkey's tectonic fault lines, it has often been affected by serious earthquakes and most of the buildings are modern.

History

Once the residence of emperors Hadrian and Diocletian, the town stands on the site of the Bithynian capital Nikomedeia, which was founded in 264 B.C. by Nikomedes I. A short distance to the north-west stood Astakos or Olbia, a city which was founded by the Megarans and later destroyed by the Thracian Lysimachos. An earthquake obliterated the old settlement in A.D. 358, but magnificent new temples and other public buildings which became famous for their statues adorned the rebuilt Nikomedeia. One life-sized ivory statue of Nikomedes was taken to Rome by Trajan. In 74 B.C., the city fell under Roman influence. Between A.D. 111 and 113, Pliny the Younger became the Roman governor of Bithynia and was resident here. In A.D. 259 after its destruction by the Goths, the city was rebuilt in its original splendour by Diocletian as the capital of his tetrarchy. Under Constantine it rivalled Rome or Alexandria in importance. In 1386 the city became a part of the Ottoman Empire.

Sights

The remains of the city walls date from Hellenistic, Roman, Byzantine and Ottoman times. The citadel ruins (acropolis) are of Byzantine origin. The Pertev Paşa Camii Mosque is the work of the famous Ottoman architect Sinan (see Famous People).

Surroundings

Adapazarı

The 19th c. provincial town of Adapazarı (pop. 174,000) is situated 20km/12½ miles to the east of İzmit and close to the River Sakarya at the western end of a wide low-lying area (Adapazarı Ovasi). It has assumed increasing economic importance as the centre of north-western Turkey's industrial heartland. The surrounding agricultural land produces potatoes, tobacco and hazelnuts. The town grew out of a weekly market on an uninhabited site ("adapazarı", island market) and there is little of interest in the town. On the southern outskirts of the town the Justinian bridge crosses a now dried-up tributary of the Sakarya (Sangarios in antiquity). Measuring 450m/492yd it dates from Roman times (A.D. 560) and has twelve arches.

Gevye

To the north-west of Gevye, about 30km/19 miles to the south of Adapazarı, a well-maintained bridge built in Ottoman times under Sultan Bayazit (1481–1512) crosses the Sakarya. The town itself lies at the northern end of a 30km/19 mile long, intensively-farmed valley, at the heart of which stands the small town of Pamukova, meaning cotton plain.

Sapanca Gölü

To the south-west of Adapazarı, at an altitude of 40m/131ft, lies the Sapanca Gölü freshwater lake (47sq.m/18sq. miles). The bottom of the lake is 20m/65ft below the level of the Sea of Marmara. It is situated in a low-lying area, Sakarya-Bosphorus, which during the Ice Age linked the Black Sea and the Sea of Marmara. Shifts in the earth's crust led to a rise in the level of the surface and the land dried up. By the end of the Pleistocene (Ice Age) period, the Sea of Marmara had flooded the İzmit/Sapanca valley to form a bay into which the Sakarya flowed. The lake slowly silted up and separated from the Gulf, but the River Sakarya continued to flow into the Gulf of İzmit through Lake Sapanca. Finally, deposits from the Sakarya and its tributaries built up in the lake and a new outlet formed to the east, flowing into the Sapanca. As a result, the river's course was altered and it now disgorges directly into the Black Sea. Picturesque villages set in extensive fruit orchards can be seen on the south side of the lake, around the town of Sapanca.

★Taraklı

About 70km/44 miles south of Adapazarı stands the small hillside village of Taraklı with its thermal waters. Since 1990 a large part of the town has been subject to a preservation order. There are many two to four storey timbered houses built in Pontic style (e.g. the Town Hall). Other interesting sights include the Yunus Paşa Camii (also known as Kurşunlu Cami, Lead Mosque), which was founded in the centre of the town after a visit by the Grand Vizier Yunus Paşa and was built between 1512 and 1521. After returning from a military campaign in Egypt the general was executed on the orders of Selim I, as he had criticised the sultan.

Gebze

Gebze (pop. 93,000) was known in Byzantine times as Dakibyza. The town which is set back from the northern side of the Gulf of İzmit at the foot of the Gazi Dağı (305m/1000ft) is noted for the splendid Orhan Gazi Camii with its tile decorations and for other Byzantine remains. Also of interest is the dome on the early Ottoman Coban Mustafa Paşa Camii, together with the polygonal türbe (mausoleum) of the founder. To the south of Gebze lay the coastal Bithynian town of Libyssa (ruins near Dif İskelesı), where in 183 B.C. the Punic general Hannibal took poison as he found himself surrounded by the Romans and the Bithynian king Prusias wished to extradite him. An interesting curiosity is to be found in an industrial estate on a small hill beneath some cypress trees. Reputed to be Hannibal's grave, it was magnificently restored by Emperor Septimius Severus (A.D. 193–211), but it is now just a pile of stones. Excavations were carried out in 1906 by Wiegand. The village of Hünkar Çayre was also situated nearby. It was here in 1481 that Sultan Mehmet II the conqueror of Constantinople died.

Hereke

On the northern side of the Gulf of İzmit lies the small town of Hereke (pop. 11,000) in a valley 30km/19 miles west of İzmit. Formerly known as Charax.

The town acquired fame when Constantine the Great died in nearby Ankyron castle (now destroyed) in A.D. 337. The main occupations of the local population are wine production and carpet-making, which follows the traditional style of İstanbul and Bursa. Here in 1891 the first factory for the production of finely-woven silk and woollen carpets was established. The carpets produced in Hereke today are made according to the specifications of the Imperial court. The special patterns are skilfully copied from old designs.

İznik E 3

Marmara region
Province: Bursa
Altitude: 90m/295ft
Population: 17,000

Notion

İznik lies on the intensively cultivated east side of the İznik Gölü, a lake (alt. 80m/260ft; area 303sq.km/117sq. miles; greatest depth 75m/245ft) occupying part of a tectonic longitudinal valley which extends from the Gulf of Gemlik into the western Pontic Mountains.

History

İznik occupies the site of ancient Nikaia (Nicaea), founded by Antigonos, Alexander the Great's General, in the 4th c. B.C. It was originaly called Antigoneia, but about 305 B.C. was renamed by Lysimachos, King of Thrace, in honour of his wife Nikaia. In 281 the town passed to the Bithynians. After suffering destruction in a number of earthquakes it was rebuilt by Hadrian and thereafter enjoyed a period of great prosperity. In A.D. 259 it was burned down by the Goths, but remained the see of a bishop. In 325 it was the meeting-place of the First Ecumenical Council (Council of Nicaea). In 364 Valens was elected Emperor in Nicaea. In the reign of Justinian the city was further developed, and in 787 the Seventh Ecumenical Council, which condemned Iconoclasm, met in Nicaea.

The city was taken by the Seljuks in 1074 but was recovered by the Crusaders 23 years later. From 1204 to 1261, when Constantinople was capital of the Latin Empire established by the Crusaders, Nicaea was the residence of the Eastern Emperor and the Orthodox Patriarch.

In 1331 the town fell to the Ottomans. Under Ottoman rule it became noted for the production of beautiful faience tiles after Sultan Selim I brought in craftsmen from Tabriz and Azerbaijan in 1514.

İznik became renowned for its faience

A photogenic group before the town walls of İznik

Sights

★★Town walls

The outstanding sight of İznik is its imposing circuit of ancient walls, reminiscent on a smaller scale of the walls of Constantinople. Although partly ruined and overgrown they are still extraordinarily impressive.

Little is left of the old Greek walls. Roman rebuilding in the 1st c. A.D. altered the original square plan to a polygon with a total extent of 4427m/4842yd. The towers flanking the old gates and the masonry superstructure were added by the Byzantines. The finest section of walls on the west side of the town, built with stone from earlier structures, dates from the reign of the Emperor Leo the Isaurian (inscription). Considerable stretches of wall were built during the Seljuk period. The inner circuit of walls is 9m/30ft high and 3.5m/11½ft thick and originally had a battlemented parapet walk. Projecting from the wall are 108 towers, with entrances within the walls. Outside this circuit, at a distance of up to 16m/50ft, is a lower wall with round towers, and beyond this again is a moat.

On the north side of the circuit stands the İstanbul Gate, which is similar in style to the Lefke gate. On the inner wall, of later construction, are two interesting human masks.

★Lefke Gate

The Lefke Gate, on the east side, was built about A.D. 70 and resembles a Roman triumphal arch. Outside the gate can be seen the end of an aqueduct, probably built in the time of Justinian, which was renovated by Sultan Orhan.

Aqueduct

Yenişehir Gate

On the south side of the town is the Yenişehir Gate, the oldest parts of which are dated by an inscription to the reign of the Emperor Claudius Goticus (3rd c. A.D.).

★Green Mosque

A little way north-west of the Lefke Gate stands İznik's finest mosque, the Yeşil Cami (Green Mosque), built in 1384–89 by Sultan Murat I's Grand

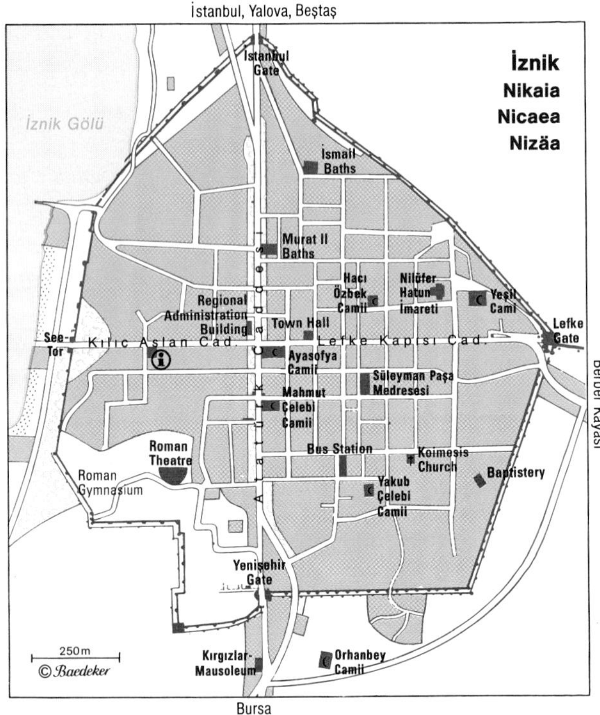

Vizier, Hayreddin. On the far side of the porch are three arches borne on two granite columns. Only a few fragments of the original marble screens have survived. Notable features of the mosque are the beautiful doorway and the windows, framed in calligraphic inscriptions.

İmaret (Museum)

Facing the Green Mosque, to the west, is the İmaret (public kitchen) of Nilüfer Hatun, built by Sultan Orhan's wife in 1388. It now houses the municipal museum (Greek and Roman antiquities, tombs, İznik tiles, calligraphy).

Hagia Sophia

The ruined Church of Hagia Sophia stands in the cente of the town, at the intersection of the two main streets which lead to the four old town gates. This was probably the meeting-place of the Seventh Ecumenical Council (787). Built in 1605 in replacement of an earlier church of the time of Justinian, it is an aisled basilica with small vaulted chambers on either side of the apse. In the reign of Sultan Orhan it was converted into a mosque and decorated with beautiful tiles.

Koimesis Church

In the south-east of the old town are the ruins of the Koimesis Church (Church of the Dormition of the Virgin), a large domed basilica built in the 11th c. to the east is a 6th c. baptistery.

Roman theatre

In the south-west of the old town is the Roman theatre, said to have been built in 112 by Pliny the Younger when Governor of Bithynia. Since there was no natural slope against which the theatre could be built, the tiers of seating were borne on massive and finely constructed vaulting.

Barber's Rock

1km/¾ mile east of the Lefke Gate rises the Barber's Rock (Berber Kayası), with the remains of a sarcophagus 4m/13ft long. From the top there is a magnificent view of the town and the lake can be enjoyed.

Obelisk of Cassius

On a hillside 5km/3 miles north-west of İznik stands the Obelisk of Cassius (Bestas), the 12m/40ft high funerary monument of C. Cassius Philiscus (2nd c. A.D.).

Kaş E 7

South-west coast (Mediterranean)
Province: Antalya
Altitude: 0–50m/0–165ft
Population: 5000

Situation and characteristics

The idyllic little port of Kaş lies near the southern tip of Lycia on a small bay off which, to the south-west, is the most easterly of the Greek islands, Kastellorizo (Megisti; Turkish Meis). The houses are built on the slopes surrounding the principal ancient harbour, which is protected by a breakwater and which is being converted into a modern marina.

The present town occupies the site of ancient Antiphellos (Lycian Habesa) and serves as the port for the Pınarbeşi hinterland and Phellos which lies opposite on a steep-sided hill.

★Holiday resort

Thanks to its beautiful setting and the facilities it offers for sailing enthusiasts, Kaş has become a popular tourist resort, with hotels, guest houses and a good camping site. Round the main harbour are a number of restaurants and souvenir shops. A good variety of boat trips can be made to interesting places on the much-indented south coast of Lycia and to the Greek island of Kastellorizo (Meis).

Fishing boats in the harbour at Kaş

★View

The principal sights are a Lycian sarcophagus in the centre of the little town, a well-preserved ancient theatre (from the top, fine view over the bay to the island of Kastellorizo) on the west side of the town, remains of the ancient town walls near the shore and Lycian rock tombs to the north-east.

Surroundings of Kaş

Bronze Age shipwreck

Off the promontory of Ulu Burun, S of Kaş, a shipwreck dating from the 14th–13th c. B.C. was found in 1984. Valuable bronze artefacts were recovered.

The Yavu mountain region

The coastline between Kaş and Kale has a wealth of historic sites. No less than seventeen large-scale settlements have been discovered in the mountain region of Yavu, along the southern section of the coast and on the offshore island of Kekova. The historical names for many of these sites are not yet known. Many interesting remains including ancient farmsteads, sarcophagi, Lycian fortresses and fortified settlements are often hidden away in the undergrowth, but the local people usually know their whereabouts.

★★Kekova

About 25km/15 miles east of Kaş is the narrow little offshore island of Kekova with many underwater ruins and the remains (choir) of a Byzantine church.

Üçağiz

The island of Kekova is best reached by boat from Üçağiz, a little fishing village on the mainland opposite the island, which in the last few years has increasingly engaged in tourism, and a good road has been built running inland from the coast.

Teimiussa

Üçağız, originally Tristoma, lies in Tristomas Bay well sheltered from the open sea. The bay is situated to the west of Kaş next to the ancient settlement of Teimiussa, which as early as 4th c. B.C. was under the command of the Lycian ruler Pericles of Limyra. As well as a few relics on the acropolis, a settlement in the east and a 50m/164ft harbour wall (outside the village underwater), there are also two burial grounds one to the north and one to the east. Many of the graves which include family tombs and sarcophagi belong to citizens of Myra and Kyaneai.

★Simena

On the eastern peninsula of Tristomas Bay, a medieval castle looks down over the tiny village of Kaleüçağız. The site of ancient Simena dating from the 4th c. B.C. usually has to be reached by boat. The castle was built on the foundations of an ancient citadel. Part of the village can be found inside the castle walls alongside the remains of a temple. Below the fortifications stands a seven-tiered theatre with space for 300 seats – an indication that the settlement was not a large one. To the west is the town and in the water on the shore line below lie the well-maintained ruins of the Titus Baths (A.D. 79–81).

Further west can be found a necropolis which contains mostly Roman sarcophagi in the Lycian style. More sarcophagi and remains are to be seen underwater.

Andriake

At the extreme south-eastern tip of the Yavu mountain region, the ancient River Andrakos meets the plain of Kale (Demre/Myra). At this point a wide marshy valley extends out on both sides of the river between the mountain region and the coastal hills of Myra and Andriake. The name of Antiochos III was linked with the town of Andriake as early as 197 B.C.

The ancient harbour is now marshland. The Andrakos flows down from its source in the karst rock passing an ancient water-mill and divides the town into north and south. The north town is mainly sand dunes with a still recognisable ruined church. Several buildings in the south town are in good condition including a warehouse, harbour wall, granarium (grain store), temple, market-place, parts of the harbour road, residences, water

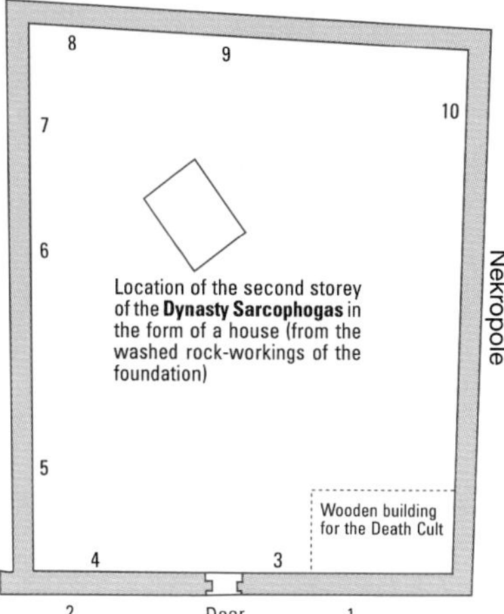

Trysa Heroon (4th c. B.C.)

MOTIFS ON THE FRIEZE OF THE TRYSA SHRINE

OUTER SOUTH WALL *right* from the door
1 Above: Seven against the Thebes
2 Below: The Landing Battle

OUTER SOUTH WALL *left* from the door
2 Above: Battle of the Amazons
Below: Battle of the Centaurs

INNER SOUTH WALL *right* from the door
3 Quadriga
Bellerphon
Rape of the Women

INNER SOUTH WALL *left* from the door
4 Above: The Freed Murderer
Below: Calydonian Hunt

INNER EAST WALL
5 left: The Landing Battle
6 middle: Town Siege
7 right: Battle of the Amazons

INNER NORTH WALL
8 left: Rape of the Leukippids
9 middle above: Hunting Scene
middle below: Battle of the Centaurs

INNER WEST WALL
10 left above: Perseus and Theseus
left below: Battle of the Centaurs

tanks, a number of churches and chapels. A wall surrounded the whole town and an aqueduct supplied water from the karst spring.

Outside the walls an extensive necropolis lies on the northern slopes behind the nymphaeum. In the south-western corner two watch towers stand on either side of a protective wall.

Trysa

Some 7km/4½ miles east of Yavu behind the village of Gölbaşı, a metalled road leads north up to the ancient town of Trysa. Located at the northern end of the acropolis stands a heroon, a 4th c. B.C. shrine of an important Trysan dynast and the site's best-known relic. The famous 20m/65ft long and 3m/10ft wide heroon frieze, showing 600 figures, was taken from inside the enclosure and can now be seen in the Kunsthistorisches Museum in Vienna.

Kyaneai

Due north of the coast road above the harbour and village of Yavu, the steep cliff of Kyaneai rises up. This Lycian town a large settlement even in the 4th c. B.C. was the see of a bishop. Three towers surmount the town walls. Interesting sights within the town include a number of sarcophagi, several rock tombs, the enormous town wall, the remains of buildings, market-place, water tanks on the acropolis and a large theatre at the foot of a gentle incline with 25 rows of seating (superb view).

Knidos — C 7

West coast (Aegean Sea)
Province: Muğla
Altitude: 0–285m/0–935ft
Nearest place: Datça

Situation

The remains of ancient Knidos (Cnidus or Gnidus in Latin), on the cost of Caria, once famed as a centre of art and learning, lie at the western tip of a peninsula, known in antiquity as the Cnidian Chersonese or Dorian Promontory and in modern Turkish as Reşadiye Yarımadası, which projects far into the Aegean towards the Dodecanese between the Kerme Körfezi (Gulf of Kos) and the Greek island of Rhodes. Long and narrow, and at two points narrowed even further, the peninsula rises to a height of 1175m/3855ft in Boz Dağı.

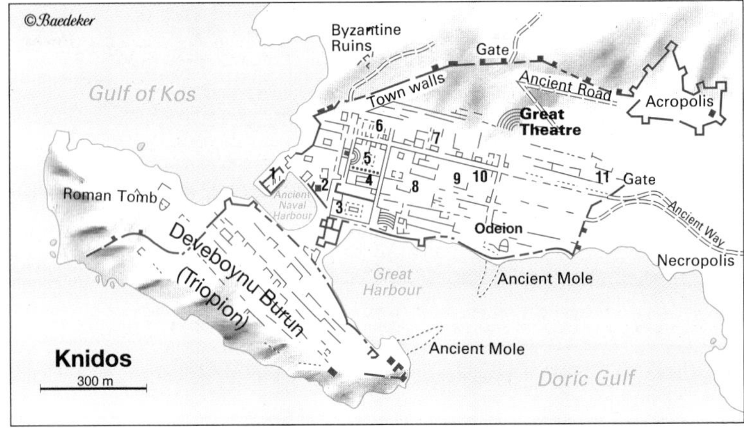

1 Agora
2 Doric Temple
3 Dionysos Temple
4 Doric Hall
5 Corinthian Temple
6 Gymnasium
7 Roman building
8 Roman structure
9 Muse Temple
10 Dorian structure
11 Sanctuary of Demeter
12 Small Theatre

The western tip of the Peninsula (the ancient Cape Triopion, now Deveboynu Burun), falling steeply down to the sea, was originally an island, but in Classical times was already joined to the mainland by a narrow strip of land. Ancient Knidos was built on the island but later extended also on to the slopes of the hill on the mainland. The site is best reached by boat from Datça or Bodrum; the modern road from Muğla ends at Datça, from which it is 35km/22 miles on a poor unsurfaced track to Knidos. There are two modest restaurants at the Great Harbour.

History

Knidos was founded, probably in the 7th c. B.C., by Laconians (Lacedaemonians) from the south-eastern Peloponnese, and rapidly developed into a place of some consequence as a result of its trading activities, its shipping and its crafts (e.g. pottery). By the 6th c. it was already sending settlers to Lipara and the Adriatic. On Cape Triopion there stood a Temple of Apollo (not yet located), the Shrine of the Hexapolis, a league of six Dorian cities whose other members were Kos, Halikarnassos, Lindos, Ialysos and Kameiros (the last three on the island of Rhodes). In 540 B.C. Knidos submitted to the Persian General Harpagos. The city continued to flourish when it became part of the Athenian Empire. Like Kos, it had a famous medical school. Later it became a Spartan base, but was liberated by the Athenian General Konon, who in 394 B.C., as commander of a Persian fleet, destroyed Spartan sea-power in a naval battle fought off Knidos (see below, Lion Monument). That art and learning continued to flourish in Knidos in the 4th c. B.C. is demonstrated by the names of the great astronomer Eudoxos and the architect Sostratos (who built the Pharos at Alexandria, one of the Seven Wonders of the World), the Cnidian Aphrodite, Praxiteles' most celebrated work (now in the Louvre), and the figure of Demeter which is now in the British Museum.

In the Hellenistic period Knidos changed masters frequently; it was long an ally of Rhodes. In Roman times it recovered its freedom; but thereafter it declined in importance and fell into decay.

Excavations

The first excavations were carried out by Sir Charles Newton in 1857–58. Work was resumed on the site by two German archaeologists, K. Sudhoff (1927) and A. von Gerkan (1930), and there was further excavation by British archaeologists in 1952 and by Americans in the 1970s.

Visiting the ★Ruins

★Harbours

Knidos had two excellent harbours, one on either side of the narrow strip of land linking the former island with the mainland. The Great Harbour, to the south, had an entrance 145m/160yd wide between two massive moles. The Trireme Harbour or Naval Harbour, to the north-west, had an entrance only 24m/26yd wide, protected by a fine round tower.

On the former island there are only remains of the town walls and ancient terracing to be seen.

The ancient city

The part of the town built on the mainland, at a date which cannot be exactly determined, had a completely regular street layout, although – as at Priene – the rising ground made terracing necessary and some of the subsidiary streets running north–south have steps.

The Agora (Market) was probably on the north side of the Naval Harbour. Near by are temples, stoas and perhaps a gymnasium. To the north of the Great Harbour are a small theatre and, halfway up the slope above the main street, the Great Theatre. At the east end of the site is a Sanctuary of Demeter, goddess of fruitfulness, and her daughter the Maiden (Kore).

★Town walls
Acropolis

To the north along the crest of the ridge above the Great Theatre and the steep slope above it, which was never built on, is a long stretch of the town walls, climbing north-east from the Naval Harbour to the acropolis (285m/935ft). This is one of the finest examples of Hellenistic fortifications, with the walls and towers surviving almost intact. Further protection was provided by a steep-sided gorge outside the walls. The ascent is fairly strenuous.

Lion Monument

6km/4 miles south-east of Knidos, on the Aslancı Burun (Lion Cape; reached only by boat), is the ruined Lion Monument, commemorating the victory won in 394 B.C. by Konon, with 90 Athenian and Persian vessels, over the 85 vessels commanded by the Spartan General Persandros. The monument was a cenotaph (an empty tomb erected in memory of those who died far from home), similar in structure to the Mausoleion of Halikarnassos, with a square base articulated by Doric half-columns supporting a stepped pyramid on which a lion (sent by Newton to the British Museum) stood guard.

Kuşadası — C 6

West coast (Aegean Sea)
Province: İzmir
Altitude: 0–50m/0–165ft
Population: 22,000

Situation and importance

This popular tourist and holiday centre lies 90km/55 miles south of İzmir in the centre of the wide Gulf of Kuşadası, on the south side of which is the Greek island of Samos (Turkish Sisam). The long sandy beaches on the adjoining coasts, the well-equipped boating harbour, the friendly atmosphere of this lively little port town (port of call for cruise ships and regular shipping lines, ferry service to Samos) and, not least, its proximity to the celebrated excavation site of Ephesus (see entry; 17km/10½ miles north) have made Kuşadası one of Turkey's leading holiday centres.

★★Holiday Centre

History

In antiquity there were in this area the cities of Neapolis, Marathesion and Anaia, of which practically no traces survive. The present town was founded in the 13th c. by Italian merchants from Genoa and Venice, who had been authorised to do so by the Imperial authorities in Constantinople. Since the old harbour of nearby Ephesus had been silted up by deposits from the Little Maeander (Küçük Menderes), they named the new port Scala Nova (in Greek, Nea Ephesos). The regular layout of the old town dates from this period. In the Ottoman period the name of the town was changed to Kuşadası (Bird Island).

Sights

Harbour

The old harbour, in the shape of a right angle, has been supplemented by two modern piers built out to the north-west, at which the larger sea-going vessels moor. At the head of the pier are the harbour-master's office and the tourist information bureau. The harbour is used by the local fishermen. Along the quay are a number of fish restaurants and shops. There is a bazaar quarter in the town.

★Caravanserai

The most prominent building in the neighbourhood of the harbour is the Caravanserai (Kervansaray) or Han, a massive battlemented structure 12m/40ft high built by Öküz Mehmet Paşa in 1618. Restored in the 1960s, it has been a hotel (the Club Caravansérail) since 1967. The courtyard with its palms and other plants is worth seeing.

Old town

Above the Caravanserai, to the south-west, there are still a few 19th c. half-timbered houses in the style typical of the region. Of the old town walls there survives only the south gate, now surmounted by the police station. Two mosques are notable, the Kale İçi Camii (of the Ottoman period; restored about 1800) and the Hanım Camii (renovated 1952).

★Güvercin Ada

A little way west of the harbour is a 350m/380yd long causeway leading to the charming island of Güvercin Ada (Pigeon Island; café-restaurant), with

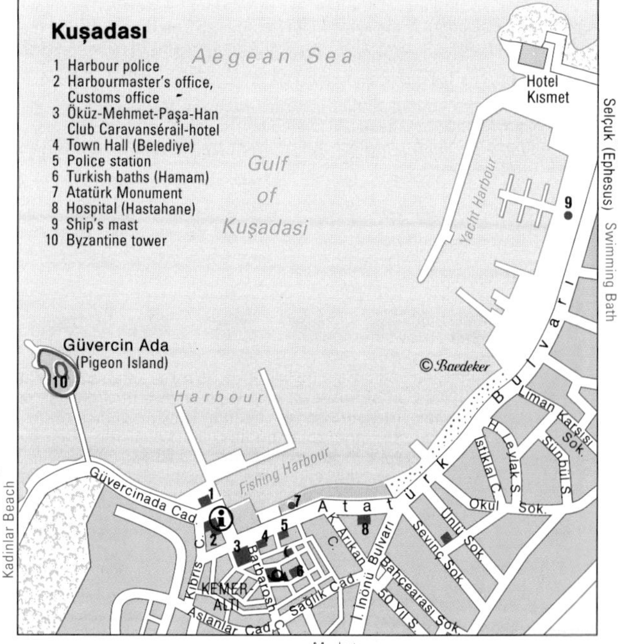

Kuşadası, one of the oldest holiday resorts in Turkey

a tower which is all that remains of a 13th c. Byzantine castle (which later became a pirates' lair). The wall round the island dates only from the early 19th c.

★Boating harbour (Marina)

From the town centre, by the old harbour, a seafront road runs north to the new boating harbour, the Turban Marina, which is one of the most modern in the country, with berthing for some 600 boats and all necessary servicing facilities. Many owners, Turkish and foreign, lay up their boats for the winter here.

Surroundings of Kuşadası

★★Bathing beaches

There are beautiful long bathing beaches on the coast both north and south of Kuşadası, with numbers of modern holiday villages.

Samsun Dağı ★National Park

The road south from Kuşadası, heading for Söke, soon turns inland and runs south-east through hilly country. To the right (south) can be seen the most westerly outlier of the Messogis range, Samsum Dağı (1237m/4060ft), known in antiquity as Mount Mykale. Now a national park, the official name of which is the "Dilek Yarımadası Milli Parkı", it is situated between the Menderes depression and the Güzelçamlı (Karaova) coastal plain, and juts out like a peninsula into the Aegean Sea. Thanks to its marble and chrystalline schists the ridge, notched by steep valleys, has an abundance of springs and so is covered by relatively lush vegetation. On the inaccessible upper slopes, today virtually uninhabited, are traces of fortifications built to protect the adjacent Strait of Samos, and the remains of monasteries.

Vegetation

Attempts at farming the peninsula in modern times have almost invariably been thwarted, as a result of which the entire 11,000ha/27,200 acre National

Park retains its original vegetation. Dense Mediterranean maquis covers up to 60% of the hillsides, in the midst of which grow stands of holm oak (*quercus ilex*; up to 10m/33ft in height), an evergreen tree with small smooth edged leathery leaves, with furry undersides and shiny dark green tops, a rarity in the eastern Mediterranean. The remainder is tall forest, with plantains, cypresses, laurels, oleander and maple, but with *pinus brutia* (brutic pine) flourishing in lower-lying areas and *pinus nigra* (black pine) higher up. In addition to wild horses and wild boar, porcupines and rock squirrels are among the varied fauna of the park.

Panionion

On the wooded northern slopes of Samsun Dağı, near the village of Güzelçamlı, the remains of the Panionion, the Sanctuary of the Panionic League dedicated to Poseidon Helikonios, were rediscovered in 1957.

Laodikya E 6

Western Anatolia (Interior)
Province: Denizli
Altitude: about 300m/985ft

Situation of the ruined site

The ruined site of ancient Laodikya (Laodicea) which is situated about 5km/3 miles north of Denizli is referred to by local people as Eskihisar or "Old Castle". The town, built on the site of an earlier settlement known originally as Diospolis and later as Rhoas, was founded by Antiochos II of Syria (261–246 B.C.), who named it after his sister Laodike. The city subsequently became the part of the kingdom of Pergamon, probably after the Treaty of Apameia in 188 B.C. and thereafter passed into Roman hands. Its commercial activities and especially its wool and textile industries made it one of the wealthiest cities in Asia Minor (Revelations 3:17). After a devastating earthquake in A.D. 60, the citizens rebuilt the city out of their own resources. It was home to one of the oldest Christian communities and ranked among the Seven Churches of Asia (Revelations 1:11; 3:14; Colossians 4:13ff). After its conquest by the Seljuks in the late 11th c., the city fell into decay and in the 13th c. the remaining inhabitants abandoned the site and moved to Ladik (Denizli).

The site

The scanty remains of Laodikya are scattered over an undulating plateau (1sq.km/½sq. mile) which is crossed by the road from Eskihisar to Goncalı. Three gates allowed entry through the walls and the ruins of an ancient bridge are visible below the north-west gate. A short distance beyond the walls lies a necropolis. This gate to Ephesus, triple arched and flanked by towers, was devoted to the Emperor Domitian (A.D. 81–96). On the south-west side stand a number of buildings built under Vespasian (A.D. 69–79) including a stadium (350×60m/380×65yd) and a large building known as the Palati which was either a gymnasium or a bath-house. An aqueduct bringing water from the spring of Baş Pınar (beside the old administrative offices in Denizli) ended in a 5m/16ft high water-tower from which water was distributed to the various parts of the city.

To the north-east an odeion stands on a hillside terrace. In the middle of the hill to the left lie the remains of a Roman nymphaeum which was excavated in 1962/63 by French archaeologists. A square water pool with a semi-circular fountain and a number of chambers is flanked on two sides by pillars. The complex was later used as a chapel. Close by the remains of a larger Ionic temple can be seen and on the north-eastern edge of the plateau lie the scanty remains of a large theatre. Further north there is a smaller and better preserved theatre. The acropolis at the northern tip is relatively small.

In the Maeander Plain

Maeander · Menderes C–E 5/6

Aegean region
Three rivers in western Anatolia
Küçük Menderes (Little Maeander)
Length: 175km/108 miles
Büyük Menderes (Great Maeander)
Length: 584km/362 miles
Küçük Menderes (Skamander; Sarımsaklı since 1987)
Length: 124km/77 miles

Situation and Importance

The first two of the rivers mentioned above flow through the deep, broad, long and extremely fertile rift valley in the 150×100km/90×60 miles Menderes massif, one of the oldest mountain ranges in the middle and southern section of the Turkish Aegean region. The third river irrigates the western part of the Biga peninsula in north-western Anatolia but all three rivers are characterised by a favourable climate, dense population and intense agricultural exploitation (cotton) in an extensive and well-irrigated area. They were of particular importance for many of the ancient towns.

Küçük Menderes

The Küçük Menderes of today is the ancient Kaystros. The source of this 175km/108 miles long river is to be found north of Kıraz on the Bozdağı (2159m/7080ft) about 80km/50 miles east of İzmir. It winds its way down to the 25km/16 miles wide and 80km/50 miles long Küçük Menderes depression disgorging into the silted, marshy delta of the Gulf of Kuşadası not far from the ancient town of Ephesus. The decline of Ephesus as a port was due largely to the river mouth which had become choked with sand.

Büyük Menderes

The Büyük Menderes is the ancient Maiandros (Maeander). This river over 500km/310 miles in length flows from a powerful karst spring near Dinar and another source south-west of Afyon ("Sağ Menderes", Right Maeander). The two streams converge south of Çivril, hurry through the mountain region of Çal and then follow a course of tiny loops (hence the term "meander") from Sarayköy through the 200km/120 miles long and up to 20km/12 miles wide Great Maeander valley, where the section to the east of Denizli is known as the Çürüksu Ovası. A very marshy and rapidly growing delta south of Kuşadası marks the spot where the river flows into the Gulf of Miletus.

The river's sedimentation has made the ancient Greek ports of Miletus, Priene and Herakleia into inland towns and cut off a part of the old bay to form Bafa Gölü (Herakleia Lake).

Sarımsaklı

The Sarımsaklı of today was also officially known as the Küçük Menderes until 1987 (in antiquity as the Skamander). It rises on the Biga peninsula some 80km/50 miles south-east of Çanakkale on the Öldüren Dağı in the Ida Mountains (Kaz Dağı 1774m/5810ft) and flows on through the fertile but in places marshy lowlands of Ezine/Bayramiç and Truva (plain and battlefield of Troy). These coastal towns also fell victim to sedimentation. The Sarımsaklı flows into the Aegean by the south-west entrance to Dardanelles near Kumkale.

Magnesia on the Maeander — C 6

West coast (Aegean Sea)
Province: Aydın
Nearest town: Ortaklar

Situation

The remains of ancient Magnesia lie on the northern edge of the wide alluvial plain of the Maeander (Büyük Menderes), 25km/15 miles inland from Kuşadası as the crow flies.

The site can be conveniently reached from the main İzmir–Milas road, bearing right at a fork just beyond Ortaklar (95km/60 miles south-east of İzmir) into a road which soon leads through the site. Although the site is not signposted it can easily be recognised by the massive remains of walls on either side of the road.

History

In the earliest times this area was occupied by the Magnates, a people whose origins and character were the subject of many later legends. About 650 B.C. a settlement established lower downstream, at the junction of the Lethaios with the Maeander, by incomers from Magnesia in Thessaly was destroyed by the Cimmerians. Thereafter the town was rebuilt by the Milesians. In 530 B.C. it was captured by the Persians, and about 522 Polykrates, the notorious tyrant of Samos, was crucified here on the orders of the Persian Satrap, Oroites. In 460 B.C. the Athenian statesman Themistokles, having fled from Athens to escape arrest, sought refuge in Persian territory and was granted possession of Magnesia as Satrap. About 400 B.C. the Spartan General Thibron compelled the Magnesians to leave their town, which was unfortified and subject to flooding, and move upstream to the present site at the foot of Mount Thorax. The new foundation, built under the direction of Hippodamos of Miletus, one of the greatest town-planners of ancient times, was slow to develop, situated as it was between Ephesus and Miletus. It began to prosper only under the Seleucids. From the time of Sulla (84 B.C.) the town was independent and an ally of Rome. On a coin issued in the reign of Gordian (first half of 3rd c. A.D.) it claimed to be the seventh city of Asia. Later it became the see of a bishop, but thereafter it decayed.

The Site

Excavations

The excavations carried out by Texier in 1842–43 and Humann in 1891–93 have since been overlaid with soil deposited during the winter floods and overgrown by vegetation, so that it is now difficult to trace the layout of the city. (Some of the material from the excavations is now in the Pergamon Museum in Berlin.)

The first remains to be seen, to the east (left) beyond the railway line, are the foundations of Roman barracks. Beyond this, on both sides of the road, is a 7th c. Byzantine wall, re-using earlier masonry.

Byzantine wall

Farther on, to the west, are remains of the once-celebrated Temple of Artemis Leukophryene, an Ionic temple built by Hermogenes of Alabanda at the end of the 3rd c. B.C. which was one of the largest in Asia Minor. It had an Amazon frieze, one of the most extensive relief compositions of ancient times, parts of which are now in the Louvre and in Berlin and İstanbul. To the west of the temple is the site of the Ionic propylon which linked the sacred precinct with the agora; to the south is a ruined Byzantine church.

Temple of Artemis

In the centre of the agora (95m/105yd by 188m/205yd), which was surrounded by colonnades, stood a small Ionic temple dedicated to Zeus Sosipolis (3rd c. A.D.). On the west side was a Temple of Athena.

Agora

On the south side of the ancient main street, which ran from east to west along the slopes of Mount Thorax, is the theatre, which had seating for 3000. It was excavated by a German archaeologist but is now overgrown.

Theatre

Farther west can be seen the remains of the Roman gymnasium. Above it, on the slope of the hill, is the stadium, in which some tiers of seating have survived.

Gymnasium
Stadium

Some remains of the town walls, 2.3m/7½ft thick, have been preserved on the hillside. They seem to have enclosed an area of some 1300m/1400yd by 1100m/1200yd.

Town walls

Outside the walls, to the west and south-east are the city's cemeteries.

Cemeteries

Manisa

C 5

Western Anatolia (interior)
Province: Manisa
Altitude: 50–100m/165–330ft
Population: 100,000

The provincial capital of Manisa lies 40km/25 miles north-east of İzmir at the foot of Manisa Dağı (the ancient Mount Sipylos; 1517m/4977ft), the highest peak in the Manisa range. To the north of the town lies the Hyrcanian Plain, through which flows the River Gediz (ancient Hermos).

Situation

Manisa has a number of notable mosques, but is worth visiting also for its picturesque situation on the slopes of a hill. The houses with their typical light-coloured hipped roofs and the minarets which soar up between them make a very attractive picture of an old Ottoman town.

Importance

Of the origins of the town, which was known in antiquity as Magnesia on the Sipylos to distinguish it from Magnesia on the Maeander (see entry), nothing is known. The Akpınar relief (see below) suggests that the region was under the influence of the Hittite Empire (after 1400 B.C.).

History

In 190 B.C. the Syrian King Antiochos III was defeated here by the Romans, who thereupon presented the city to King Eumenes II of Pergamon. In A.D. 17 it suffered severe destruction in an earthquake, but was soon rebuilt. Manisa escaped the Arab raids, and it achieved some prominence in the time of the Byzantine Emperor John III, who retired here during the Latin occupation of Constantinople (1204). In 1313 Manisa was occupied by the Seljuks and in 1390 by the Ottomans, who thereafter retained possession of the town apart from a temporary occupation by the Mongols in 1402. Sultans Murat I and II resided here as well as in Bursa. In the 18th c. Manisa was ruled by the Karaosmanoğlu family, who were not finally deposed until 1822, in the reign of Mahmut II.

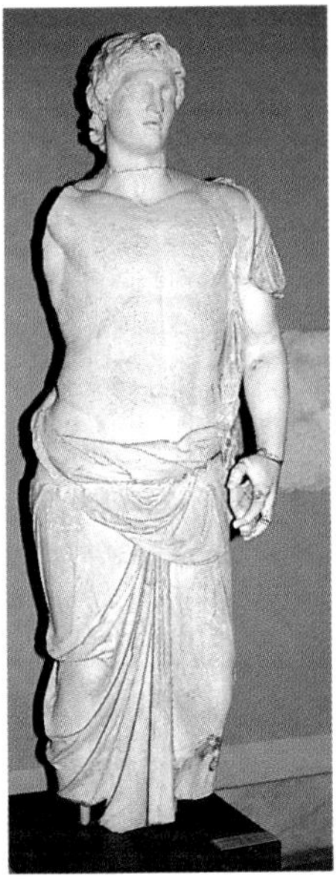

Alexander the Great

Sights

★Mosques

The two principal mosques are the Great Mosque (Ulu Cami), built in 1366, which has antique columns with Byzantine capitals supporting the arcading round its courtyard, and the Muradiye Camii (1583–86), now a museum, which is surrounded by an imaret (public kitchen), a library and a former medrese.

Near these two mosques is the Sultan's Mosque (Sultan Camii; 1552), with a school and a hospital.

Beside the Halk Evi (People's House) can be seen the ruins of an old 15th c. library. Here, too, are the Hatuniye Camii (1485) and the Çesniğir Camii (1475).

Citadel

On the hill of Sandık Tepesi, to the south of the town, are the walls of the old Citadel. Three circuits of walls can be distinguished. The outermost ring dates from the time of the Byzantine Emperor John III (1222–54). The middle and upper rings, both also of the Byzantine period, are much dilapidated. The upper ring must be built on the foundations of the ancient acropolis, of which nothing is left. From the top of the hill there are fine views of the town and the plain of the Gediz.

★View

Niobe Rock

On the south-western outskirts of the town a crag in the rough shape of a human head has been popularly identified as Niobe weeping for her father Tantalus – a legend traditionally located in this area.

Surroundings of Manisa

★Akpınar relief

On the hillside to the left of the Salihli road, 6km/4 miles east of Manisa, can be found a badly weathered figure of a seated goddess carved from the native rock. Referred to by Pausanias as "the oldest sculptured image of the Mother of the gods", it is dated by inscriptions to the period of the Hittite Empire.

Marmara, Sea of — B–E 2/3

Marmara region

11,500sq.km/4440sq. miles) inland sea between Thrace and Asia Minor

Situation and Origins

The Sea of Marmara separates European Turkey from Asia Minor. In antiquity it was known as Propontis. 280km/173 miles long and 80km/50 miles wide, it extends from the Bosphorus to the Dardanelles and links the Black Sea with the Aegean Sea. Tectonic movement in the Early Quaternary period created a rift valley with large parts of the old land surface ending up only 200m/650ft under water. The deepest water is to be found in an underwater trough which extends 1300m/4250ft below the surface and which follows the line of a broken shelf into the Gulf of İzmit (İzmit Körfezi). This rift valley is part of the long North Anatolian fault line, which is responsible for making the Sea of Marmara and northern Anatolia an area where earthquakes are frequent.

★Coasts

The southern coast in particular consists of bays, peninsulas and low-lying lakeland and these troughs and ridges include the Gulf of Gemlik, Erdek, Bandırma, Kapıdağ peninsula and Samanlı Dağ. Most of the protected ports such as İzmit, Gemlik, Bandırma and Mudanya are situated along this part of the coastline. The northern coastline on the other hand is relatively straight, there are few natural harbours and what were once high mountains are now islands. Close to İstanbul in the east lie the Princes' Islands (see İstanbul).

Marmara Adalari

In the south-west a number of small islands are clustered around the island of Marmara and the Kapıdağ peninsula, which in antiquity was an island. Of the 23 islands the very mountainous Marmara Adasi (Marmara Island) is the best known, and with 118sq.km/46sq. miles is also the largest. From it the Marmara Sea takes its name. It became famous for its marble quarries (marmara = marble) which provided building material for Roman sarcophagi and Ottoman mosques. The economic basis of the island was built around the abundance of fish found in the surrounding waters. Today the island is popular for seaside holidays. Also popular for its attractive coastline is Avşa, only 21sq.km/8sq. miles in area, lying three sea-miles south of Marmara Island. Its two simple villages are known for producing a good wine. Boat connections run from Erdek or Bandirma.

Climate

The summer climate in the Marmara region has many attractions as it stays relatively cool in high summer with frequent northerly and northwesterly

Turtles in Dalyan Bay

winds (meltem) and also cooling currents from the Black Sea. In winter, however, the Sea of Marmara is subject to cold and stormy weather, but the olive groves in the region rarely fall victim to sudden frosts.

Resorts on the north coast

In the last ten years the northern coastline of the Sea of Marmara has become very popular with holidaymakers from the major Turkish cities. Holiday villages, chalets and apartment blocks line the coast between Tekirdağ and the western outskirts of İstanbul and also for 100km/60 miles on the eastern side of the Bosphorus. With building work continuing unabated, almost the whole length of coast is now devoted to tourism, but the western section and the area between Marmara Ereğlisi and Kumburgaz are most affected. The sandy beaches south-west of Tekirdağ remain as yet untouched with the exception of the Barbaros and Kumbağ regions (10km/7 miles) and, after the coast-road was extended, Sarköy (55km/34 miles).

Tekirdağ

The provincial town of Tekirdağ (pop. 63,000) is a busy place on the northern coast of the Sea of Marmara with a small commercial port. Previously known as Rodosto, it was called Bisanthe in antiquity and later Rhaidestos. The Turkish name Tekir Dağ (Slate Mountain) refers to the Isıklar Dağı range of slate mountains which line the coast to the south-west. Tekirdağ was the birthplace of the Turkish poet Namık Kemal (see Famous People).

The Phrygians set out across the Sea of Marmara from Tekirdağ in their conquest of Asia Minor. For many years the town was under control of the Thracians who gave their name to the whole region. In 46 B.C., the Romans under Vespasian occupied Tekirdağ and the rest of Thrace but the town continued to play an important part during Byzantine times.

The birthplace of the Hungarian prince Rakóczi has been converted into a small museum and the Damat Rüstem Paşa complex which comprises a mosque and bedesten (covered bazaar) was built about 1565 by the famous architect Sinan.

Çorlu

The regional centre of Çorlu (pop. 59,000) is a picturesque town set on a hillside some 36km/22 miles north-east of İstanbul on the main transit route from İstanbul to Bulgaria and beyond. The famous Roman road known as the Via Egnatia which linked İstanbul with the Adriatic coast passed through Çorlu and the Roman bridge behind the town was a part of the road.

Marmaris D 7

South-west coast (Mediterranean)
Province: Muğla
Altitude: 0–50m/0–165ft
Population: 12,000

Situation and characteristics

The port town of Marmaris lies 60km/37 miles south of the provincial capital, Muğla, at the head of Marmaris Bay, an inlet sheltered from the sea by a number of rocky islets. Thanks to its beautiful situation in lush green surroundings (pine woods), its sheltered harbour and the long, beautiful beaches round the shores of its bay, Marmaris has developed into a popular holiday resort, with modern hotels, guest houses and holiday homes (sometimes a long way from the town). It is easily accessible by way of the regional airport at Dalaman, 100km/60 miles east. A marina for over 1000 yachts had recently been built.

★Holiday resort

History

The modern town's predecessor was Physkos (Physcus), a dependency of Rhodes, scanty traces of which, dating from Hellenistic times, can be detected on the Hill of Asartepe, outside the present built-up area.

During the 14th c., under the Seljuks, Marmaris was ruled by Emirs of the Menteşe dynasty from Milas, and thereafter was incorporated in the

Ottoman Empire. Many of the present inhabitants are the descendants of Turks from Crete.

★The Town

The half-timbered houses of the old town huddle round a medieval castle on a peninsula projecting into the bay. At the foot of the hill lies the well-equipped harbour, with berths for yachts, landing-stages (car ferry to Rhodes; boat trips to Datça, Knidos, Bodrum, etc.), restaurants and cafés and the tourist information bureau.

Old Town

Harbour

There is a lively bazaar in the old town. The İbrahim Paşa Mosque dates from the 18th c.

Surroundings of Marmaris

80km/50 miles west of Marmaris is the growing holiday resort of Datça, which can be reached either by boat or on a winding hill road which runs along the narrow Resadiye Peninsula (known to the ancients as the Cnidian Chersonese), affording beautiful views of the sea on both sides and passing beautiful bathing beaches (large camping sites).

Datça

Datça, situated in the bay of the same name on the site of ancient Stadeia, has a pleasant boating harbour (boat charter), new hotels and other accommodation for visitors, restaurants and shops.

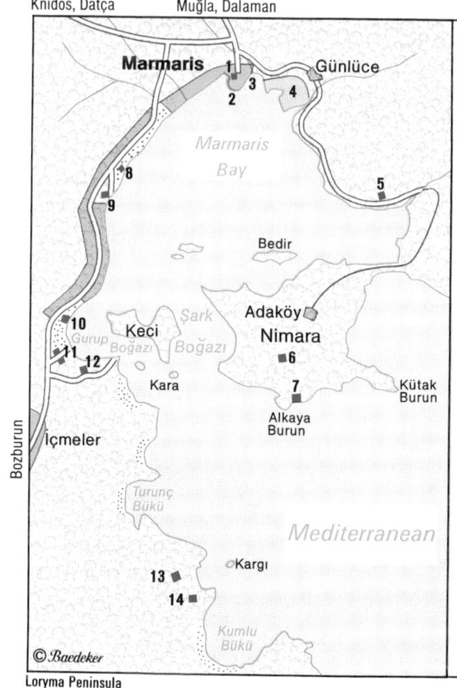

Marmaris and Surroundings

1 Citadel
2 Harbour
3 Boatyard
4 Günnücek Park
5 Camping motel
6 Ruins
7 Phosphorus Cave
8 Lidya Hotel
9 Marmaris holiday village
10 Camping site
11 Martı holiday village
12 Mineral springs
13 Tombs
14 Ruins

3 km
2 miles

The rock tombs of Kaunos, most easily reached by water

From a point about 10km/6 miles north-west of the town, on the north coast of the peninsula, there is a regular ferry service (cars carried) to Bodrum (see entry; Halicarnassus).

★Knidos

See entry.

Kaunos

30km/20 miles east of Marmaris as the crow flies can be seen the site of ancient Kaunos. The road to the site runs north to Gökova, at the head of the long Gulf of Gökova, and then east to Köyceğiz, on a coastal lagoon which is linked with the open sea by a winding channel. Roughly half way between the lagoon and the sea is the village of Dalyan, where a boat can be taken across the channel, here flowing through a marshy plain, to the monumental rock tombs of Kaunos on the west side. The tombs (4th c. B.C.), hewn from the steep rock face in the form of temples, can be seen from a considerable distance. Investigation of the site by Turkish archaeologists since 1960 has suggested a dating in the first millennium B.C. (acropolis, amphitheatre, etc.).

★Rock tombs
★View from the Dalyan Delta (protected area for birds and the loggerhead turtle)

Menderes

See Maeander.

Mersin K 7

South coast (Eastern Mediterranean)
Province: İçel
Altitude: 0–10m/0–35ft. Population: 422,000

Mersin, capital of the province of İçel, is a modern town, only 150 years old. It was partly built with stone from the remains of ancient Soloi.

Situation and importance

On the east side of the town are the large harbour, modernised in the 1950s, which ships the produce of the Çukurova or Cilician Plain (mainly cotton, wheat, timber and citrus fruits), and an oil refinery. It has beautiful seafront gardens with a palm walk; the Atatürk Recreation Park is worth a visit.

There is a car ferry to Gazi Mağusa (Famagusta; North Cyprus).

Surroundings of Mersin

Yümüktepe

3km/2 miles west is the Yümüktepe, where excavations by John Garstang between 1938 and 1949 brought to light 33 settlement levels, ranging in date from the period of the earliest, unpainted, pottery (*c.* 6000 B.C.) to Early Islamic times.

Soloi

14km/9 miles south-west of Mersin lies the village of Viranşehir, near which, on the coast, are the remains of the ancient port of Soloi. The town was founded about 700 B.C. as a Rhodian colony, later captured by the Persians and in 333 B.C. by Alexander the Great. During the sebsequent struggle between the Ptolemies and the Seleucids the town was several times destroyed. In the 3rd c. B.C. it was the birthplace of the Stoic philosopher Chrysippos and the mathematician and astronomer Aratos, who wrote a didactic poem on the constellations ("Phainomena"). In 91 B.C. the town was destroyed by King Tigranes of Armenia (95–60 B.C.), who devastated Cappadocia and Cilicia and carried off the inhabitants of Soloi to populate his city of Tigranokerta beyond the Tigris. Soloi also suffered much destruction during the wars against the Mediterranean pirates.

Pompeiopolis

After defeating the pirates Pompey resettled them in Soloi, rebuilt the town and called in Pompeiopolis. Thereafter it developed into a flourishing commercial town. In A.D. 527 or 528 it was destroyed by an earthquake.

Since the site was used as a quarry of building material for the construction of Mersin there are only scanty remains of the ancient city. The main feature is a colonnaded street 450m/490yd long running north-west from the harbour through the centre of the site. Of the original 200 columns 44 were still standing in 1812; in 1913 only 24. Other features which can be identified are a gate in the town walls, of which only foundations survive, an almost completely destroyed theatre, probably built against an artificial hill on the north-east side of the town, an aqueduct outside the town and the harbour wall, with a semicircular ending; the harbour itself is almost totally silted up. To judge from the capitals of the colonnaded street, it was begun in the middle of the 2nd c. A.D.

There is a good bathing beach, with camping facilities.

Miletus C 6

West coast (Aegean Sea)
Province: Aydın
Altitude: 2–63m/7–205ft
Place: Yeniköy

Situation and ★★importance

The remains of the celebrated ancient commercial city of Miletus (Miletos), the largest of the Ionian cities, lie near the little village of Yeniköy in a narrow bend of the Büyük Menderes (ancient Maeander), 40km/25 miles south of Söke and some 150m/95 miles from İzmir. In ancient times this was the region of Caria.

Until the 5th c. the city lay on a peninsula projecting into the Latmian Gulf and had four harbours, which shipped locally made textiles and Pontic corn. Thereafter the silt deposited by the Maeander filled in the whole of the Latmian Gulf and pushed the coastline 10km/6 miles away from the city, leading to its decline and eventual abandonment. The remains, now isolated in the alluvial plain, still bear witness to the greatness of this one-time economic, cultural and political centre and make this one of the most interesting archaeological sites in Turkey. During the rainy season the ground is frequently marshy.

History

Miletus is believed to have originally been founded by settlers from Crete (on which there was a city of the same name) on a site adjoining the Theatre Harbour and then refounded in the 11th c. B.C. by Ionians under the leadership of Neleus on the hill of Kalabak Tepe, father south. Thanks to its favourable situation on a peninsula in the Latmian Gulf, at the meeting-place of important trade routes, it soon became the principal port for large territories in the hinterland. The city also built up a large trade in the Black Sea. By the beginning of the 6th c. B.C. it had established in the Black Sea area, on the Aegean islands and in Egypt something like 80 colonies, some of which grew into important towns.

During the 7th and 6th c. Miletus successfully withstood a number of long sieges by the kings of Lydia, who finally had to be content with making the city an ally. The Cimmerians are said to have taken Miletus on one of their raiding expeditions in the 7th c. B.C.

Miletus reached its period of greatest splendour at the end of the 7th c. B.C. under a tyrant named Thrasyboulos, a friend of the Corinthian Prince Periander. The city began to mint coins, and the alphabet was perfected.

The death of Thrasyboulos was followed by long and bloody civil wars, and the city's power and trade declined. In 546 B.C. it entered into an alliance with the Persian King Cyrus. Then about 500 the city's tyrant Histiaios, who had been of assistance to Darius during his campaign against the Scythians (513) by holding back the fleet of the Greek cities in Asia Minor at the Danube crossing but had later fallen out of favour, urged his successor Aristagoras to persuade the Ionian cities to rise against the Persians. Herodotus tells us how Aristagoras travelled to Sparta with a bronze tablet showing "the whole circuit of the earth" – one of the earliest references to a map – and how the rising, which was supported by Athens and Eretria, eventually collapsed. The war drew closer to Miletus, and after a naval defeat off Lade the city was taken by storm in 494 and subjected to severe retribution. Thereafter it never recovered its former power.

The city, which had been completely destroyed, was rebuilt about 460 B.C. in accordance with Hippodamian principles on a new site to the north-east of its previous position. In 479 it shook off Persian control and became a member of the Athenian maritime league known as the Confederacy of Delos. Art and industry flourished, and Milesian beds, chairs and textiles were widely renowned. The Milesians themselves became notorious for good living and effeminacy.

In 412–411 Miletus broke with Athens and until the end of the Peloponnesian War was a Spartan base. In 401, during the rising by Cyrus the Younger against his brother Artaxerxes II, Tissaphernes, the Persian Satrap of Sardis, secured the city for Artaxerxes. During the 4th c. it fell for a time under the control of King Mausolos of Caria; then in 334 B.C. Alexander the Great took the city after a long siege and restored its independence. The subsequent period is still obscure. In 313 B.C. Antigonos freed the city from its tyrant. Thereafter it had a variety of masters – Lysimachos, the pharaohs of Egypt, the Seleucids of Syria – with an interlude of independence.

Soon after 200 B.C. Miletus became an ally of Rome and had its independence and its possessions confirmed. Caesar, Antony and the Apostle Paul (Acts 20:15) visited the city. Under the Empire it had a further period of prosperity, as the remains of the huge theatre and other public buildings attest.

From the middle of the 3rd c. A.D. onwards Miletus was harried by Barbarian raids. Under Byzantine rule it became the see of a bishop and later of an archbishop. Above the theatre was built a castle, referred to as

Kastrion Palation in a document of 1212 issued by the Monastery of St John on Patmos (which had had rich possessions in this area until the end of the 11th c.).

Shortly before the First Crusade the city was taken by the Seljuks, who may have established another settlement here. It belonged to the Princes of Menteşe (to the south) and ranked as the most important commercial town on the coast after Altoluogo (Ephesus). The Princes concluded commercial treaties with Venice and allowed the Venetians to build a church (St Nicholas) and establish a consulate to look after their interests. It may be concluded that Miletus was not yet completely cut off from the sea, though it had already an outer harbour on the coast. Under the Ottomans (who built the mosque in 1501) Miletus at first maintained its importance; but conflicts between the Ottomans and the Byzantines and Venetians, together with the steady retreat of the coastline which increasingly hampered its maritime trade, led inevitably to its decline. Since the Ottoman Sultans took little interest in its fate, Miletus decayed and finally was abandoned.

Famous Milesians

Miletus was the birthplace of a number of notable figures of the Ancient World – the great philosopher Thales (*c.* 625–545 B.C.); Anaximander and Anaximenes; a certain Kadmos, to whom the first historical records in prose are attributed; Hekataios (Hecataeus; *c.* 500 B.C.) a distinguished historian; Timotheos, a noted poet and musician of the first half of the 4th c. B.C.; Hippodamos, the great town-planner, who designed the gridiron layouts of Piraeus, Thouroi in southern Italy and Rhodes and is said to have been responsible for the regular plan of his native city. The celebrated Aspasia, the witty hetaira (courtesan) who was Pericles' companion, is said also to have been a native of Miletus (*c.* 470 B.C.).

Excavations

Excavations were begun by Theodor Wiegandt in 1899, and have been continued since 1955 by other German archaeologists. They have revealed a circuit of Mycanaean walls (partly restored) on the south side of the town, Mycenaean settlement levels of the 2nd millennium B.C. and a Roman ceremonial avenue.

Visiting the ★Ruins

The layout of the site is difficult to follow, since the scanty remains are scattered about in the alluvial plain of the Büvük Menderes (Maeander) and cannot be related to the original coastline of the peninsula on which the city stood.

The practice of laying out a town on a strict rectangular grid probably originated in Miletus. The principle was consistently applied in the rebuilding of the city in the 4th c. B.C., probably under the direction of the great architect and town-planner Hippodamos of Miletus. With its regular blocks and rectangular open spaces the layout is clear and simple to follow (on the plan, if not now on the site).

★★Theatre

The best-preserved and therefore most prominent structure in the ancient city is the Roman theatre, which with its 140m/460ft long façade and a circuit of almost 500m/1640ft round the semicircular auditorium, still rising to a height of 30m/100ft above the plain (and originally surmounted by a 10m/33ft high gallery), is a visible symbol of the city's former greatness. Greeks, Romans and Byzantines contributed to its building. An earlier Greek theatre was replaced in the time of Trajan (2nd c. A.D.) by a Roman theatre, which was enlarged in the 3rd and 4th c., giving it a total capacity of some 25,000 spectators. The seating is arranged in three tiers of 18 rows each, divided by stairways into 5, 10 and 20 wedge-shaped blocks. The seats were reached by a series of stairway tunnels. The theatre was lavishly decorated with a facing of many-coloured marble, which covered the seating (in white marble), the 34m/112ft long orchestra and the stage building. In the middle of the lowest tier of seating was the Imperial box,

Miletus: the ancient theatre, overlooked by a Byzantine castle

with a canopy borne on columns. The stage building had three rows of columns of red, black and white marble and was decorated with numerous statues. The acoustics of the theatre were said to be excellent.

★Byzantine castle

On the hill 32m/105ft above the theatre is a ruined Byzantine castle, built of reused ancient masonry. It was linked with the town walls, which formerly crossed the stage of the theatre but have since been removed. There may originally have been a Greek fortress on the hill.

From the top of the hill there is a good general view of the site. The peninsula on which the town lay – less than 1km/1100yd wide at its broadest point – had two inlets on the north side, so that the theatre had a harbour on either side – the Theatre Harbour, on the shores of which the Cretan settlers had established themselves, and the Lions' Bay, which can still be clearly distinguished when the river floods.

Above the theatre to the east, on the highest point of the hill, was a heroon (tomb of a hero), a circular structure with five tombs.

Lions' Bay

The Lions' Bay, to the north-east of the theatre, cut deeply into the peninsula and was flanked by two massive marble lions, the city's heraldic animals. Across the head of the bay ran the 160m/175yd long harbour colonnade, with a 32m/35yd long section projecting at right angles at the north-west end. In the angle between the two colonnades stood the Harbour Monument erected in the time of Augustus, the plinth of which can still be seen. The monument had a circular base supporting the rectangular plinth of finely dressed stone, on which was a stone representation of a boat, surmounted by a stone disc which in turn was crowned by a stela-like stone cylinder.

Harbour Monument

Delphinion

At the south-east end of the harbour colonnade was the Delphinion, the city's principal shrine, dedicated to Apollo Delphinios, protector of ships and harbours, with parts dating from the Archaic, Hellenistic and Roman periods. The superstructure, built on earlier foundations, consisted of a three-sided colonnade which, together with a plain end wall, enclosed the temenos or sacred precinct, measuring 50m/165ft by 60m/200ft. Within the precinct were a circular structure 10m/33ft in diameter, altars and a variety of votive gifts. The ground-level was built up in Roman times, using marble blocks which have yielded about 100 important inscriptions (including lists of officials for 434 years).

Harbour Gate

Between the harbour colonnade and the Delphinion stood the Harbour Gate, with 16 columns, which gave access to a colonnaded street running south-west for some 200m/220yd; 30m/100ft wide, it had pavements 5.8m/19ft wide.

Northern Agora

In the angle between this street and the harbour colonnade lay the Northern Agora (90m/98yd by 43m/47yd), surrounded by two-storey colonnades. In the colonnades on both sides of the street were shops. Numerous stone bases, presumably for statues, were found in the Agora. On the left-hand side of the street, on a six-stepped base, was a 140m/155yd long Ionic colonnade presented to the city by Cn Vergilius Capito about A.D.50, with arcading along the street and a pediment over the entrance; the rear wall has been reconstructed to a height of 4m/13ft for a distance of 12m/40ft.

Ionic colonnade

Baths of Vergilius Capito

Beyond this colonnade (to the south of the Delphinion) were the Baths of Vergilius Capito, dating from the time of the Emperor Claudius (A.D. 41–54), the walls of which are still standing. The baths, originally faced with marble, consisted of a palaestra 38m/125ft square surrounded by two-storey colonnades, in front of which was a semicircular swimming pool. From this pool bathers went directly into the tepidarium (warm bath), flanked on right and left by changing rooms. Beyond the tepidarium were the two rooms of the caldarium (hot bath); to the right was the laconicum (sweating room).

Gymnasium

Also beyond the Ionic colonnade, immediately south-west of the Baths of Vergilius Capito, was a gymnasium of about 150 B.C., with a Doric colonnade on three sides and a higher Ionic colonnade on the fourth side.

The end of the Ionic colonnade and the gymnasium form the north-east side of the square which is surrounded by the remains of a number of major public buildings. On the south-east side of the square was a nymphaeum (shrine of the fountain divinities) dating from the reign of Titus (A.D. 79–80). The three-storey reservoir, 20m/65ft wide, was decorated with marble friezes and numerous statues in niches. it was fed by an aqueduct bringing water from a plateau south of the city, and also supplied the baths. Besides the nymphaeum stood a 10m/33ft high Corinthian gateway of the time of Diocletian. To its right was a marble Temple of Asklepios (Aesculapius), on the foundations of which an Early Byzantine church was later built.

Bouleuterion

On the opposite side of the square are the remains of the Bouleuterion (Council Chamber), a building 35m/115ft wide erected between 175 and 164 B.C. (as an inscription records) by two Milesians, Tinarchos and Herakleidos, for their patron King Antiochos IV Epiphanes of Syria.

The interior of the council chamber is in the form of a theatre. The orchestra had a diameter of 8m/26ft, and the auditorium, divided into four sections by stairways, could seat about 5000 people. It was enclosed within four high walls, on the outside of which were Ionic half-columns with Doric capitals; alternating between the columns were window-openings and carved circular shields. The building originally had a timber saddle roof. On the east side, entered through four large doors, was a colonnaded court (35m/115ft by 31.5m/105ft), in the centre of which was a relief-decorated altar dedicated to Artemis measuring 9.5m/31ft by 7m/23ft. On the east side of the court was a Corinthian doorway leading into the ceremonial avenue.

Market Gate

Southern Agora

From the little square between the nymphaeum and the bouleuterion the Market Gate (165 B.C.; now in the Pergamon Museum in Berlin), a magnificent gateway 29m/95ft wide, with three openings, led into the Southern

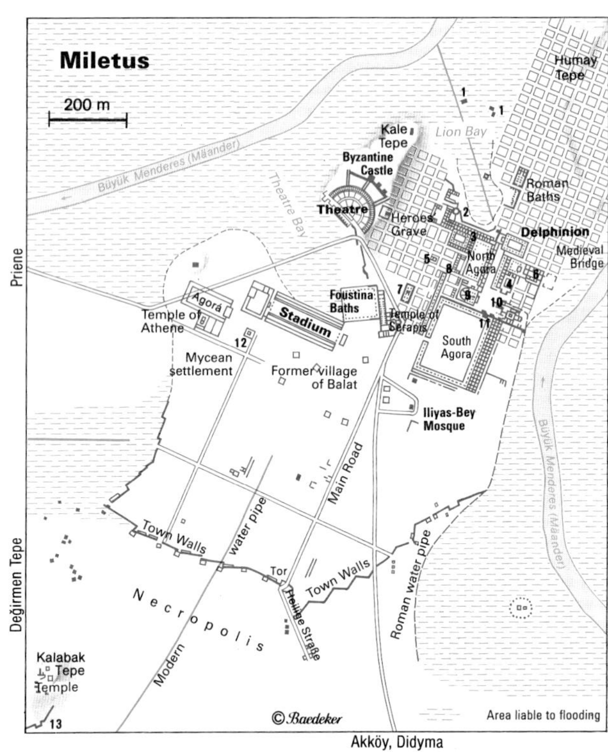

1 Lions
2 Harbour monument
3 Hellenist Harbour Hall
4 Hellenist Gymnasion
5 Byzantine Church of St Michael
6 Baths of Vergilius Capito
7 Palästra
8 Prytaneion
9 Buleuterion
10 Nymphaeum
11 Market Gate (original in Berlin)
12 Temple of Eumenes II
13 Town walls of ancient Miletus

Agora, which was similar in layout to the Northern Agora. This colonnaded square, the largest known Greek agora (196.5m/215ft by 164m/180ft), was built in several stages and completed about the middle of the 2nd c. B.C.

Along the south-west side of the agora was a long building (163m/535ft by 13m/45ft) which served as the municipal grain-store. Immediately south-west of this building was the Temple of Serapis, a prostyle temple (i.e. with a portico at the front end; 23m/75ft by 13m/54ft) of the Roman period (3rd c. A.D.). The temple was converted into a church in Byzantine times, but later collapsed during an earthquake.

Baths of Faustina

To the west of the Temple of Serapis were the Baths of Faustina, of which considerable remains survive. They are named after the Empress Faustina, wife of Antoninus Pius, in whose reign (*c.* A.D. 150) they were built.

The baths, which had a large palaestra on the east side, followed the characteristic pattern of Roman baths. From the palaestra a doorway led into the apodyterium (changing room), a long hall with recesses along the sides for rest and relaxation. At the right-hand end was a door into the tepidarium (warm bath), to the left of which was the frigidarium (cold room); in the central section of this was a large swimming-pool. To the right of the tepidarium was the laconicum (sweating-room), and beyond this the two large rooms of the caldarium (hot bath).

Stadium

West of the Baths of Faustina is an area now occupied by modern building, part of the site of the large Roman Stadium, of which some remains survive. It was over 230m/250yd long and 74m/80yd across; the length of the track between the three water-clocks at each end was 185m/200yd. At the east end was a gate 22.8m/75ft wide (3rd c. A.D.), at the west end a small gate of the Hellenistic period.

North-west of the stadium, on what had been a peninsula, was a third agora, probably of the Roman period.

Gymnasium
Temple of Athena

To the west of the stadium was a gymnasium. Still farther south-east stood an Archaic Ionic Temple of Athena (6th c. B.C.), under which the excavators found sherds of Mycenaean pottery and the walls of houses built by the earliest Cretan settlers on the site.

Peristyle house

Between the Temple of Athena and the south side of the stadium are the remains of a handsome peristyle (colonnaded) house, in the courtyard of which stood a small temple dedicated to King Eumenes II of Pergamon. There is a base which once bore a colossal statue of gilded bronze.

Main street

From the Lions' Bay the ancient main street ran almost directly south, cut by cross streets at intervals, to the gate giving access to the Sacred Way to Didyma. It was only 4.3m/14ft wide, with 60cm/2ft wide pavements. Of the side streets the one cutting across the old village of Balat, for example, was – as rebuilt in Roman times – 8m/26ft wide, including two 2m/6½ft wide pavements. Under the main street ran a drain 1.5m/5ft wide and 2m/6½ft deep, joined by side drains 60cm/2ft deep from the buildings on either side – a drainage system similar to that of a modern town.

On either side of the main street were the magnificent public buildings which have already been described; farther south there were also handsome private houses. The poorer inhabitants were probably huddled together at the northern tip of the peninsula on the hill of Humay Tepe, while the best residential quarter lay south-east of the stadium, in the area now occupied by the İliyas Bey Camii, a mosque built in 1404 which is still impressive in spite of its dilapidated state. The rectangular street grid (breadth of streets 4.5m/15ft, distance between east–west streets 29m/32yd, between north–south streets 55.5m/61yd) is Hellenistic; the older Hippodamian layout had a slightly different orientation.

İliyas Bey Mosque

Gate to Sacred Way

The gate giving access to the Sacred Way, as found by the excavators, was a Trajanic restoration; on the left-hand side of the passage an inscription in the name of Trajan recorded the beginning of the construction of the road in A.D. 100. Below this were substantial remains of the Hellenistic gate and below this again remains of the Greek gate, in the town walls, only 2m/6½ft thick, which were stormed by Alexander the Great in 334 B.C.

Town walls

On either side of the gate rose the massive Hellenistic town walls, renovated by Trajan, which were 5–10m/16½–33ft) thick. In the section to the east were three other gates protected by towers, while the section to the west, the one most exposed to attack, was divided into eight lengths of curtain-wall reinforced by seven projecting towers, with flights of steps and ramps for artillery on the inside. At the low ground on either side the two sections turned north, reached the sea and continued alongside it. Under the Empire these walls were abandoned, and in Byzantine times the whole of the southern part of the town was given up.

In A.D. 538 a makeshift wall reusing older material was built, running in front of the theatre and along the north side of the southern agora. When it was removed during the excavations this wall yielded large numbers of architectural fragments, inscriptions and works of sculpture.

Necropolis

To the south of the town walls lay a large necropolis, remains of which are visible over a large area. this whole sector, extending south-west from the

Kalabak Tepe

gate for a distance of some 800m/880yd, was part of the Archaic settlement of Miletus, the acropolis of which was on Kalabak Tepe (Cup Hill; 63m/207ft, 1.5km/1 mile from the theatre. The sea was barely 100m/110yd from the foot of the hill. How far the Archaic town, still known to Strabo as Old Miletus, extended over the peninsula in its heyday in the 7th and 6th c. B.C. has not yet been established, but the remains of Archaic sanctuaries have been found on the Theatre Harbour and Lions' Bay. it was only after the destruction of the town by the Persians in 494 B.C. that the inhabitants abandoned this area to the dead and moved farther north.

Walls of Old Miletus

On the south side of Kalabak Tepe a section of the town walls of Old Miletus, 3–4m/10–13ft thick and originally over 12m/40ft high, was brought to light by the excavators and dated by the pottery found to before 650 B.C.; the section excavated included a north-east and south-west gate, another smaller gate and a tower.

On the plateau east of the hill were found remains of a sacred precinct with a small temple, and all over the slopes of the hill, extending as far as the Hellenistic town walls, were the foundations of Archaic houses.

Museum

On the road running south from the theatre is the site museum, with material recovered in the modern excavations (architectural fragments, pottery, etc.). In front of the theatre is a stall selling refreshments.

Nazilli D 6

Western Anatolia (Menderes valley)
Province: Aydın
Altitude: 87m/285ft
Population: 80,000

Situation and Place-names

Nazilli, halfway between Kuşadası and Pamukkale, was probably founded in Seljuk times *c.* 1176 by Emir Yazır the leader of an Ogusan tribe. In Ottoman times the village was first known as Cuma Yeri (Friday Square) or Pazarköy (Weekday Market). The town was only later referred to as Nazlıköy. According to legend, the son of Aydın's provincial governor fell in love with a young woman from Pazarköy but was rejected by the girl's father. The young man later named the town Nazli İli (Nazlı's Home) after his loved one. Evliya Çelebi mentions the town as Nazlu. By the 19th c. (1836) Nazilli consisted of two settlements: the larger one Aşaği Nazilli or Büyük Nazilli (Lower or Great Nazilli) was the seat of an Aga and stood on the edge of the Maeander plain, while by today's main road on the slopes of the valley 2km/1¼ miles further north lay the smaller settlement of Nazilli Pazarı or Yukarı Nazilli (Nazilli Market or Upper Nazilli) which had a huge bazaar.

Mastaura

North of Nazilli on the road to Ödemis, about 1km/½ mile from Bozyurt, lie the remains of Mastaura, the early settlement of Nazilli. The ruins include a theatre, polygonal stones in the bed of the Mastaura Çayı, remains of a vault and a castle but little is known of the town's history.

Surroundings

Başalan/ Antiochia on the Maeander

The town of Başalan (formerly Çiftlik Köyü) is situated in the valley of Vandalas Çayı (formerly Dandalas Çağğ, Morsynos or Orsinos in antiquity) on the route from Nazilli to Aphrodisias (see entry). On the foothills to the north between Morsynos and the Maeander (see entry), where even in ancient times a bridge crossed the river, lie the remains of Antiochia, a town on the Maeander. The town was founded by Antiochos I Soter in honour of his mother on the site of two settlements which Pliny referred to as Symaithos and Kranaos. The site is signposted from Başalan and from the main road between Nazilli and Kuyucak.

★Nysa (Sultanhisar)

North-west of the regional centre of Sultanhisar 14km/9 miles west of Nazilli lies the ruined site of Nysa, which probably developed from three towns founded either by the Spartan leaders Athymbros, Athymbrados and Hydrelos or by the Cretan Athymbros under its original name of Akara (see below). The town prospered under the Roman Empire and was described in some detail by the geographer and historian Strabo (XIV, 1,43ff) from Amasya who studied grammar and rhetoric here between 50 and 45 B.C.

Nysa enjoys a superb location on the lower slopes of the Malkac Dağı (Mesogis), split in two by the Tekkecik Çayı and protected by the steep Beylik Deresi gorge in the east and the Asar Deresi in the west.

The site

To find the site of Nysa, first of all follow the traces of an ancient paved track which climbs out of Sultanhisar towards the eastern side of the town. After a short distance a piece of the old fortified Byzantine walls with some encased marble pillar drums will be found. Higher up on the right lie the remains of the agora, recognisable from the numerous pillar stumps. Opposite the north-west corner to the left of the path and in the middle of a cluster of olive trees stands the bouleuterion which consists of a large council chamber (20×23m/22×25yd) with five well-preserved rows of seats. To the south-west close to the gorge which separates the east and west town stands a large ancient Greek building (40×50m/43×55yd) with stone blocks up to 4.5m/5yd long in the north side and two beautiful gate pillars in the south-east corner. Further up the valley a stadium was built at the foot of the gorge with rows of seats cut into the steep hillside. The stream was bridged for the race track as at Pergamon. Higher up, a bridge crosses the gorge.

Theatre

To the rear by a bend in the valley the gorge is bridged again by a 115m/125yd long tunnel, 10m/11yd high and 9m/10yd wide and this creates space for the 35-row theatre. Most of the south- facing auditorium is cut out

The Roman theatre of Nysa

of the sloping sides of the gorge. The front length measures 110m/120yd with proskenion and paraskenia constructed from enormous stone blocks. The top of the theatre offers a superb view over the Maeander plain with the Madran Baba Dağı forming a backdrop to the south. Above the theatre a large water cistern can be found. A narrow path leads from the theatre through the west town to the village of İletmes (Erekmes) which lies at the end of the gorge. This route passes Roman and Byzantine buildings including what is reckoned to be the finest library in Asia Minor after Ephesus and, between the town and the necropoles, a church from whose west side a Sacred Way to Akaraka (see below) begins.

Gymnasium

The large 30×95m/33×104yd gymnasium can be reached from above the steep slope on the third lowest terrace. The stonework some 3m/10ft wide and 5m/16ft high is of Roman-Byzantine origin and in the middle of the north side stands a well-preserved propylon and a cistern.

Salavatlı (Akaraka)

Barely 1½km/1 mile from both Nysa and Salavatlı, a village a short distance to the west of Sultanhisar, the site of the ancient village of Acharaka (Akaraka) can be found. Linked with Nysa by a Sacred Way, it was home to the Nysean Shrine to Pluto and Persephone with a dream oracle and sulphur springs. The remains of the marble temple lie well to the east of the village. Lined with a double row of vaulted tombs of which some remains are preserved, a sacred path led from the necropolis on the west side of Nysa to this plutonium.

Yakızent

To the south of Nazilli about 40km/25 miles along the eastern side of the Akçay (Harpassos) valley near the village of Yakızent (İnebolu) lie the ruins of the ancient town of Neapolis (İnebolu Kalesi, Arpaş Kalesi). It was here in 229/228 B.C. that the Seleukid prince Antiochos of Attalos was defeated by troops from Pergamon, leading to the fall of Asia Minor to the Attalids.

Pamukkale E 6

Western Anatolia (interior)
Province: Denizli
Nearest town: Denizli
Altitude: 350m/1150ft

Situation and ★★Landscape

The site of ancient **Hierapolis**, known as Pamukkale, lies on the borders of Caria, Lydia and Phrygia some 20km/12 miles north of Denizli on a plateau of chalky deposits nearly 3km/2 miles long, up to 300m/330yd wide and about 160m/525ft above the Lykos valley. Gleaming white limestone deposits cascading down the steep hillside like a petrified waterfall and flanked by oleanders, the inviting warm water baths and the remains of the ancient city of Hierapolis combine to create one of Turkey's most fascinating sights. Apart from a number of motels and souvenir shops there is nothing here but the ancient remains.

Origin of the ★Limestone terraces

The calcareous deposits come from a warm spring which has large quantities of calcium bicarbonate in solution. When it reaches the surface the calcium bicarbonate, already partly dissociated in the water, breaks down into carbon dioxide, calcium carbonate and water. The carbon dioxide escapes into the atmosphere and the calcium carbonate is deposited in the form of a hard greyish-white layer. These deposits gradually fill up the water channel, so that the water spreads out in all directions and the continuing deposits create a series of fan-like formations. The process continues as the water flows downhill, producing in course of time a terraced hillside of calcareous deposits. Water dripping over the edge of the fan formations creates bizarre stalactitic patterns, while the masses of deposits have something of the appearance of piles of cotton: hence the modern name of the site, which means "Cotton Castle".

History of Hierapolis

The thermal spring, which in addition to limestone contains sulphuric acid, sodium chloride and some iron and magnesium was famed from the earliest times for its healing powers and was revered as a shrine; and no doubt it was this, as well as the excellent situation, that attracted the first settlers.

A town was founded here by King Eumenes II of Pergamon soon after 190 B.C. Intended as a rival to Laodikeia, the new foundation was a fortified military colony. It may have been named after Hiera, wife of Telephos, the mythical ancestor of the Pergamenes. This first town was destroyed by an earthquake in the time of Nero (A.D. 60) and is now represented only by the scanty remains of a theatre on the north of the site. A new town was built, with State assistance, on a new site to the south. The surviving remains, however, are later still, since the town had again to be rebuilt after further severe earthquakes, particularly in the reigns of Antoninus Pius (d. A.D. 161) and Alexander Severus (d. A.D. 235). The city's heyday lay between these two dates, in the reigns of Septimius Severus and Caracalla (whose tutor was the sophist Antipater of Hierapolis).

The existence of a large Jewish community in Hierapolis led to the early arrival of Christianity (Colossians 4:13). In A.D. 80 the Apostle Philip was martyred here, and later a church (perhaps the basilica outside the north gate) was dedicated to him. Hierapolis became the see of a bishop and a metropolitan, but after the coming of the Seljuks it gradually decayed and was abandoned.

Importance

Like Laodikeia, Hierapolis owed its prosperity to the various branches of the wool industry, and cattle-farmers, shearers, dyers (who used the water of the spring), spinners, weavers and cloth-dealers made up a large proportion of its population. Their products were exported as far afield as Italy: the tomb of one merchant records that he had sailed 22 times to Italy round Cape Malea.

Ancient spa

The city was also a much-frequented spa, in which brilliant festivals and games were held to entertain visitors. The extraordinary qualities of the spring also attracted many tourists. In Roman times the water came from the Plutonium, a cave under the Temple of Apollo, who was the city's principal divinity. The priests of Kybele, who was venerated here long before Apollo, were in charge of the cave, and it was their practice of bringing in birds, and perhaps also oxen, and let visitors see how they were immediately killed by the rising carbon dioxide while they themselves, to the astonishment of the beholders, survived unharmed, their heads being above the level of the gas. The cave – similar in character to the Grotta del Cane at Cumae, near Naples – is no longer in existence, and the water now emerges below the theatre. After many centuries of activity it has covered the whole of the lower part of the city with 2m/6½ft of calcareous deposits.

Excavations

The first archaeological investigation of the site was carried out in 1887 by a German expedition under the leadership of Carl Humann. There were further excavations by Italian archaeologists from 1757 onwards.

Sights in Pamukkale and Hierapolis

★★Limestone terraces

The road which winds its way up from the Çürüksu Plain to the plateau affords superb views of the "petrified waterfall", the terraces of calcareous deposits. It leads to the south-west side of the plateau, where, on the left, is the Tusan Motel, with a bathing-pool supplied with water by the pool containing hot springs (see below).

Near here, on the edge of the terrace, are the remains of an 11th–12th c. castle, whose name of Pamukkale (Cotton Castle) was extended to cover the whole terrace and the site of ancient Hierapolis. From here there are fine views of the limestone terraces cascading down the steep slope below.

Baths

Farther east are the ruins of the Great Baths, the walls of which, with vaulting up to 16m/52ft high, are reminiscent of the great buildings of

Rome, though the effect is somewhat spoiled by the thick layer of calcareous deposits. Beyond the baths, in an area now densely overgrown by oleanders, was a courtyard for training and games. Round the courtyard are various rooms, their area broken up by pillars. Several rooms have been roofed and now house the Pamukkale Museum.

★Museum

To the east of the baths, approximately in the centre of the plateau, is a pool containing hot springs (about 36°C/97°F), now the bathing-pool of a motel. In the pool are a number of antique columns and other architectural fragments.

★Hot spring pool

Arcaded street

Just beyond the motel are the remains of an arcaded street running in a dead straight line from the north-west to south-east for a distance of some 1200m/1300yd. Going south-east from the motel in the direction of the south gate, it passes on the right a Byzantine church and the barely recognisable site of the Agora. The street is 13.5m/45ft wide, and was lined on both sides by arcades 6m/20ft deep which contained shops opening off the street. It extends outside the north and south gates (passage only 3m/10ft wide; niches for statues) for a distance of 160m/175yd in each direction. Outside the gates, on both sides of the street, are pillars with Doric half-columns, now buried in calcareous deposits to a height of 1.5m/5ft; at some points there are also remains of the architrave. These are probably the insides of covered passages. At both ends of the street are round towers with three vaulted passages.

The city was laid out on a strictly rectangular grid. At various points on the main street the beginnings of side streets can be seen.

Theatre

Some 300m/330yd east of the hot spring pool, higher up, is the large and well-preservd Theatre, which had a façade over 100m/330ft long. The auditorium, entered by two broad passages, had two tiers of seating, of 26 rows each, separated by a gangway and divided into sections by eight stairways. The orchestra and the two-storey stage building (which had five doors) are now a mass of rubble from which protrude architectural fragments and reliefs.

A little to the west of the theatre can be seen the remains of a Temple of Apollo.

Town walls

Some 150m/165yd east of the theatre are substantial remains of the old town walls. Inside and outside the walls are the collecting-tanks of two aqueducts. Outside the walls to the north and south are two large necropolises.

Martyrium of St Philip

500m/550yd north-east of the theatre stands the octagonal martyrium (burial church; 5th c. A.D.) of the Apostle Philip, erected on the spot where the Apostle and his children were martyred.

Gates

From the hot spring pool the arcaded street leads north-west, past another Byzantine church, to the Byzantine north gate, which – like the Roman gate 160m/175yd north-west – shows the same structure as the corresponding south gates.

Basilica

★Necropolis

The road continues to a large three-aisled basilica, beyond which lies an extensive necropolis, one of the largest and best-preserved necropolises of the Roman period.

Surroundings

Kolossai

25km/15 miles south-east of Pamukkale, near the village of Honaz, which lies below the north side of Honaz Dağı (the ancient Mount Kadmos;

◀ *Endangered limestone terraces at Pamukkale*

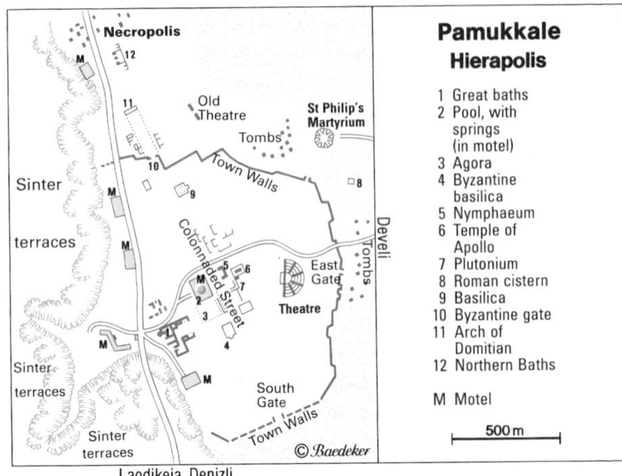

2571m/8435ft) is the site of ancient Kolossai (Colossae). The scanty remains are on a hill above the south bank of the Çürüksu (Lykos), which here cuts through a limestone plateau, partly in an underground channel and partly in a 4km/2½ mile long gorge (Boğaz Kesen).

The once great Phrygian city of Kolossai, which is referred to by Herodotus (Bk 7, ch, 30) and in the time of Xenophon ("Anabasis", Bk 1, ch. 2 and 6) was still a place of some consequence, was increasingly overshadowed

The ancient main street of Hierapolis

A circular tomb in the necropolis

by Laodikeia and Hierapolis, though its name remained familiar because of Paul's epistle to its Christian community. In Byzantine times the town of Chonai (Honaz), 4km/2½ miles south, was of more importance: it was the scene of a famous miracle attributed to the Archangel Michael, patron saint of the little town.

Laodikeia — See entry

★★Aphrodisias — See entry

★Nysa — See Nazilli

Tralles — See Aydın

Pergamon C 4

West coast (Aegean Sea)
Province: İzmir
Altitude: 50–333m/165–1095ft
Population of Bergama: 45,000

Situation

The site of the celebrated ancient city of Pergamon, once capital of a kingdom which was one of the most powerful in Asia Minor, lies some 30km/20 miles from the west coast in the old region of Mysia, overlapping the modern town of Bergama. The remains of the Roman city are for the most part under the modern town, while the Greek city with the imposing ruins of its royal stronghold occupies a magnificently impressive situation on the summit and the terraced slopes of the hill which rise above Bergama on the east. To the east of the hill flows the Kestel Çayi (Ketios in antiquity) and to the west the Bergama Çayi (Selinus).

Bergama

Situation and importance

Although Bergama cannot claim the importance of ancient Pergamon as capital and commercial centre of a great kingdom, it is a busy modern town with carpet-weaving, textiles and leather-working industries. Cotton, tobacco and vines flourish in the subtropical climate of the fertile surrounding area.

At the entrance to Bergama, at an information bureau, a road goes off on the left to the Asklepieion (2km/1¼ miles). In the plain on the right are three tumuli (burial mounds) of the Pergamene period. One of them, Maltepe, is 30m/100ft high, with a diameter of 160m/535ft; a passage leads to the interior.

Archaeological Museum

The main road continues past a stadium (on right). Some 600m/650yd from the road to the Asklepieion, on the left, is the Archaeological Museum, with a large collection of material from the Stone Age to Byzantine times and an Ethnographic department. Farther on, a narrow street on the left

Seljuk Minaret

passes through the bazaar quarter to the Seljuk Minaret, all that remains of a 14th c. mosque.

Continuing north-east on the main road through the busy streets of

★Red Basilica

Bergama, we come to the massive brick-built ruins of the Red Basilica (Kızıl Avlu, red Courtyard), originally built by Hadrian (A.D. 117–138) as a temple, probably dedicated to Serapis, and converted in Byzantine times into a church dedicated to the apostle John. The lower half of the building was clad with marble slabs; in the upper part the red-brick walls from which the building takes its popular name were left bare but relieved by bands of marble. The scale of the building is exemplified by the huge block of marble by the entrance, which is said to weigh 35 tons.

The interior of the Red Basilica is divided into three aisles by two rows of columns. The central aisle ended in an apse, under which was a crypt. Above the lateral aisles were galleries. After the destruction of the basilica by the Arabs in the early 8th c. a smaller church was built within the ruins. At the west end of the basilica was a large courtyard (260m/285yd by 110m/120yd) which spanned the Bergama Çayi on barrel vaulting and was surrounded by colonnades with more than 200 columns. The main road continues north-west from the Red Basilica for another 200m/220yd to a car park at the foot of the Castle Hill which is the starting-point for a tour of the upper town and the acropolis.

Excavations of ★★Pergamon

History

From the 5th to the early 3rd c. B.C. Pergamon was a small fortified settlement on the summit of the hill, and may well have belonged in its early days to large Persian landowners. In 400–399 B.C. it was occupied by Xenophon. The Seleucid King Lysimachos (305–281) kept a treasure of 9000 talents (worth many million pounds) in the city, in the charge of one Philetairos; but when Lysimachos died Philetairos contrived to hold on to the treasure, defend it against all attacks and finally establish himself as ruler of an independent State of Pergamon (283–263). His nephew Eumenes I (263–241) and Eumenes' nephew Attalos I (241–197) successfully defended it against the Syrian kings and the Galatians, a Celtic people who had made their way into Asia Minor and been employed by Syria as mercenaries. Attalos I assumed the title of King. He erected victory monuments richly decorated with sculpture and made a collection of ancient works of art – the first known collection of its kind. The city steadily increased in size, and a new circuit of the walls was built half-way down the hill.

During the reign of Eumenes II (179–159) an alliance with Rome brought the Attalid dynasty to the peak of its power and the kingdom to its greatest extent. A new and massive ring of walls was built round the foot of the hill. The city and its acropolis were decked with splendid new buildings, and Eumenes created a great library of 200,000 volumes (which subsequently, presented by Antony to Cleopatra, went to enrich the rival library of Alexandria). Learning flourished in Pergamon, and there was a great flowering of sculpture and painting. Pergamon is credited, too, with the invention of parchment.

Eumenes was succeeded by his brother Attalos II (159–138). Then followed his nephew Attalos III (138–133), who bequeathed the Pergamene kingdom to Rome; and after the defeat of a rival claimant, Aristonikos, the kingdom became the Roman province of Asia.

Under Roman rule, from the time of Augustus (to whom a temple was dedicated in Pergamon), the city expanded into the plain, unfortified, during the long period of peace. Christianity gained a foothold, and Pergamon is listed as one of the Seven Churches of Asia (Revelation 1:11 and 2:12 ff.).

When insecurity increased in the second half of the 2nd c. a new wall was built round the hill, higher than the wall of Eumenes II and containing little ancient material.

The town of Bergama with the Red Basilica

Statue of Nike in Archaeological Museum

View from the Red Basilica

In Byzantine times, about A.D. 1000, another wall was built higher up the hill, enclosing a still smaller area. 6m/20ft thick and almost entirely constructed of stones from ancient buildings, it provided protection against Seljuk and later Ottoman attack.

The Pergamon region was occupied by the Ottomans in the 14th c., and thereafter the city on the hill was abandoned and fell into decay, while the new town of Bergama grew up below the south side of the hill.

Excavations

The ruins of ancient Pergamon, like those of other Hellenistic cities, were used for many centuries as quarries of stone for building and for the production of lime. When the German engineer Carl Humann visited Pergamon in the winter of 1864–65 he found only a few inscriptions. After gaining the support of the Department of Antiquities of the Berlin Museums for his excavation plans, he began systematic research on the site in 1878, and within a short time had recovered 11 pieces of sculpture in high relief and 30 fragments of relief friezes. Between 1878 and 1886, with A. Conze, he excavated the altar precinct, the Sanctuary of Athena, the palaces of the Trajaneum, the theatre terrace and the upper agora on the acropolis. Thereafter, between 1900 and 1914, Conze and W. Dörpfeld excavated the

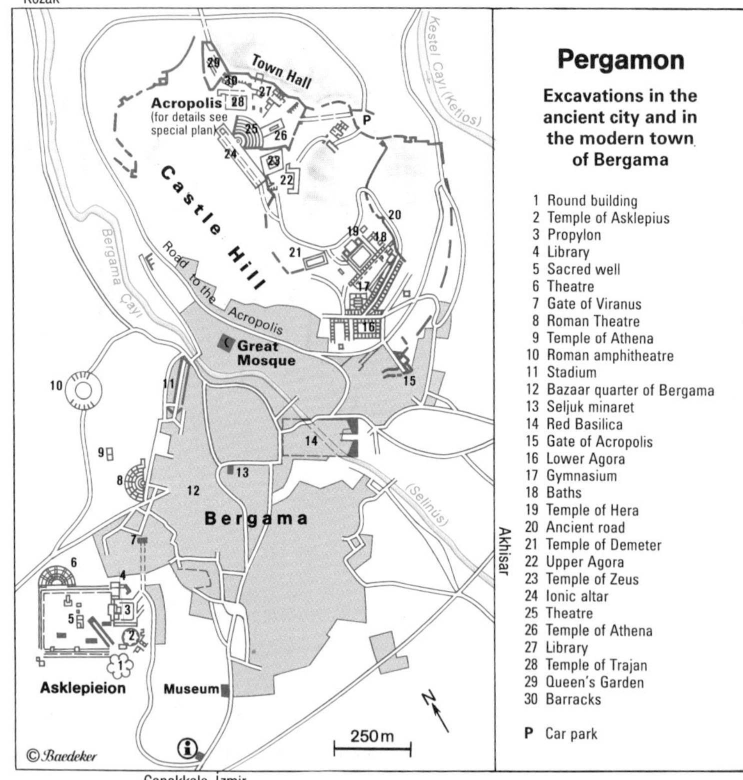

Temple of Trajan

middle and lower town. Further excavations from 1927 onwards finally led to the discovery of the Asklepieion. German archaeologists under the direction of E. Boehringer worked at Pergamon between 1957 and 1968, and German excavations are still in progress on the Demeter terrace and in the Temple of Trajan.

Visiting the ruins

Lower Agora

We come first to the Lower Agora, built by Eumenes II at the beginning of the 2nd c. B.C. to supplement the existing Upper Agora. The paved square (80m/260ft by 50m/165ft) was surrounded by two-storey colonnades in which the merchants offered their wares. A Byzantine church was built in the middle of the square in the 6th c.

Gymnasium

To the north of the Lower Agora was the Gymnasium, built on three terraces. On the lowest terrace was the children's gymnasium – the gymnasium of the paides (aged between 6 and 9); above this was the gymnasium of the ephebes (between 10 and 15); and on the highest terrace was the largest and finest of the three, the gymnasium of the neoi (young men over 16). This had a courtyard measuring 107m/350ft by 90m/295ft surrounded by colonnades with Corinthian columns containing marble shower-rooms, artists' studios and various cult rooms.

Odeion

On the north-west side of the Lower Agora was the Odeion, a lecture and concert hall which could accommodate an audience of 1000. On the south-west side was a covered stadium 212m/700ft long by 12m/40ft across.

Roman baths

North-east of the uppermost gymnasium were Roman baths, lavishly decorated with marble cladding, mosaic pavements and numerous statues in niches.

Temple of Hera

A little to the north-west of the baths was an Ionic Temple of Hera built in the reign of Attalos II, with a beautiful mosaic pavement.

Sanctuary of Demeter

The ancient road winds its way up to the acropolis in a wide S-shaped curve (motor road round the north side of the hill to the upper car park, 4km/2½ miles). Half-way up the ancient road, on the left, are the remains of the Sanctuary of Demeter. Built in the 3rd c. B.C. on a site which was then outside the acropolis, this is thought to be one of the oldest structures in Pergamon. Passing through a propylon (gateway) built by Apollonia, wife of Attalos I, with two columns still standing, we enter the sacred precinct containing the Temple of Demeter. On the south side of the courtyard was a colonnade 90m/295ft long by 4m/13ft deep; on the north and east sides were nine tiers of seating for the participants in the Eleusinian mysteries which were celebrated here. Only the initiate could take part in these ceremonies, designed to strengthen the believers' faith in a better life in the hereafter.

★★Acropolis

From the Sanctuary of Demeter the road goes up in a wide right-hand curve to the acropolis, which is laid out in terraces in an arc round the large theatre on the south side of the hill.

Upper Agora

The road comes first to the Upper Agora, 84m/275ft long by 44m/145ft across, with colonnades on the south and east sides. On the west side was a small Temple of Dionysos.

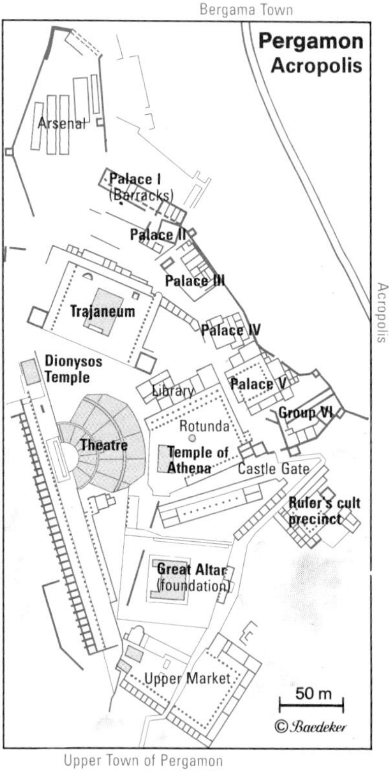

Terrace of Altar of Zeus

Above the agora is a trapeziform terrace with massive retaining walls, once occupied by Pergamon's celebrated Altar of Zeus, built by Eumenes II between 180 and 160 B.C. Only the foundations of the temple now remain, but there is a full-scale reconstruction, with part of the original frieze, in the Pergamon Museum in Berlin. On a substructure measuring 36.4m/120ft by 34.2m/110ft was a horseshoe-shaped platform or podium, with a sculptured frieze 120m/395ft long and 2.3m/7½ft high, supporting a superstructure surrounded by Ionic colonnades. A broad (20m/65ft) flight of steps led up to the rear colonnades. The frieze round the podium is a vigorous representation of the battle of the gods and giants, symbolising the victory of Greek civilisation over the barbarians and no doubt reflecting Pergamene pride in their defeat of the Galatians. The frieze which encircled the colonnade was devoted to the myth of Telephos and the legendary descent of the Pergamenes from Herakles.

To the north of the altar terrace are a number of other terraces within the old acropolis walls bearing remains of ancient buildings. The walls, probably built by the kings of Pergamon and rebuilt in Roman and Byzantine times, are well preserved. This area is entered through a gate on the east side. Along the north wall are the scanty remains of several palaces, most notably the palace of Eumenes II. This is laid out round a courtyard, on the far side of which are two porticoes each 22m/72ft long.

Temple of Athena

On the terrace to the west of the citadel gate stood the Temple of Athena, a peripteral Doric temple of the 4th c. B.C., which must have presented a particularly imposing appearance, situated as it was on a terrace above the precipitous slope of the hill, surrounded on three sides by a Doric colonnade. To the east of the temple was a cistern.

Library

Adjoining the north colonnade of the Temple of Athena was the famous Library of Pergamon, built about 170 B.C., which with its 200,000 volumes ("volumes" in the sense of folded sheets of parchment rather than the older parchment rolls) was one of the largest libraries in the Ancient World. The collection was later presented by Antony to Cleopatra and carried off to Alexandria. The main hall of the library contained a copy of Phidias' "Athena Parthenos".

★Temple of Trajan

To the west of the library, beyond an intervening square, stood the Temple of Trajan, a peripteral Corinthian temple (9 by 6 columns) of white marble, built in the reign of Trajan but later destroyed by an earthquake, which stood on a colonnaded terrace 100m/330ft long by 70m/230ft wide. On the north side of the terrace were two exedras (benches) with recesses for statues. From the front of the terrace there is a magnificent view of the lower terraces of the acropolis, the theatre on its large terrace to the south-west, the town of Bergama and the hills beyond the alluvial plain of the Bergama Çayı.

Queen's Gardens

In the north-west corner of the acropolis, north-west of the barracks, are the so-called Queen's Gardens, where excavation has revealed an ancient arsenal. The walls show Greek, Roman and Byzantine features.

★★Theatre

The most striking feature on the acropolis is the Theatre on the steep south-west slope of the hill, which is reached from the Temple of Athena on a narrow ancient flight of steps. The theatre, built in the time of the Pergamene kings, could accommodate some 15,000 spectators on its 80 rows of seating. Two horizontal gangways and five steep stairways (six in the lowest tier) gave access to the seats. The royal box was in the centre of the lower gangway. The stage building, originally of timber and later of stone, stood on the upper level of a terrace built on several levels. Along the outside of the 216m/710ft long upper terrace was a colonnade, which, with the beautiful hilly countryside and the deep blue of the sky, must have formed an impressive backdrop to performances in the theatre.

Temple of Dionysos

At the north-west corner of the theatre terrace stood a prostyle Ionic temple, probably dedicated to Dionysos, the mythical ancestor of the Pergamene royal house. After its destruction in the 3rd c. A.D. it was rebuilt by Caracalla.

The return to Bergama can be either on the ancient road through the middle town or on the motor road which skirts the north side of the hill from the car park at the gate of the acropolis.

★Asklepieion

Ancient healing town

On the western outskirts of Bergama (military area, with restrictions on photography) is the site, well excavated by German archaeologists, of the

Asklepieion

Asklepieion, the Sanctuary of Asklepios (Aesculapius), god of healing, which ranked with Epidauros and Kos among the most celebrated places of healing in the Ancient World. An inscription records that it was founded in the 4th c. B.C. by a citizen of Pergamon named Aristarchos in thanksgiving for being cured of a broken leg at Epidauros. The sanctuary flourished particularly in Roman times, when Galen (A.D. 129–199), the most celebrated ancient doctor after Hippokrates, practised here. The Emperor Caracalla was one of the many who came to the Asklepieion in hope of a cure. The methods of treatment included preparations of herbs and honey, water-baths and sun-baths, blood transfusions, "incubation" (in which patients slept in the temple and were either cured or had treatment prescribed on the basis of their dreams) and suggestion. The Asklepieion was also a centre of teaching by the leading philosophers of the day.

Altar of Asklepios

Sacred precinct

From the Sacred Way we cross a colonnaded forecourt, in the centre of which is the Altar of Asklepios, a stone bearing the Aesculapian snake, and pass through a large propylon (entrance gate) into the sacred precinct, a large rectangular area which was surrounded on the north, west and south by colonnades.

Library

Theatre

The northern colonnades, relatively well preserved with 17 columns still standing, leads from the Library at the north-east corner to the Theatre, built into the slope of the hill, which could accommodate an audience of 30,000 in its 14 tiers of seating. It has been restored and is used for the annual Bergama Festival (performances of Classical plays). Of the colonnades on the west and south sides there are only scanty remains. At the south-west corner were latrines.

In the square, which was originally paved with flagstones, were the sacred well, with a pool, and the incubation rooms. The sacred precinct was linked by a tunnel with a two-storey round building just outside it known as the Temple of Telesphoros, in the basement of which treatment by bathing and incubation was carried out.

Immediately north of this, beside the propylon, is the Temple of Asklepios, a 20m/65ft high building with a domed roof which was visited by patients before leaving the sanctuary.

Temple of Asklepios

Between the Asklepieion and the Bergama Çayı is the site, still hardly explored, of the Roman city, which has been covered with silt deposited by the river and partly built over. 300m/330yd north-east of the car park are the meagre remains of the Gate of Viranus, at the starting-point of the Sacred Way leading to the Asklepieion. To the north of this was a large Roman theatre with seating for 30,000. 100m/110yd north-west stood a Temple of Athena, and 200m/220yd beyond this a Roman amphitheatre with seating for 50,000. Farther east, near the Bergama Çayı, was a sports arena (circus).

Roman city

Perge F 7

South coast (eastern Mediterranean)
Province: Antalya
Altitude: 10–50m/35–165ft
Place: Murtuna

Situation of the ★★ruins

The remains of ancient Perge (Pergai, Pergae), a city in Pamphylia which was of particular importance in Roman Imperial times, lie on a steep-sided hill on the north-western edge of the alluvial plain of the Aksu Çayı (the ancient Kestros) near the village of Murtuna, 18km/11 miles north-east of Antalya. The site is 4km/2½ miles from the river, which was navigable in ancient times, and 12km/7½ miles from the Mediterranean.

The situation of Perge is typical of the sites chosen by Greek settlers for their colonies – a steeply scarped flat-topped hill with room for an acropolis (to which a lower town was usually later added), rising above an easily cultivable plain, near the coast and linked with the sea by a navigable river. Like most of the Greek colonies on the west and south coasts of Asia Minor, Perge saw one of the bases of its existence gradually being destroyed as the harbour silted up, leading in Byzantine times to its final decline. Since in Strabo's day the winding River Kestros still took 8km/5 miles from Perge to reach the sea, the mouth of the river must have moved 4km/2½ miles farther away since his time.

History

The alluvial plain of the Aksu Çayı was probably settled by Greeks from the Argolid and Lacedaemon at a very early period. The first reference to Perge is in the middle of the 4th c. B.C. Alexander the Great passed this way several times during his Persian campaign, and the inhabitants, who had maintained friendly relations with the Macedonians, provided him with guides when he set out to attack Aspendos and Side. It is not certain whether after the collapse of Alexander's empire Perge fell to the Ptolemies; certainly at the end of the 3rd c. B.C. it was under Seleucid influence.

Perge was the home of Apollonios (262–190 B.C.), one of the great geometricians of antiquity, who wrote a fundamental work on conic sections and irrational numbers which has survived.

In 188 B.C. Perge was taken by the Romans, who then presented it to King Eumenes II of Pergamon. Perge returned to Roman control when Pergamon was bequeathed to Rome by its last King, but until Pompey's campaign against the pirates the Mediterranean coast of Asia Minor was highly insecure. About 80–79 B.C. Verres, guided by a Pergaean doctor named Artemidoros, plundered the Temple of Artemis, which ranked with the temples at Ephesus and Magnesia on the Maeander as one of the goddess's most celebrated shrines.

Under the Empire Perge rose to great importance, as is attested by honorific inscriptions naming Caligula, Claudius, Trajan, Hadrian and Gordian I, II and III. It also had one of the oldest Christian communities in Asia Minor. Paul and Barnabas came here after their flight from Antioch in Pisidia and "preached the word in Perga" (Acts 14:25). Many bishops of Perge are recorded in the history of the Church.

Little is known about the later destinies of Perga, which in Byzantine times shrank into a small settlement on the acropolis hill. It is uncertain whether its final decline was the result of earthquake or Arab raids, or whether these merely completed a process which was already under way.

Visiting the ★★ruins

Lower town

The lower town of Perge is bounded on the north by the acropolis hill, on the west by a ridge of hills extending down to the sea and on the south-east by another long flat-topped hill. It was surrounded on the west, east and south by a circuit of walls and towers, remains of which can be seen at the three gates and various other points.

The site, some parts of which are marshy, is entered through a gate in the walls, immediately beyond which are the remains of two round towers belonging to a gateway of the Hellenistic period. To the right of these towers lies the (relatively small) Agora, with a circular temple.

Hellenistic gate
Agora

Colonnaded street

Across the centre of the site runs a colonnaded street 20m/65ft wide (many columns re-erected), which is continued at the foot of the acropolis by two branches leading east and west. Little is known of the buildings on either side of the colonnaded street. Remains of baths and of Byzantine churches have been identified at various points.

Palace of Gaius Julius Cornutus

On the north-west of the site are the excavated remains of the palace of Gaius Julius Cornutus.

Acropolis

On the acropolis hill, 50m/165ft above the plain, was the original walled settlement of Perge, the only access to which is on the south side of the hill. It is not certain whether the remains at the south-east corner of the plateau are those of the famous Temple of Artemis to which Strabo refers.

Remains of the ruins at Perge

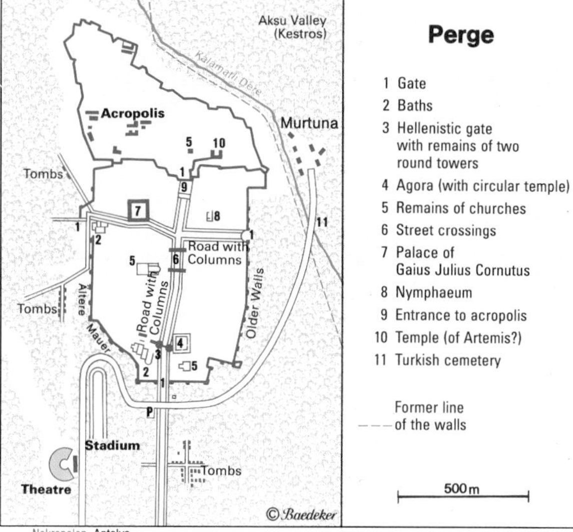

Nekropolen, Antalya

To the south-west, outside the walls of the lower town, is the well-preserved Roman Stadium (2nd c. A.D.) – 234m/256yd long by 34m/37yd across, it could seat some 12,000 spectators. The south end of the stadium was used for the gladiatorial combats which were then popular. Under the seating on the east side are 30 rooms, originally used as shops.

★Stadium

200m/220yd farther south-west, built into the hillside, is the Theatre, which dates from the 3rd c. A.D. Built of travertine and faced with marble, it has 40 rows of seating, with a gangway between the upper and lower tiers, and could accommodate an audience of 13,000. According to Texier the structure was still completely intact about 1835, but in the 1920s the people of Murtuna used it as a quarry of building-stone, and of the stage building, which had numerous niches for statues on the outside wall, only the ground floor is left.

Theatre

To the west, south and east of the lower town are extensive necropolises. A test dig in the western necropolis in 1946 yielded 35 sarcophagi of the 3rd c. A.D. with Greek and some Latin inscriptions.

Necropolises

Priene C 6

West coast (Aegean Sea)
Province: Aydın
Altitude: 36–130m/120–425ft
Nearest place: Güllübahçe

The remains of the Carian city of Priene, 15km/9 miles south-west of Söke and 130km/80 miles from İzmir, lie on a lonely rock terrace on the Milesian Peninsula, below the south side of a marble crag 371m/1217ft high, an offshoot of the Samsun Dağı (Mykale) Massif. To the south extends the wide alluvial plain of the Büyük Menderes (Maeander), created by the silting up of the Latmian Gulf, which in ancient times reached far inland.

Situation of the ★excavations

The terrace must have seemed a very attractive site for a city, while the crag above it, protected by a sheer drop of almost 200m/650ft, was admirably suited for the acropolis. The sea may never have reached right up to the city, which probably had as its port Naulochos, on the north side of Gaidonis Limne, a large lagoon to the south-west. In Strabo's day the Maeander had already pushed the coastline 40 stadia away from Priene.

Seen from the plain, Priene must have had the same kind of picturesque aspect as Assisi has today. It was built on a series of terraces, with the town walls, the residential quarters, the stadium and the gymnasium at a height of 36m/120ft, the agora at 79m/260ft, the Temple of Athena at 97m/320ft, the Sanctuary of Demeter at 130m/425ft and the acropolis on its crag providing a majestic culmination. But even in ruin Priene still holds a powerful attraction, both for the beauty of its setting and for the impression it gives, in rare completeness, of a Hellenistic country town of 4000–5000 inhabitants.

History

Priene – the name is Carian – is said to have been founded by Aigyptos, son of Neleus. It was a member of the Panionic League. After being captured by King Ardys of Lydia it became a stronghold of Lydian power in this area, and under the leadership of Bias (*c.* 625–540 B.C.), one of the Seven Sages, it grew and prospered. About 545 B.C. it was taken by Cyrus' Persians. As one of its smaller cities in the region (it contributed only 12 ships to the Ionian fleet for the Battle of Lade) it was in constant conflict with its powerful neighbours – Samos, Miletus and Magnesia on the Maeander – the inhabitants of which sought to eliminate it either by military action or by appeals to the Panionic League or other States as arbiters. Later Priene was incorporated in the Athenian Empire, and in 442 B.C. Athens handed it over to Miletus.

The site of Ionian Priene is not known; probably it lies deep under the alluvial plain of the Maeander. It certainly did not occupy the site of the new Priene which Athens founded in the mid 4th c. B.C. as a rival to Miletus and which Alexander the Great helped to complete after 334 B.C. The principal temple was dedicated to Athena by Alexander himself.

A period of peace and prosperity was followed by troubled times during the struggle between Alexander's successors, the Diadochoi, and continuing conflicts with the city's neighbours. The city was faced with a grave crisis in the middle of the 2nd c. B.C., when Ariarathes V of Cappadocia, having deposed his brother Orophernes, called on Priene to hand over 400 talents of gold which Orophernes had deposited for safe keeping in the Temple of Athena. When the city remained loyal to its old patron it was besieged by Ariarathes and his ally Attalos II of Pergamon and was saved only by the intervention of Rome. At this time the western part of the town was destroyed by fire, and part of it was never rebuilt. Orophernes recovered his money and showed his gratitude by dedicating a cult image of Athena and by erecting various buildings in the city.

Under Roman rule Priene was a place of very modest importance. Inscriptions reflect the life of a Graeco-Roman provincial town, the inhabitants of which suffered from the exactions of the tax-gatherers and clung to their surviving municipal liberties, honours and festivals. That it was still a place of some limited importance in Byzantine times is indicated by the existence of a number of churches, the extension of the acropolis and the building of a castle. Under Turkish rule (from the end of the 13th c.) Priene, now called Samsun Kalesi, declined and decayed.

Excavations

Systematic excavations were begun in 1895 by Carl Humann, working for the Royal Museums in Berlin. After his death they were continued by Theodor Wiegand and completed in 1898. Material from the site is in the British Museum, the Louvre, the Pergamon Museum in Berlin and the Archaeological Museum in İstanbul.

Visiting the ★ruins

Town walls

The beautifully coursed town walls, 2m/6½ft thick, have a total extent of 2.5km/1½ miles. The lower part of the walls is given a jagged outline by a series of offsets; the upper part is reinforced by towers. On the south side of the city the walls run along the lowest terrace and turn north at both ends to run up to the acropolis. After interruptions at the steepest part of the hill they continue on the summit plateau, enclosing a roughly square area which in Byzantine times was extended to the north. Apart from the walls themselves there are practically no ancient remains on the summit, and no trace of the sanctuary of the hero Telon, after which the citadel was known as the Teloneia. A barely practicable stepped path leads up to the acropolis, the place of refuge in dire emergency. From the top there are extensive views.

Acropolis

Layout of the town

The lower town was laid out on a grid plan, with streets intersecting at right angles to produce some 80 rectangular building plots measuring 35m/38yd by 47m/51yd. Public buildings might occupy several blocks; private houses were usually allotted a quarter of a block. The main streets, running east and west, were 5–6m/16–20ft wide. Two of them led to the main east and west gates, another to a subsidiary gate which gave access to a spring. The lesser streets, leading north and south, were about 3.5m/11½ft wide. The streets were paved with breccia (a rock composed of angular fragments),

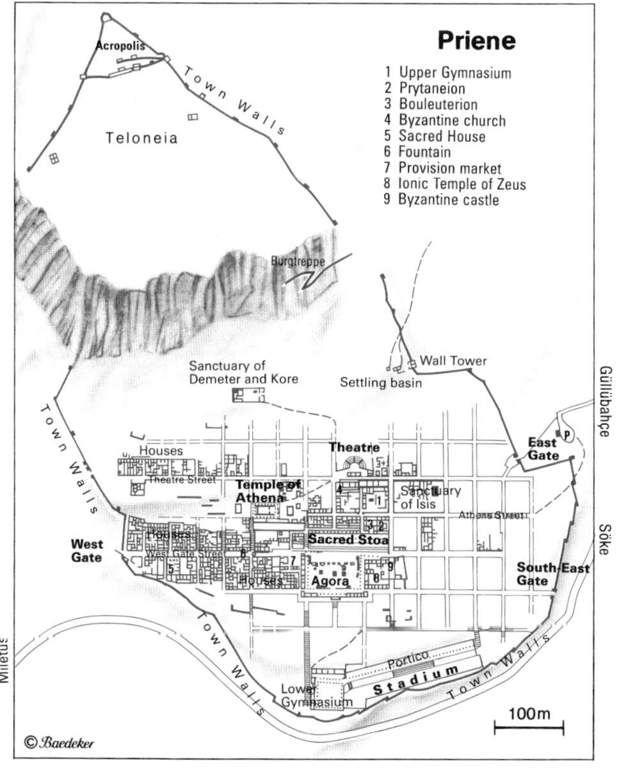

but had no pavements. There was a water-supply system, with fountains at street corners, and a system of drains. The building of the town must have involved a vast effort in levelling the ground, hewing out the native rock, building terrace walls and constructing flights of steps – all carried through with the energy characteristic of the period.

Lower town

From the car park at the end of the road from Güllübahçe (Söke) the entrance to the site is through the East Gate. From here we keep straight across the town to the West Gate, where the following description begins.

Immediately on the right of the gate, which was originally vaulted, is the gate-keeper's lodge, consisting of a single room preceded by an antechamber. The angle between the street and the town walls is occupied by a Sanctuary of Kybele, the entrance to which is on the east side, in the first side street; built of large blocks of stone, this contains an offerings pit. Beyond the next block, in the second side street, is a sacred precinct consisting of a courtyard, a double-aisled hall with a dais at the east end and a number of other rooms. This Sacred House may have been a dynastic shrine.

★Houses

From this point up to the Agora the main street is flanked on both sides by private houses, of great interest because they date back to the 4th c. B.C. and give us some idea of what a dwelling-house of the Classical period was like.

The plans of the houses, built on such difficult and valuable terrain, show great variety and are often much simplified in layout. Common to all of them is a rectangular courtyard on which the life of the family was centred; on the north side of the courtyard is an antechamber open in front, and beyond this the main living-room. Round these are a wide exedra (stone bench), a dining-room, bedrooms and other apartments. Some houses had an upper floor, usually containing the women's apartments, over part of the ground floor. The outer walls, often still standing to the height of a man, are built of fine rusticated masonry or of rubble revetted with plaster; they had no windows. The entrance, leading directly into the courtyard, is usually in a side street.

Interiors

The interior of the houses were light and cheerful, with wall decorations in the First Pompeian style. Remains of fine marble stucco-work, with traces of colouring, were found by the excavators, and the walls might be relieved by Ionic half-columns, cornices with dentil (rectangular toothed) mouldings, friezes of triglyphs (alternate grooved tablets and spaces) or figural ornament. In the courtyards were marble tables and water-basins on high feet, as in Pompeii. Among domestic furnishings found were parts of bedsteads, bronze candelabra and lamps, bronze and earthenware vessels, bathtubs and stone hand-mills. The ornaments recovered included numbers of terracotta figures – Eroses (cupids) and goddesses of victory designed to be suspended on cords, human masks and animal heads which would be fixed to the wall and genre figures (figures of ordinary life) standing on cornices.

Fountain

Food market

Agora

At the corner of a stepped lane leading up to the Temple of Athena is a handsome fountain. Beyond this the main street continues through a cutting in the rock and past the small meat and vegetable market (on the right; 30m/98ft by 16m/52ft) to the large Agora (128m/140yd by 95m/105yd), which is all the more impressive in such a relatively small town. The agora was surrounded on three sides by Doric colonnades, to the rear of which, except in the middle of the south side, were a series of rooms. In the centre of the square, which would be the scene of festivals and sacrifices, there was probably an Altar of Zeus. In front of the colonnades and along the street skirting the north side of the square were honorific statues, the bases of which were often in the form of circular or rectangular benches (exedras).

Priene: Temple of Athena at the foot of the acropolis

Sacred Stoa

On the north side of the street, on a seven-stepped base, stood a double-aisled stoa (roofed colonnade) 116m/380ft long by 12.5m/40ft deep, with an outer row of Doric columns and an inner row of Ionic columns. This was the Sacred Stoa, probably built by the grateful Orophernes about 150 B.C., in which, and in the rooms to the rear, the political business of the city was transacted. The inside end walls were covered with honorific inscriptions which give an interesting insight into political life in the 2nd and 1st c. B.C. One inscription records that one Stephanophoros, the highest civic dignitary, treated all the inhabitants to a meal in the stoa to mark his assumption of office. There is a reconstruction of the west wall, the better preserved of the two, in the Pergamon Museum in Berlin. To the rear of the stoa is a series of rooms of some size, probably the offices of city officials.

At the east end of the Sacred Stoa are the Bouleuterion and the Prytaneion.

★Bouleuterion

The Bouleuterion or Ekklesiastrion, the Council Chamber in which the popular assembly and the council of the city met, is one of the best-preserved buildings in Priene, thanks to its situation in the shelter of a steep slope, and one of the most interesting. Built about 200 B.C., it resembles a small theatre.

In the centre of the room is an altar decorated with reliefs, and on three sides are 13 rows of seating, reached from stairways in the corners and also from above, with room for 640 people. The tiers of seating are bounded on the south side by oblique walls, with doors to right and left leading into passages under the seating. Between these, in the middle of the south side, is a 5m/16½ft wide recess topped by a round arch – one of the earliest known examples of a masonry arch. The upper part of the niche was open, forming a window which gave light to the chamber. The building had a timber roof structure covered with tiles bedded in clay. Round the top of the seating runs a narrow passage. The square pillars supporting the roof originally stood along this passage, but were later moved inwards to reduce the span of the roof – which even so was greater than that of the Parthenon. In the window recess, on a dais, is a marble bench, with two other benches flanking it on ground-level – the seats of the president, secretaries and officials. When addressing the meeting speakers stood by the altar.

Prytaneion

The Prytaneion (offices of the civic authorities), a courtyard with rooms opening off it, was altered in Roman times. In the courtyard are a marble table and a water-basin. In one of the rooms can be seen a large masonry hearth, perhaps the civic hearth with the eternal fire.

Temple of Zeus

On the east side of the agora is the Ionic Temple of Zeus. An entrance in the side street to the east led into the courtyard, with Doric colonnades to right and left. The temple had a portico of four Ionic columns but lacked a frieze. In front of it was the altar. It was destroyed by the construction of a Byzantine castle.

★Temple of Athena

Going up the side street from which the Temple of Zeus is entered and turning left (west) along "Athena Street", above the prytaneion and bouleuterion, we come to the city's principal sanctuary, the Temple of Athena, which stood on a high terrace borne on finely built retaining walls. According to an inscription on one of the pillars in the pronaos (entrance hall), now in the British Museum, the temple was dedicated to Athena Polias by Alexander the Great in 334 B.C. Built by Pytheos, architect of the Mausoleion at Halicarnassus, it was an Ionic peripteral temple (with a colonnade on all four sides) of 6 by 11 columns (5 of which have been re-erected), with no frieze above the architrave. The cult image, a copy of Phidas' "Athena Parthenos" almost 7m/23ft high, was presented by Orophernes. Outside the entrance, at the east end, was a large altar with figures in high relief between Ionic columns. Farther east an entrance gateway was built in Roman times; part of the south wall of this still stands to a height of 4.5m/15ft. The broad colonnade on the south side of the temple, open to the front but closed on the side facing the temple, goes back to Hellenistic times.

Upper Gymnasium

From here we return along "Athena Street" and turn into the side street by which we reached it. To the left is the Upper Gymnasium, dating from an earlier period but rebuilt in Roman times. To the right is the Sanctuary of Isis and her associated divinities, with a small propylon at the north-west corner, a colonnade on the west side and a large altar.

★Theatre

Going west along the street from the East Gate, above the Sanctuary of Isis, we come to the most impressive of Priene's ancient buildings, the excellently preserved Theatre (3rd c. B.C.). Only eight rows of seating have been excavated in the auditorium, which was divided into two tiers by a horizontal passage (diazoma) and into five wedge-shaped sections by stairways. Round the orchestra (diameter 18.65m/60ft), which was separated from the auditorium by a channel for the drainage of rainwater, was a bench of honour, into which were later inserted five marble thrones with lions' feet and ivy-leaf ornament and a marble altar, presented by the agonothete (president of the games) Pythotimos. The 18m/60ft long stage building originally consisted of three 2.5m/8ft high rooms with their rear walls on the street, surmounted by an upper storey. Only the front of the walls is dressed to a smooth finish; the rear side was left rough. Each room had a door opening into the proscenium, which has Doric half-columns 2.7m/9ft high, originally painted red, supporting a Doric entablature. Between the half-columns are the three doors into the rooms; the other intercolumniations (spaced columns) could be closed off by pinakes (painted wooden screens). Later statues were set up in front of the second intercolumninations from the right and the left. The action of a play originally took place in front of this wall. When a character had to appear on the roof of a house he could make his way up on the top of the proscenium, a 2.74m/9ft wide podium with low lateral balustrades at the ends, on an external staircase at the right-hand (west) end. In Roman times the rear wall of this podium (i.e. the front wall of the upper storey of the stage building) was pulled down and the usual elaborately articulated stage wall built 2m/6½ft farther back. In order to support this wall three strong brick vaults and a wall of undressed stone were built in the old rear rooms.

The intercolumniations, apart from the three doors, were walled up and painted (remains of painting at west end). Thereafter the action took place on the higher level.

To the south of the theatre, reached through the middle of the stage building, is the city's principal Byzantine church. Farther west some fine private houses have been excavated.

Sanctuary of Demeter and Kore

Near the church is a path which runs up the Sanctuary of Demeter and Kore. Of the two statues of priestesses which stood outside the entrance one is now in Berlin. The sanctuary itself, a temple *in antis* of unusual form, is badly damaged. A bench-like podium and two tables for the divine meal were found in the temple, together with pottery votive statuettes. To the left of the temple is an offerings pit.

Water-supply

To the east of the Temple of Demeter, adjoining a tower on the town walls, is a settling basin from which water (brought from Mount Mykale) could be distributed throughout the town, enabling the water to be purified without any interruption of the supply. From here it is possible to climb up the steps leading to the summit of the hill or down to the East Gate.

Stadium

On the lowest terrace, just within the town walls, are the Stadium and the Lower Gymnasium, built in the 2nd c. B.C. Given the nature of the ground, the Stadium, 191m/210yd long, has seating only on the north side; above it was a portico. The starting-sill at the west end is partially preserved.

Lower Gymnasium

To the west of the stadium is the Hellenistic Lower Gymnasium. The square courtyard is surrounded by colonnades, with changing-rooms and wash-rooms to the rear on two sides.

The colonnade opening to the south is double, in accordance with Vitruvius' prescriptions. In the centre, to the rear, is the ephebeum (room for military training of young men), with large numbers of names carved on the walls. In the left-hand corner is a handsome room with a wash-basin running along the wall, supplied with water by elegant lion's-head spouts.

Princes' Islands — D/E 3

Marmara region
Province: İstanbul
Area: 10sq.km/4sq. miles
Population: 15,000

Situation
19–28km/12–17 miles South-south-east of İstanbul

Boat services:
Several times daily to and from İstanbul and Yalova

A boat trip to the beautiful Princes' Islands (Kızıl Adalar) in the north-east of the Sea of Marmara is a very rewarding experience.

With their carefully tended gardens and parks, their first-rate facilities for water-sports and their excellent roads, they offer a welcome change from the hectic pace of life in İstanbul.

There is no motor traffic on the Princes' Islands: the principal means of transport is provided by horse-drawn carriages, which can be hired for drives round the islands.

Sights

★Büyük Ada

Büyük Ada (Greek Prinkipo), the island "rich in figs" and the largest and most populous of the Princes' Islands, has developed into a holiday resort of first-rate importance, with villas, clubs, hotels and a wide range of leisure activities which attract large numbers of visitors.

On İsa Tepe (163m/535ft), the Hill of Christ, at the north end of the island, is the Monastery of the Transfiguration; on Yüce Tepe (201m/659ft), at the south end, the fortress-like Monastery of St George, from the terrace of which there are magnificent panoramic views.

★Heybeli Ada

This island takes its Geek name of Chalki from its deposits of copper (remains of a mine in Çalimanı Bay in the south of the island). It is now the headquarters of the Turkish Naval Academy. In the harbour, in front of the Academy, is the "Savarona", once Kemal Atatürk's private yacht.

In the saddle between the island's two highest hills, at its north end, stands the former Orthodox theological seminary. On the western hill is the only surviving Byzantine church in the Princes' Islands (15th c.; quatrefoil plan; for permission to visit, apply to Commandant, Naval Academy).

★Burgaz Ada

Burgaz Ada (Greek Pyrgos or Antigoni), an island of beautiful and varied scenery, probably takes its name from a tower which once stood on its highest hill (165m/541ft). Its excellent facilities for water-sports and its well-maintained country roads (ideal for excursions in horse-drawn carriages) attract many visitors. Near the Greek Orthodox church is the former home of the Turkish poet Sait Faik (1907–54), which is now a museum.

Kınalı Ada

Kınalı Ada (Greek Proti), the nearest of the islands to İstanbul, has a number of small bathing beaches. The monasteries on the island, now in ruin, were once used for internment of members of the Imperial family. From the highest point on the island (115m/377ft) there are fine panoramic views.

Sivri Ada

The rocky islet of Sivri Ada (great Oxia), rising out of the sea to a height of 90m/295ft, is notable only for the fact that in 1911 thousands of ownerless dogs which had been rounded up on the streets of İstanbul were marooned here and left to starve.

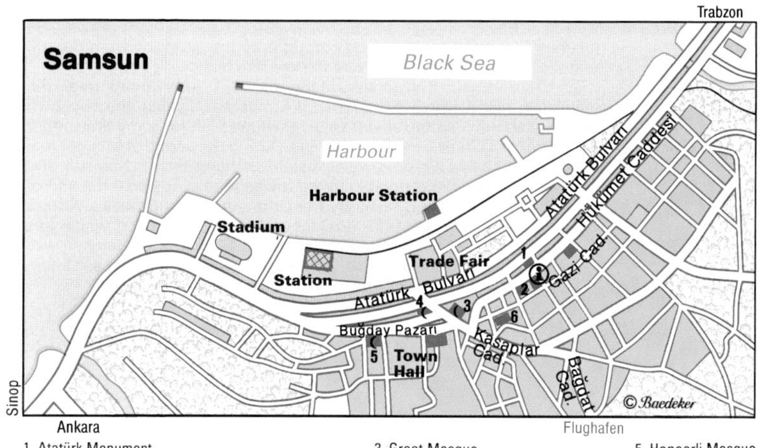

1 Atatürk Monument
2 Air terminal (airport buses)
3 Great Mosque
4 Yalı Mosque
5 Hançerli Mosque
6 Gazi Museum

Samsun

M 2

North coast (Black Sea)
Province: Samsun
Altitude: 0–40m/0–130ft
Population: 305,000

Situation and importance

The provincial capital of Samsun, half-way along the Turkish Black Sea coast, is the largest city on the north coast and its principal port and commercial centre. The importance of Samsun's well-equipped port depends mainly on its good communications with the Central Anatolian Plateau, with a convenient gap between the Eastern and Western Pontic Mountains affording passage to a trunk road and a railway line. Thanks to these communications it rivals Mersin on the Mediterranean coast as the principal port for the shipment of the produce of Central Anatolia. Tobacco (the best in Turkey), corn, cotton, poppies and other oil-producing plants are grown in the coastal plain round Samsun, between the delta of the Kızılırmak (Red River) to the west and the Yeşilırmak (Green River) to the east, processed (large tobacco and foodstuffs factories) and exported from the port of Samsun.

Samsun conveys the impression of a friendly and thriving modern town. It plays an important part in the holiday and tourist trade through its situation at the west end of the beautiful coast road below the East Pontic Mountains. The sandy beaches in the vicinity of the town offer excellent bathing.

History

The site of ancient Amisos, founded in the 7th c. B.C. by Greek settlers from Miletus, lay some 3km/2 miles north-west of present-day Samsun, where an earlier Bronze Age site has been identified. Later the site was occupied by Athenian settlers and called Peiraieus (Piraeus). From the early 4th c. B.C. the town was held by the Persians, but in the time of Alexander the Great recovered its freedom. After Alexander's death it was involved in the struggle of the Diadochoi for his succession, and finally fell to the kingdom of Pontos. Mithradates Eupator built temples in the city and resided in it for a time. During the conflict with the Romans the inhabitants set their city on fire just before it was taken by Lucullus. After many vicissitudes in subsequent years the town rose to prosperity in the time of Augustus as a transhipment point for the goods brought by the caravans from Central Anatolia. In Byzantine times it was the see of a bishop.

The name Samsun first appears in the year 1331. After its capture by the Seljuk ruler Kılıç Arslan II in the 12th c. the town was divided: the new town fell to Sultan Rukn-eddin, while the old town was left for some time under the control of a Greek Governor, Sabbas. During the period of Mongol rule Genoese merchants were allowed to establish themselves in Samsun, and their activities proved profitable to the townspeople. Towards the end of the 14th c. the town was taken by the Ottoman Sultan Beyazit I. After a second Ottoman attack in 1425 the Genoese set fire to the town, which was finally incorporated in the Ottoman Empire in 1470. In 1806 Samsun was again burned down, this time by the Turkish fleet after the town had shown opposition to the Sublime Porte.

Samsun is associated in modern Turkey with the beginning of the Republican era. It was here that Mustafa Kemal Paşa (later Atatürk) landed on May 19th 1919 to begin his fight against the foreign occupying forces. This date is celebrated throughout Turkey as the "Day of Youth".

Sights

Atatürk Monument
Gazi Museum

Mustafa Kemal Paşa's historic landing in 1919 is commemorated by a large equestrian statue in the Municipal Park and by the Gazi Museum (with library) in the former hotel in which Kemal Paşa stayed while in Samsun.

Mosques

The most notable of the town's older mosques are the Pazar Camii or Market Mosque, built by the Mongolian governors in the 14th c., the Great Mosque (Ulu Cami; 18th–19th c.), the Hacı Hatun Mosque and the Yalı Mosque.

Archaeological Museum

The Archaeological Museum displays material from the site of ancient Amisos on the hill of Düdar Tepe. It also has an interesting Ethnographic section.

Trade Fair

A Trade Fair is held annually in July in the Trade Fair grounds near the harbour.

Sardis D 5

Western Anatolia (interior)
Province: Manısa. Place: Sart

Situation

The site of the ancient Lydian capital, Sardis, once celebrated for its proverbial wealth and for its Sanctuary of Artemis, lies some 100km/60 miles east of İzmir at the little village of Sart in the valley of the Sart Çayı (the ancient Paktolos), a tributary of the Gediz (Hermos). The Lydian and Greek city lay on the west side of a steeply scarped acropolis hill some 200m/650ft high, while the later Roman town, laid out in the form of a semicircle, occupied a low terrace below the north side of the hill.

History

The development of Sardis (Sardeis) was closely dependent on the emergence and growth of the Lydian Empire. It is not yet established, however, whether the Lydians, a Semitic people whose rulers claimed descent from the Assyrian sun god, themselves founded the town or whether they conquered and incorporated in their kingdom an already existing Maeonian settlement. The town had a period of great prosperity from the reign of King Gyges (*c.* 685 B.C.) to that of Kroisos (Croesus; 560–546 B.C., thanks to its situation at the end of an ancient trade route, the winning of gold from the River Paktolos and a busy trade with the East. In 546 B.C. Sardis was conquered by the Persians under Cyrus, and until 499 B.C. was the residence of a Persian satrap. From here the great Royal Road of the Persian kings, with posting stations at four-hour intervals, ran by way of Ankyra (Ankara) to Susa.

In 499 B.C. Greeks from Ephesus occupied the city. After the Battle of the River Granikos in May 334 B.C. Alexander the Great captured Sardis without a fight and developed it into an important stronghold. During the struggle between the Diadochoi it was destroyed by Antichos III but was soon rebuilt. It then became part of the kingdom of Pergamon and thereafter passed under Roman control, when it enjoyed a period of prosperity. The town was ravaged by an earthquake in A.D. 17 but was rebuilt by Tiberius. Christianity came to Sardis at an early stage, no doubt through the missionary activity of Paul. It is mentioned in Revelations (1:11 and 3:4) as one of the Seven Churches of Asia.

Towards the end of the 11th c. Sardis passed under Seljuk rule. Thereafter it declined rapidly, until its final destruction by the Mongols of Tamerlane (Timur-Leng) in 1402.

The present village of Sart was not established until the beginning of the 20th c.

Excavations

The first excavations were carried out by Princeton University, and further work was done on the site by Harvard University from 1958 onwards.

Visiting the ★★ruins

★Temple of Artemis

On a low hill within the Lydian and Greek city are the remains of the celebrated Temple of Artemis built by King Kroisos (Croesus) of Lydia in the 6th c. B.C., destroyed by the Greeks in 498 and rebuilt in the reign of Alexander the Great. The temple is unusually large, measuring 100m/330ft long by 48m/155ft across. Along each side were 20 Ionic columns, at each end 8, of which 2 at the east end are completely preserved and 6 are preserved to half their height. The temple proper was divided into two parts by a transverse wall. A Lydian inscription with an Aramaic translation which was found near by provided a key for the decipherment of the Lydian language.

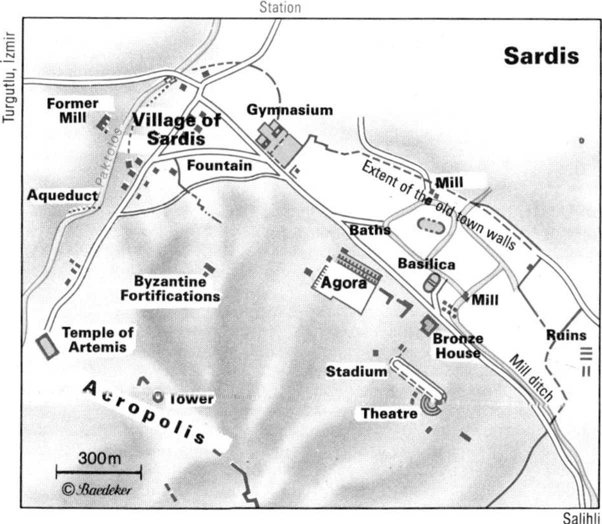

On the south-east side of the temple hill is a ruined Byzantine chapel of the 8th c.

Near the temple can be seen a necropolis of the Lydian period.

Acropolis

★★View

As a result of heavy weathering and the washing-down effect of rain practically nothing has survived on the Acropolis apart from scanty remains of walls on the south and east sides. From the top of the acropolis hill, however, there are superb views.

The Roman city

The Roman city is represented by the remains of a few houses, a theatre (fine view from top) and a stadium measuring 230m/250yd – probably all dating from after the great earthquake of A.D. 17.

Gymnasium

North-east of the village of Sart on the road to Salihli the American excavators brought to light a gymnasium of the 2nd c. A.D.; to the south-east they found other buildings (a synagogue, Byzantine shops), and, some 650m/710yd east of the gymnasium, baths. A little way north of the stadium is the so-called Bronze House.

Necropolis

Some 10km/6 miles north-west of Sart is another large necropolis, in the area known as Bin Tepe (Thousand Hills). Here, scattered over an undulating plateau are more than 60 conical burial mounds of varying size. Among them is an unusually large mound (69m/225ft high), traditionally believed to be the Tomb of Alyattes, father of Kroisos, which is described by Herodotus (Bk 1, ch. 93).

Side G 7

South coast (eastern Mediterranean)
Province: Antalya
Altitude: 0–15m/0–50ft
Place: Selimye

Situation

The remains of the once-important Hellenistic city of Side in Pamphylia lie on a rocky peninsula 300–400m/330–440yd wide, which is flanked by sandy beaches and which projects some 800m/880yd into the Mediterranean (Gulf of Antalya), approximately half-way between Antalya and Alanya. The peninsula reaches its highest point a little way inland in the bare limestone crag of Ak Dağı. This platform of rock in the middle of a featureless but relatively fertile stretch of coast, with the additional advantage of a little bay at the tip of the peninsula to serve as a harbour, was bound to attract human settlement.

★Selimiye (holiday resort)

In the heart of the ancient city, now much overgrown and covered by drifting sand, lies the charming little fishing village of Selimiye, which has developed into a busy holiday resort. Many of the inhabitants are the descendants of Cretans who settled here about 1900. There are hotels of all categories and a variety of restaurants and shops.

History

There was already a settlement on the Side Peninsula by about 1000 B.C. In the 7th or 6th c. Greek settlers from the city of Kyme on the west coast of Asia Minor established a colony here, but they soon merged with the local population. The little bay at the end of the peninsula was made into a harbour, and the men of Side soon built up a reputation for skilful and daring seamanship. After a period when it was a pirates' lair and a slave market Side developed in Roman times into an important and prosperous commercial city with many handsome public buildings of which only ruins remain. As at Perge and other coastal cities, however, the coastal currents gradually caused the silting up of the harbour, and this, combined with the collapse of Roman rule, led to the decay of the city. It was finally abandoned

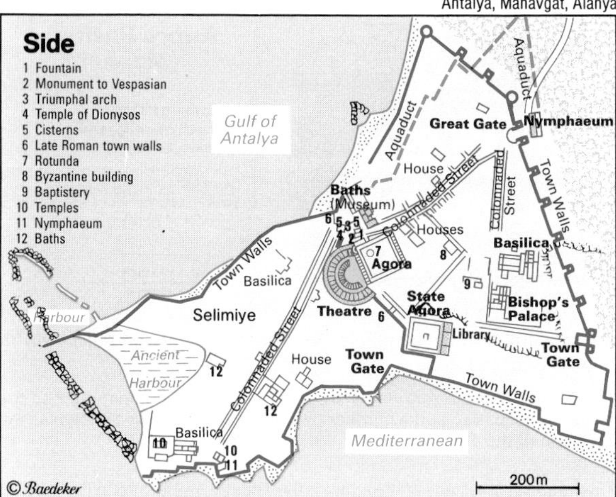

between the 7th and 9th c., and the Arab geographer Edrisi, visiting the site in the 12th c., found nothing but ruins and named the place Old Antalya.

Excavations

Systematic excavations were carried out by the Archaeological Institute of İstanbul between 1947 and 1967. The excavated remains give an excellent impression of the size and appearance of this Hellenistic city.

Visiting the ★ruins

Town walls

Nymphaeum

Along the east end of the peninsula extend the Byzantine town walls, once reinforced by towers, Outside the North Gate or Great Gate (which was originally of several storeys) is a nymphaeum (fountain house; 2nd c. B.C.), fed by an aqueduct coming in from the north.

Colonnaded street

Agora

From the Great Gate two colonnaded streets laid out in Roman times ran through the town, one leading due south, the other south-west. The latter comes in some 350m/380yd to the Agora, which was approximately square and was surrounded by colonnades housing shops. At the west corner the foundations of a small round Corinthian temple are clearly discernible. Some 30m/35yd north of the agora are two Roman peristyle houses (2nd–1st c. B.C.) with remains of mosaics.

★Agora Baths (Museum)

Facing the north-west side of the agora stand the imposing Agora Baths, now housing an interesting museum which contains the finest of the statues, reliefs, sarcophagi, urns, etc., recovered during the 20-year Turkish excavation campaign (1947–67). The exhibits are displayed in the various rooms of the baths (restored) and in the garden.

Items of particular interest are two Roman altars, a Hittite column base, a Roman sundial and a carving of weapons from the East Gate in the frigidarium (cold room); figures of girls and women, including the Three Graces, in the caldarium (hot room); a magnificent sarcophagus with a frieze of Eroses, statues of Herakles (with the apple of the Hesperides in his hand), Hermes and the Emperor Licinius in the large tepidarium (tepid room); a large statue of Nike, goddess of victory in the small tepidarium; and

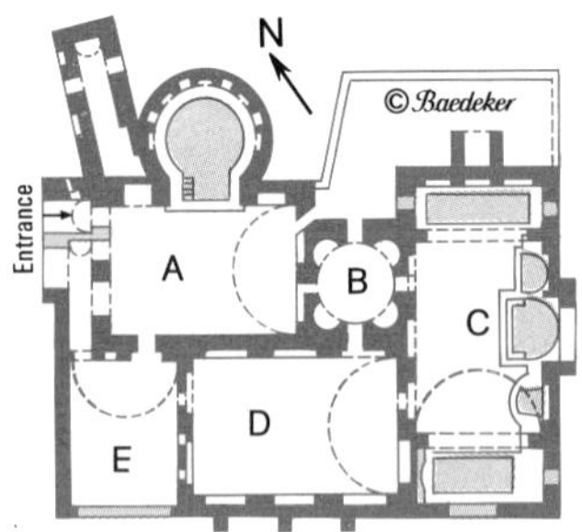

Side
Agora Baths
(Museum)

A Frigidarium (cold bath)
B Laconicum (sweating-room)
C Caldarium (hot bath)
D Large Tepidarium (warm bath)
E Small Tepidarium (anteroom of museum)

15 m
50 ft

architectural fragments, reliefs, Medusa heads, etc., in the palaestra garden.

Triumph arch
Vespasian
Monument
Fountains

South-west of the Agora Baths are a triumphal arch, a Monument to the Emperor Vespasian and a number of fountains, notably one known as the Fountain of the Three Basins.

★Theatre

On the south-west side of the agora is the Theatre, the largest in Pampyhlia, which could accommodate an audience of 15,000 in its 49 rows of seating. Although several of the supporting arches have collapsed, bringing down parts of the auditorium, this is stil a remarkable example of Roman architectural skill.

Selimiye

From the theatre the colonnaded street continues south-west across the peninsula, passing through the village of Selimiye (many restaurants and

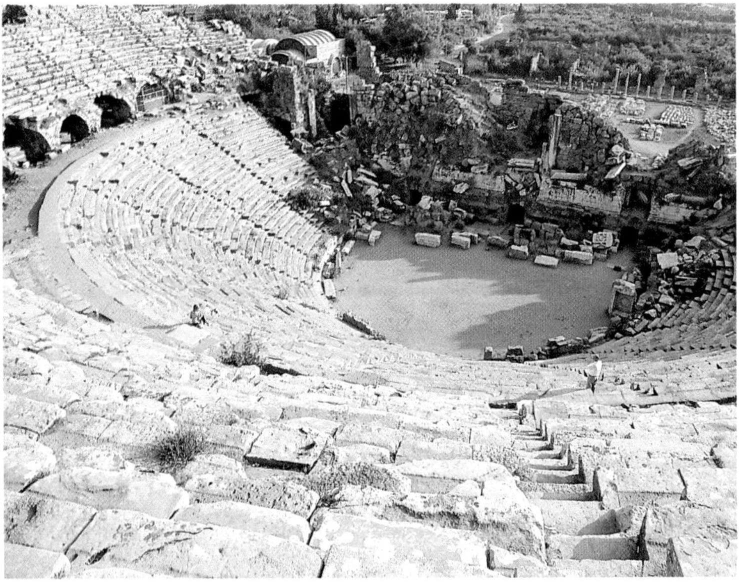

Side: the largest ancient theatre in Pamphylia

Manavat Waterfalls near Side

souvenir shops) and ending at a semicircular temple by the sea dedicated to the moon god Men. West of this, at the tip of the peninsula, are the remains of the city's two principal temples, probably dedicated to Athena and Apollo; adjoining on the east are the ruins of a Byzantine basilican church.

Temples

At the south-west end of the peninsula is the ancient harbour, now largely silted up. Its outline is marked by the steep scarp of the coastal rocks.

Ancient harbour

Following this scarp to the north-east, we come to the remains of Byzantine baths.

On the eastern part of the city, some 200m/220yd south-east of the theatre, is the so-called State Agora. Its east side is occupied by an imposing building, originally two-storeyed, which has been interpreted as a library. In a columned niche, still *in situ*, is a figure of Nemesis, goddes of fate.

State Agora

Between the State Agora and the eastern town walls are the extensive ruins of the Byzantine bishop's palace, principal basilica and baptistery, dating from the 5th–10th c.

Byzantine churches

Surroundings of Side

In the immediate vicinity of the ancient site and the village of Selimiye are long sandy beaches which are much frequented by holiday-makers. They begin immediately below the ancient town walls on the edge of the cliff and continue for miles along the coast of the Gulf.

★Bathing beaches

8km/5 miles north-east of Side, a little way in from the coast, lies the little town of Manavgat (alt. 30m/100ft) on the river of the same name (the

Manavgat

ancient Melas), a stream with an abundant flow of water which rises in the Seytan range of the Taurus. 5km/3 miles upstream (access road) are the beautiful Manavgat Falls (Şelâlesi). The area is laid out as a garden, and visitors can make their way on various paths and gangways to the immediate vicinity of the falls, the roar of which can be heard a long way off.

★Manavgat Falls

Silifke

I 7

South coast (eastern Mediterranean)
Province: İçel
Altitude: 50m/165ft
Population: 47,000

Situation and ★importance

Silifke (formerly Selefke), chief town of its district, lies some 10km/6 miles from the Mediterranean on the right bank of the Göksu Nehri (ancient bridge). It occupies the site of ancient Seleukeia Tracheia, one of the cities founded by Seleukos Nikator (312–281 B.C.), an important road junction in "Rough" Cilicia (Kilikia Tracheia, Cilicia Aspera). It had a famous oracle of Apollo and flourished up to the end of the Roman Imperial period.

Sights

Konak

The visible remains date from the Roman period. The Konak contains a collection of archaeological material (inscriptions, statues, architectural fragments, etc.).

Camardesium

On the hill to the west are the ruins of the Crusader Castle of Camardesium, successor to the ancient acropolis. On the southern slope of the hill and on the neighbouring hill is the ancient necropolis, with numerous sarcophagi and rock tombs. The Christian cemetery is on the hill of Meriamlık.

Necropolis

Surroundings of Silifke

Göksu Nehri (Saleph)

The Göksu Nehri (Blue Water), the sources of which are on the slopes of the mighty Ak Dağı range to the north-west, was known in antiquity as the Kalykadnos, in medieval times as the Selef or Saleph. In this abundantly flowing stream the Emperor Frederick I Barbarossa was drowned on June 10th 1190 while on the march from Laranda (now Karaman) to Seleukeia (Silifke) during the Third Crusade. The river formerly reached the sea to the west of the town, but now flows to the south-east. In consequence of the predominantly westerly direction of the marine currents the river delta is extending southward in a long narrow sand spit, creating areas of marsh, small lakes and coastal lagoons.

Meriamlık

A good half-hour's walk south of Silifke, on a stepped footpath hewn from the soft local rock, lies Meriamlık, on a hill projecting to the east. This was one of the most-frequented places of pilgrimage of the Early Christian period, where St Thekla, a disciple of the Apostle Paul, was said to have lived in a cave and to have disappeared into the earth to escape her oppressors. Of the numerous churches, monasteries and associated buildings only the apse of the great columned basilica at the south end of the plateau remains above ground. The huge structure (90m/295ft by 37m/120ft), which had a forecourt, narthex, three aisles and sacristies in addition to the apse, was built by the Emperor Zeno (474–491) on the site of an earlier basilica. Below the church are the sacred caves, which in the 2nd c. were reconstructed to form a three-aisled crypt; they are still visited by pilgrims.

Baedeker Special

Death in the Raging Torrent

On June 10th 1190, a Sunday, the German army of Crusaders stood some 8km/5 miles from the present coastal town of Silifke. The army, made up of 15,000 men including 3,000 knights, had set out from Regensburg in Germany on May 11th 1189 with the aim of restoring Christian rule to the Holy Sepulchre. After arriving in Asia at the entrance to the Dardanelles near Gallipoli (now Gelibolu), the army took less than six weeks to complete its exhausting forced march through western Turkey. The soldiers were led by a man who came close to epitomising knighthood and leadership – the 67 year-old German King and Holy Roman Emperor Frederick I, who was later nicknamed Barbarossa (redbeard) because of his full red beard.

On the day in question the heat descended very early. The army had a difficult climb to the coast ahead and gradually became broken up into a number of sections. "As we marched on . . . we came to the Saleph river . . . Taking a short cut through the valleys the Emperor led us across a raging torrent and we came safely to the other bank. After the interminable and exhausting forced march we had endured he finally stopped so that we could rest and eat. He decided to wash in the river and to swim in it to refresh himself but, by the will of God, drowned as the result of a terrible accident", reported an anonymous crusader in a letter home. In the eyes of another chronicler Frederick I died a hero's death: "The Emperor was anxious to give us relief from the unbearable heat and to find a way round the mountain ridge, so he tried to swim across the raging river . . . Even though we all tried to dissuade him, he entered the water and dived into a whirlpool, to be seen no more. He who had survived so many dangers thus died an awful death."

To this day it remains uncertain how the Emperor really died – possibly he suffered a heart attack while bathing. His unexpected death signalled the end of the Third Crusade. Many of his comrades-in-arms owed allegiance more to him than to the crusading ideals, and shortly after his death the first crusaders returned home. Of those who marched on under the command of Barbarossa's son Duke Frederick of Swabia, many died from disease; only a few hundred Germans reached their final goal, the town of Akko (now in northern Israel), which was occupied by their Muslim adversary, the Sultan Saladin.

It was the custom in the Middle Ages for various parts of the bodies of important people to be buried in different places. Duke Frederick had his father's heart interred in Tarsus Cathedral; his flesh, boiled to free it from his skeleton, was buried in the Cathedral of Antiochia (Antakya), while his bones were taken to Tyrus for interment. However, there is no memorial to Frederick Barbarossa in the mosque which was later built on the site of Tarsus Cathedral; Antiocha Cathedral was soon destroyed; a new town was built over the ruins of Tyrus, and somewhere underneath it rest the bones of the Emperor.

Source: Peter Milger, "The Crusades", Munich 1988.

Diocaesarea: columns of the Temple of Zeus

Demirçili

About 7km/4 miles north of Silifke, the road to Uzuncaburç passes a number of 2nd and 3rd c. tombs in different styles. There are three basic architectural styles: towers, temples and houses: the square towers are mostly simple and relatively slender, the temple tombs are so called because of their Corinthian columns, while the plain house-tombs have a rather squat appearance. The last two often display sculptures of the deceased on the gabled wall. These tombs are a part of the necropolis of the ancient Roman town of Imbriogon, dating from the 2nd/3rd c.

★★Olba Diocaesarea

Some 30km/20 miles north of Silifke in the rolling uplands of the Southern Taurus (alt. 1110m/3640ft), to the right of the old road to Karaman (on the right, a number of temples), are the well-preserved remains of ancient Olba (Diocaesarea), known in Turkish as Uzuncaburç (high tower), once the seat of the priestly Teucrid dynasty which ruled western Cilicia in the 3rd and 2nd c. B.C. To the north is the five-storey tower (*c.* 200 B.C.) from which the place gets its present name. To the south are remains of dwelling-houses, and beyond these a colonnaded street of the Hellenistic and Roman periods running from east to west. At the east end of the street are the Theatre (A.D.164–165) and a Byzantine church. To the west, on the south side of the colonnaded street, is a Temple of Zeus built soon after 300 B.C. with 6 by 12 Early Corinthian columns, 30 of them still standing and 4 still retaining their capitals. The cella was pulled down in the 5th c. when the temple was converted into a church; at the west end was a portico. From here a cross street leads 70m/75yd north to a well-preserved Roman gate with three passages. At the west end of the colonnaded street is the Tychaion, a temple of the 1st c. A.D. with an unusual plan; five of the six columns on the façade are still standing. 110m/120yd south of the Temple of Zeus is a large public building (*c.* A.D. 200), on the upper floor of which was a colonnaded hall.

From the high tower a paved ancient road lined by cemeteries runs east to another ancient site in the Ura Basin (975m/3200ft), the residential part of

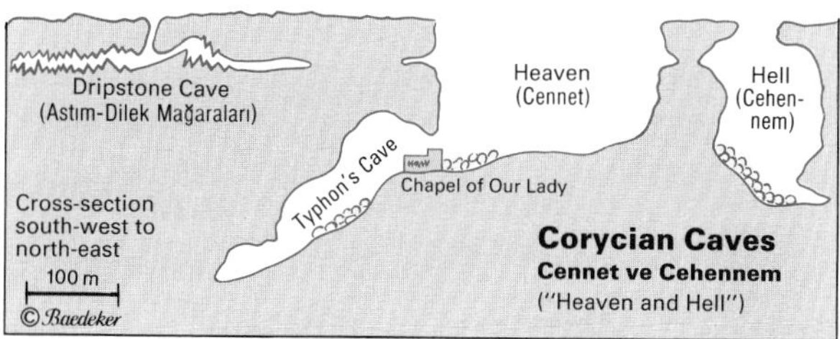

Olba, with numerous remains of churches, houses, tombs, a water-tower and a large aqueduct built in the reign of the Emperor Pertinax.

★Narlıkuyu

6km north of Susanoğlu lies the small coastal town of Narlıkuyu (pomegranate fountain) with the remains of ancient baths and a finely coloured 4th c. mosaic on display in a small covered museum. The mosaic represents the "Three Graces" with the goddesses Aglaia (Grace), Euphrosyne (Merriment) and Thalia (Charm). According to the inscription it was presented by the governor of the Princes' Islands, Poimenios, who controlled the flow of water from the spring and built a bath here. Another inscription reads: "Whoever drinks this water will become wise and live long, the ugly will become beautiful."

★Corycian Caves
Cennet ve Cehennem

A side road on the left (3km/2 miles) goes up to the two Corycian Caves or in Turkish Cennet ve Cehennem (Heaven and Hell) with a chapel and various ancient remains. The two huge, collapsed sink-holes (obruk) are sited above a cave system with an underground lake that extends under the sea in the Bay of Narlıkuyu emerging as a karst spring. When the sea is calm, the flow of water can be seen from the surface. While the round 120m/393ft Cehennem (Hell) cave 75m/80yd further east is not accessible, steps lead down to the larger Cennet (Heaven) cave which is 100m/325ft wide and 550m/1800ft long. What is initially an open pit leads to a deeper cave at the rear. Known as the Typhon Cave (300m/984ft long and 75m/246ft high), the 5th c. Chapel of St Mary stands at the edge, guarding the entrance to the underworld where the monster Typhon with a hundred dragon heads and snake feet lived.

Korykos
★Kızkalesi

4km/2½ miles north-east of Narlıkuyu the massive remains of the citadel of ancient Korykos face the picturesque island fortress of Kızkalesi (Maiden's Castle). During the Middle Ages this fortified islet became one of the most notorious pirates' lairs on the coasts of the Mediterranean. The present name derives from an old legend. A sultan was told by a soothsayer that his daughter would die of a snakebite, whereupon he built a castle, hoping that the sturdy walls would protect her. The prophecy was fulfilled however, when he himself sent her a basket of fruit and she was bitten by a snake concealed inside.

Ayaş
Elaiusa-Sebaste

4km/2½ miles further north lies Ayaş with the widely scattered remains of ancient Elaiusa-Sebaste. Partly covered by drifting sand, there are remains of a five-aisled basilica on the mainland and various ruined parts of the city including a temple, theatre, grain-stores, etc. In a wide arc around the city lie several necropolises with house-tombs and sarcophagi.

Adamkayalar

Above the Cennet ve Cehennem Caves some 3km/2 miles from Kızkalesi in the direction of Hüseyinler some interesting rock tombs and carvings with human figures can be seen.

★Kanlıdivane

About 40km/25 miles north-east of Silifke a side road forks off to the left to the ruined site of ancient Kanytelleis (3km/2 miles). It was discovered by Langlois in 1852 and lies around a deep sink-hole (obruk) which it is

The island stronghold called "Maiden's Castle" (Kiskalesi)

possible to descend by a narrow footpath. The ruins of many of the town's sacred and secular buildings can still be seen, including five churches (two large 8th/9th c. basilica). On the south side stands a huge Hellenistic tower, which the priestly prince Teukros of Olba Diocaesarea (Uzuncaburç) built around 200 B.C. in honour of Zeus Olbios who was revered in Olba. Extensive necropoles with sarcophagi, temple tombs and house-tombs can be found around the town.

Several decades ago the town was settled by the Yürüks (a nomadic or semi-nomadic tribe), whose simple dwellings and cemetery can be found inside the ruined site.

Liman Kalesi

About 20km/12 miles west of Silifke beside the large bay of Taşucu (Boğsak Körfezi) stands the octagonal castle of Liman Kalesi. Cisterns and dwellings can be found hidden behind the walls. At the beginning of the 19th c. it was almost certainly used as a pirates' lair.

Sinop — L 1

North coast (Black Sea)
Province: Sinop
Altitude: 0–25m/0–80ft
Population: 26,000

Situation and importance

The provincial capital of Sinop, Turkey's most northerly town, is charmingly situated on the Boztepe Peninsula, in the central section (which is also the most northerly) of the Turkish Black Sea coast. It has the most sheltered harbour on the coast. It is now a place of little consequence compared with its importance in antiquity, when it was a busy commercial city situated at the end of important caravan routes from Cappadocia and

The Port of Sinop

the lands on the Euphrates and also oriented towards the sea; nowadays communications with the Anatolian Plateau are rendered difficult by the intervening barrier of the West Pontic Mountains.

History

The history of ancient Sinope extended well before the establishment of a colony by Miletus in the 8th c. B.C., but as a Milesian colony it had a leading position among the cities on the Black Sea. Here in 401 B.C. Xenophon and his Ten Thousand took ship for Byzantium after their long and toilsome Anabasis (up-country march). In 413 B.C. the Cynic philosopher Diogenes (the one who lived in a tub; not to be confused with Diogenes of Apollonia) was born in Sinope. In the 2nd c. B.C. it was the residence for some time of Mithradates VI, last King of Pontos. In 63 B.C. it came under Roman rule, and later belonged to the Byzantine Empire. In 1214 it was taken by the Seljuks, and in 1301 it passed into the hands of the Emirs of Kastamonu. The Genoese established a trading-post here, as they did at Samsun. In 1458 the town was occupied by Mehmet II's Ottoman forces. On November 30th 1853 Russian warships launched a surprise attack, destroyed a Turkish flotilla off Sinop and bombarded the town, an event which led to the outbreak of the Crimean War (1853–56).

Sights

No buildings survive from the great days of ancient Sinope, apart from scanty remains of the citadel and of a Temple of Serapis. The town is notable for its woodcarving craft.

Town walls

A stretch of the town walls approximately 3km/2 miles long and up to 30m/100ft high is in part preserved; in the harbour district it is possible to walk along the walls. They were restored by the Genoese in the 13th c.

Mosques

The Alaeddin and Alaiye Mosques are fine examples of Seljuk architecture.

Museum

The Museum of Sinop contains archaeological material and a number of icons painted on a gold ground.

Harbour

★View

The ancient city had two harbours, one on either side of the narrow strip of land linking the Boztepe Peninsula with the mainland. Of these only the one on the east side is now used by coastal shipping and the brightly painted local fishing-boats. From the highest point of the peninsula, on which there is a small mosque, there are beautiful panoramic views.

Gerze

40km/25 miles south-east of Sinop lies the little port of Gerze, with a beautiful park, a number of fishermen's cafés and restaurants and a good bathing beach.

Tarsus K 7

South coast (eastern Mediterranean)
Province: İçel
Altitude: 0–15m/0–49ft
Population: 191,000

Situation and importance

The city of Tarsus, in a rather damp and unhealthy situation, surrounded by gardens, on the Tarsus Çayı (the ancient Kyndos) in the hot Cilician Plain, at the foot of the Tarsus, is one of the few towns in the eastern Mediterranean which can trace its history back without interruption for 3000 years. Its importance in ancient times depended on its situation at the south end of the celebrated pass through the Taurus known as the Cilician Gates and on a lagoon on the Mediterranean coast. Since then the lagoon has been completely silted up and the coastline has moved away from the town, destroying its maritime trade, while the main road from Ankara through the Cilician Gates to Adana, İskenderun and Syria now runs some distance to the east of the town. Tarsus is now a commercial and market centre (cotton export), with no features of any great interest to the tourist.

History

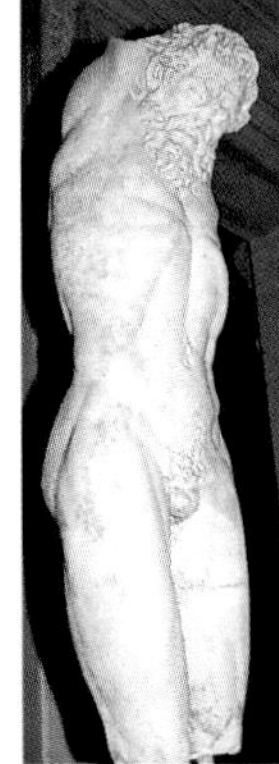

Marayas statue

Excavations on the Gözlü Kale have brought to light occupation levels extending from about 5000 B.C. into Roman times. The first town walls were built in the 3rd millennium B.C. In the 5th c. B.C. the town passed under Persian control. The Greek General and historian Xenophon (430–354 B.C.) tells us that about 400 B.C. Tarsus, then a flourishing city, was plundered by Cyrus' forces. In 333 B.C. Alexander the Great put an end to Persian rule, and after his death it belonged to the kingdom of the Seleucids. During the Third Syrian War (246 B.C.) it was conquered by Egypt. In 64 B.C. it became Roman and was made capital of the province of Cilicia.

Under the Empire Tarsus had an important harbour in the lagoon, and in its university (particularly the school of philosophy) vied with the great schools of Athens and Alexandria. In the last century B.C. the Apostle Paul was born in Tarsus, the son of a tent-maker; but there was no large Christian community there until the end of the 4th c. Thereafter the archbishops of Tarsus played a prominent part in the Councils of the Church.

After the occupation of Syria by the Arabs Cilicia became a frontier area, and the decline of Tarsus began. It was taken by the Syrian Caliph El Mahmun in 831 but recovered by the Byzantine Emperor Nikephoros Phokas in 965. About the middle of the 11th c. the Seljuks took the town, but in 1097 they were dislodged by the Crusaders, who returned the town to the Byzantines. During the 13th and 14th c. the Armenians who had been driven out of eastern Asia Minor by the Seljuks established a kingdom in Cilicia with the agreement of the Byzantines. In 1266 and 1274 Tarsus was plundered by the Arabs, and in 1359 it was taken by the Mamelukes. With the conquest of the town by the Ottomans in 1515 its political history came to an end. Thereafter it lived on as a place of little consequence, having lost its function as chief town of a region and an important port.

Sights

Of the great buildings of antiquity, particularly those of the city's heyday in the early Christian centuries, practically nothing remains. The ancient city now lies buried 6–7m/20–23ft deep under the alluvial plain of the Tarsus Çayi, and little excavation has so far been carried out. A town gate of the Roman period is given the name of Paul's Gate. Remains of a stoa and a Roman theatre have been found south-east of the present town.

Paul's Gate

In the market square is the Ulu Cami (Great Mosque), with a türbe.

Great Mosque

Near the town, on the right bank of the Tarsus Çayı, is a massive structure 5–6m/16–20ft high known as the Dönik Taş or as the Tomb of Sardanapalus, after the legendary founder of Tarsus. It is probably the substructure of a huge temple (108m/355ft by 52m/170ft; 10 by 21 columns) of the Roman Imperial period.

Tomb of Sardanapalus

About 20 minutes' walk above the town is a şelâle (waterfall) of the Tarsus Çayı, where Alexander the Great nearly drowned while bathing in the Kydnos.

Waterfall

Surroundings of Tarsus

Just over 50km/30 miles north of Tarsus the valley of the Tarsus Çayı narrows into the defile now called Gülek Boğazı but famed in ancient times as the Cilician Gates (in Latin Pylae Ciliciae) – a rocky gorge several hundred metres high but barely 20m/65ft wide. The ancient road, which frequently features in history and was used by such noted figures as Semiramis, Xerxes, Darius, Cyrus the Younger, Alexander the Great, Haroun al-Rashid and Godfrey de Bouillon, followed the east side of the gorge, partly hewn from the rock face and partly borne on projecting beams. A modern road has been blasted out of the cliffs on the west side. The new long-distance highway bypasses the gorge on the east.

★Cilician Gates

Immediately south of the Cilician Gates rises the fortress-like crag of Gülek Kale Dağı, with the ruined Castle of Assa Kaliba crowning the hill 600m/2000ft higher up.

Trabzon

P 2/3

North coast (Black Sea)
Province: Trabzon
Altitude: 0–36m/0–120ft
Population: 145,000

The port town and provincial capital of Trabzon (formerly better known as Trebizond) is the most important town on the eastern Black Sea coast and the third largest (after Samsun and Zonguldak) of the Turkish Black Sea towns. It has a University of Technology.

Situation and importance

The coastal scenery in the vicinity of Trabzon is particularly beautiful. The steeply scarped peaks of the Eastern Pontic Mountains, which reach their highest point in Tatos Dağı (3937m/12,917ft), 100km/60 miles east of Trabzon, leave room for only a narrow coastal strip on the Black Sea, with a climate, mild in winter and ofter oppressively close in summer, which produces a luxuriant subtropical vegetation such as is found scarcely anywhere else in Turkey. The road from Trabzon over the Gümüşhane Pass (Zigana Pass 2030m/6660ft) through the Pontic Mountains to the Eastern Anatolian plain has been a major factor in the development of the port.

Trabzon took its Greek name of Trapezous (Latin Trapezus) from the shape of its flat-topped acropolis hill (trapeza×table). Founded perhaps as early as the 8th c. (according to Xenophon in the 5th c.) by settlers from the Greek

History

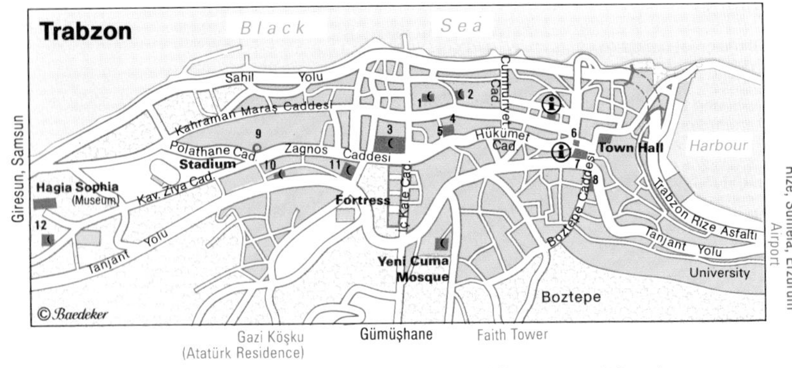

1 Pazar Kapı Mosque
2 Bazaar Mosque
3 Orttahisar (Fatih) Mosque (Panagia Chrysokephalos)
4 St Basil's Church (Büyük Ayvasıl Kilise)
5 St Anne's Church (Küçük Ayvasıl Kilise)
6 Atatürk Monument
7 Air terminal (airport buses)
8 Bus station
9 Fountain
10 Pir Ahmet Mausoleum
11 Gülbahar Hatun Mosque
12 Yeni Fatih Mosque

colony of Sinope, it soon developed into a flourishing city. It lay at the end of an important caravan route on which Persian goods were brought to the Black Sea for onward transport to the Mediterranean. This was also the route by which Xenophon and his Ten Thousand fought their way back to Trapezous after serving in Cyrus the Younger's campaign against Artaxerxes II (see Xenophon's "Anabasis"). During the war between King Mithradates Eupator of Pontos and the Roman General Lucullus (*c.* 70 B.C.) the city remained neutral and was spared the ravages of war; and it

Hagia Sophia in Trabzon

Sumela Monastery

remained a free city after Rome gained control of Asia Minor. In A.D. 260 Trapezous was captured by the Ostrogoths after putting up a fierce resistance. In Byzantine times it was the seat of a provincial governor and its defences were strengthened as an eastern outpost of the Empire.

After the capture of Constantinople by the Crusaders in 1204 Alexius Comnenus V proclaimed himself Emperor and made Trapezous capital of the reduced Greek Empire of the Comneni. The city flourished during this period, and after the re-establishment of the Byzantine Empire in Constantinople the Emperor granted Trapezous its independence. In 1461 it fell to the Ottomans under Sultan Mehmet II. In recent decades Trabzon has shared in the general upturn in the economy of eastern Turkey, and the harbour has been improved to enable it to handle vessels of greater draught.

Sights

The town

Trabzon consists of three districts built on low hill ridges – the commercial district or İskander Paşa quarter immediately west of the harbour, the Cumhuriyet quarter adjoining it on the north-west, and an old-world quarter of irregular little streets and old wooden houses still farther west.

Armenian churches

In the İskander Paşa quarter is St Anne's Church (Küçük Ayvasıl Kilise, the Little Armenian Church) and near this is St Basil's Church (Büyük Ayvasıl Kilise, the Great Armenian Church). Both churches date from the 8th c.

Ortahisar Mosque

Beyond the Tabakhane Deresi (fine views from viaduct), beginning on the old citadel hill, lies the Cumhuriyet quarter. The most notable building in this district is the Ortahisar Camii or Fatih Camii, originally a 13th c. Byzantine church known from the gilded dome over the crossing as Panagia Chrysokephalos (the Church of the Virgin with the Golden Head). It has a Latin cross plan, with a nave flanked by lower aisles and cut by the transept. The galleries over the aisles, which are marked off from the nave by triforia, were the gynaecea, the areas reserved for women, which could be reached either from within the church or from the narthex. Outside the main doorway are a fountain and marble basin for şadırvan (ritual ablutions).

★Hagia Sophia

Some 3km/2 miles west of the harbour, charmingly situated on a hill near the coast, is the Church of Hagia Sophia (Ayasofya), probably built by the Emperor Alexius Comnenus immediately after coming to Trabzon from Constantinople in 1204. In Ottoman times it was converted into a mosque; it is now a museum. Like other Byzantine churches in Trabzon, Hagia Sophia has a cruciform plan, with a nave flanked by aisles and a transept (wall-paintings). Over the crossing is a dome. Along the base of the south doorway is a frieze depicting the story of Adam, in a style which shows clear Eastern influence.

Boztepe

On the north side of the hill of Boztepe (244m/800ft; views) is the Monastic Church of Panagia Theoskepastos, built in the 13th c. on the site of an ancient temple (old frescos). The church is partly hewn from the rock.

Surroundings of Trabzon

Hezıt İlys

The former Monastery of St George in Peristera can be reached from the village of Esiroğlu (Yesiroğu in the Maçka valley) which lies 28km/17 miles south of Trabzon. A local guide is advisable and the walk will take at least three hours. This monastery and look-out post for Trabzon was built in the reign of Justinian (532). A famous collection of manuscripts was destroyed by a fire in 1906 and in 1923 the monks had to abandon the monastery.

Kaymaklı

About 5km/3 miles south of Trabzon a steep track off the main Erzurum road leads to the Monastery of Kaymaklı, where Armenian monks lived until 1923. The two-storey building with an arcaded façade stands alongside the ruins of a bell-tower. In the vicinity two chapels can be found: one (1424) is now used as a hay barn and the other (1622) contains the remains of some paintings.

Kiremitli

Kücük Konak, a village 46km/29 miles south of Trabzon, is the starting point for a 10km/7 mile walk to the Vazelon Monastery (St John of Vazelon) which is set on a rock high above the Değirmendere valley. It is one of the most important Pontic monasteries and was used by Justinian as a look-out post to warn of attacks from hostile mountain tribes. The monastery was linked with Trapezunt by a cobbled road (King's Road). The main building which has been altered many times stands in front of a cave. The nearby Chapel of St John (John the Baptist), which was built by Manuel III in 1410, contains the remains of some paintings.

★★Sumela Monastery

Some 62km/38 miles south-east of Trabzon in the Altındere Vadisi Milli Parkı (Gülden Valley National Park) the Meryam Ana Manastiri (St Mary's Monastery) clings to a rock high above the Altındere. During the summer months visitors are admitted each day at 9am, 11am, 2pm and 4pm. There are two ways to get there. One very steep track leads directly up from the car park, while another longer, more leisurely route initially follows the valley upwards, but then at the first bend to the left a path runs back almost parallel to the monastery. The old Greek name for the monastery was Hagia Maria tou Mela (St Mary from the Black Mountains). 67 steps lead to the inner courtyard well back behind the entrance doorway. Directly above the precipice are the main living quarters and the old library, while beneath a rock face several other monastery buildings, including the painted cave chapel, huddle around the courtyard. The monastery in its present form with cells for 75 monks, a refectory, visitors' house and fountain (miracle-working water) dates from 1860.

According to legend, the monastery was founded in the 5th c. by two Greek monks (Barnabas and Sophronios) who had intended it to house an icon (Mary) painted by St Luke. They claim the site, with a spring on the rock face, appeared to them in a dream. When the monastery was destroyed in the 12th c. this icon was said to have survived all attempts to destroy it.

The Sumela Monastery remained a popular place of pilgrimage until the 19th c. In 1923 the monks abandoned the burnt out monastery and buried the relics of the cross and St Luke's icon in the monastery's Chapel of St Barbara. The monk's successors now live some 100km/70 miles west of Salonica in Greece. In 1931 the icon, the relics of the cross and Abbot Fazelon's four-volumed gospel book (644) written on gazelle skins were taken to the Benaki Museum in Athens.

Zigana Pass

The main road from Trabzon to Erzurum and Erzincan, runs south-west through the Eastern Pontic Mountains and climbs the 2030m/6660ft Zigana Pass. It was perhaps on a mound near here (about an hour's walk) that Xenophon and his Ten Thousand caught their first glimpses of the Black Sea ("Thalatta!").

Troy — B 4

West coast (Aegean Sea)
Province: Çanakkale
Altitude: 8–40m/25–130ft
District: Hisarlık

Northern Schliemann excavations

Situation and ★★importance

Troy (Greek Ilion or Ilios, Latin Ilium Novum, Turkish Turuva, Truva, sometimes Trova), the excavated site of the chief town of the ancient Troad, made famous by Homer's "Iliad", lies on a hill now some 35m/115ft high a little to the south of the junction of the Dardanelles with the Aegean. The hill is a wedge-shaped outlier of an area of high ground which broadens out towards the east, rising steeply to the alluvial plain of the Küçük Menderes (the Scamander of the Greeks) and the Dümrek Çayı (the ancient Simois).

The hill rising out of the surrounding plain offered a good strategic site for a fortress, far enough away from the sea to be safe from surprise attacks but near enough to be able to keep a watch on the entrance to the Dardanelles. No doubt only the acropolis was on the hill, with the rest of the town extending over the river plain. This situation enabled the settlement to achieve early prosperity but also exposed it to repeated attacks and frequent destruction. There are, therefore, no buildings left standing on the site; all that the visitor will see are the excavators' trenches and the settlement levels they have brought to light – though what he does see is extraordinarily impressive both as a revelation of a history going back 5000 years and as a demonstration of what archaeology can achieve in unravelling the distant past.

Access

To get to this rather remote site, take a bus or car to Çanakkale from İstanbul via Tekirdağ and the Dardanelles ferry (380km/235 miles) or via Bursa, Bandırma (580km/360 miles); from Çanakkale by minibus or long-distance bus to Edremit/İzmir, alight at the fork to Troy and take a taxi (5km/3 miles).

The Troy periods

Troy I 10 levels (3000–2500 B.C.)

Excavations have shown that there was a fortified settlement of large, long houses on the rocky hill of Hisarlık some 5000 years ago.

Troy

Nine periods in the settlement-hill of Hisarlık

Ilios
Ilion
Ilium
Truva

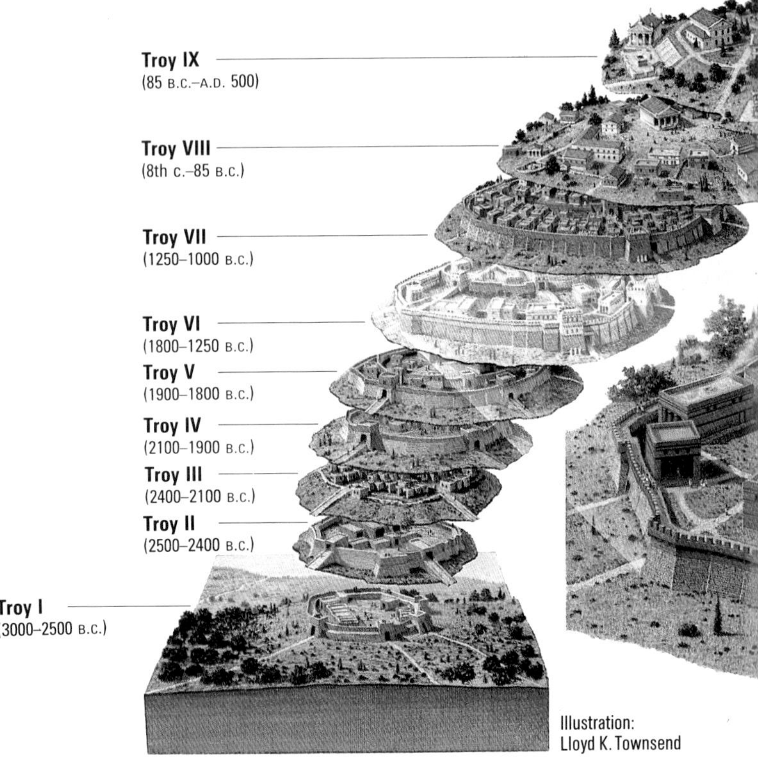

Illustration: Lloyd K. Townsend

Troy II
7 levels
(2500–2400 B.C.)

About the middle of the 3rd millennium the Troy I settlement was extended towards the south-west. An area of 8000sq.m/9500sq.yd was surrounded by a fortified wall which was rebuilt three times. To the south-west stood a huge entrance of stone blocks. In the centre of the circuit of walls stood the palace of the ruler. In the upper section of Troy II (i.e. the "Burnt Town") Schliemann found what he called the Treasure of Priam (gold and silver vessels, gold jewellery etc.). This treasure has been dated to around 2400 B.C. and is linked with the fire. Schliemann was convinced until shortly before his death that this was Homer's Troy.

Troy III–V
13 levels
(2400–1800 B.C.)

The fire mentioned above which destroyed Troy II left a 2m/6½ft thick layer of rubble and ashes. Later settlers dwelt in primitive huts, living from hunting and little is known about them. Some vessels with depictions of human faces and thin goblets with opposing handles have come to light. The last layer here indicates that this settlement was also destroyed by fire.

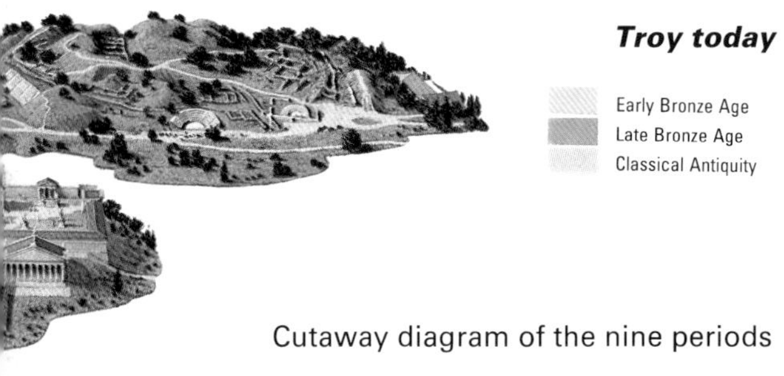

Troy today

Early Bronze Age
Late Bronze Age
Classical Antiquity

Cutaway diagram of the nine periods

Homeric Ilios

It is the new town's huge walls of large smooth-faced irregular blocks which form the most impressive of Troy's remains. In the years between the 15th and 13th c. B.C., the town enjoyed its greatest period of prosperity. The area (200×300m/220×330yd) was surrounded by a wall once 10m/33ft high. Inside the walls the foundations of a number of palaces have been preserved. No trace has yet been found of a lower town in the plain below.

Troy VI
8 levels
"Homer's Troy"
(1800–1250 B.C.)

The cemetery which contains the funerary urns with the ashes of the dead is situated some 500m/550yd to the south.

The town seems to have been rebuilt soon after an earthquake. The inhabitants' way of life remained unchanged. A century later the town was destroyed again.

Troy VII a
(*c.* 1250–1180 B.C.)

After the destruction of Troy VIIa the site was occupied by settlers from the Balkans. It is thought that the last people to settle here during this period were the Dardanians who gave their name to the Dardanelles.

Troy VIIb
(*c.* 1180–1000 B.C.)

Troy VIII
(8th c.–85 B.C.)

After an interruption the site became a Greek colony. About 730 B.C. Homer described the events of the Trojan War which is dated at sometime in the 13th c. B.C. Since then Troy has been regarded as a "sacred site".

In 652 B.C. the Cimmerians after defeating King Gyges of Lydia, moved into Troad but without displacing the Greeks. In 547 B.C. King Cyrus of Persia incorporated Troy into the Persian satrapy of Phrygia.

In 334 B.C. Alexander the Great crossed the Dardanelles and took Troy where he offered a sacrifice to Athene Ilios. About 300 B.C. Lysimachos built a harbour for the town at the mouth of the Scamander and replaced the old Temple of Athena by a splendid new one in marble. At least by the time of this construction work, the main buildings from the periods of Troy VII and Troy VI on the surface of the hill had been levelled. Between A.D. 278 and 270 the town was held by the Galatians, a Celtic people.

Troy IX
(85 B.C. to A.D. 500)

Whereas the importance of Troy had hitherto depended on its Temple of Athena, which was ranked equal in status to the Temple of Artemis, it now enjoyed Roman favour as the city of Aeneas – Rome seeing itself as the political heir to Troy.

There was now a period of great building activity.

Until the incursion of the Goths about A.D. 262 Troy flourished and this prosperity continued into Early Byzantine times. Constantine the Great even contemplated making Troy his capital. With the recognition of Christianity as the State religion, however, the old temples fell into ruin and Troy's glory rapidly faded.

Troy X
(12th to 14th c. A.D.

In the Middle Ages Troy still had a fortress and until the 13th c. it was the see of a bishop, but after its conquest by the Ottomans in 1306 the town rapidly decayed. The ruins were used by the Turks as a source of building stone for their homes and tomb stelae. Grass grew over the site and Troy fell into oblivion.

History of the excavations

The first Westerner to visit Troy seems to have been a French traveller named Pierre Belon (before 1553). In 1610 and Englishman, George Sandys, looked for the ruins of Troy on the hill of Hisarlık. Between 1781 and 1791 the Comte de Choiseul-Gouffier and a French archaeologist named Lechevalier explored the Troad and localised Homer's Troy on the hill of Balıdağ, at Bunarbaşı, 8km/5 miles south-east of Hisarlık. Helmuth von Moltke, then a Captain on the Prussian General Staff, also saw Bunarbaşı as the site of Troy.

From 1859 onwards Frank Calvert, an Englishman who owned part of the hill of Hisarlık, carried out excavations there. In 1868 Heinrich Schliemann (1822–90), a German businessman who had made a large fortune in St Petersburg, came to the Troad to look for Troy, and after a brief exploratory excavation on Bunarbaşı, which yielded only a thin layer of rubble, turned his attention to Hisarlık. Thereafter, in a series of excavation campaigns between 1871 and 1890, he was able to prove the correctness of his choice and to defend his case against the passionately held views of other archaeologists. Until 1882, it is true, his excavations showed little concern with exact observation or the conservation of the remains, and much evidence was destroyed for ever, particularly by the broad trench which he drove across the site from north to south; but thereafter, with the collaboration of the German archaeologist Wilhelm Dörpfeld (1853–1940), the work was carried on more scientifically. Unfortunately Schliemann himself did not live to see the final result of his excavations. After discovering, on June 14th 1873, the so-called "Treasure of Priam" (which was shipped to Germany in dramatic circumstances and from 1945–94 locked away in the Pushkin Museum in Moscow) he held Troy II to be the city of Priam. It was only his 1890 excavations and Dörpfeld's excavations of 1893–94 (after Schliemann's death) that suggested that Troy VI should be assigned to the Mycenaean period. Excavation was continued in 1932–38 by Carl W. Blegen of Cincinnati University and broadly confirmed earlier findings.

Recently restored stone ramp

According to legend Troy fell after Greek soldiers emerged from within a hollow horse dedicated to the earthquake god Poseidon; consequently scholars such as Schachermeyr have identified Troy VI as the city of Priam. Other researchers regard Troy VIIa as the more likely level. Since 1988 the German archaeologist Professor Manfred Korfmann from Tübingen University has been continuing the work of Schliemann, Dörpfeld and Blegen. Excavations have been continuing on Beşiktepe and in Beşik Bay west of Troy near Yeniköy, already identified as a port for Troy (1982–87). Recently the area south of the hill (lower town), indeed the whole landscape around Troy, has come under the archaeologists' spotlight. In 1992 houses from Troy II were uncovered. Demands are being made that this area, identified as a historic national park as well as part of the world's most important heritage, be put under protection.

Trojan Horse

★Tour of the site (see pages 272 and 273)

Information Point 1

Visitors to the site follow a recommended route which comprises twelve information points. Information Point 1 is the starting point of the tour, from where a flight of steps leads to Information Point 2 on the wall which encompasses the area of the Roman Temple.

Information Point 2

This point offers a view over the whole site. The East Wall, a part of the hill's defences in Troy VI, consisted of an embanked substructure some 6m/20ft

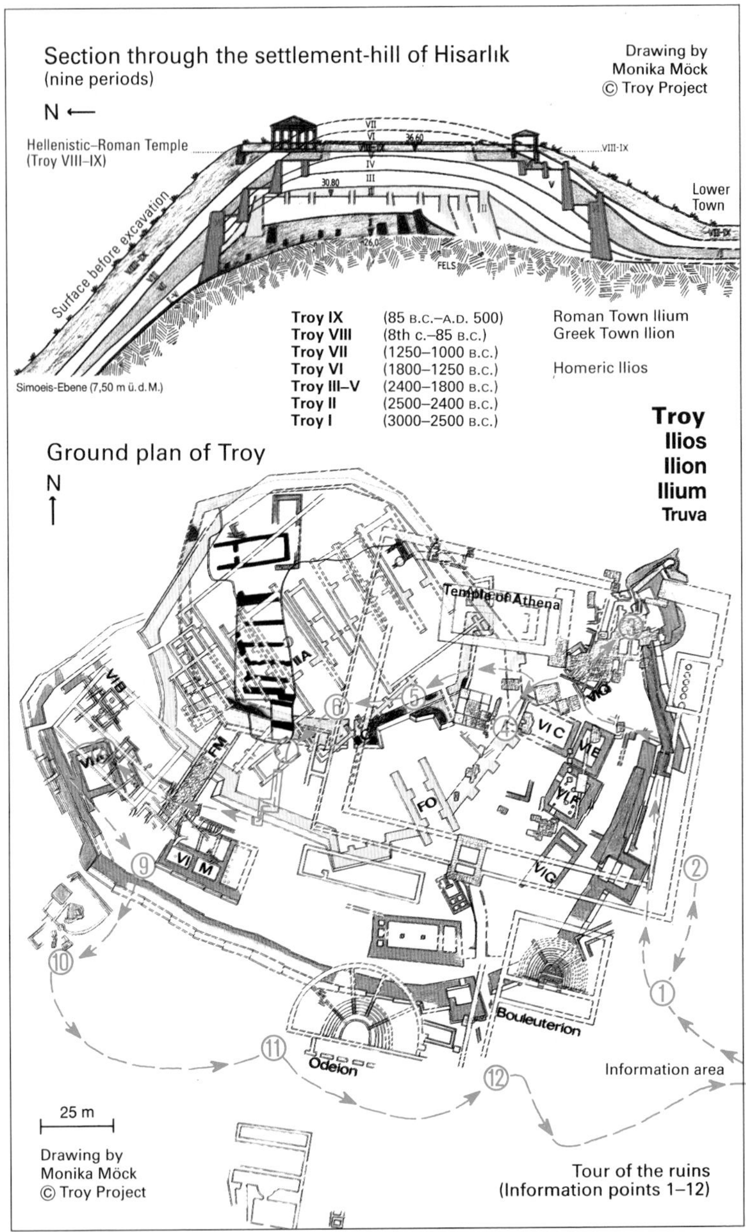
Section through the settlement-hill of Hisarlık
(nine periods)
Drawing by
Monika Möck
© Troy Project
N ⟵
Hellenistic–Roman Temple
(Troy VIII–IX)
VII
VI
36,60
VIII–IX
IV
III
30,80
II
V
Lower
Town
Surface before excavation
26,0
FELS
Simoeis-Ebene (7,50 m ü. d. M.)
Troy IX (85 B.C.–A.D. 500) Roman Town Ilium
Troy VIII (8th c.–85 B.C.) Greek Town Ilion
Troy VII (1250–1000 B.C.)
Troy VI (1800–1250 B.C.) Homeric Ilios
Troy III–V (2400–1800 B.C.)
Troy II (2500–2400 B.C.)
Troy I (3000–2500 B.C.)
Troy
Ilios
Ilion
Ilium
Truva
Ground plan of Troy
N
Temple of Athena
IIA
VIB
VIA
FM
VIQ
VI C
VIE
VIF
FO
VIG
VI M
Bouleuterion
Odeion
Information area
25 m
Drawing by
Monika Möck
© Troy Project
Tour of the ruins
(Information points 1–12)

Aerial view of the ruins of the Castle of Troy with marked points 1–12.
Photo: H. G. Jansen – Project Troia

high, 5m/16ft thick and exposed on the outside. On top of this, 1m/40in above the ground level of the settlement, was a vertical superstructure of flat rectangular stones, almost regularly dressed. The surface has been rebuilt with clay bricks.

South-East Tower

The South-East Tower was originally two-storeyed. One of the characteristic features of the wall, the vertical offsets, can be seen in this area. They are spaced out at regular 9–10m/30–33ft intervals.

Mycenaean houses Troy VI

Beyond the wall and the tower, large houses of the Mycenaean settlement are visible: first House VI G, then to the north-east away from the wall House VI F and further north Houses VI E and VI C. The houses of Troy VI were built round the hill on a number of concentric terraces with almost certainly the king's palace on the highest point.

Building VI F had pillars suggesting a second floor. Passing through the gate it will be clear that House VI E was particularly well built. It needs to be remembered that at the time these grandiose buildings were built, iron or steel had not been discovered. The quality of the stonemasonry is therefore all the more impressive.

East Gate

The wall projecting from the East Gate is overlaid with a Roman wall of dressed stone which bore the columns at the east end of the temple. The defensive wall from the south helped to form a curving passage some 10m/33ft long and 1.80m/6ft wide.

Information Point 3

From one of more than 20 limestone altars which surrounded the Temple of Athena, it is possible to see the massive tower of the North-East Gate in the Mycenaean walls.

North-East Bastion

The 8m/26ft high substructure of fine dressed stone with a receding embankment once bore a clay brick superstructure giving the gate a commanding height. Within the gate is a square well hewn from the rock and descending to a considerable depth. It remained in use for a long period.

In the Troy VIII period a flight of steps was constructed on the north side of the tower leading down to another well outside the tower. The great retaining wall to the south-east dates from the Roman period. In the background, the auditorium of the Greek and Roman theatre can be seen with the Dümrek Çayı plain (Simois) beyond.

Information Point 4

Temple of Athena

Only the altars and mounds give any indication of the existence of the Temple of Athena. It has to be imagined lying to the west and north of the altars. The magnificent new temple which had been promised by Alexander the Great was built by Lysimachos but little survives. Columns, parts of the coffered ceiling, as well as other marble fragments from the temple built by Augustus, "strayed" into the levels of Troy II during the course of the excavations.

These fragments were gathered together there by the researchers so that they could discover more information on the construction of the temple.

View

From these heights there is a fine view over the Dardanelles, European Turkey and the Menderes (Skamander) river plain. In the foreground lie remains of the "Burnt Town" (Troy II), which Schliemann believed was the city of Priam.

Information Point 5

Fortified wall

At Information Point 5 stands a cross-section of Troy I's fortifications with a tower-like projection behind which the then South Gate was situated. The gateway was only 2m/6ft wide. Troy I was built directly on to the rock floor and layers 4m/13ft deep would suggest that this period endured for many years (*c.* 3000 to 2500 B.C.). Troy I covered the smallest surface area and in the course of time this settlement spread out to the south. Further finds from Troy I can be found at Information Point 7. Immediately above the tower stands a small propylon from Troy III. Its massive 3m/10ft long and 1.1m/3½ft) wide stone threshold is still in place.

Information Point 6

Residence of the ruler

The propylon was the entrance to a group of buildings in the centre of Troy II citadel which were probably occupied by the city's ruler. The dwellings of the ruler and his family led off a gravelled courtyard. The main building directly opposite the propylon known as the Megaron consisted of a porch and a main hall with a hearth in the middle. The structure of the walls (1.44m/4ft 9in) can be clearly seen here, but the height cannot be ascertained. It would have had a flat roof with an opening over the hearth. To the right was a smaller building with a porch, main room and rear chamber. On either side were buildings of a similar type opening off the courtyard but they were all destroyed by fire, leaving a 2m/6½ft thick layer of stone and ash (Schliemann's "Burnt Town"). Many interesting finds have been unearthed in this level (see Information Point 7).

The Troy II era (*c.* 2500 B.C.) was characterised by major cultural and technological changes: a stratified society as witnessed by these buildings with the forerunner to the Greek temple ("megaron", porch and main room), the mixture of copper and tin to make bronze as well as the invention of the potter's wheel. So impressed was Schliemann by the astonishing finds, he believed that he had found the "Treasure of Priam" but he was wrong by at least 1000 years.

Information Point 7

Schliemann's trench

The great north–south trench which Schliemann drove across the site passes between the first and second groups of Troy II houses and it is possible to see house walls and parts of ancient settlements, made from stones bound together with earth mortar. The restored supporting wall on the east side which is made from air-dried clay bricks marks the limit of the long, spacious buildings. A wooden bridge crossing the three ring walls of Troy II leads past the base of the ramp to Information Point 8.

Information Point 8

Prehistoric settlement

From the corner of House M6 A a stone ramp to the Gate FM can be seen at a lower level. It leads from a lower settlement area (discovered in 1992) up to the inner citadel hill. The pre-historic citadel of Troy II which was destroyed by fire was at first thought by Schliemann to be the citadel of Priam. It had a circumference of some 300m/330yd and is now almost completely exposed. The layers of rubble range from a thickness of 1m/40in to 2m/80in.

Ramp

The citadel's ring of walls stretches out on both sides of the ramp. It consists of a substructure 1m/40in. to 4m/13ft high made from roughly hewn limestone and earth mortar and has recently been restored (1992). It now resembles the condition it was in before the first excavations about 100 years earlier.

Treasure of Priam

Some 6m/20ft north-west of the ramp Schliemann found the so-called "Treasure of Priam" built into a cavity in the brick superstructure of the ring wall. It later found its way into the Museum of Pre- and Early-history in Berlin but disappeared at the end of the Second World War. It was recently discovered in the Pushkin Museum in Moscow and in 1994 for the first time since it was taken to there part of the treasure was put on display. An exhibition is planned for 1996. Other items are in the Hermitage in St Petersburg. Similar finds of jewellery, vessels, weapons and tools made of gold, silver, electron (an alloy of gold and silver) and bronze have been made elsewhere in the Troy II level ("Burnt Town") and also in the layer of fire debris in Troy III. At present the finds from Troy are spread throughout seven countries of the world.

Information Point 9

The remains of Troy III, IV, V are of little to interest the ordinary visitor. The citadel's principal monuments from Troy VI have been preserved and of Troy VII some house walls survive, chiefly those between the citadel wall of Troy VI and the first palace walls, which were also terrace walls. These can be divided into two completely different periods. First the walls and gates of Troy VI (VIIa) were repaired by simple country-dwellers who still used "Mycenaean" pottery. These were subsequently destroyed in a catastrophic fire. In the period that followed peoples of completely different Balkan cultures settled on and in the ruins (VIIb and VIIb2), and visitors can recognise their houses in the small building remains above the wide wall fortifications of Troy VI and to the west of the citadel VI.

Kitchen building Palace VI M

Inside the ring wall stands the impressive 27m/30yd long supporting wall of Palace VI M which certainly formed a part of Troy VI's citadel.

This large building of the Mycenaean period on a 4m/13ft high terrace is named after the large *pithois* ([pottery storage vessels) and other finds from one of the rooms known as the "kitchen buildings". Inside a flight of steps led to a second floor. Following the unearthing of the upper section of its foundations in 1994 the course of the wall of Troy VI can easily be followed.

Information Point 10

Shrine

The shrine altars in the south-west show that soon after the Greek settlement and continuing well into the Roman phase, cult rituals took place outside the wall of "Sacred Ilios". The latest excavations reveal that the marble altar higher up dates from the time of Augustus, when the whole site of Ilios was renovated. A tribune and more shrines are situated beyond.

The large supporting wall and the older altars lower down all originated in Hellenistic times (Troy VII).

The older shrine complex is divided into two sections. In the west, during the course of the latest excavations, the foundations of large Hellenistic (and older) buildings were unearthed; these were apparently linked with the ritual complex. Of particular importance here, however, is the discovery of a town quarter from the "Trojan Wars" era (Troy VI-Late/Troy VIIa; not open to visitors).

Information Point 11

Odeion and bouleuterion

At the edge of the former agora stood the odeion a small theatre for musical performances and a little further east the bouleuterion, the Roman town hall. The odeion consists of a semi-circular orchestra which is separated from the skene or the stage building. A marble statue of the Emperor Hadrian, who had visited Troy in 124 A.D., was discovered here in 1939; it is now in the museum in Çanakkale. The rows of seating are divided into wedge-shaped blocks. Some of the fragments belonging to the odeion are gathered together nearby.

The bouleuterion about 70m/75yd away was built above Troy VI's fortified wall. The interior was surrounded by a wall on all sides, enabling the city fathers to conduct their business uninterrupted.

Information Point 12

South Gate

The South Gate was probably the main entrance to the town, but only the paved roadway to the right of the tower (1.3m/50in. wide) remains. A covered water channel can be seen in the middle. To the left behind the South Tower, a pillar marks the location of the "Pillar House", which with a surface area of 27×12.5m/29×13yd was one of the largest houses of Troy VI. Set in front of the tower are two vertical stones, no doubt serving some cult purpose.

Lower town

The lower town (not open to visitors) situated on the plateau to the south below the citadel hill was, as excavations since 1988 show, inhabited towards the end of the 2nd millennium B.C. (Troy VI/VII). Defensive ditches safeguarded it from attack. Traces of an enclosing wall have been found and some historians have recently suggested that this settlement and its citadel constituted an important seat of power and a commercial centre covering an area of some 20ha/50 acres. As the surrounding countryside was suitable for arable farming and the breeding of cattle, some 7000 people could have lived here, an extremely high figure for the Bronze Age. Excavations are continuing both here and inside the citadel. The area of the lower town on the plateau to the south and east of the hill has so far been little explored, but a small township was established here in the Hellenistic period and then expanded in Roman times, particularly in the reign of Augustus. It was planned and laid out in traditional style with a ring wall which totalled 3.5km/2 miles in length and was 2.5m/8ft thick. Ritual events held here were of national importance, and the large theatre in the north used for such purposes could accommodate some 6000 spectators.

Surroundings of Troy

Alexandreia Troas

33km/21 miles south-west (reached also by way of Ezine, near the main road) is the lonely site of ancient Alexandreia Troas (also called simply Troas). Now known as Eskiistanbul, which dates from the time of Lysimachos. The imposing remains (baths with handsome doorways) mostly date from Roman times.

Assos

See entry

Xanthos

E 7

South-west coast (Mediterranean)
Province: Muğla
Altitude: 80–150m/260–490ft
Place: Kınık

Situation

The remains of ancient Xanthos, once capital of the kingdom of Lydia, lie in the valley of the River Xanthos (now Koca Çayı), which separates the mountains (Ak Dağı, 3024m/9922ft) from the upland region which falls away towards the coast. The Lycians were a non-Greek people of unknown origin with an Indo-European language, which at a later stage was written in the Greek alphabet with some supplementary letters. The art of Xanthos is in the Ionian/Milesian tradition. It is noted particularly for its pillar-tombs, in which the grave-chambers are on the top of tall monolithic pillars.

Xanthos is reached from road 30, which runs from Fethiye via Kemer (22km/14 miles) to Kestep (Eşen; another 24km/15 miles). 12km/7½ miles farther on, on the left, is the village of Kınık, from which there is a road to the site.

History

Lycia has been called "the oldest republic in the world" – a league of 20 cities governed by a popular assembly and a president. In the 7th c. B.C. Xanthos came under the control of the kings of Lydia. In 545 B.C., it was destroyed by the Persians under the leadership of Harpagos, and Lycia remained under Persian domination until the end of the 5th c. During the Peloponnesian War Xanthos fought against Athens. In 333 B.C. it was taken by Alexander the Great, and in the 3rd c. it passed to the Seleucids. In 188 B.C. it was conquered by Rhodes. Later it gained Roman support against the Rhodians, and when Rome won control of Asia Minor Xanthos enjoyed a period of renewed prosperity.

★Pillar-tombs

The most notable monuments of Xanthos, its Lycian pillar-tombs, have no parallel either in Greek or in Oriental art. They first appear in the 6th c. B.C. and disappear from the scene in the middle of the 4th.

Excavations

The site was discovered in 1838 by Sir Charles Fellows, and in 1842 the reliefs from the so-called Harpy Tomb and the Nereid Monument were taken to London, where they can now be seen in the British Museum. Excavations were carried out by Austrian archaeologists from 1881 to 1901 and by a French expedition from 1951 onwards.

The Site

The road bisects the site from north to south, 200m/220yd beyond the line of the town walls, to the right, is a 5.75m/19ft high pillar with inscriptions, shown by recent investigations to have been a pillar-tomb originally 9m/30ft high. Round the top ran a frieze of warriors, now in the Archaeological Museum in İstanbul. The Lycian inscription has not yet been completely deciphered; the Greek inscription extols the exploits of the dead man in Oriental fashion.

Agora

Harpy Tomb

Immediately south is the Roman Agora (50m/165ft square), which was originally surrounded by columns. On its south-west side are two tall pillar-tombs. The more northerly of the two is the so-called Harpy Tomb (480 B.C.), a tower-like monolith 5m/16½ft high on a rectangular base. The grave-chamber, with room for a number of urns, was decorated with reliefs (now replaced by casts) depicting two seated figures of women and three standing figures of men being honoured by their relatives, while their souls are carried off by harpies. This belief in bird-demons which carry the dead up to heaven may be the explanation of the pillar-tombs. The pillar-tomb to the south is topped by a house-shaped sarcophagus with a pitched roof (probably 4th c. B.C.).

Theatre

South of the agora is the theatre, which dates from the Roman period but incorporates some Hellenistic work. To the right, above the path, is the Theatre Pillar, a 4.3m/14ft high limestone monolith of the mid 4th c. B.C. with a Lycian inscription recording the exploits of a Lycian prince.

Lycian acropolis

★Nereid Monument

South of the theatre is the Lycian acropolis, with remains of buildings of the Archaic, Classical and Byzantine periods. 260m/285yd farther on, to the left of the road, stands the so-called Nereid Monument, an Ionic temple which had rich sculptural decoration (now in the British Museum). To the right of the road is the Hellenistic town gate. The town walls, considerable stretches of which are still visible, probably date originally from the 3rd c. B.C.; they were later renewed, incorporating the Roman acropolis, and were again rebuilt in Byzantine times.

Roman acropolis

To the north of the Nereid Monument are the ruins of a Byzantine church, and beyond this, to the east of the north end of the road, the Roman acropolis. On the summit of the hill (150m/490ft) are the ruins of a large Byzantine monastery. On a spur of rock on the north-east side of the hill is the well-preserved Acropolis Pillar (mid 4th c. B.C.), a limestone monolith 4.75m/16ft high with a three-stage top section. On the top is a band of marble 1.13m/44in. high enclosing the 2.28m/7½ft high grave-chamber, which is partly hewn from the interior of the pillar. Below the pillar are three rock tombs with splayed window-like façades.

There are also numbers of small rock tombs outside the town walls (handsome Lycian sarcophagi with high-pitched lids which are often decorated with reliefs).

Surroundings of Xanthos

Letoon

5km/3 miles south of Xanthos (side road 1km/¾ mile from Kınıkı) is the Letoon, an important Lycian sanctuary excavated from 1962 onwards. The remains include temples of Leto, Artemis and Apollo and a theatre. A trilingual inscription found here made an important contribution to the decipherment of the Lycian language.

Patara

15km/9 miles south of Kınık lie the remains of ancient Patara, once an important city in the Lycian League and later, according to legend, the birthplace of St Nicholas of Myra (see Finike – Surroundings). There was still a port here in Byzantine times. Outside the area of the city are a Roman and a Lycian necropolis. The city itself is entered through a triple-arched gate of about A.D. 100. The theatre (2nd c. A.D.) is also excellently preserved. other remains include the foundations of baths (Baths of Vespasian), a temple and a granary (near the former harbour, now silted up).

Kalkan

The coast road from Kınık continues to the little fishing village of Kalkan (former Greek name Kalamaki), picturesquely situated in its bay.

Yalova E 3

Marmara region
Province: İzmit
Altitude: 0–130m/0–425ft
Population: 25,000

Situation

The little port of Yalova is beautifully situated on the south side of the Gulf of İzmit, 45m/28 miles south-east of İstanbul as the crow flies. There are ferries from İstanbul and Kartal to Yalova which considerably reduces the distances to Bursa.

★Baths of Yalova

A few kilometres south-west of the town centre, in a wooded valley, are the thermal springs (containing iron, carbon dioxide and sulphur; temperature up to 65°C/149°F which have been famed since ancient times for their medicinal properties. Featuring in the Argonaut legend as Pythia and known in Byzantine times as Soteropolis, the place is now called Yalova Kaplıcalar, Baths of Yalova (formerly Kury, or in French Coury-les-Bains). Many Greeks and Romans sought healing here, and visitors in later times included Constantine the Great, Justinian and his wife Theodora and many Seljuk and Ottoman potentates. Kemal Atatürk frequently came to Yalova to take the cure (Atatürk House). The waters are recommended for the treatment of a wide range of complaints, from kidney and bladder conditions to rheumatism and nervous diseases. The spa has recently been brought into line with modern requirements (new hotels and treatment facilities) and has one of the highest reputations in the Near East.

Pythia
Soteropolis
Kury

Zonguldak G 2

Western Black Sea region
Province: Zonguldak
Altitude: 5m/16ft
Population: 120,000

Situation and ★importance

The Zonguldak mountains 800m/2620ft high and 50km/32 miles long are situated to the north-east of the lower Pontic mountains of Bolu and Akçakoca and extend along the coast from the mouth of the ancient Filyos (Yenice İrmağı). Seams of coal rise to the surface and an important coal-mining industry has grown up in the deep mountain valleys. The absence of work-place safety regulations means that Zonguldak mine counts as one of the most dangerous mines in the world. The last serious mining disaster occurred in March 1992.

Until 1850 Zonguldak was a small village but the coal fields, the steel-works in neighbouring Karabük (with a rail link for transporting coal) and Karadeniz Ereğlisi and the resulting expansion of the original 1899 harbour have transformed the place into the second-largest town on the Black Sea coast. Nestling in the steep wooded areas to the west and east of the town are the mining communities of Kozlu, Kilimli and Çatalağzi. The name Zonguldak derives from "zongalık" meaning reeded marshland. The small port of Sandaraca stood here in antiquity. In the Hittite times it was known as Palla.

The coastal region to the east of Zonguldak beyond the Yenice İrmağı offers fine sandy beaches with Karpuz and İnkum (İnkumu) 70km/43 miles to the east worth a special mention. Other excellent beaches can be found near Kuzlu (e.g. İliksu) 18km/11 miles west of the town.

Surroundings

★Amasra

This coastal resort with an old town is located in a picturesque spot on a peninsula 60km/37 miles north-east of Zonguldak. Established in the 6th c. B.C. by Milesian colonists during the 3rd c. B.C. renamed Amastris after a niece of Darius III of Persia. She became the regent of Herakleia Pontike (Karadeniz Ereğlisi) upon her marriage to Lysimachos the king of Thrace. It is said that she planned to lay out hanging gardens here like those of Semiramis in Babylon.

After its destruction, it was rebuilt by the Byzantines, but in the 14th c. it fell to Genoese trading companies who extended the citadel. Mehmet II (the Conqueror) acquired Amastris for the Ottomans in 1485. A local museum displays finds of historical interest.

The town is a popular seaside resort for nearby city dwellers and the preferred home of wealthy families connected with the Zonguldak mining industry. More recently the steelworks has also grown in importance. Little remains of the old town apart from the ruins of a Roman theatre and baths. A castle on a narrow strip of land protected the old town and peninsula, which is still linked to an offshore island by a Roman bridge and an ancient tunnel. Within the fortress site near the West Gate stands the Kilise Mescidi, a small church mosque which served as the chapel for the castle commander. Parts of an ancient cemetery extend above the western beaches (Büyük Liman; 500m/550yd) and below what was once the acropolis.

In some fields about 2km/1¼ miles inland stands a well-preserved Roman store-house over 100m/110yd long.

Bartın

The busy administrative town of Bartın (pop. 25,000) on the Kocağrmak 70km/43 miles east of Zonguldak is the former Parthenios. Traditional wooden houses help to give the town a pleasant atmosphere.

To the north-west near the towns of İnkum, Mugadar and Güzelcihisar (Hisar), other attractive beaches can be found but unfortunately some are not easy to reach.

Çatalağazı

The longest caves in Turkey are situated just a few kilometres to the south-west of Çatalağazı, a small coastal town about 20km/12 miles east of Trabzon. The entrance, Kizılelma Mağarası, can be found by the border with the neighbouring district of Gelik, while the northern exit 10km/6 miles to the north is known as Cumayanı-Mağarası. Because of the long underground siphon within the watercourse, it is not possible to pass through the cave network from one end to the other.

Near the exit the cave opens out into a large cavern with travertine terraces and basins similar to those at Pamukkale. The cavern is open to the public.

Çayğrköy

The village of Çayğr (pop. 1648 in 1985) lies 10km/6 miles past the village of Güdüllü on the road from Çaycuma to Zonguldak. The 1km/½ mile long Çayğrköy Mağarası can be found close to the village. The cave was surveyed by a Swedish explorer in 1951 and there are plans to open it up to the public.

Erğli
(Karadeniz Ereğlisi)

Situated around 50km/30 miles to the south-west of Zonguldak, at first sight there seems to be little of interest for visitors to the coal port and industrial town of Ereğlisi (formerly Herakleia Pontike; pop. 55,000) with steelworks and coalfields to the south and dominated by a ruined Genoese fortress. The old town nestling below, however, has much to commend it.

About 558 B.C. the town was founded by colonists from Megara. For a short time it came under Lysimachos and then became a part of the Pontic Empire. The Romans destroyed the town in the war with Mithradates as the townsfolk took sides against the Roman army. It was rebuilt as a Roman garrison. Until 1922 Karandeniz was almost entirely Greek. Few ancient remains can be seen today.

The Caves of Hercules

The Caves of Hercules lie north-west of Ereğli in the valley of ancient Acheron about 100m/110yd upstream. According to Xenophon in his "Anabasis", it was here that Hercules, hero and demigod, descended into the underworld and brought out Cerberus the three-headed dog which guarded the entrance to Hades.

Plundered ancient stones can be seen at the entrance to the cave. The valley which leads to the mouth of the cave is known in local parlance as the "Valley of the Infidels". This description harks back to Byzantine times when a Christian resurrection cult used the caves and a floor mosaic in the first cave provides some evidence of their existence. The actual entrance to the underworld was believed to be in the second cave as a narrow staircase leads down from there into a dark chamber 50m/55yd wide. There is an underwater lake and also traces of painting and other workings.

Üzülmez

A 1km/½ mile long cave known as Gökgöl Mağarası can be found near the mining town of Üzülmez just a few kilometres south-east of Zonguldak. An underground river flows through the cave and it is not yet open to the public.

Practical Information from A to Z

Practical Information

Accommodation

See Camping, Hotels, Youth Accommodation

Air Travel

International Flights

The national airline, Türk Hava Yollan (THY; Turkish Airlines), İstanbul Airlines and many other carriers operate international flights to and from Turkey (see Getting to Turkey).

Airports

Turkey's main airport is İstanbul's Atatürk Airport at Yeşilköy;
tel. (212) 663 63 63, fax (212) 663 47 44.
A regular bus service runs between the airport and the THY terminal in the city centre (Şişhane, Meşrutiyet Caddesi 26).

Other international airports include:

Adana: Şakirpasa; tel. (322) 435 91 86
Antalya; tel. (242) 330 32 21
Dalaman; tel. (252) 692 58 99
İzmir: Adnan Menderes Airport; tel. (232) 274 24 24
A relatively cheap hourly train service connects the airport with İzmir's Alsançak station, close to the big hotels.
Trabzon; tel. (462) 325 67 38

Internal flights

THY and THT, the domestic airline, also operate internal flights to:

Batman, Denizli, Diyarbakır, Elazığ, Erzurum, Kars, Kayseri, Malatya, Muş, Samsun, Şanlıurfa, Trabzon and Van.

Airlines

Turkish Airlines
Türk Hava Yolları
THY

Australian office: Level 16, Suite 1602, 388 George St., Sydney, NSW 2000;
tel. (61–2) 233 21 05
Irish office: c/o Aer Lingus, Dublin Airport, Dublin; tel. (3531) 37 00 11
South African office: c/o South African Airways, P.O. Box 7778, Johannesburg; tel. (713) 22 06
UK office: 11–12 Hanover Street, London W1R 9HF;
tel. (0171) 499 9249
USA office: 437 Madison Avenue, New York, NY 10022; tel. (212) 339 96 50

THY also has representatives at all Turkish airports.

İstanbul Airlines

In İstanbul THY has several offices in town.
Cumhuriyet Cad. No. 27 Kat. 2, Taksim Parki Karsısi, Taksim, İstanbul
tel. (212) 25 56 70
Cumhuriyet Cad. No. 199–201, tel. (212) 225 05 06
İncirli Caddesi 50, İstanbul-Bakirköy; tel. (212) 543 62 58/59
Taksim, tel. (212) 252 11 06
Atatürk Airport, Yeşilköy;
tel. (212) 663 63 63 (international flights)
tel. (212) 574 42 71 (internal flights)

◀ *The yacht harbour at Antalya*

In İzmir THY has a town office at Gasios Man Pasa Bul. No. 1/F, İzmir-Alsançak; tel. (232) 484 12 20
and at Adnan Menderes Airport; tel. (232) 274 24 24

Offices also in Adana, Antalya, Dalaman, Marmaris and Trabzon.

Air Canada

Mete Cad. No. 24/1, Taksim, İstanbul; tel. (212) 251 61 30

American Airlines

Cumhuriyet Cad. Taksim, Okay Apt. 47/2, İstanbul; tel. (212) 237 20 03

British Airways

Cumhuriyet Caddesi 10, İstanbul; tel. (212) 234 13 00
Yasar Holding, Şehit Fethi Bey Caddesi 120, İzmir; tel. (232) 13 92 59, 14 17 88, 12 22 00

QANTAS

Cumhuriyet Caddesi 155/1, Elmadag, İstanbul; tel. (212) 240 50 32

TWA

Cumhuriyet Caddesi No. 193, Elmadag, İstanbul; tel. (212) 234 53 27

Other airlines operating from the UK include
İstanbul Airlines – tel. (0171) 499 4499 – fly all year to İstanbul from Heathrow (twice weekly) and from Gatwick (weekly). In summer they fly to İstanbul weekly from Stansted and Manchester, and to İstanbul, İzmir, Antalya and Dalaman from Gatwick.

Onur Air – tel. (0171) 499 99 19 – fly all year (twice weekly) to İstanbul from Gatwick, Manchester and Stansted; April–October weekly to Dalaman and İzmir.

There are several charter companies operating flights during the summer months.

Beaches

Turkey's coastline, full of bays and inlets, guarantees a wonderful holiday by the sea, with a choice of sandy or pebble-strewn beaches, most of them in settings of great natural beauty. The season for swimming is from early April to late October in the southern Aegean and the Mediterranean, and from June to September in the Black Sea, northern Aegean and Sea of Marmara.

It is possible to swim in the sea in winter in southern Turkey at resorts such as Antalya, Alanya and Dalaman, and Side and Kemer.

Turkish beaches are public and open to everyone. Hoteliers usually try to keep the beach clean in front of their hotels but the weather and tides can bring in tar, rubbish and other pollutants, so take some footwear for swimming, especially if the beach is likely to be stony.

Facilities

Hotels provide simple wooden sunbeds, usually free of charge, but charge for the covers to go on them. Water sports equipment tends to be the province of private operators on the beach, and outside the peak season the supply of sailboats, surf boards, etc. is more limited.

Nudism

Swimming and sunbathing in the nude is definitely against the strict moral code of Islam, and on rare occasions can even mean getting arrested. Even going topless is not aceptable.

Bathing beaches

Sea of Marmara

The Sea of Marmara's best developed bathing beaches are mostly on its southern shore. The most distinctive are: Büyük Ada, one of the Prince's Islands; Yalova on the south coast with a very fine sandy beach and a spa some 20km/12½ miles inland; Gemlik, a popular resort in a beautiful setting, but with a rather stony beach; Tirilye; Eşkel with a sheltered beach of fine sand; the little port of Bandırma with a flat but exposed sandy beach; the lovely little peninsula town of Erdek; Tatlısu with a sheltered sandy beach; the islands of Avşar and Marmara, both with lovely beaches; and, on the north coast, Tekirdağ and Silivri, the latter with a long sandy beach.

Aegean coast

Bathing beaches on the Aegean coast include Çanakkale at the narrowest point of the Dardanelles, with beaches at Çamlık Intepe (thermal springs) and the islands of İmroz and Bozcaada south of the Dardanelles; then, along the Gulf of Edremit, Akltınoluk on the north side, Ören, near Burhaniye, at the head of the gulf, and Ayvalık on the south side with many small offshore islands and pine woods close to the beach. The best beaches around İzmir are between Yenifoça and Foça (quiet little coves) and at the west end of the Çeşme Peninsula, especially near Ilıca. Kuşadası (Ephesus) has long stretches of beach, with a number of holiday villages, then come Altınkum south of Didyma, Bodrum (Halicarnassus) with several beautiful coves and good diving waters, the sheltered Bay of Marmaris, and Fethiye, with good beaches on the adjoining coastline, the islands in the bay and the lovely Ölüdeniz lagoon.

Mediterranean coast

Tourism has grown considerably along the Mediterranean coast, especially around the Gulf of Antalya with its magnificent mountain backdrop, because of the long beaches along the western shore between Antalya and Çamyuva and Kemer. Farther east Manavgat (Side) and Alanya have also become popular with holidaymakers, but the stretch from Alanya to Silifke is less developed although this part of the coast, extending beyond Silifke to Mersin, also has its attractions.

Black Sea coast

Places worth recommending going westward along the Black Sea coast include Kilyos, on the western part of the Bosphorus, which has miles of beaches of fine sand and is a favourite with the people of İstanbul; Sile, which has a sandy beach on the eastern part of the Bosphorus; Karasu, the little town with another long beach of fine sand at the mouth of the Sakarya, and on a wooded coastline with a number of lakes further inland; then Akçakoca with a particularly lovely beach 8km/5 miles further west; Abana to the north-east with a long sandy beach; the little port of İnebolu with its scenic beach; Ayancık in its forest setting with a beach stretching for 10km/6 miles; the old port of Samsun; Çamlık with a particularly good bathing beach of fine sand; and the little ports of Ordu, Giresun, Trabzon and Rize, all with bathing beaches and on a superb mountainous coastline.

Buses

Buses (otobüs) are far and away Turkey's most important form of public transport, and bus fares are relatively cheap. Various kinds of bus services operate between nearly all the major towns and cities, and the buses themselves are for the most part clean, modern – many of them brought in second-hand from Western Europe – and reasonably comfortable, albeit often quite overcrowded.

In the larger places there are usually one or more bus stations (otagar, garaj), often on the edge of town, for the lines covering the long-distance routes.

Business Hours

See Opening Times

Camping and Caravanning

Compared with Europe and North America camping and caravanning in Turkey is still relatively underdeveloped. The largest concentration of campsites is along the Aegean and the Mediterranean coast and on the Sea of Marmara (just over 100 sites).

Experienced campers will find that these have retained much of their uniquely Turkish flavour, especially those established by the State around the National Parks (see entry) and other conservation areas.

Campsites tend to be located on main roads close to towns and holiday centres. For detailed information ask the Tourist Office for the leaflet "Camps in Türkiye".

Opening times

Campsites are normally open from April/May through to October. Some stay open all year round.

Facilities

Some campsites also have their own guest houses and private beaches. However, problems with access roads, insufficient drinking water and inadequate sanitation, not to mention the all-pervading dust, make many sites unsuitable for a long-term stay. Recommended sites include those operated by BP Mocamps.

Warning

Off-site camping and stopping overnight by the roadside and in lay-bys, etc. is usually allowed but is inadvisable for safety reasons.

Caravans

If you plan to take a caravan or motorhome on a ferry check beforehand on the maximum vehicle size permissible with the ferry company or the travel agent making the booking.

Motorhomes

See Car Rental under Motoring

Car ferries

International car ferry services

Italy–Turkey (April to November)

Route	Frequency	Operator
Venice–İzmir (both ways)	once a week	Turkish Maritime Lines
Venice–Antalya/Marmaris (both ways)	once a week	Turkish Maritime Lines
Venice–Çeşme (both ways)	once a week	Turkish Maritime Lines
Brindisi–Çeşme (both ways)	twice a week in summer	Medlink Lines (via Patras)
Brindisi–Çeşme	once a week	European Seaways
Otranto–Çeşme	once a week	Rainbow Lines
Ancona–Kuşadasi	once a week	Marlines (via Heraklion)

See also Coastal Shipping.

The following offices of the ferry companies and their agents should be able to supply you with further information.

Turkish Maritime Lines

Türkiye Denizcilik İşletmeleri (TDI):
Central Office: Rıhtım Cad., Karaköy, İstanbul
tel. (212) 245 53 66–244 02 07, fax (212) 251 90 25
Denizyolları Acentiliĭ, Yeni Liman Alsancak, İzmir
tel. (232) 421 14 84, fax (232) 421 14 81

Agents in United Kingdom:
Sunquest Holidays Ltd., 23 Princes Street, London W1R 7RG; tel. (0171) 499 9919, fax (0171) 499 9599 is the agent for Turkish Maritime Lines.
Viamare Travel, 2 Sumatra Road, London NW6 1PV; tel. (0171) 431 4560, fax (0171) 431 5456 is the agent for Marlines, Medlink, European Seaways and Rainbow Lines.

Medlink Lines

İzmir port: tel. (232) 712 72 30

Car Rental

International and local car-rental firms have representatives or offices at the airports and in all the tourist resorts. Bookings can also be made at some hotels. Local firms often have jeeps, convertibles, motorbikes, mountain bikes, etc. for hire as well, and charge lower rates than the better known names, but the vehicles they supply are not always up to the same standard.

Drivers usually need to be over 25 and have held a driving licence for at least two years. As a rule insurance and free mileage are included.

To hire a car in the peak holiday season it is advisable to book it before leaving home, either with the hire company direct or through a travel agent.

Where to book

The following firms operate a computerised service for making bookings before leaving home. We list the UK phone numbers of major car hire companies and centres in Turkey where they operate. Airports are at Adana, Antalya, Dalaman, İstanbul and İzmir.

Avis

UK reservation tel. 0990 900 500
Head office in Turkey: Tramvay Cad. 74, Kuruçeşme 808820, İstanbul; tel. (212) 257 76 70
Other offices in Turkey: Adana, Alanya, Antalya, Ayvalik, Bodrum, Bursa, Çeşme, Dalaman, Fethiye, Foça, İzmir, İzmit, Kemer, Kuşadasi, Marmaris, Mersin, Side, Trabzon.

Budget

UK reservations tel. 0800 181 181
Head office in Turkey: İstanbul Airport; tel. (212) 663 08 58
Other offices in Turkey: Alanya, Antalya, Bodrum, Bursa, Fethiye, İzmir, Kuşadasi, Marmaris, Side.

Eurodollar Rent a car

UK reservations tel. 0990 565 656
Head office in Turkey: Kalamis Sener Cad. No. 30/2, Kadiköy 81030, İstanbul; tel. (216) 349 36 87
Other offices in Turkey: Adana, Antalya, İzmir.
Eurodollar operates in Turkey via franchise company "Yes rent a car".

Europcar Interrent

UK reservation tel. 0345 222 525
Head office in Turkey: Cumhuriyet Cad. No. 47/2, Taksim, İstanbul 80090; tel. (212) 254 77 88
Other offices in Turkey: Adana, Alanya, Altinkum, Antalya, Bodrum, Bursa, Dalaman, Fethiye, İzmir, Kemer, Kuşadasi, Marmaris, Mersin, Side.

Hertz

UK reservations tel. 0990 996 699
Head office in Turkey; İstanbul Airport; tel. (212) 663 08 07
Other offices in Turkey: Adana, Antalya, Bodrum, Dalaman, İstanbul (town), İzmir, Kuşadasi, Marmaris, Mersin.

Coastal Shipping Services

Turkish Maritime Lines (Türkiye Denizcilik İşletmeleri; TDİ)

The State shipping line, Turkish Maritime Lines (Türkiye Denizcilik İşletmeleri; TDİ), operates regular passenger services – some of which take cars – along the Mediterranean, Marmara and Black Sea coasts all year round. They have agents in every port of call who can provide timetables and ticket prices (see also Car Ferries).

TDİ Central Office in İstanbul:
Rıhtım Caddesi, Karaköy, İstanbul;
tel. (212) 245 53 66, fax (212) 251 90 25
Denizyolları Acentiliĭ, Yeni Liman Alsancak, İzmir;
tel. (232) 421 14 84, fax (232) 421 14 81

Black Sea coast

There are services from İstanbul to the Black Sea ports of Sinop, Samsun, Ordu, Giresun, Trabzon and Rize.

Sea of Marmara

Around the Sea of Marmara car ferries run between İstanbul to Mudanya and Bandırma.

Marmara and Bosphorus boats depart from Eminönü quay in İstanbul and minicruises start at Kabataş on Beyoğlu.

Sea-bus service

Catamaran sea buses (*deniz otobüsleri*) are a speedy but rather more expensive way of getting from İstanbul to the Marmara destinations of Yalova, and the islands of Büyükada, Marmara and Avşa. The sea-bus also goes from Kartal, 20 mins east of İstanbul, to Yalova on the Asian side.
Information from the sea-bus central office in İstanbul;
tel. (212) 362 04 44.

Dardanelles

Car ferries operate across the Dardanelles between Eceabat and Çanakkale and between Gelibolu and Lâpseki.

Aegean and Mediterranean coasts

Ports in services along the Aegean west coast and the Mediterranean south coast are Dikili, İzmir (also direct service to İstanbul), Kuşadası, Bodrum, Marmaris, Taşycy/Silifke and Mersin.

Car ferries also operate from Kabatepe to the island of Gökçeada and from Odunluk, 60km south-west of Çanakkale, to the island of Bozcaada.

Another car ferry on the Aegean south-west coast sails from the port of Bodrum to the ferry terminal at Körmen, not far from Datça, on the Resadiye peninsula.

Cruises, yachts

See Sport

International ferries

Excursions on local ferries between places on the Turkish coast and the Greek islands in the eastern Aegean have been put virtually out of reach by steep rises in the taxes levied at either end by the Greek and Turkish authorities. For further information see Car Ferries, Getting to Turkey.

Conculates

See Diplomatic Representation

Cruises

Cruise ships operating in the Aegean and the eastern Mediterranean usually call in at ports on the Turkish coast such as Kuşadası, Bodrum, Marmaris, Kaş and Alanya. Travel agencies which specialise in sea cruises will be able to provide more detailed information. See also Coastal Shipping.

Currency

The unit of currency is the Turkish lira (TL, also known as the Turkish pound and originally subdivided into 100 kuruş or 4000 paras). Banknotes currently in circulation are for 10,000, 20,000, 50,000, 100,000 and 250,000 TL; coins are for 500, 1000, 2500 and 5000 TL.

Because of the high rate of inflation – currently around 70% – it is advisable to check with the banks for the very latest exchange rates.

Banks

Open: Mon.–Fri. 8.30am–noon and 1.30–5pm

On weekends and public holidays money can be changed at the international airports (see Air Travel) and İstanbul's Sirkeci Station.

Changing money

As is usually the case for countries with a weak currency, it is better to change money in Turkey rather than at home, and then only in banks or official exchange bureaux such as those in post offices and the larger hotels. Private exchange deals in the street are forbidden, and there is also the risk of ending up with money which is counterfeit!

Be sure to keep the official receipts since these must be produced before rechanging Turkish money back into your own currency, and they are also needed for checks at the frontier to prove that goods purchased in Turkey have been paid for with money that has been exchanged legally.

Import and export of currency

There are no limits on the amount of foreign currency that may be brought into Turkey, but no more than the equivalent of US$5000 may be brought into or taken out of the country in Turkish lira.

The locals in the tourist resorts quite often like to be paid in a hard currency, so it is worth carrying a few pounds or dollars in small denominations to avoid having to change larger ones. But do remember not to change money illegally.

Eurocheques, traveller's cheques

There are plenty of banks in the main towns and tourist centres which cash Eurocheques (on production of a Eurocard) and the major traveller's cheques, although only in the larger branches. Post offices (PTT) will also cash traveller's cheques.

Ordinary cheques will take longer since it may take several days to clear them with the bank of origin.

Credit cards

In the main towns and tourist centres the Turks are becoming increasingly used to payment for goods and services with credit cards such as American Express, Eurocard/Mastercard, Visa/Bank Americard, Diners Club, etc.

Lost/stolen cards

Be sure to put an immediate stop on credit cards, cheque cards, etc. if they are lost or stolen. Inform the relevant issuing authority straightaway, giving all the necessary details except your pin number, and also tell your own local bank. Always keep the receipt for traveller's cheques separately from the cheques themselves.

Customs Regulations

On entry

A verbal declaration is all that is required on entry into Turkey but items of value, including portable TV sets, camcorders and jewellery worth over £10,000/15,000 US dollars, have to be entered in your passport and will be checked again on leaving.

The following items can be taken into the country without payment of duty: personel effects, camping and sports gear, spare parts for the car (to be entered in passport), a camera and 5 rolls of film, a cine-camera and 10 (8mm) films, tape-recorder, one portable CD player, transistor radio, walkman, one TV, one video recording camera (camcorder), 5 video cassettes,

5 records, 5 tape cassettes or compact discs, one video player, one slide projector, one pocket computer (max. 128mb RAM memory), 3 musical instruments, 200 cigarettes and 50 cigars, 200g tobacco, 1.5kg coffee, 500g tea, 5 litres spirits or wine, 5 120ml bottles of perfume and presents up to the value of £200/US$330. Special permission is needed to take in weapons and knives of any kind, including those for camping, etc.

Drugs are illegal in Turkey so do not take them in, do not deal in them and do not use them while in the country – the penalties are very severe.

On exit

Souvenirs can be exported from Turkey free of duty up to a total value of £71 (to the UK).

Valuable personal items can only be taken out if they were entered in the owner's passport on entry or can be shown to have been bought with currency which had been exchanged legally (see Currency). New carpets must be accompanied by proof of purchase and old items also require a certificate from a museum directorate.

The export of antiques is forbidden.

Minerals may only be exported with a special permit from MTA, the General Directorate of Mining Exploration and Research.

Re-entry to EU countries

For persons over 15 the allowances for travellers returning direct from Turkey and other non-member states are 500g coffee or 200g powdered coffee and 100g tea or 40g teabags, 50g perfume and 0.25 litre toilet water and for persons over 17 1 litre spirits over 22% proof or 2 litres spirits under 22% proof or 2 litres sparking wine and 2 litres table wine and 200 cigarettes or 100 cigarillos or 50 cigars or 250g tobacco.

Re-entry to non-EU countries

For countries outside the European Union the allowances are as follows: Australia 250 cigarettes or 50 cigars or 250g tobacco, 1 litre spirits or 1 litre wine; Canada 200 cigarettes and 50 cigars and 1 kg tobacco, 1.14 litre spirits or wine; New Zealand 200 cigarettes or 50 cigars or 250g tobacco, 1.125 litres spirits and 4.5 litres wine; South Africa 400 cigarettes and 50 cigars and 250g tobacco, 1 litre spirits and 2 litres wine; USA 200 cigarettes or 100 cigars or 2 kg of tobacco or proportionate amounts of each, 1 litre spirits or 1 litre wine.

Private yachts

See Sport

Travel Documents

See entry

Diplomatic Representation

Australia

Embassy: Nenehatun Caddesi 83, Gaziosmanpaşa, Ankara; tel. (312) 445 11 80
Consulate: Tepecik Yolu 58, Etiler, İstanbul; tel. (212) 257 76 50

Canada

Embassy: Nenehatun Caddesi 75, Gasiosmanpaşa, Ankara; tel. (312) 436 12 75/79
Consulate: Büyükdere Caddesi, Begün Han 107, Kat. 3, Gayrettepe, İstanbul; tel. (212) 272 51 74

Eire

Consulate: Honorary Consul-General Mr Ferruh Verdi, Cumhuriyet Caddesi, Pegasus Evi 26a, Harbiye, İstanbul; tel. (212) 246 60 25

South Africa

Embassy: Filistin Sokak 27, Gaziosmanpaşa, Ankara; tel. (312) 446 40 56

United Kingdom

Embassy: Şehit Ersan Caddesi 46a, Çankaya, Ankara; tel. (312) 468 62 30
Consulates:
Kızılsaray Mah., Dolaplıdere Cad., Pırıltı Sitesi, Kat. 1, Antalya; tel. (242) 247 70 00

Atatürk Cad., Adliye Sok. 12C, Bodrum; tel. (252) 316 49 92
Cantoni Maritime Agency, Mareşal Çatinak Cad. 28/D, İskenderum; tel. (326) 613 03 61
Mesrutiyet Caddesi 34, Tepebası, İstanbul; tel. (212) 293 75 40
1442 Sokak 49, Alsancak, İzmir; tel. (232) 463 51 51
Yeşil Marmaris Turizm ve Yat İsletmeciliği A.S., Barbaros Cad., Marina, Marmaris; tel. (252) 412 64 86
Çakmak Cad., 124 Sok., M. Tece İş Merkezi, A Blok, Kat 4, Mersin; tel. (324) 232 12 48

USA

Embassy: Atatürk Bulvarı 110, Kavaklıdere, Ankara; tel. (312) 468 61 10
Consulates:
Atatürk Caddesi, Vali Yolu, Adana; tel. (322) 453 91 06
Mesrutiyet Caddesi 104–108, Tepebaşı, İstanbul; tel. (212) 251 36 02
Amerikan Kültür Derneği, 2 Kat, İzmir; tel. (232) 421 36 43

Electricity

Turkey has 220-volt 50 cycles AC. Most European standard plugs will fit but North American ones are likely to need an adaptor.

Power failures are quite common

Embassies

See Diplomatic Representation

Emergency Services

Emergency calls nationwide

Medical emergency: tel. 112
Fire brigade: tel. 110
Traffic police: 154
Police: 155
Local police: 156

Information: 118 – you can use this number to find out which doctors (*doktor, hekim*) and pharmacies (*eczane*) are on duty.

Breakdown service

See Motoring

Events

The following list covers a number of festivals, fairs and other special events. For information about the precise dates check with the tourist information centres (see Information). See also Public Holidays.

January

Selçuk: Camel Fighting Festival

March

Çanakkale: 1915 Sea Victory Celebrations

April

İstanbul: International Film Festival
İstanbul: International Theatre Festival
İzmir: International Film Festival
Manisa: Mesir (traditional festival)

April/May

İstanbul: Tulip Festival

Anamur: International Tourism Festival Giresun: Aksu Culture and Art Festival İstanbul: International Music Festival Marmaris: International Yachting Festival Samsun: Culture and Arts Festival Selçuk: Ephesus International Festival Silifke: International Music and Folklore Festival	May
Alanya: Tourism Festival Bergama: Bergama Festival Çeşme: Sea and Music Festival Foça: Music, Foklore and Watersports Festival Marmaris: Marmaris Festival Rize: International Tea Festival	June
İstanbul: International Art and Culture Festival	June/July
Adana: Sea Festival Antakya: Culture and Arts Festival Bursa: International Festival Iskenderun: Tourism and Culture Festival Samsun: International Folk Dance Festival	July
Çanakkale: Troy Festival	August
İzmir: International Fair	August/ September
Ayder (Black Sea): Alpine pasture cattle drive with beautifully decorated cattle Antalya: Altın Portakal Film Festival Kemer: Carnival Manisa: Grape Harvest Festival Mersin: International Fair Safranbolu: Heritage and Folklore Week	September
Antalya: Akdeniz International Song Contest Mersin: Art and Culture Festival	September/ October
Bodrum: International Gulet Regatta (Bodrum Cup)	October
Marmaris: International Yacht Race	November
Demre, Antalya: International St Nicholas Symposium	December

Ferries

See Car Ferries, Coastal Shipping

Folklore

Folk music

Turkish folk music originates from the steppes of Asia and its rhythms, harmonies and tonal intervals differ fundamentally from those of European music and from the Turkish classical music of the Ottoman court.

In the late Baroque period Ottoman military music, also with its origins in Central Asia, found its way into European music through composers such as Gluck and Mozart, albeit freely adapted to suit the tastes of the time. It is still performed today by İstanbul's authentically costumed Janissary Band, principally on kettle drums, clarinets, bells (Turkish crescents) and cymbals.

Folk dances

Each of Turkey's regions still has its own special folk dance. The best known include the "Zeybek" of the Aegean coast, performed by male dancers only and symbolising their courage and heroism, Bursa's "Kılıç Kalkan" sword and shield dance, another men-only dance, representing the Ottoman conquest of the city, "Kasık Oyunu", a spoon dance for men and women in colourful traditional costumes found between Konya and the coastal town of Silifke, and, finally, the "Horon" of the Black Sea coast, also for men only.

Traditional sports

"Yağlı Güres", greased wrestling, is the Turkish national sport, and wrestling championships are held in July every year at Kırkpınar, outside Edirne, close to Turkey's western border. The wrestlers grease their bodies to make the holds more difficult.

Camel fighting is another traditional sport and contests where the male beasts square up to one another take place in Selçuk in January and in many small towns on the Aegean coast in the spring.

Food and Drink

All Turkish food is prepared from fresh ingredients, and the national cuisine is among the best in the world, with dishes to suit even the most jaded Western palate. Dinner in a good Turkish restaurant (see Restaurants) is a meal to linger over, so allow plenty of time.

Snacks on the street

Street vendors are everywhere, selling dried fruit, hazelnuts, pistachios, sunflower seeds, etc. In summer all kinds of fruit, especially melons, are plentiful. Other food on sale includes corn on the cob, twists of sesame seed bread (*simit*), fried fish and tripe soup (*işkembe çorbaşı*). Be wary of water and lemonade; in winter *çay*, the national beverage of hot sweet tea, and hot chestnuts are both cold weather favourites.

Breakfast

Breakfast usually consists of bread, butter, feta cheese, tomatoes, cucumber, olives, jam, honey, tea and/or (instant) coffee. The better hotels (see entry) provide a buffet with plenty of choice.

Aperitif

Rakı, an aniseed liqueur, 45% proof, which can be drunk neat or with water which it turns milky-white (hence the name "lion's milk"), is Turkey's typical pre-dinner aperitif and also the accompaniment to starters (meze) and fish dishes.

Meze for starters

Favourite starters include various kinds of *dolma*, i.e. stuffed vegetables with a filling of rice or minced meat, such as *biber dolması* (stuffed peppers), *kabak dolması* (stuffed squash), *lahana dolması* (stuffed cabbage leaves), *yaprak dolması* (stuffed vine leaves) and *domates dolması* (stuffed tomatoes). Other starters are *zeytin* (olives), *tarama* (fish roe creamed with oil and lemon juice), *beyaz peynir* (goat's cheese), *kabak kızartması* (thinly sliced fried zuccini/courgettes dressed with yoghurt), *patlıcan kızartması* (fried eggplant/aubergine with yoghurt).

Soups

Popular soups include *dügün çorbası* (wedding soup, lamb broth with lemon juice and beaten egg yolks), *iskembe çobası* (mutton tripe soup), *yayla çobası* (rice soup thickened with whipped yoghurt and egg yolk, flavoured with mint leaves), and *tarhana çobası* (a thick soup of yoghurt, tomatoes, peppers and onions).

Main courses

The main course will usually be something with lamb or mutton or, near the coast, fish or seafood. Turks do not eat pork because it is against their religion, and beef is relatively rare because few cattle are raised for their meat, which makes it expensive. On the other hand, there is plenty of chicken.

Turkey's best-known speciality is probably the kebab, pieces of meat grilled on skewers. *Şiş kebabı* is diced shoulder of lamb grilled between pieces of onion, tomato and peppers and served with rice. *Döner kebabı* is lamb or mutton grilled on a revolving vertical spit then thinly sliced as it cooks. *Güveç* is meat casseroled with rice, vegetables, peppers and tomatoes, *kuzu kapama* is braised lamb with onions, *kuzu dolması* is roast lamb stuffed with rice, sultanas and pinenuts, *çomlek kebabı* is mutton steamed with vegetables, and *kuzu* or *koyun külbastısı* is a spit-roast joint of lamb or mutton.

Chicken dishes include *çerkes tavuğu*, Circassian chicken, served in a thick sauce of paprika and walnuts.

Accompaniments

One of the most popular accompaniments is *cacık*, yoghurt prepared with cucumber, olive oil, dill, salt and garlic. Other side-dishes include *piyaz* (haricot beans and onion salad), *taze fasulya* (green beens), and *zeytinyağlı fasulya* (beans in tomato sauce). Rice may be served plain (*sade pılav*), or with nuts and currants (*İç pılav*).

Dessert

Anyone with a very sweet tooth will enjoy the typical Turkish desserts (*deser*) and sweetmeats, of which *lokum*, or Turkish Delight, is only one. Equally famous is *baklava*, flaky pastry filled with chopped almonds or pistachios and soaked with honey. Other specialities are *kabak tatlısı*, pumpkin slices boiled in milk and sprinkled with grated nuts, *güllaç*, waffles dipped in milk filled with grated almonds and *sütlaç* (cold rice pudding).

Turkey also has wonderful fresh fruit, and is famous for its strawberries from the Bosphorus and Ereğli, figs and grapes from İzmir, peaches from Bursa, apricots from Eastern Anatolia, cherries from Giresun, citrus fruit from the Mediterranean, and pears from around Ankara, while melons of all kinds are found throughout the country.

Turkish dishes (in alphabetical order)

A kind of pudding made from cooked wheat, raisins, dried figs and nuts in jelly.	Aşure
Diluted yoghurt	Ayran
Sweet flaky pastry	Baklava
Stuffed pepper	Biber dolması
Cucumber in garlic-flavoured yoghurt	Cacık
Circassian chicken	Çerkes tavuğu
Salad with tomato, onion, pepper, cucumber	Çoban salatası
Spit-roast lamb or mutton	Döner kebabı
Ice cream	Dondurma
Wedding soup (meat broth with egg yolks)	Düğün çorbası
Bean salad with hardboiled eggs and onions	Fasulye piyazı
Waffles with almond filling	Güllaç
Fried sardines	Hamsı tavası

Baedeker Special

Why did the Imam faint?

Just what made the Imam faint is still open to question when it comes to *Imam Bayıldı* ("the Imam fainted away"), a Turkish dish of aubergines cooked in olive oil and stuffed with onion and tomatoes. Was it because, as a thrifty cleric, he was so appalled that his wife had used a whole litre of olive oil? Or was he bowled over, as some malicious tongues would have it, by the strong reek of garlic? Or was he so enraptured that he was robbed of his senses?

Certainly many Turkish dishes are made with olive oil but that doesn't mean everything is swimming in it, at least not where good Turkish cuisine is concerned. Nor is the Turkish chef heavy on the garlic. It usually plays a large role and is highly prized, not least for health reasons, but is used sparingly for flavouring and then only in certain dishes – its anti-social effects are well-known. The Prophet Mohammed even foreswore garlic and onion out of consideration for his fellows. (Hence the affronted reaction of the Turkish press to a foreign dignitary who greeted a delegation from their country by saying he had been eating garlic so they would feel at home.) Incidentally, the inclusion of fresh parsley is supposed to help with bad breath, and the same goes for chewing cloves after you've eaten garlic.

So did the Imam swoon with pleasure over the wonderful aubergine dish? Quite likely! Turkish cuisine is amongst the best and most imaginative in the world, reflecting the far-flung Ottoman Empire which once stretched from Central Asia to Morocco and from Yemen almost to Vienna. Besides borrowing and refining the food of other cultures, it also left its mark on their cuisine, with Greece's moussaka, the shashlik of the Balkans, not to mention rissoles and yoghurt, all hailing from Turkey. A Turkish chef once calculated his country had over 1500 different dishes. No wonder, then, that many of them have such fanciful names – *karnıyarık* ("slit belly", aubergines stuffed with mince), *güzel hanım çorbaşı* ("lovely lady soup", noodle soup with meatballs), *kadınbudu köfte* ("lady's thigh", elongated meat and rice rissoles), and *hünkar beğendi* ("fit for a Sultan", lamb or beef stew).

Sultans often appeared to be great eaters; they say that Mahmut (1730–54), for example, frequently ordered 72-course meals. When visiting Sultan Abdülaziz in İstanbul Empress Eugenie, the wife of Napoleon III, was so enchanted by the said *hünkar beğendi*, and especially its aubergine purée accompaniment, that she asked whether her personal chef could be taught how to make it. The Sultan gave his permission but the next day the French chef asked to be relieved of this duty since, as he recounted, when he presented himself to the Sultan's head chef, notebook and scales at the ready, the latter hurled them out the window, declaring that a royal chef cooks by feel and with his eyes and his nose. In fact the Turks do tend to rely on taste, feel and experience rather than exact measures when they cook – and the Empress returned to France without her recipe.

Very little animal fat is used in the preparation of Turkish dishes, nor are they as a rule very highly seasoned. The meat is mainly mutton and lamb, a little beef and chicken, but never pork. And of course there are the vegetables – the Turks are master chefs with vegetables!

Cutlery is confined almost exclusively to the use of a spoon, easy to eat with since everything is cut up so small. When a lot of people are invited for a meal they bring their own spoons because they think the host will not have enough. Hence someone who goes out to eat often will get a name for "carrying his spoon in his belt". In some places the spoon has a special significance. In Anatolia when a young man sticks his spoon into the food then gets up and leaves the table he is telling his family he wants to marry, leave home, and set up house for himself.

Snack bar in Antalya

Although restaurants provide a knife and fork as well, the Turks themselves don't use them, since a fork must convey food to the mouth with the left hand, an unclean and ill-mannered practice for a Muslim. As for other table manners, what is not frowned upon is slurping, smacking your lips or, within limits, blowing your nose.

The Turks have a very sweet tooth, and from cradle to grave they call for sweet things to mark every occasion. Hence a visitor's arrival is celebrated by an exchange of sweet gifts, and a present to a friend is always accompanied by a box of sweets, which is why they have so many desserts and sweetmeats, many of them with romantic names like *dilber dudağı* ("lovely lady's lips"), *hanım gobeği ("lady's navel") and kız memesı tel kadayıfı* ("maiden's breasts"), little round crescent cakes, swimming in syrup . . . bon appetit!

Although the Koran forbids the drinking of alcohol, statistics show that every year the Turks get through 300 million litres of beer and 100 million litres of rakı, their 45% proof aniseed liqueur. And if you should succumb not to Imam Bayıldı but to too much rakı then the ideal pick-me-up for the morning after, or so they reckon, is not an aspirin but a bowl of *işkembe çorbası* ("mutton tripe soup").

Food and Drink

Hünkâr beğendi ("fit for a Sultan")	Meat stew with aubergine purée
Hurma tatlısı	Sweet dessert
İç pilav	Spiced rice with raisins and pistachios
İmam bayıldı ("The Imam fainted")	Aubergines, onions and tomatoes, cooked in olive oil and served cold
İşkembe çorbası	Mutton tripe soup thickened with egg
Kabak dolması	Cucumber stuffed with meat and rice
Kabak kızartması	Fried courgettes
Kabak tatlısı	Squash cooked with sugar
Kadın budu ("lady's thighs")	Meat balls dipped in egg
Kadin Göbeği ("lady's navel")	Syrup-covered doughnut
Kılıç şiş	Fried swordfish
Kuzu dolması	Roast lamb with spiced rice
Midye dolması	Mussels stuffed with spiced rice
Patlıcan kızartması	Roast aubergines
Pirzola	Lamb chops
Revani	Semolina soaked with syrup
Sangı burma ("twisted turban")	Sweet dessert
Şiş kebabı	Shish kebab, grilled meat on a skewer
Şiş köfte	Grilled meatballs
Su böreği	Pastry filled with mincemeat or grated cheese
Sütlaç	Cold rice pudding
Tarama	Fish roe
Tel Kadayıf	Shredded wheat covered with syrup and nuts
Tütün balık	Smoked fish
Vezir parmağı ("vizier's finger")	Sweet dessert
Zerde	A kind of rice pudding with saffron, usually served at weddings
Zeytinyağlı fasulye	Green beans in tomato sauce
Patlıcan dolması	Aubergines stuffed with rice and cooked in olive oil

Drink

Yoghurt (*ayran*)	In the dry areas of Asia Minor yoghurt made from slightly salted goat's milk forms a staple part of the Turkish diet, either as an ingredient in many dishes or diluted with water and drunk as "ayran".

Although the precepts of the Koran mean that the Turks are not great wine-drinkers, there is plenty of good wine to be had in the areas which cater for tourists. Popular brands are Doluca (red and white), Kavaklıdere (red and white), Yakut Damlası (red) and Lâl (rosé).

Most of Turkey's grapes are grown in Thrace and on the Aegean coast but the majority are sold as dessert fruit and only a fraction is made into wine.

Wine (*sarap*)

Local beers ("Efes" is one of the most popular) are good quality and relatively light. Foreign beers and lagers which are brewed in Turkey under licence are also available.

Beer (*bira*)

Carbonated mineral water and bottled water is cheap and worth recommending, but be wary of ordinary water, and the same goes for lemonade sold on the street.

Mineral water (*maden suyu*)

Since fruit juice is made from nearly every kind of fruit grown in Turkey there is a wonderful range to choose from.

Fruit juice (*meyva suyu*)

Tea (drunk black) is nowadays the Turks' national beverage. It is in greatest demand in summer when everyone flocks to the gardens of the tea-houses (*çayhane*).

Tea (*çay*)

Turkish coffee is relatively expensive. In good coffee-houses the mocca coffee is individually prepared on a side-table – a heaped coffee spoon of very dark roast ground coffee beans is placed in a little copper pot, the desired amount of sugar is added (the Turks like their coffee very sweet) and this is all stirred together with some water, boiled up on an open flame as more water is added, allowed to bubble up several times and then served.

Coffee (*kahve*)

Besides rakı (see Aperitif above) Turkey also produces its own local brandy and gin.

Spirits (*alkollü ičkiler*)

Getting to Turkey

By air

The best way to get to Turkey is by air, especially for a short visit. Turkish Airlines (THY) and British Airways operate daily flights from London Heathrow to İstanbul, while THY also operate regular flights to Ankara, İzmir, Antalya, Adana, Trabzon and Dalaman from many of the world's other major cities. In fact most international airlines have scheduled flights to Turkey's international airports and during the holiday season there are charter flights as well.

See also Air Travel

By sea

A number of cruises (see entry) have ports of call along the Turkish coast, with Alanya, Antalya, Bodrum, Çeşme, Dikili, İskenderun, İstanbul, İzmir, Kuşadası, Marmaris, Mersin, Samsun and Trabzon among the most popular; information is available from local travel agents (see also Coastal Shipping).

If you are staying on a Greek island and planning an outing by sea to Turkey you will need to pay a very high exit tax.

By car

Although the ending of hostilities in former Yugoslavia means that Turkey is again accessible by the overland route it is not really to be recommended.

London to İstanbul is about 3000km/1850 miles by road. The best route from Northern Europe is undoubtedly the southern one, via Belgium, Germany, Austria then Italy and a ferry direct to Turkey (see Car Ferries).

By bus

Various coach operators offer package tours to Turkey which have the advantage of taking the worry out of making arrangements for meals, accommodation, etc. Try to ensure that the vehicle is comfortable and preferably with air conditioning

By rail

During the summer there are daily through trains from Munich to İstanbul which take about 1½ days, including two nights on the train.

Venice Simplon Orient Express

The old Orient Express which used to run from London to İstanbul has been renamed the Venice Simplon Orient Express (VSOE) and now only runs from London to Venice, from where it is possible to join a cruise ship or take a ferry. For details contact: VSOE, 20 Upper Ground, London SE1, tel. (0171) 620 0003.

Health Care

Medical care is ensured by having a hospital (*hastane*) in every provincial capital.

Since many Turkish doctors have trained abroad they usually speak at least one foreign language.

Hospitals

İstanbul and İzmir have foreign hospitals as well as Turkish clinics:

American Hospital
Güzelbahçe Sokağı 20, Nisantaşı, İstanbul; tel. (212) 231 40 50
1375 Sok., Alsancak, İzmir; tel. (232) 484 53 60

French Lape Hospital (Hôpital Français)
Şişli, İstanbul; tel. (212) 246 10 20, fax (212) 233 69 89

German Hospital (Alman Hastanesi)
Sıraselviler Caddesi 119, Taksim, İstanbul;
tel. (212) 293 21 50, fax (212) 252 39 11

International Hospital
Çınar Oteli Yanı 82, İstanbul Cad., Yeşilköy, İstanbul;
tel. (212) 663 30 00, fax (212) 663 28 62

Italian Hospital (Ospedale Italiano)
Defterdar Yokuşu 37, Tophane, İstanbul; tel. (212) 249 97 51

St. George's Austrian Hospital (Sen Jerj Hastanesi)
Bereketzade Sokağı 5/7, Beyoğlu, İstanbul; tel. (212) 243 25 90

Vaccinations

No vaccinations are necessary but check with your doctor or travel clinic before leaving home about precautionary measures (it is well worth getting protection against malaria and hepatitis).

Emergency number (police)

Tel. 155

Emergency doctor

Tel. 112

Pharmacies

Call 118 for information. The operator can advise you which doctors (*doktor, hekim*) and pharmacies (*eczane*) are on duty. Pharmacies carry the sign of the red crescent. Medicines are not expensive but anyone on regular medication should take sufficient to last the holiday.

Health insurance

It is generally advisable to take out additional short-term health and accident insurance to cover the cost of, for example, being flown home in an emergency.

Holiday Villages

See Hotels

Hotels

The recent building boom means that there are now over 250,000 beds for visitors to Turkey's tourist areas.

Alpine-style holidays

The best-known areas for Alpine-style holidays, with high mountain pastures and their annual festivals (see Events), include those on the Black Sea such as Ayder by Rize, Kadırga by Trabzon, and Kümbet by Giresun. Details of these holidays are available from the tourist offices listed in the Information section.

Nightlife

The big hotels and holiday villages have night clubs with belly dancers, folk dancing, etc., as well as bars and discos.

Many holiday resorts have their own casinos (passports must be shown).

Holiday villages

Holiday villages such as those run by Club Aldiana, Club Méditerranée, Robinson Clubs, Sunsail Clubs, etc., are very popular, due largely to the range of sporting facilities on offer.

Classifications

The following list gives the official categories for hotels (oteli) and other types of accommodation:

HL	luxury hotel	APRT	holiday apartments
H1	1st class hotel	O	hostel, inn
H2	2nd class hotel	P	pension, guest house
H3	3rd class hotel	TKA	1st class holiday village
H4	4th class hotel	TKB	2nd class holiday village
M1	1st class motel	S	Special (historic building)
M2	2nd class motel	HV	Holiday Village

Prices

Although most accommodation in Turkey is subject to state control those responsible will not commit themselves on prices for short or longer term stays. Because of Turkey's high rate of inflation prices are often given in German marks (DM) or US dollars.

Generally speaking, the price level tends to be well below what is usual in more highly developed countries. This particularly applies to accommodation in the lower categories, but the degree of comfort is usually less than adequate.

Room reservation

If your holiday is not pre booked and you want to travel around Turkey independently you would be well recommended, for the summer months at least, to book your room well ahead and come to a binding agreement on the price directly with the place concerned.

List of hotels

Following Turkey's recent intensive drive to promote itself as a holiday destination many private and foreign investors have put in new hotels and other visitor accommodation. Because of the timelag in updating the official lists it has not yet been possible to include a number of these newer hotels in the selection which follows (international dialling code for Turkey: 90).

b.=number of beds

Bul.	= Bulvarı (boulevard)	Mev.	= Mevki (square)
Cad.	= Caddesi (street)	Mey.	= Meydan (square)
Kat.	= Bina katı (floor)	Sok.	= Sokak (street, alley)

List of hotels (a selection)

Adana

Seyhan Oteli, HL, 300 b., Reşatbey M.T. Cemal Beriker Bul. 30;
tel. (322) 475 18 10, fax (322) 454 28 34
(a luxury hotel with every comfort, plus swimming pool, night club, two restaurants, etc.)
Zaimoğlu Oteli, H1, 156 b., Özler Cad. 72;
tel. (322) 351 34 01, fax (322) 351 68 11
(modern, air-conditioned centrally located hotel but with a garage)
İpek Palas Oteli, H2, 102 b., İnönü Cad. 103;
tel. (322) 351 87 41, fax (322) 351 87 45
(central location but with quiet rooms at the back)

Alanya

Club Alantur, H1, 811 b., Dimçayı Mevkii 07400;
tel. (242) 518 17 40, fax (242) 518 17 56
(4 miles east of the town, right on the beach; very comfortable)
Bedesten Hotel, H1 S, 46 b., İçkale;
tel. (242) 512 12 34, fax (242) 513 79 34
(luxurious accommodation on the castle hill, in an old caravanserei, Alanya's most unusual hotel)
Club Castalia, TKB, 484 b., Konaklı Mev. 07400;
tel. (242) 565 13 15, fax (242) 565 14 28
(about 6 miles west of the town)

Anamur

Eser Pansiyonu, P, İskele Makallesi
(small, comfortable guest house; good food in the roof restaurant)

Antakya

Büyük Antakya Oteli, H1, 144 b., Atatürk Cad. 8;
tel. (326) 213 58 60
(central location, night club)

Antalya

Aspen Oteli, O S, Kaledibi Sok. 16–18;
tel. (242) 247 05 90, fax (242) 241 33 64
(complex of old houses in the heart of the Old Town, super de luxe)
Perge Oteli, H1, 52 b., Perge Sokak 5;
tel. (242) 242 36 00, fax (242) 241 75 87
(outstanding service, rooms with sea view, spic and span kitchen)
Tütay Türkevleri Oteli, H1 S, 50 b., Mermerli Sok. 2;
tel. (242) 248 65 91, fax (242) 241 94 19
(hotel consisting of three renovated Ottoman houses in the heart of the Old Town; wonderful view of the sea, harbour and Taurus mountains; swimming pool)

Ayvalık

Grand Temizel Oteli, H1, Sarımsaklı;
tel. (266) 324 20 00, fax (266) 324 12 74
(very grand, but a bit off the beaten track)
Cunda Hotel, H1, 92 b., Alibey Adası;
tel. (266) 327 15 98, fax (266) 327 19 43
(1993 chalet village, 2½ miles out of town, small private beach)
Murat Reis Club Hotel, H1, 400 b., Altınkum Mevkii;
tel. (266) 324 14 56, fax (266) 324 14 57
(one of the oldest and most famous hotels, on a lovely bay with private beach and naturalistic swimming pool in the rocks)
Berk Oteli, H3, 98 b., Ortaçamlık 23;
tel. (266) 312 15 01, fax (266) 312 13 45
(renovated in art deco style in 1993 with lovely view of the bay)

Bergama

Tusan Motel, Yolacti Mev.;
tel. (232) 663 11 73, fax (232) 633 19 38
(4 miles out of town, idyllic garden)
Berksoy Oteli, H2, 120 b., PK 19, İzmir Yolu;
tel. (232) 633 25 95, fax (232) 633 53 46
(large mountainside hotel complex)

Bodrum

Ambrosia Oteli, H1, 142 b., Bitez-Bodrum;
tel. (252) 343 18 86, fax (252) 343 18 79
(about 4 miles from the town centre)
Marina Vista, H1, 174 b., Neyzen Tevfik Cad. 226;
tel. (252) 316 22 69, fax (252) 316 23 47
(elegant, with large garden courtyard and swimming pool)
Metem Holiday Village, TKA, 456 b., Gumbet 48400;
tel. (252) 316 25 00, fax (252) 316 15 00
Baraz Oteli, H3, 76 b., Cumhuriyet Cad. 70;
tel. (252) 316 18 57, fax (252) 316 44 30
(in the Old Town; can be noisy)

Bursa

Artıç Oteli, H4, 137 b., Atatürk Cad. 95;
tel. (224) 224 55 05, fax (224) 224 55 09
(good, centrally located but not particularly quiet)

Çanakkale

Akol Oteli, H1, 300 b., Kordonboyu 17100;
tel. (286) 217 94 56, fax (286) 217 28 97
(grandest place in town)
Anafartalar Oteli, H3, 140 b., İskele Mey;
tel. (286) 217 44 54, fax (286) 217 44 57
(large hotel on the harbour, sea rooms with balcony, rather noisy)
Iris Oteli, H2, 162 b., Mola Cad. 48 (in Güzelyalı)
tel. (286) 232 81 00, fax (286) 232 80 28
(comfortable, with sandy beach, about 6 miles from Çanakkale)

Çeşme

Altın Yunus Holiday Resort, H1, 1000 b., Boyalık Mevkii;
tel. (232) 723 12 50, fax (232) 723 22 52
(large complex of four hotels – Dolphin, Mermaid, Marina and Beach Oteli; all kinds of sports facilities, own marina, fitness centre, casino and beach)
Kervansaray Kanuni, O, S, 66 b., Çeşme Kale Yanı 35930;
tel. (232) 712 71 77, fax (232) 712 64 92
(comfort in an old building dating from 1528, near the harbour)
Framissima Boyalık Beach Hotel, H1, Boyalık;
tel. (232) 712 70 81, fax (232) 712 73 31
(grand de luxe, right on the beach, two restaurants with Turkish and European specialities)

Datça

Club Datça, TKB, 270 b., (at north end of town) İskele M.;
tel. (252) 712 31 70, fax (252) 712 33 80
(large holiday village with own beach)

Didim (Didyma)

Kardelen Oteli;
tel. (256) 813 31 57
(modern; beach location)

Fethiye

Letoonia Holiday Village, PK 63, Fethiye, Muğla/Tatil Köyü HV and TKA, 1502 b., Paçarız Burnu;
tel. (252) 614 49 66, fax (252) 614 44 22
(modern complex, on a tongue of land in a lovely bay, swimming pools)
Meri Motel, HL, 150 b., Ölüdeniz
tel. (252) 616 60 60, fax (252) 616 64 56
(with lovely garden and own beach)
Belcehan Hotel, H4, Ölüdeniz;
tel. (252) 616 69 75, fax (252) 616 69 53

Foça

Leon Oteli, H3, 160 b., I Mersinaki, Karaçina Mevkii;
tel. (232) 812 29 60, fax (232) 812 23 56
(modern and well-equipped hotel on the sea front; lots of amenities)

Giresun

Giresun Oteli, H3, 100b., Sultanselim Meydanı 3;
tel. (454) 212 30 17, fax (454) 212 60 38
(fine view of the sea and the town)

Hopa	Cihan Oteli, H4, 68 b., Ortahopa Cad. 7; tel. (466) 351 48 97, fax (466) 351 48 98
İstanbul	Çirağan Palace (Kempinski), HL, 648 b., Çirağan Cad. 84, Beşiktaş; tel. (212) 258 33 77, fax (212) 259 66 87 (in a restored Ottoman palace, grandest hotel in the city) İstanbul Hilton, HL, 758 b., Cumhuriyet Cad., Harbiye; tel. (212) 231 46 46, fax (212) 240 41 65 (in a lovely park, with every conceivable comfort) Palace Hotel, H2 S, 273 b., Meşrutiyet Cad. 98/100; tel. (212) 251 45 60, fax (212) 251 40 89 (stylish Belle Epoque hotel with very well preserved art nouveau décor, former Orient Express tied hotel) Hidiv Kasrı Oteli, H2 S, 36 b., Çubuklu; tel. (216) 331 26 51 fax (216) 322 34 34 (former palace of the Egyptian Viceroy, superb view of the Bosphorus, extremely comfortable) Splendid Palace, H2 S, 134 b., 23 Nisan Cad. 71, Büyük Ada; tel. (216) 382 69 50, fax (216) 382 67 75 (on an island so no noise problems)
İzmir	Grand Efes, HL, 885 b., Gazi Osman Paşa Bul. 1; tel. (232) 484 43 00, fax (232) 441 56 95 (oldest luxury hotel, one of Turkey's best, with every conceivable comfort; dinner by the large swimming pool) İzmir Etap, HL, 168 rooms, Cumhuriyet Bul. 138; tel. (232) 489 40 90, fax (232) 480 40 89 (despite luxury category relatively moderate prices) Karaca Oteli, H2, 146 b., 1379. Sok. 55, Alsancak; tel. (232) 489 19 40, fax (232) 483 14 98 (central location but in a quiet side street, very comfortable; small pool on roof terrace)
Kalkan	Hotel Pirat, H1, 270 b., Kalkan Marinası; tel. (242) 844 31 78, fax (242) 844 31 83 (very comfortable; water sports)
Kas	Ekici Hotel, H1, 168 b., Arisan SK. 1; tel. (242) 836 14 17, fax (242) 836 18 23 Medusa Oteli, H2, 80 b., Küçüçakil, Kaş; tel. (242) 836 14 41
Kemer	Türkiz Hotel, HL, 300 b., Yalı Cad. 3; tel. (242) 814 41 00, fax (242) 814 248 33 Otem Hotel, H1, 120 b., Yat Limanı Karşışı; tel. (242) 814 31 81, fax (242) 814 31 90
Kızkalesi	Club Hotel Barbarossa, H1, 250 b., Kızkalesi Mevkii 33790; tel. (324) 523 23 64, fax (324) 523 20 90 (very grand; the hotel restaurant is highly recommended)
Köyceğiz	Kaunos Oteli, H3, 100 b., Çengiz Topel Cad; tel. (252) 262 42 88, fax (252) 262 48 36 Özay Oteli, H3, 70 b., Kordon Boyu 11; tel. (252) 262 43 00, fax (252) 262 43 61
Kuşadası	Atınç Oteli, H1, 155 b., Atatürk Bul. 42; tel. (256) 614 76 08, fax (256) 614 49 67 Club Caravanserai, H1, 80 b., Atatürk Bul. 2, Kuşadası-Aydın; tel. (256) 614 41 15, (256) 614 24 23 (luxury hotel in an old caravanserai dating from 1618) Surtel, H2, 200 b., Atatürk Bul. 20; tel. (256) 612 06 06, fax (256) 614 51 26 (by the old city wall and palm-fringed promenade)

Marmaris

Lidya Oteli, H2, 672 b., Siteler MH 130;
tel. (252) 412 29 40, fax 252 412 14 78
(lovely palm gardens and private beach)
Martı Holiday Village, TKA, 835 b., İcmeler;
tel. (252) 455 34 40, fax (252) 455 34 48
(holiday hotel complex with lots of sports facilities)
Robinson Club Maris, 602 b., Hısarönö Mevkii, Muğla 48700;
tel. (252) 436 92 00, fax (252) 436 92 28

Ölü Deniz

Otel Dedeoğlu, 101 b., İskeler Meydanı;
tel. (252) 614 40 10
(older, by the harbour)

Ordu

Turist Otel, H3, 72 b., Atatürk Bul. 134;
tel. (452) 214 42 73, fax (452) 214 19 50

Pamukkale

Richmond Oteli, HL, Karahayıt Köyü;
tel. (258) 271 42 94, fax (258) 271 40 78

Patara

Bayhan Patara Hotel, 252 b., Gelemiş Köyö;
tel. (242) 843 52 96, fax (242) 843 50 97

Rize

Keleş, H3, 56 b., Palandöken Cad. 2;
tel. (464) 217 46 12, fax (464) 217 86 41
(by the harbour)

Samsun

Turban Büyük Samsun Oteli, H1, 226 b., Sahil C.;
tel. (362) 431 07 50, fax (362) 431 07 40
Burç Oteli, H4, 72 b., Kazım Paşa Cad. 36;
tel. (362) 431 54 80, fax (362) 431 37 88

Sarıgerme

Magic Life, HL, 454 b., Muğla/Ortaca;
tel. (252) 286 80 63
(hotel park, in woodland; with swimming pool, tennis courts)

Selçuk

Otel Tamsa, H1, 300 b., Pamucak, Sahil;
tel. (232) 892 61 90, fax (232) 892 27 71
(about 6 miles from Selçuk)

Side

Kleopatra Hotel, H1, 84 b.;
tel. (242) 753 10 33

Silifke

Altınfoz Banana, H1, 232 b., Atakent Susanoğlu;
tel. (324) 722 42 11, fax (324) 722 42 15
Çadir Oteli, H4, 50 b., Atatük Cad. 8;
tel. (324) 714 24 49, fax (324) 714 12 44

Sinop

Melia Kasım Oteli, H3, Gazi Cad. 9;
tel. (368) 261 42 10, fax (368) 261 16 25

Trabzon

Özgür Oteli, H3, 100 b., Atatürk Alanı 29;
tel. (462) 321 13 19, fax (462) 321 39 52;
(on the Taksim, with its own restaurant)
Usta Oteli, H4, 140 b., Telgrafhane Sok. 3;
tel. (462) 321 21 95, fax (462) 322 37 93

Yalova

Turban Termal, O, Termal-Yalova;
tel. (216) 835 74 00

Information

Australia

Suite 101, 280 George Street, Sydney NSW 2000;
tel. (61–2) 92 23 30 55, fax (61–2) 92 23 32 04

Information

Canada	Constitution Square, 360 Albert Street, Suite 801, Ottawa, Ontario K1R 7X7; tel. (613) 230 86 54, fax (613) 230 36 83
United Kingdom	Turkish Tourism and Information Office 170–173 Piccadilly (1st floor), London W1V 9DD; tel. (0171) 629 77 71, fax (0171) 491 07 73
United States	821 United Nations Plaza, New York NY 10017; tel. (212) 687 21 94, fax (212) 599 75 68
	Culture and Tourism Office, Turkish Embassy, Suite 306, 1717 Massachusetts Avenue NW, Washington DC 20036; tel. (202) 429 98 44, fax (202) 429 56 49

Turkish Tourist Information Centres

The following is a list of local tourist offices on the Turkish coast.

Adana	Atatürk Cad. 13; tel. (322) 359 19 94, fax (322) 352 67 90 Şakirpaşa airport; tel./fax (322) 436 92 14
Akçay	Edremit Caddesi Karabudak Apt. 2; tel./fax (266) 384 11 13
Alanya	Damlataş Mağarasi Yani, Damlataş Cad. 1; tel. (242) 513 12 40, fax (242) 513 54 36
Anamur	Otogar Binası Kat. 2, 2 tel. (324) 814 40 58, 814 35 29, fax (324) 814 40 58
Antakya (Hatay)	Vali Ürgen Alanı 47; tel. (326) 216 06 10, fax (326) 213 57 40
Antalya	Cumhuriyet Caddesi 2, Özel İdare İşhanı Altı; tel./fax (242) 241 17 47
	Airport; tel. (242) 330 32 21, 330 32 30
Aydın	Yeni Dörtyol Mevkii; tel. (256) 225 41 45, fax (256) 212 62 26
Ayvalık (Balıkesir)	Yat Limanı Karşisı; tel./fax (266) 312 21 22
Bergama	Zafer Mah., İzmir Caddesi 54; tel./fax (232) 633 18 62
Bodrum	Baris Meydanı; tel. (252) 316 10 19, fax (252) 316 76 94
Bursa	Orhangazi Altgeçidi, Heykel; tel./fax (224) 220 18 48
Çanakkale	İskele Meydanı 67; tel./fax (286) 217 11 87
	Vilayet Konağı; tel. (286) 217 50 12, 217 37 91, fax (286) 217 25 34
Çeşme	İskele Meydanı 8; tel./fax (232) 712 66 53

Dalaman Hava Limanı (airport); tel. (252) 692 58 99	**Dalaman**
Hükümet Binası, İskele Mah.; tel. (252) 712 31 63, fax (252) 712 35 46	**Datça**
Atatürk Cad., Ufuk Apt. 8; tel. (258) 261 33 93, fax (258) 264 76 21	**Denizli**
see Selçuk	**Ephesus**
Yalı Mah., 1 Nolu Sokak Şeref Apt. 2; tel./fax (266) 835 11 69	**Erdek**
İskele Karşısı 1; tel./fax (252) 614 15 27	**Fethiye**
Atatürk Bulvarı, Foça Girisi 1; tel./fax (232) 812 12 22	**Foça**
Cemal Gürsel Caddesi, Hafız Avni Ögütçü Sok. 11; tel. (454) 212 31 90, fax (454) 216 00 95	**Giresun**
see Antakya	**Hatay**
Atatürk Bul. 49B; tel. (326) 614 16 20, fax (326) 613 28 79	**İskenderun**
Meşrutiyet Cad. 57/1, Tepebaşi, Beyoğlu; tel. (212) 245 01 09 Hilton Oteli Girişı, Taksim; tel. (212) 245 68 76 Taksim Meydani/Maksem; tel. (212) 245 68 76 Sultanahmet Meydanı; tel./fax (212) 518 18 02 Yesilköy, Atatürk Airport; tel./fax (212) 663 07 93	**İstanbul**
Gazi Osman Pasa Bulvarı 1/F, Büyük Efes Oteli Altı; tel.fax (232) 489 92 78 Adnan Menderes Airport; tel. (232) 274 24 24, fax (232) 274 20 51	**İzmir**
Belediye İşhanı Kat 1; tel./fax (224) 757 19 33	**İznik**
Cumhuriyet Meydanı 5; tel./fax (242) 836 12 38	**Kaş**
Belediye ve Turizm Örgüt Binası; tel. (242) 814 11 12, 814 15 37, fax (242) 814 15 36	**Kemer**
Atatürk Kordonu; tel./fax (252) 262 47 03	**Köyceğiz**
Liman Cad. 13 tel. (256) 614 11 03, fax (256) 614 62 95	**Kuşadası**
Özel İdare İşhanı Doğu Caddesi 14/3; tel. (236) 231 25 41, fax (236) 232 74 23	**Manisa**
İskele Meydanı 2; tel. (252) 412 10 35, fax (252) 412 72 77	**Marmaris**

Mersin	İsmet Inönü Bul. 5/1, Liman Girişi; tel. (324) 238 32 71, fax (324) 238 32 72
Muğla	Marmaris Bulvarı 24; tel. (252) 214 12 61, fax (252) 214 12 44
Ordu	Hükümet Konağı, A Blok, Kat 1; tel. (452) 223 16 07, fax (452) 223 29 22
Pamukkale	Örenyeri; tel./fax (258) 272 20 77
Pergamon	see Bergama
Samsun	19 Mayıs Mah. Talimhane Cad. 6; tel. (362) 431 12 28
Selçuk	Atatürk Mah., Agora Çarşısı 35; tel. (232) 892 63 28, fax (232) 892 69 45
Side	Side Yolu Üzeri, Manavgat; tel. (242) 753 12 65, fax (242) 753 26 57
Silifke	Gazi Mah., Veli Gürten Bozbey Caddesi 6; tel. (324) 714 11 51, fax (324) 714 53 28
Sinop	Hükümet Konağı, Kat 4; tel. (368) 261 52 07, fax (368) 260 03 10
Trabzon	Atatürk Alanı, Meydan Parkı Köşesı 37/A; tel./fax (462) 321 46 59

Insurance

General

Visitors are strongly advised to take out adequate holiday insurance, including cover against illness, accident, etc., loss or damage to luggage loss of currency and jewellery and, particularly if a package holiday has been booked, cancellation insurance.

Arrangements can be made through a travel agent or an insurance company. Many companies operating package holidays now include insurance as part of the deal.

Vehicles

Visitors travelling by car should make sure that their insurance is comprehensive and covers use of the vehicle in Turkey.

See also Travel Documents.

Language

Turkey's official and spoken language is Turkish. The most westerly member of the Turco-Tataric language family, this is believed to have been originally related to the non-Indo European family of Ural-Altaic languages, and can trace its origins back to the 12th c. In the centuries that followed Turkish borrowed many words and much grammar from Persian and Arabic, and these only began to be systematically eliminated in the 19th c. On the other hand, it has since absorbed many words of European origin, especially French and particularly in the technical field.

Latin script replaced Arabic in 1928 when some diacritic marks were also added, the most notable being "ı", the dotless i which gets back its dot as a capital letter (eg. İstanbul).

Alphabet

Turkish	Pronunciation
a	a
b	b
c	j
ç	ch as in "church"
d	d
e	e
f	f
g	g (hard, as in "gag")
ğ	(barely perceptible; lengthens preceding vowel)
h	h (emphatically pronounced, approaching ch in "loch")
ı	a dark uh sound
i	i
j	zh as in "pleasure"

Turkish	Pronunciation
k	k
l	l
m	m
n	n
o	o
ö	eu, as in French "deux"
p	p
r	r
s	s
ş	sh
t	t
u	u
ü	as in French "une"
v	v
y	y, as in "yet"
z	z

Numbers

Number	Turkish
0	sıfır
1	bir
2	ıki
3	üç
4	dört
5	beş
6	altı
7	yedi
8	sekiz
9	dokuz
10	on
11	onbir

Number	Turkish
20	yirmi
21	yirmibir
30	otuz
40	kırk
50	elli
60	altmiş
70	yetmış
80	seksen
90	doksan
100	yüz
200	ıkiyüz
1000	bin

Useful words and phrases

English	Turkish
Do you speak English?	Ingilizce biliyor musununz?
yes	evet
no	hayır
please	lütfen
thank you	teşekkür ederim, mersi
excuse me	affedersiniz
hello	merhaba
good morning	günaydın
good evening	İyi akşamlar
good night	İyi geceler
goodbye	Allahaısmarladık, güle güle
men	erkekler/baylar
women	kadınlar/bayanlar
where is . . . ?	nerede . . . ?
when?	ne zaman?
how much?	bu ne kadar?
open	açık
shut	kapalı
right	sağ
left	sola, solda
straight ahead	doğruca doğru/direk
what time is it?	saat kaç?

Turkish	English
bahçe	garden
bedesten	indoor market
delediye	town hall
benzin istasyonu	filling station
caddesi (Cad.)	street
cami	mosque
çarşi	bazaar, market
çeşme	(drinking) fountain
dağ	mountain
eczane	pharmacy
ev	house
gemi	ship
hamam	bath-house
han	inn, caravanserai
hesaplama	bill
hisar	castle, fortress
iskele	landing-stage
kapı	gate
kervansaray	caravanserai
kıbla	wall pointing to Mecca
kilise	church
kitapçı	bookshop
köşk	pavilion, kiosk
köy	village
kule	tower
kütüphane	library
mektup	letter
mihrab	mosque prayer niche
müzes	museum
okul	school
opus sectile	mosaic
otobüs durağİ	bus stop
otogar	bus station
plaj	beach
polis	police
saray	palace
sebil	fountain-house
şehir	town
sokağ (sok.)	lane
su	water
tarmirhane	garage
tren istansyonu	railway station
tuvalet/umumî	WC
vapur	boat
yol	road

Motoring

Roads

Turkey has quite a good road network which it is constantly extending and improving. All the main roads – about 40,000km/25,000 miles of them – are tarmac but relatively few stretches rank as motorways. Most of these are around the conurbations of İstanbul, İzmir, Adana and Ankara. Many other roads are surfaced with gravel chippings and are not really suitable for driving on except in the summer. Roadworks are frequent and often involve long detours. If touring away from the main highways a good sturdy vehicle is necessary.

Although the main roads are numbered they are not always systematically signed, but it is relatively easy to find your way provided you pay careful attention. Toll highways are being built in some areas.

Coast roads

A good main road runs along the whole of Turkey's Aegean and Mediterranean coastline, but places on the western Black Sea coast as far as Sinop can often only be reached from the İstanbul–Samsun road further inland.

Traffic regulations

In Turkey vehicles travel on the right and overtake on the left.

Two warning triangles must be carried to place behind and in front of the vehicle in the event of a breakdown and a supply of spare bulbs for front and rear lights should also be carried.

The wearing of seat belts is compulsory.

There is a total ban on drinking and driving.

Speed limits are 50kph/31mph in built-up areas (40kph/25mph for cars with trailers) and 90kph/56mph elsewhere (70kph/44mph for motorcycles and cars with trailers).

Road signs

Road signs follow the usual international pattern (yellow shields denote sites of archaeological or historical interest), but there are also some written in Turkish:

Bozuk yol	Bad road surface
Dikkat	Attention!
Dur	Stop
Düşüt banket	Unstable verge
Girilmez	no entry
Park edilmez	No parking
Şehir merkezi	City centre
Tamirat	Roadworks in progress
Tek yön	one way
Viraj	Bend
Yavaş	Slow down

Standard of driving

Turkish drivers tend to be none too careful about traffic discipline. Although they are not unduly aggressive at the wheel, lorries and buses in particular can be guilty of some risky overtaking and of a tendency to stop without warning on open roads to pick up prospective passengers.

The possibility of encountering farm machinery or straying livestock means you also need to take special care when driving on country roads. Driving at night can also be hazardous on account of the number of vehicles driving with poor lights or no lights at all, and the sudden changes in road surface, not to mention the potholes.

Accidents

In the event of an accident always notify the police immediately even if no-one is injured, since by law there has to be a police report. If your vehicle is a total write-off or has to stay in Turkey for repairs for longer than six months you must notify the appropriate customs office so that the entry for the vehicle in your passport can be altered accordingly (see Travel Documents).

Vehicle theft

If your vehicle is stolen you must get a certificate to that effect from the provincial authority (valı), so that the entry in your passport can be cancelled when you leave Turkey.

Fuel/gas

There are filling/gas stations at regular intervals along the main trunk roads. These stay open 24 hours a day and usually have their own repair shop and restaurant as well.

If travelling away from the main roads you should carry a full spare can of fuel and top it up again as soon as possible if you have to use any.

Ordinary leaded petrol (benzin, 91 octane), super leaded petrol (süper, 95 octane), diesel (motorin), and engine oil (motor yağı) are available. Motoring organisations can supply a list of filling stations which have unleaded petrol (kurşunsuz benzin).

Breakdowns and repairs

The Turkish Touring and Automobile Club (TTOK) can provide assistance for members of other motoring organisations, so it is advisable to check on how this can be arranged before leaving home:

Turkish Touring and Automobile Club
Türkiye Turing ve Otomobil Kurumu (TTOK)
Oto Sanayi Sitesi Yani 4, Levent;
tel. (212) 282 81 40, fax (212) 282 80 42
Antalya: tel. (242) 247 06 99
İskenderun: tel. (326) 617 74 62
İzmir: tel. (232) 421 35 14
Mersin: tel. (324) 232 12 47

The charge for a call-out is according to the distance covered to get there.

Garages, repair shops

There are garages and repair shops (*bir tamirci*) on the main highways and the edge of towns, but it can take time to get spare parts for some makes of car.

Emergency calls

See Emergency Services

Museums

The major museums are covered in the A to Z section under the headings for where they are located.

Opening times

Museums are usually open between 9am and 4.30pm except on Mondays, when they are closed. The main exceptions to this in İstanbul are Dolmabahçe Sarayı, where the palace is closed all day Thursday as well as Monday, and Topkapı, which is closed on Tuesdays. Since lunchtime closures and the hours of late visiting times can vary considerably you should check beforehand either on the spot or at tourist information centres (see Information).

Museums are also closed on the first day of the religious holidays (Ramadan: three days; Holy Days of Sacrifice: four days).

Filming and photography

An extra charge is made for filming or photographing at some archaeological sites and museums. If the pictures are for publication or of items which have not been cleared for copyright a special permit from the General Directorate of Antiquities and Museums in İstanbul is necessary.

National Parks

Turkey has a large number of national parks which have been created for the protection of the indigenous flora and fauna, the conservation of archaeological sites and national monuments, and to honour the fallen. We list some of them below.

Altındere

In Trabzon province (highway 885)
Lovely mountain scenery known for its natural beauty, Sumela monastery; cafés, picnic sites, post office

Beydağları Olympos

Antalya province (Highway 400)
Ruins of Phaselis and Olympos, wooded mountains
Museum, post office, restaurants, picnic and camp sites, holiday village, motels, beach

Dalyan

Muğla province, just east of Marmaris
Beach used for breeding by loggerhead turtles from May to October

Dilek Yarımadası

Aydın province, on the E87, 28km/17 miles east of Kuşadası
Peninsula with Mount Samsun; sea turtles; bobcats, wild horses and tortoises in park. Note: much of the park is a military area.
Picnic and camp sites, hiking, climbing, water sports
April–December

Gelibolu Yarımadası

Gallipoli peninsula north-west of Çanakkale
History park dedicated to the fallen of the First World War (Australian, British, French, Australian, New Zealand and Turkish war memorials)
Information stands at the Kilitbahir and Kabatepe entrances; beaches, campsite, hotel, motel, restaurants

Güllük Dağı/Termessos

Antalya province (E87)
Rugged mountain scenery, flora and fauna, open air museum
Picnic sites, restaurant, camping
April–October

Karatepe-Aslantaş

Adana province, Ceyhan valley (E90 or highway 825)
Hittite and Roman remains
Picnic and camp sites; April–November

Köprülü Kanyon

Antalya province (Highway 400)
Deep river canyon (14km/8 miles long 92km/58 miles NE of Antalya), Roman bridge, woods; site of ancient Selge (open air museum)
Picnic and camp sites, fishing, restaurants; summer

Spil Dağı

Manisa province
Thermal springs, interesting flora and wildlife. At foot of mountain is mythical "Weeping Rock of Niobe", caves and canyons
Picnic and camp site, walking and climbing
April–November

Ulu Dağ

South of Bursa
Ancient Mysian Olympus (1800–1900m/5908–6236ft); forests and lakes; variety of flora and wildlife; campsite, walks and picnics June–September; winter sports centre with skilifts, hotels, chalets, restaurants, post office
December–April

Opening Times

As a result of Kemal Atatürk's secular reforms Turkey differs from other Muslim countries by having Sunday as its day of rest rather than Friday.

Banks

See Currency

Government and other offices

Mon.–Fri. 8.30am–12.30pm and 1.30–5.30pm
Along the Mediterranean and Aegean coasts many offices and other facilities remain closed in the afternoon during the summer months.

Museums

See entry

Post offices

See Postal Services

Shops

Mon.–Sat. 9.30am–1pm and 2–7pm

Shops in the bazaars and small retailers, especially food stores, often stay open during lunchtime and well into the evening.

Shops (and museums) are closed on the first day of the religious holidays (Ramadan, three days; Holy Days of Sacrifice, four days).

Postal Services

Post offices, PTT

Turkish post offices (postane) are identified by a yellow sign with the letters PTT in black. Postboxes are also yellow. The large main post offices are open Monday to Saturday from 8am to midnight and Sundays from 9am to 7pm. Small post offices have the same hours as government offices (see Opening Times).

Express postal service, special stamps

Turkey operates and express postal service (Acele Posta Servisi–APS) to 72 other countries for letters, documents, and small packages.

Stamp collectors will find a wide range of special stamps.

Poste restante/ General delivery

Poste restante (general delivery) letters should be sent to the head post office (*Merkez Postanesi*) of the place in question marked "postrestant". You will need to show your passport or some other form of identification when collecting letters.

Changing money

Post offices will also change money at the current rate as well as cashing postal orders and all kinds of travellers' cheques. See Currency for further details.

Public Holidays

Day of rest

Following Atatürk's secular reforms Turkey observes Sunday as the weekly day of rest rather than Friday as is usually the case in Muslim countries.

Official holidays

January 1st (New Year's Day)
April 23rd (National Independence and Children's Day)
May 19th (Atatürk Commemoration and Youth and Sports Day, usually extended to two or three days)
August 30th (Victory Day, celebrating Turkey's 1922 War of Independence from Greece)
October 29th (Republic Day, anniversary of the declaration of the Republic in 1923)

Religious festivals

Ramazan (Ramadan): Muslim month of fasting and prayer, based on the Islamic lunar calendar and beginning ten days earlier every year, with a holiday on the 24th day (1997 from midday Feb. 8th–Feb. 11th)

Şeker Bayramı (Sugar Holy Days): three-day festival following the end of Ramadan

Kurban Baramı (Holy Days of Sacrifice): four-day festival around the date of Mohammed's birth, when sheep are sacrificed and distributed to the poor. This festival also occurs ten days earlier every year (1997 from midday Apr. 17th–Apr. 21st).

Shops and museums close on the first day of Ramadan, the Sugar Holy Days and the Holy Days of Sacrifice. Local beauty spots and attractions get very crowded during these religious festivals.

Radio and Television

Tourism Radio

Tourism Radio is aimed at promoting Turkey to foreign visitors and broadcasts feature and news programmes daily in English, French and German from 7.30am to 12.45pm and from 6.30 to 10pm local time.

TRT Radio on the FM band puts out the news in English at 9am, midday, 2, 5, 7 and 10pm.

For further information contact:

The Voice of Turkey
TRT (External Services) Türkiyenin Sesi Radyosu
POB 333, Yenişehir, Ankara, 06443 Turkey
tel. (312) 490 98 17, fax (312) 490 98 06

TV news in English

TRT TV2 puts out the news in English shortly after 10pm and the news in English on television's international channel (TV INT) is broadcast shortly after 11pm.

Railways

TCDD

The Turkish rail network, which is operated by Turkish State Railways (Türkiye Cumhuriyeti Devlet Demiryolları, TCDD), is not very highly developed and does not really lend itself to tourist travel – it only carries about 10% of the country's passenger traffic. The other public transport options are to travel by bus or by boat (see Buses, Coastal Shipping). Because of a shortage of rolling stock the trains on the relatively small number of main routes tend to be overcrowded and often none too clean, but the fares are extremely cheap.

The only rail routes featured in this guide are to the Aegean and Mediterranean coasts, İstanbul–Eskişehir (change)–İzmir, and İstanbul–Eskişehir–Ankara–Adana (Bagdad line). There is no line along the Black Sea coast, but trains run to Samsun from Sivas and to Zonguldak from Ankara.

Steam trains

Steam trains operate on regular tours in Western Turkey between İzmir and Aydın. They can also be chartered for tours by large groups anywhere in Turkey.

For further details contact the tourist offices listed under Information.

İzmir (Alsancak) airport rail link

Trains run hourly between İzmir's Alsancak railway station (tel. (232) 421 01 14) and Adnan Menderes airport (see Air Travel) and cost a fraction of the price of a taxi.

Restaurants

Besides the restaurants in the better hotels (see Hotels) which usually serve international as well as local dishes, Turkey has a good range of restaurants and other eating places in its larger towns and tourist resorts providing the delicious food for which Turkey is justly famous (see Food and Drink). Along the coast you will also find plenty of smaller places on the seafront or by the harbour where you can eat outdoors in summer.

Categories

In the following selection of established restaurants in Turkish coastal resorts the numbers (1) and (2) after the name give an indication of the standard you can expect. Based on the official Turkish categories, (1) stands for "above average" and (2) for "average".

Adana

Seyhan Oteli (2), Turkan Cemal Beriker Bul. 30; tel. (322) 457 58 10
(best in the place)

Alanya

Mahperi Sultan Restoran (1), Gazi Paşa Cad.; tel. (245) 513 10 99
(best and most expensive in town; top Turkish food)
Yakamoz Restaurant (2), Iskele Cad. 39; tel. (242) 512 23 03
(traditional Turkish food and fish dishes, with a wonderful view of the bay)

Restaurants

Anamur
Oba Restoran
(nice beach restaurant with garden terrace)

Antakya
Andolu Restoran (2), Saray Cad.; tel. (326) 215 15 41
(large choice of starters; friendly service; meals served in the garden in summer)

Antalya
Favorit Restoran (2), Uzunçarşı Sok. 19; tel. (242) 247 98 55
(garden restaurant in the heart of the Old Town, very good service)
Blue Parrot Café (2), İzmirli Ali Efendi Sok. 10; tel. (242) 247 03 49
(in a lovely old building; international cuisine)
Ahtapot (2), in front of the harbour mosque
(big choice of fish and seafood)

Assos
Athena Restaurant (2), in the old village centre; tel. (286) 712 70 37
(large helpings; reservation recommended)

Aydın
Pino Restaurant (2), İzmir Yolu
(on the western edge of town; big choice; very popular with drivers)

Ayvalık
Acar Kanelo (2), Gazinolar Cad. 1; tel. (266) 312 46 63
(on the tip of the harbour mole, in a fine classical building; delicious fish dishes)
Artur Restaurant (2), Sahil Boyu; tel. (266) 327 10 14
(by the harbour; fresh-caught fish)

Bergama
Kardeşler Restaurant (2), İzmir Cad.; tel. (232) 633 10 50
(best in the place)
Meydan Restaurant (2), İstiklal Meydani 4; tel. (232) 633 17 93
(good value for money)

Bodrum
Amphora Restaurant (1), Neyzen Tevfik Cad. 172; tel. (252) 316 23 68
(by the marina; outstanding food, with prices to match)
Han Restaurant (2), Kale Cad.; tel. (252) 316 16 14
(right in the bazaar in an old caravanserai; fish and starters; belly dancing)
Sandal Restaurant (2), Atatürk Cad. 74; tel. (252) 316 74 49
(Turkey's first Chinese restaurant; Thai food as well)

Bursa
Kebapçı İskender (2), Ünlü Cad. 7; tel. (224) 221 46 15
(birthplace of the döner kebab)

Çanakkale
Yeni Entellektüel Restaurant (2), Rıthım Boyu 17
(small place but one of the best fish restaurants, near ferry landing stage)

Çeşme
Körfez Restaurant (2), Yalı Cad. 12; tel. (232) 712 67 18
(fish specialities and seafood)
Sail Restaurant (2), Cumhuriyet Meydanı; tel. (232) 712 66 86
(harbour fish restaurant very popular with tourists)

Datça
Akdeniz Restaurant (2), İskele Meydanı; tel. (252) 712 33 92
(the fish is highly recommended)

Fethiye
Rafet Restaurant (2), Kordon Boyu; tel. (252) 614 11 06
(this restaurant has been specialising in fish and local dishes for over 40 years; lovely sea view)
Uysallar Restaurant (2), Hamam Sok. 14; tel. (252) 614 65 24
(Turkish food, eaten outdoors on the edge of the lively bazaar quarter)

Finike
Petek Restoran (2), at the harbour entrance
(big choice of starters; excellent service)

Foça
Çetin Restaurant (2), Küçükdeniz Sahil; tel. (232) 812 23 55
(by the harbour; seafood)

İstanbul

Urcan Balik Lokantası (1), by Sariyer harbour; tel. (212) 242 16 27
(Istanbul's best fish restaurant)
Sarnic Lokantası (1), Soğukçeşme Sok., Sultanahmet; tel. (212) 512 42 91
(gourmet shrine in a restored Byzantine cistern next to Hagia Sophia; reservation highly recommended)
Reshad Pasha Palace Restaurant (1), Kozyatağı Mh. Bağlamaşı Cad. 34, Erenköy; tel. (212) 361 34 11
(Turkish cuisine; elegant Ottoman décor)
Rendezvous Restaurant (2), Lamartin Cad. 7; tel. (212) 255 33 77
(very smart, moderate prices)

İzmir

Kemal Usta'nin Yeri (1), 1453 Sok. 20, Alsancak; tel. (232) 422 31 90
(outstanding cuisine, not cheap)
1888 Restaurant (1), Cumhuriyet Bul. 248; tel. (232) 421 66 90
(elegant restaurant in an old house from 1888; Turkish food; live music Wednesdays and at weekends)
Yeni Cati Restoran (2), Şehit Fethibey Cad. 56; tel. (232) 489 04 03
(fish; mostly Turkish patrons)

Kalkan

Akın Restaurant (2), over the harbour
(most popular restaurant in the place)
Belgin's Kitchen (2), Yalı Boyu 1; tel. (242) 844 36 14
(real oriental atmosphere)

Kaş

Mercan Restaurant (2), Cumhuriyet Medanı; tel. (242) 836 12 09
(by the marina; Turkish dishes; not exactly cheap, very smart)
Pizzeria Funghi (2), by the theatre
(excellent Italian pizza, straight from the oven)

Kuşadası

Toros Canalı Balık Restaurant (1), by the cruise-ship landing stage; tel. (637) 614 11 44
(fish and seafood specialities)
Ali Baba (2), by the harbour
(very popular fish restaurant; big choice of shellfish)

Manisa

Dorlan (2), near the Sultaniye
(simple but plenty of choice; popular with the locals)

Marmaris

Okimo (1), Netsel marina; tel. (252) 412 27 08
(in the new marina; very grand décor)
Özyalçin Kebab (2), Gözpinar Sok.; tel. (252) 412 29 34
(in the Old Town by the mosque; cheap Turkish specialities)

Mersin/İçel

Sahil Restoran (2), İsmet İnönü Bul.
(worth recommending; with sea view)

Ordu

Mıdı Restaurant (2), Sahil Cad.; tel. (452) 214 03 40
(top class; on the seafront)

Patara

Antalya Restoran (2)
(very idyllic, with garden under eucalyptus trees)

Selçuk

Hitit Restoran (2), on the edge of town on the Aydın road
(popular with tourist groups; extensive choice)

Side

Soundwaves (2), east promenade
(international dishes; expensive and almost always full)

Silifke

Piknik Restaurant (2), İnönü Cad. 58; tel. (324) 714 26 80
(in the town centre; music and dancing sometimes)

Baedeker Special

Of Prayer Rugs and Kız Kelims

The magnificence of the Anatolian carpets in the Sultans' palaces was already being remarked on by Marco Polo back in the 13th c. Turkey is also a leading producer of prayer rugs. On these the tympanum recalls a mihrab (prayer niche) and when the faithful kneel on their rugs to pray five times a day they position them so that the mihrab points towards Mecca. Since the Koran forbids the depiction of living creatures, motifs are primarily geometric or architectural (e.g. mihrab, house) with the influence of carpet-makers from Persia reflected in the use of medallions and floral patterns.

Until the discovery of aniline dyes in 1865 only vegetable dyes were used, with their formula a closely-guarded family secret. The old dyes have often kept their lustrous colours for centuries. Chief among them are red, symbolising wealth and good fortune, and blue, for nobility and splendour. In remote mountain regions Kurdish nomads still use plant dyes for their sheep's wool rugs.

The reputation of Anatolian carpets has become tarnished as some workshops have tried to satisfy the growing demand for old carpets by artificially ageing new ones, using methods such as leaving them out to be bleached by the sun or soaking them in chlorine, a process which actually destroys the fibres and shortens the life of a carpet.

Most of Hereke's sumptuous silk carpets, usually with Persian floral designs on an ivory ground, go for export, but when the workshops were founded in 1844 their products were intended for the Sultan and his court.

Colourful flat weave kelims with their bright zigzag patterns on a dark background are found everywhere as wall-hangings, throws and floor-coverings. Konya's kız kelims – made as gifts by the bride (kız = maiden) – are particularly fine examples.

Carpets for sale in Marmaris

Shopping and Souvenirs

Souvenirs

Among the many traditional wares which Turkey has to offer carpets and kelims (see Baedeker Special), often produced locally on or near the coast, make particularly good souvenirs. Another national speciality is the nargile, the Turkish version of the hubble-bubble water pipe, and this comes in many different shapes and sizes. Meerschaum is also found everywhere in the form of pipes and smoker's accessories, as are embossed wares in non-ferrous metals, leather goods, especially jackets, bags, etc., and textiles.

There is an amazing choice of gold and silver jewellery too, but you should insist on a certificate to show that what you are getting is the genuine article.

Food and drink

Sweetmeats and candied fruits such as Turkish delight (*lokum*) and marrons glacés, make good presents for someone with a really sweet tooth, and bottles of rakı, the national drink, are also worth considering.

Antiques

Buying antiques and antiquities is not a good idea. The export of genuine items is illegal and will be drastically punished, so avoid the temptation.

Bazaars

Foreign visitors usually have high hopes of Turkish bazaars as places with a particularly wide range of traditional wares, and this is certainly true of the ones in İstanbul, but elsewhere – even in İzmir – you will find them a sad disappointment.

The fact is that generally speaking the local bazaars are there to cater for the needs of local people and are not likely to provide much of any interest for collectors of good quality souvenirs.

Beware of imitations

Clever copies of internationally famous names – from designer clothing to perfume and cosmetics – are touted for sale throughout the country but especially around the tourist resorts, so if you are asked to pay a high price for anything of that kind find out first if it is genuine.

Tourist touts

Visitors not travelling with an organised tour will find themselves the target of persistent locals wanting to act as guides. Since they usually speak English it is easy to accept their offer, but the tour usually finishes in a shop where visitors will be pressurised to buy rugs, jewellery or some other souvenir – and will have to be very firm indeed to leave without buying anything.

On leaving Turkey

If you are taking out any new carpets you will require proof of purchase. You also need to be able to present exchange slips to show that your souvenirs have been bought with legally converted currency (see also Currency, Customs Regulations).

Spas

Turkey has over a thousand thermal springs; some of the spars are listed below with the water temperatures in brackets. Accommodation is provided at many of these resorts.

Balçova

10km/6 miles west of İzmir
For rheumatism, gynaecological conditions, sciatica
Facilities: Ege University treatment centre; Turkey's largest indoor thermal pool (62°C/143°F); drinking and bathing cures

Bursa/Çekirge

South of İstanbul
For rheumatism, gynaecological conditions, dermatological and metabolic disorders
Facilities: drinking and bathing cures (47–78°C/116–172°F); hotel cures under medical supervision

Çeşme

On Route 300, west of İzmir (7km/4 miles east of Çeşme)
For rheumatism, gynaecological conditions, dermatological and urinary disorders
Facilities: drinking and bathing cures (42–55°C/108–131°F)

Pamukkale and Karahayıt

Denizli province 20km/12 miles north-east of Denizli
For heart and circulatory complaints, rheumatism, digestive, gall bladder and kidney diseases
Facilities: drinking and bathing cures (33–56°C/91–133°F)

Yalova

İstanbul province, springs 11km/7 miles south-west of Yalova
For rheumatism, gynaecological conditions, urinary and nervous complaints, control of cholesterol and lipid levels
Facilities: drinking and bathing cures (55–60°C/131–140°F)

Sport

Many of the hotels featured in packaged tours to Turkey have a wide range of sports facilities, although the tennis courts, etc. are not always up to European standards. The facilities elsewhere also tend to be rather limited outside the peak holiday season. Leaflets on climbing, trekking and rafting are available from the tourist offices listed in the Information section. Turkey's own more esoteric traditional sports include greased wrestling, camel fights (see Folklore) and *cirit oyunu*, the "javelin game" played on horseback.

Aerial sports

Anyone interested in aerial sports such as flying, gliding, hang-gliding, para-sailing, etc. should contact the Turkish Flying Association (THK) in Ankara (Türk Hava Kurumu Genel Başkanlığı, Havacılık Müdürlüğü, Atatürk Bulvarı 33, Opera, Ankara; tel. (312) 310 48 40, fax (312) 310 04 13). Courses in these activities can be provided for groups of ten or more people provided they speak the same language.

Diving

Snorkelling and scuba diving with amateur equipment is permitted in certain areas for leisure purposes, but since the rules governing diving vary from place to place it is best to find out about them from a national Turkish tourist office (see Information) before leaving home and also to check again with the appropriate authorities, such as the local harbour-master's office, when you get to Turkey.

Fishing

Fishing for sport is allowed in non-prohibited areas, using non-commercial lines and nets not weighing more than 5kg, and does not require a licence. Details of permitted fishing zones, minimum fish size and how many fish may be caught per person are obtainable from the Ministry of Agriculture's Fisheries Department in Ankara (Orman Bakanlığı, Koruma ve Kontrol, Gen. Müdürlüğü, Akay Cad. 3 Bakanlıklar, Ankara; tel. (312) 417 41 76, fax (312) 418 80 05). Commercial fishing by foreigners is strictly forbidden.

Football

Football is one of Turkey's favourite spectator sports. For visitors there is also a holiday football school, organised between June and October by Club Palmariva at Kemer where soccer enthusiasts can take part in many other sporting activities as well, such as tennis, squash, sailing, water-skiing, etc.

Golf

The Turkish coast has several 18-hole golf courses. For information contact:
Classis Golf and Country Club, Silivri, İstanbul;
tel. (212) 727 40 49, fax (212) 266 94 50

Kemer Country and Golf Club, Göktürk Köyü, Kemerburgaz, İstanbul
tel. (212) 239 79 13, 239 81 55/56, fax (212) 239 70 76

National Golf Club, Belek, Antalya;
tel. (242) 725 46 20, fax (242) 725 46 24

Hiking

Many parts of Turkey lend themselves to walking and hiking, although there are no marked trails as such. Some of the best areas are the Black Sea coast, the Ulu Dağ mountains around Bursa (see National Parks) and the countryside around Marmaris. You should take good footwear, a rucksack and waterbottle, warm clothing and protection against the sun and the rain. Enquire about trail maps in bookstores or specialist shops before leaving for Turkey. Visitors planning to climb mountains should inform the local mountaineering club.

Hunting

Private hunting is banned in Turkey, and foreign visitors can only hunt in parties organised by Turkish travel agencies which have been authorised by the Ministry of Agriculture, Forestry and Rural Affairs. For a list of these agencies contact the Union of Turkish Travel Agencies (TÜRSAB, Gazeteciler Sitesi, Haberler Sokak 15, Esentepe, İstanbul; tel. (212) 275 13 61, fax (212) 275 00 66).

Sailing

Private yachts require a transit log before entering Turkey's territorial waters where they may remain for up to two years for maintenance or for wintering. Once you have entered Turkish waters you must make your way immediately to an official port of entry to present your transit log and get it endorsed by the proper authorities. These ports of entry are İskenderun, Botaş (Adana), Mersin, Taşucu, Anamur, Alanya, Antalya, Kemer, Finike, Kaş, Fethiye, Marmaris, Datça, Bodrum, Güllük, Didim, Kuşadası, Çeşme, İzmir, Dikili, Ayvalıık, Akçay, Çanakkale, Bandırma, Tekirdağ, Körfez, İstanbul, and, on the Black Sea, Zonguldak, Sinop, Samsun, Ordu, Giresun, Trabzon, Rize and Hopa.

Rules of navigation

International navigation rules must be followed. The Turkish courtesy flag should be flown from 8am to sunset. Avoid zigzagging between Turkish and Greek territorial waters to prevent any misunderstanding, and above all refrain from taking any "archaeological souvenirs" from coastal waters and keeping them on board – the penalty is confiscation of the boat.

Wind and weather conditions

Be sure to check on wind and weather conditions. There is a meteorological bulletin on VHF 16 and 67 for the Mediterranean and Aegean region in English and Turkish, repeated three times, which is broadcast daily at 9am, noon and 3, 6 and 9pm. Further information is also available from: Çevre Bakanlığı, Devlet Meteoroloji Genel Müdürlüğü, 06120 Kalaba, Ankara; tel. (312) 359 75 45, fax (312) 359 34 30 (see also When to Go in this section and Climate under Facts and Figures).

Gulet cruises and sailing holidays

Sailing holidays cruising around the Turkish coastline and islands of the Aegean and Mediterranean are becoming very popular, especially in the form of *gulet* cruises, using new motor yachts modelled on the traditional wooden gulets of Bodrum and Marmaris, with a local crew and providing full board and accommodation for up to twelve people.

"Blue Voyage" (Mavi Yolculuk)

The "Blue Voyage" is a popular week-long sailing cruise along the coast from Çeşme to Antalya operated by various agencies between April and October for groups of 8 to 12 people. There are also all kinds of yachts available at Marmaris on which to enjoy the scenic coast between here and Bodrum.

Surfing The best surfing conditions are in the bays of the Aegean at Çeşme, Bodrum and on the Datça peninsula, and on the Mediterranean coast at Antalya. There are a number of places where surf boards and surfing lessons are available.

Winter sports Anyone who wants to combine skiing in the morning with a swim in the Mediterranean in the afternoon should opt for Saklıkent (2000–2400m/6564–7877ft; chair-lifts etc., ski hire, ski school) in March and April since this is within easy distance of the sandy beach at Olympos, west of Antalya.

Taxis

All Turkey's larger towns and cities have plenty of taxis. These are yellow and easy to recognise by the "Taksi" sign on the roof. They are relatively cheap and mostly fitted with meters but it is wise to ask how much the fare will be before starting the journey.

Dolmuş Turkey's communal taxi, the dolmuş, is even cheaper than an ordinary taxi. Identifiable by their yellow band, they follow set routes with fixed stops and charge set rates which are fixed by the local authority. A typical route would be from the centre of town to the airport or out to the suburbs and often other places nearby. "Dolmuş" means full and they will carry on picking up passengers until there's no more room. Each passenger pays a set amount according to the distance travelled and gets off where convenient.

Minibuses Minibuses are another cheap way to travel. They stop on request – but only if there's enough room inside – and follow no particular route.

Tipping See entry

Telephone

Turkey's telephone system is still being improved and extended but nearly all the main towns have STD and direct dialling. However, since the area codes have recently been reorganised it is advisable to check locally on the latest situation. Long-distance calls through the operator can be either normal, urgent or "lightning".

Public phone boxes are yellow and there are plenty of them; there is always one near a post office. To make a call either tokens (*jetons*) or a phonecard (*telefon kartı*), both available from post offices, are needed. When dialling direct lift the receiver, wait for the tone, then dial 9 and wait for another tone before dialling the area code followed by the number required.

Long-distance calls via the operator can mean a long wait running into several hours in some cases.

Within Turkey the area code for İzmir, for example, is 232. To dial an İzmir number from abroad dial the international network access code (00) followed by 90 for Turkey then 232 and the number you want.

International dialling codes from Turkey First dial 00 then the following numbers to:

Canada, United States	1	South Africa	99 27
Eire	99 353	United Kingdom	99 44

Telegrams See Postal Services

Time

Turkey observes Eastern European Time which is two hours ahead of Greenwich Mean Time (GMT). From the beginning of April until the end of September the clocks are put forward an hour to Turkish Summer Time which is three hours ahead of GMT.

Tipping

In hotels and at barbers and hairdressers the tip is usually up to 10% of the bill and in restaurants up to 15%. Taxi drivers expect a rounding up of the fare.

For hotel porters, etc. the tip is between 500 and 1000 TL but often the amounts for some services (e.g. lavatory attendant) are posted up.

Tourist Guides

Official tour guides

All tour operators are required to provide professional interpreter/guides on their tours, and Ministry of Tourism offices and travel agents can also provide professional guides for independent travellers.

Self-appointed guides

See Shopping and souvenirs, Tourist touts

Travel Documents

Passport

Nationals of EU countries, Australia, Canada, the United States and most Western countries normally only require a valid passport to enter Turkey for a stay of up to six months. If travelling overland transit visas are also required for countries such as Rumania and Bulgaria. Children under sixteen may be included on their parents' passport but only if they are entering and leaving Turkey at the same time.

Driver and vehicle papers

Drivers must have their driving licence and vehicle registration papers and cars must bear the oval nationality disc. On entering Turkey, all vehicles – from caravans and minibuses to motorbikes and mopeds, and including luggage trailers and towed boats – will be entered in the driver's passport. Make sure this is cancelled again when you leave (see also Motoring). If you intend to keep a vehicle in Turkey for longer than three months or to continue on into the Middle East you also require a triptyque or "carnet de passage". These are obtainable in advance from motoring organisations.

Vehicle insurance

All vehicles must have at least third party insurance. The international green card is compulsory and it must expressly state that it covers the Asian as well as the European part of Turkey. Otherwise you will have to take out a short-term insurance at the frontier.

Because of the poor performance of Turkish insurance it is advisable to try to avoid doing badly out of claims for damage in local accidents by taking out an additional short-term comprehensive and passenger insurance in advance which must be written to cover the whole of Turkey. You should definitely carry written confirmation from your home insurers that the policy cover is valid throughout the country. A police report is necessary for the settlement of any claims.

Turkish Baths

Because of Islam's strict rules regarding ritual purification and cleanliness, the "hamam" or public bath-house has been part of Turkish life since the Middle Ages. There are usually separate baths for men and women, or, when there is only one bath house in town, they are allocated different days or times.

The central hot room, which is surrounded by open cubicles, has a heated slab in the middle – the "göbek taşı" or belly stone – where you sweat wrapped in a "peştamal" (a kind of bath apron) before being rubbed down and massaged by a male or female attendant (*tellak* or *natır*) as the case may be. This not only leaves you much cleaner but also gets the circulation going.

There are over a hundred Turkish baths in İstanbul alone, some of them well worth visiting, if only for the architecture (see also Art and Culture, Typical Islamic Buildings).

Turkish Society and the Visitor

Islam

The vast majority of Turks are followers of Islam, one of the world's great monotheistic religions (see Facts and Figures, Religion), and their lives as Muslims (believers prefer Muslim or Moslem to the term Mohammedan) are wholly governed by the tenets of their faith. These are based on the rules laid down in the Koran, their holy book, which prescribes absolute obedience to the will of Allah, their one and only God. The precepts of the Koran also embrace the laws derived from the words and deeds of Islam's founder, the Prophet Mohammed (born in Mecca in 570 A.D. and died in Medina in 632). Every area of Muslim society is ordered by laws, rules and customs based on the five fundamental duties of the Islamic faith:

Duties of the faith

1. Profession of faith (Shahidah): "there is no God but Allah and Mohammed is his prophet".
2. Duty of prayer (Salat): this must be performed five times a day, preceded by ritual cleansing, facing Mecca and using preordained prayers, in Arabic if possible, and in strictly prescribed prayer positions.
3. Almsgiving (Sakat): every Muslim must regularly give alms to the poor and needy (between 2.5 and 10% of their income).
4. Fasting (Saum): Muslims are required to abstain from food and drink and worldly pleasures such as smoking between sunrise and sunset during Ramadan (Ramasan), the ninth month of Islam's lunar calendar.
5. Pilgrimage to Mecca (Hadj): every Muslim who is of age, unless prevented by sickness or poverty, must make the pilgrimage to Mecca once in their lifetime to visit the Kaba, Islam's holiest shrine.

Islamic codes of conduct

Other religious ordinances include bans on drinking alcohol and eating pork, as well as the prohibition of usury and all forms of gambling. Animals must be slaughtered according to fixed rules and no blood or blood products may be consumed. There are also detailed rules governing bodily purification and the relationships between married people and parents and children.

The husband is the prime member of the family for which he alone is responsible both in fact and in law. The wife remains in the background and her domain is the home and the family. The extended family is the Muslim's accepted territory, and thoughts, feelings and behaviour are geared to the communal unit. The Islamic world is currently showing a growing awareness of its own values and potential; greater emphasis is again being placed on cultural and religious tradition, but in the big cities you also encounter modern, more western lifestyles – like any other movement Islam has its progressive forces as well as its conservative fundamentalists.

How to behave as a visitor

If you want to understand the way Muslims behave and to avoid offending them you should bear in mind that they have a different lifestyle and way of thinking from those who are not of their faith. Thus the Turks have different values and customs which, as a visitor to their country, you should respect if you want them to respect you.

Since their religion is so closely bound up with every other aspect of Turkish society, any dismissive remark will readily be regarded as a criticism of the Islamic faith.

Avoid wearing revealing clothing, especially in rural areas, and particularly if you are visiting a mosque. Always remove your shoes before entering, never wear shorts, and, if you are a woman, cover your head with a scarf. Non-Muslims are excluded from mosques during prayers.

In the more conservative parts of Turkey avoid public displays of affection between the sexes since this will be regarded as promiscuous; eye-contact by foreign women with Turkish men is taboo.

Refrain from taking photographs of women, children, poor people or beggars. Muslims consider this a slur on a person's dignity and it can meet with a very hostile reaction.

Needless to say you will cause offence if you make fun of the sound of the muezzin or Muslim behaviour at prayer, and during Ramadan you should avoid eating, drinking or smoking in public in the daytime.

The Turks are immensely hospitable and it is considered impolite to refuse an invitation. If you do, be very apologetic about it. The Islamic code means that friendships are taken very seriously.

If you are invited into a Turkish home you will be treated like a member of the family, and the same generous hospitality will be expected of you if you receive a visit in return.

As a guest, do not ask for pork or any alcoholic drinks, but you can eat or drink these items if they are put in front of you. An appropriate gift of flowers for the hostess or some other token will be expected when you leave. Never offer money.

When to Go

The spring is the best time to make a tour of Turkey if you want to enjoy the scenery at its freshest and greenest. In summer the heat, dust and drought can make travelling very wearing, and it may often prove difficult to get a room during the peak season. Autumn is also a good time to go if you are prepared not to see the countryside at its best. For the best time for swimming see Beaches.

Out of season

Although prices are lower on both sides of the peak holiday season this also has its disadvantages, such as more building work and routine maintenance and repairs. There are often fewer people about to cater for visitors which means having to wait longer, and many shops, restaurants, etc. are closed.

Spring

After the heavy winter rains spring comes to the Mediterranean coast between İzmir and Antakya in early March when the countryside is in bloom with fresh new growth and beautiful wild flowers. Spring reaches the coast between İzmir and the Bosphorus in mid-March, and the Black Sea coast in April. On the other hand the mountain peaks of the Taurus and the Pontus are capped with snow until well into June and this contrast between the white of the mountain tops and the azure blue of the sea makes the Mediterranean coast particularly attractive in April and May.

Swimming is possible in the Sea of Marmara from mid-May onwards and in the Black Sea from June.

Summer

The summer drought sets in as early as June and the heat on the coast is only occasionally tempered by sea breezes. This is the time to opt for the Sea of Marmara or the Black Sea, although it can get oppressively close on the eastern part of the Black Sea coast where the warm wet winds from the sea meet the mountain barrier of the Pontus. The summer months in central and south-eastern Anatolia are hot and dry, but it can become quite chilly in the evenings on the central plateau.

Autumn

Temperatures become tolerable again in the autumn but the heat of summer will have dried everything up, leaving the landscape sere and barren.

Winter

Winter tourism in Turkey is still in its infancy. Although the Turkish Riviera and the Aegean coast often enjoy spring temperatures at this time of year, so far they tend to be short of wintertime facilities. The best months for winter sports (see Sport) are from December to March around Bursa and Ankara and from November to April near Kayseri.

Climate

See Facts and Figures, Climate

Youth Accommodation

Youth hostels

Turkey is not a member of the International Youth Hostel Federation since it only has a few youth hostels (e.g. in İstanbul, Bursa, Çanakkale, and İzmir). Young people travelling on a tight budget can also easily find a cheap bed for the night in the more modest hotels and guest houses.

Information

Information about accommodation for young people is available from the following organisations:

Yüksek Öğrenim Kredi ve Yurtlar Kurumu Genel Müdürlüğü
(Youth Hostel General Directorate)
Kıbrıs Cad. 4, Kurtuluş, Ankara;
tel. (312) 431 11 00, fax (312) 435 03 29

International Youth Hostel Federation Center, IYHF
Alemdar Cad. 26, Sultanahmet, İstanbul;
tel. (212) 520 95 94, fax (212) 511 45 97

A number of other agencies can also help with arranging stays at youth camps, host families, cheap travel, etc. These include:

Gençtur Turizm ve Seyahat Acentesi
Yerebatan Caddesi 15/3, Sultanahmet, İstanbul;
tel. (212) 520 52 74, fax (212) 519 08 64

7 TUR Turizm Ltd.
İnönü Caddesi 37/2, Gümüşsuyu, Taksim, İstanbul;
tel. (212) 252 59 21, fax (212) 252 59 24

Renk Turizm Seyahat Acentası
Halaskargazı Caddesi 105, Harbiye, İstanbul;
tel. (212) 232 23 02, fax (212) 248 39 15

Seventur Turizm Seyehat Acentası
Alemdar Caddesi 2/C, Sultanahmet, İstanbul;
tel. (212) 520 95 94, fax (212) 511 45 97

Index

Principal Places of Tourist Interest at a Glance

Note on spelling: Greek place-names and personal names are normally given in a direct transliteration from the Greek rather than in the Latinised form often used in English: e.g. Thourioi rather than Thurii. But where the Latinised form is in general use and the Greek form would appear unduly pedantic the Latinised form is used: Thucydides rather than Thoukydides.

Imprint

118 colour photographs
12 town plans, 12 plans of ruined sites, 9 general plans, 12 ground plans, 10 graphic drawings, 9 sectional drawings, 1 large map of Turkish Coasts

Text: Dr Peter Baumgarten, Achim Bourmer, Astrid Feltes, Dr Volker Höhfeld, Prof. Dr Manfred Korfmann

Editorial work: Baedeker Stuttgart

English language edition: Alec Court

Design and layout: Creativ GmbH; Ulrich Kolb, Stuttgart

General direction: Dr Peter Baumgarten, Baedeker Stuttgart

Cartography: Gert Oberländer, Munich; Christoph Gallus, Lahr; Hallwag AG, Berne (fold-out map)

English translation: James Hogarth

Revised text: Wendy Bell, David Cocking, Margaret Court

Source of illustrations: Archiv für Kunst und Geschichte (1), Baumgarten (1), Bildagentur Schuster (1), Börner (1), Feltes (65), Fotoagentur Lade (4), Hackenberg (7), Historia-Photo (7), Höhfeld (8), IFA-Bilderteam (2), Information Department of the Turkish General Consul, Munich (1), Jansen (1), Mauritius Bildagentur (3), Paysan (2), Schäfer (1), Stetter (2), Strobel (8), Süddeutscher Verlag (1), Ullstein Bilderdienst (1)

4th English edition 1996

Published in the United States by:
Macmillan Travel
A Simon & Schuster Macmillan Company
1633 Broadway
New York, NY 10019–6785

Macmillan is a registered trademark of Macmillan, Inc.

Distributed in the United Kingdom by the Publishing Division of the Automobile Association, Fanum House, Basingstoke, Hampshire RG21 2EA

A CIP catalogue record of this book is available from the British Library

Licensed user:
Mairs Geographischer Verlag GmbH & Co.,
Ostfildern-Kemnat bei Stuttgart

Printed in Italy by G. Canale & C.S.p.A – Borgaro T.se –Turin

ISBN 0–02–861353–8 USA and Canada
0 7495 1419 1 UK

Notes

Notes

Notes

Notes

Notes